South Carolina

South Carolina

Page Ivey
with photographs by the author

The Countryman Press ✳ Woodstock, Vermont

Explorer's Guide South Carolina

ISBN: 978-0-88150-931-1

Interior photographs by the author unless otherwise specified
Maps by Erin Greb Cartography, © The Countryman Press
Book design by Bodenweber Design
Composition by PerfecType, Nashville, TN

Published by The Countryman Press, P.O. Box 748, Woodstock, VT 05091

Distributed by W. W. Norton & Company, Inc., 500 Fifth Avenue, New York, NY 10110

Printed in the United States of America

10 9 8 7 6 5 4 3 2

DEDICATION

To Mom and Aunt Betty, who taught me that laughter smooths
all traveling wrinkles, and to Jan for showing me that it's not
where you go that matters, it's who you go with.

EXPLORE WITH US!

Welcome to the first edition of *Explorer's Guide South Carolina*, the most comprehensive travel guide covering the state. We've included attractions, accommodations, restaurants, and shopping on the basis of merit (primarily through the personal knowledge of the author) rather than paid advertising. The following points will help you understand how we've organized the guide.

WHAT'S WHERE

The book starts out with some highlights to the major attractions in the state and some things you should know about the peculiar institution that is South Carolina.

LODGING

All selections for accommodations in this guide are based on merit. No businesses were charged for inclusion in this guide. Most places don't accept pets, so I mention it when they do; if they don't take children (many bed & breakfasts), I mention that as well. Many locations along the coast require a minimum stay during summer, and those are noted.

RATES

Rate ranges were accurate as of early 2011 and show the cheapest that two people could stay in a particular location and the most expensive rate quoted. Some places offer deals for booking and paying in advance. Rates will vary greatly depending on time of year; those also have been noted. Each section will tell you the prime seasons for that area. For example, summer is high season for the beaches surrounding Charleston, but for the city, spring is the most expensive time.

RESTAURANTS

Our distinction between *Eating Out* and *Dining Out* is based mainly on price. Typically, if a restaurant has no entrée offerings under $15, it's in *Dining Out*. These also tend to be slightly dressier locales, though it is rare that a person is turned away for dress. If it's in the *Dining Out* section and jackets or reservations are required, that is typically noted. To be safe, you can call ahead. Smoking is still allowed in some restaurants and bars in South Carolina (the state's number one cash crop still is tobacco, after all). But by and large, the major tourist destinations of Hilton Head, Charleston, Greenville, and Columbia are smoke-free.

KEY TO SYMBOLS

🐾 **Pets.** The dog-paw symbol appears next to venues that accept pets (usually with prior notice).

🖍 **Child-friendly.** The crayon symbol appears next to lodgings, restaurants, activities, and shops of special interest or appeal to youngsters.

♿ **Handicapped access.** The wheelchair symbol appears next to lodgings, restaurants, and attractions that are partially or completely handicapped accessible.

Did we miss someplace great? Drop us a line at explorersguidesc@gmail.com, or follow us on Twitter at ExploringSC; we're also on Facebook under Explorer's Guide: South Carolina.

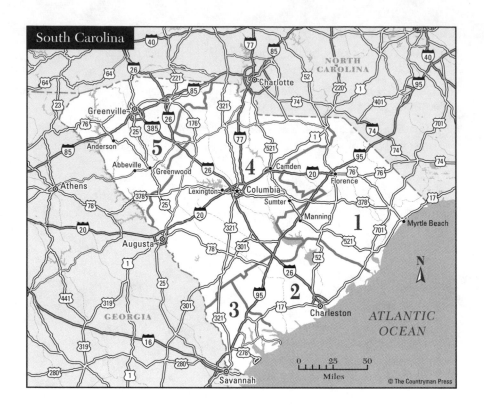

CONTENTS

5   Upstate / 321

INTRODUCTION

Whe most people think of South Carolina as a travel destination, they think Myrtle Beach, Hilton Head Island, or Charleston. To be sure, those are the hot spots in the state's $18-billion-a-year tourism industry. But for those who like to take the long way home rather than setting the GPS for the fastest interstate route, there is much more to South Carolina.

Much of what there is to see and do in the Palmetto State revolves around more than 400 years of history since European settlers arrived at Charles Towne Landing. An independent streak runs through that history, from a 1739 slave rebellion along the Stono River near Charleston to the American Revolution to the Civil War.

Visitors can see battlefields from both the Revolution and Civil War. The scars of that last war are prominently displayed on the state capitol, where cannon fire hit the still-under-construction building in 1865.

The cypress swamps that helped Francis Marion, the Swamp Fox, hide as he attacked the British can still be seen along roadways and preserved at Cypress Gardens near Charleston.

Of course, South Carolina has miles and miles of sandy beaches from Myrtle Beach to the sea islands off Charleston and Beaufort. Back from the beaches but still along the coast is the Gullah/Geechee Cultural Heritage Corridor, spotlighting the language and culture of freed slaves in the late 19th century. St. Helena Island was home to one of the first schools dedicated to educating freed slaves and was a stopping point for the Reverend Martin Luther King Jr. during the civil rights movement of the 1960s.

The Upstate is for nature and art lovers. Some of the most rugged and remote areas of the 425-mile Palmetto Trail wind through Jocassee Gorges in South Carolina's northwest corner. The trail forms a spine for a series of hiking, walking and biking paths that run along many of the state's lakes and rivers on its way from the mountains to the sea. The Greenville Museum of Art in the heart of the city's downtown houses more Andrew

CAESARS HEAD STATE PARK NEAR CLEVELAND

SC Department of Parks, Recreation & Tourism, DiscoverSouthCarolina.com

SOUTH CAROLINA FAVORITE SHRIMP AND GRITS

Wyeth paintings than any other museum in the Southeast. The Bob Jones University Museum and Gallery has an often overlooked collection of religious artwork, including 400 paintings by the Old Masters, Gothic furniture, textiles, and ancient artifacts.

South Carolina's one national park located on the Congaree Swamp is a wonderland for canoers. Countless lakes, rivers, and streams make the state a fishing, hunting, and boating paradise.

The state also has produced a number of entertainers, including Hootie and the Blowfish, Dizzy Gillespie, Eartha Kitt, James Brown, and Chubby Checker; their hometowns proclaim them proudly on signs. When entering North Myrtle Beach, for example, the welcome sign tells you that you are entering the hometown of *Wheel of Fortune* star Vanna White.

As a native of South Carolina, I love sharing tidbits about surprising things people don't know about the state and about little out-of-the-way places with memorable food and characters. Finding such places is, I suspect, why we all love to travel.

WHAT'S WHERE IN SOUTH CAROLINA

AREA CODES 864 in the Upstate, 803 in the Midlands, and 843 along the coast.

AIRPORTS AND AIRLINES
Charleston International Airport (843-767-7007; chs-airport.com) offers connections to several major U.S. airports and is served by carriers Air Tran (800-247-8726 or 678-254-7999; airtran.com), American Eagle (800-433-7300; aa.com), Continental Airlines (800-525-0280; continental.com), Delta Air Lines (800-221-1212; delta.com), Northwest Airlines (800-225-2525; nwa.com), United Express (800-241-6522; united.com), US Airways (800-428-4322; usairways.com).

Columbia Metropolitan Airport (803-822-5000 or 888-562-5002; columbiaairport.com) offers connections to several major U.S. airports and is served by carriers American Eagle (800-433-7300; aa.com), Continental Airlines (800-525-0280; continental.com), Delta Air Lines (800-221-1212; delta.com), Northwest Airlines (800-225-2525; nwa.com), United (800-241-6522; united.com), US Airways (800-428-4322; usairways.com).

Florence Regional Airport (843-669-5001; florencescairport.com) offers daily flights to Atlanta, Georgia, through Atlantic Southeast Airlines (800-221-1212; flyasa.com), and Charlotte, North Carolina, through US Airways Express (800-428-4322; usairways.com).

Greenville-Spartanburg International Airport (864-877-7426; gspairport.com) offers direct flights to four Florida cities through Allegiant Airlines (702-505-8888; allegiantair.com) and connections to most major airports through carriers American Eagle (800-433-7300; aa.com), Continental Airlines (800-525-0280; continental.com), Delta Air Lines (800-221-1212; delta.com), Northwest Airlines (800-225-2525; nwa.com), United Express (800-241-6522; united.com), US Airways (800-428-4322; usairways.com).

Hilton Head Island Airport (843-689-5400; bcgov.net/Airport _HHI/) has daily flights to and from Charlotte, North Carolina, and Washington, DC, through US Airways Express (800-428-4322; usairways.com), and seasonal flights through Delta Connection (800-221-1212; delta.com).

Myrtle Beach International Airport (843 448 1589; flymyrtle beach.com) offers direct and connecting flights through U.S. carriers Allegiant Airlines (702-505-8888; allegiantair.com), Continental Airlines (800-525-0280; continental.com), Delta Air Lines (800-221-1212; delta.com), Northwest Airlines (800-225-2525; nwa .com), Myrtle Beach Direct Air (877-432-3473; visitdirectair.com), Spirit Airlines (800-772-7117; spiritair.com), United Express (800-241-6522; united.com), US Airways (800-428-4322; us airways.com).

AMTRAK (800-872-7245; amtrak .com). The Silver Service (Silver Meteor and Silver Star) and the Palmetto offer rail service among New York City, Georgia, and Florida with stops in eight different South Carolina cities and towns. The Silver Meteor follows Interstate 95 and makes stops in Florence, Kingstree, Charleston, and Yemassee. The Palmetto makes those same stops plus one in the town of Dillon south of the North Carolina state line. The Silver Star comes inland with stops in Camden, Columbia, and Denmark. The Crescent runs from New York to New Orleans with stops in Spartanburg, Greenville, and Clemson in the Upstate.

AMUSEMENT PARKS
⚓ **Carowinds Amusement and Water Park** (803-548-5300; carowinds.com), 14523 Carowinds Boulevard, Fort Mill. Open daily June through mid-August; weekends only from March through May and September through October. Park opens at 10 AM, and closing times vary. Closed late October through mid-March. When this theme park opened in 1973, the highlight was the gold-paved North Carolina–South Carolina state line running through the middle. Over the years, the park has paid tribute to its Carolina stock car roots with ride names such as Thunder Road, White Lightning, and, new in 2010, The Intimidator, after famed NASCAR driver Dale Earnhardt. The 112-acre theme includes the 20-acre Boomerang Bay water park and offers 13 roller coasters as well as other rides, attractions, and shows. Admission: $45.99 adults; $19.99 juniors shorter than 48 inches tall and seniors 62 and older. Children younger than 3 admitted free.

⚓ **Family Kingdom Amusement Park & Oceanfront Water Park** (843-626-3447; familyking domfun.com), 300 S. Ocean Boulevard, Myrtle Beach. Open March through September, 4 PM–midnight. Water park open Memorial Day to Labor Day at 10 AM. Myrtle Beach's oldest operating amusement park is located on 16 acres by the ocean and has more than 30 rides, including the historic Swamp Fox wooden roller coaster. The water park includes a 400-foot lazy river. Admission to the park is $23.50; water park wristband is $18.95. Combo deals are available.

⌀ **The Pavilion Nostalgia Park** (843-913-9400; pavilion nostalgiapark.com), 1325 Celebrity Circle, Myrtle Beach. Open daily 11 AM weather permitting. The park has a sampling of rides from the former Myrtle Beach Pavilion that was the hallmark of the beachfront for decades. Admission is free, but rides cost $3 each.

ANTIQUES Antiquarian Book Dealers' Association of South Carolina (803-791-8002; abdasc .org). This group works to develop a code of ethics for dealers of rare and out-of-print book editions. Its members also will appraise the value of old editions at book festivals.

APPLES South Carolina Apple Growers' Association (864-638-5648), 140 Hawthorne Lane, Mountain Rest. The best place to find apples in South Carolina is along the Cherokee Foothills Scenic Highway (SC 11), which runs north and east from Lake Hartwell on the Georgia state line to Gaffney.

AQUARIUMS ⌀ **The South Carolina Aquarium** (843-720-

1990; scaquarium.org), 100 Aquarium Wharf, Charleston. Open daily 9 AM–5 PM March through August. Closes at 4 PM September through February. Opened in 2000 on Charleston Harbor, the South Carolina Aquarium has more than 60 exhibits, including the Great Ocean Tank with 385,000 gallons of water and more than 450 animals. Special programs include behind-the-scenes tours of the tank and the aquarium's sea turtle hospital. Admission: $17.95 for adults (12 and older), $16.95 for seniors (62-plus), $10.95 for children 11 and younger. Toddlers are free.

⌀ **Ripley's Aquarium** (843-916-0888; myrtlebeach.ripley aquariums.com), 1110 Celebrity Circle, Myrtle Beach. Open 9 AM–10 PM, seven days a week. Admission: $18.99 for adults; $9.99 for children ages 6–11, and $3.99 for ages 2–5. Exhibits include a 750,000-gallon tank and Ray Bay, which lets visitors see stingrays from all angles and even touch some. Freshwater exhibits highlight life in the Amazon rain forest, and a 10-foot cylindrical exhibit shows species native to South Carolina coastal waters.

ARTISTS AND GALLERIES Blue Sky Gallery (803-779-4242; blueskyart.com), 733 Saluda Avenue, Columbia. Open 11:30 AM–5:30 PM, Wednesday through Saturday, or by appointment. Shop features work by famed muralist and Columbia native Blue Sky.

His artwork can be seen around the city, and his gallery has photographs and smaller versions of some of his most memorable murals and installations.

ART MUSEUMS South Carolina's larger cities—Columbia, Charleston, and Greenville—have fine art museums, as do some of the smaller cities, such as Greenwood. Greenville is home to a large collection of religious art at Bob Jones University, which also has a satellite location at the city's Heritage Green.

"BALD PEANUTS" If you stop at a small-town convenience store as you drive through the state, you might hear one of your fellow shoppers ask whether the store has any "bald peanuts." They're not asking for hairless peanuts, though that is a plus; they are asking for *boiled* peanuts, peanuts that have steeped in a pot of briny boiling water for several hours. They can be eaten hot, warm, or cold. I have a friend who buys them by the 5-pound bag and keeps them in her freezer. She takes them out a few at a time, lets them thaw at room temperature, and voilà, the official snack food of South Carolina.

I have heard that some people, upon tasting their first boiled peanut, are a little taken aback. I have no such recollection of my first experience with the soft, salty legumes, but I guess for the uninitiated, it can be a little off-putting. Another friend of mine—not from around here—described it as having the texture of a peanut that someone else held in their mouth for a while then decided they didn't want after all. Most roadside stores that advertise these little beauties do a fine job of cooking them up, but for the "Guaranteed Worst in Town," you will need to see **Cromer's P-Nuts Inc.** (803-779-2290; cromers.com), 1700 Huger Street, Columbia.

BALLOONING ✍ **Freedom Weekend Aloft** (864-399-9481; freedomeweekend.org), Simpsonville. This event typically is held on a Friday through Monday in May and features hot-air balloon competitions and kid-friendly entertainment and activities. Admission is $10 a day for adults (13 and older); Monday is free admission, but parking is $5 every day.

BEACHES South Carolina is blessed with a bevy of beaches. From north to south, they are Cherry Grove, Ocean Drive, North Myrtle Beach, Atlantic Beach, Myrtle Beach, Surfside, Garden City, Murrells Inlet, Litchfield, Pawleys Island, Isle of Palms, Sullivans Island, Folly Beach, Kiawah Island, Seabrook Island, and the Beaufort-area sea islands: Edisto, Lady's, Hunting, Fripp, and Hilton Head.

BED & BREAKFASTS South Carolina Bed & Breakfast Association (864-949-7230; scbba.net), 110 Ridge Road, Lyman.

many set here. Pat Conroy is one of the state's most famous writers with a collection of fictional stories—including *The Lords of Discipline, The Prince of Tides, Beach Music,* and *South of Broad*—set in the state. A memoir, *My Losing Season,* chronicles Conroy's senior season as the starting point guard on The Citadel's basketball team. Sullivans Island native Dorothea Benton Frank has written almost a dozen novels set in the South Carolina Lowcountry, including *Sullivans Island, Isle of Palms,* and *Pawleys Island.* Sue Monk Kidd lives in Charleston and set *The Secret Life of Bees* and *The Mermaid Chair* in the state.

The organization inspects all the B&Bs and inns listed on its website.

BIRDING Hundreds of species of birds have been seen in South Carolina—and the **Carolina Bird Club** (carolinabirdclub.org) keeps a list of all of them. The website also has a great listing of some of the best bird-spotting areas in the state and information on field trips.

BOATING In addition to the raft of beaches and access to the Atlantic Ocean, South Carolina has an abundance of freshwater lakes, rivers, and streams for skiing, pontoon boating, or paddling. The **South Carolina Natural Resources Department** (803-734-385; dnr.sc.gov/boating.html) has information about bringing your own boat and safety requirements on state waters.

BOOKS There are many books written about South Carolina, and

BUS SERVICE Greyhound offers bus service to the following South Carolina cities: Aiken, Anderson, Beaufort, Camden, Charleston, Columbia, Dillon, Duncan, Florence, Fort Jackson, Georgetown, Greenville, Manning, Myrtle Beach, Orangeburg, Spartanburg, Summerville, Sumter, and Walterboro.

CAMPING AND CABINS The best camping is at state parks. **The South Carolina Department of Parks, Recreation and Tourism** (803-734-1700; south carolinaparks.com) has a complete listing of all parks and natural areas, including information about camping, cabin rentals, and activities at the parks. You can make reservations online, get a yearlong pass for entry into all state parks, and book tee times at the two golf

CABIN RENTALS

South Carolina's cabins are one of the state parks' most popular features. There are 230 cabins statewide that can be reserved up to 11 months in advance. Some folks are ready to call on the first business day of each new year to get in their reservations.

The state parks agency offers three ways to book a cabin: Online at southcarolinaparks.reserveamerica.com, by calling toll-free at 866-345-PARK (7275), or by contacting the individual parks. Last-minute reservations made less than three days in advance have to go through the park. The website offers the best way to see availability at all parks. Half the total rental cost must be paid when the reservation is made.

Cabin check-in is 4 PM at most parks, 3 PM at Hickory Knob. Checkout is 10 AM at most parks, 11 AM at Hickory Knob. Prices start at $48 a night at Barnwell State Park in the offseason and range up to $172 a night at Devils Fork or Hunting Island during the peak season.

Typically, you can rent a cabin for as few as two days, but many parks may require weekly rental during the peak season from Memorial Day to Labor Day. Pets are not allowed in or around the cabins or cabin areas. For those who want to stay in a state park with their furry family members, pets are welcome in most parks' camping areas.

Amenities for those staying at the cabins include water bodies for swimming, fishing, and paddling. Hickory Knob and Cheraw parks offer golf courses with greens fees of $20 on weekends, $15 weekdays. Cart fees are $13 per person.

Christy Watts Gentry

25 percent locally grown produce in their restaurants and can use the FRESH ON THE MENU sticker.

CRABBING A very popular type of crab that's easy to catch along the South Carolina coast is the blue crab. Recreational fishermen can put out two crab pots without a license, but you have to write your name on an attached yellow buoy that will float at high tide. Traps should be checked at least once a day—twice a day for the best catch. The best bait is chicken necks. Blue crabs can be caught year-round. The state **Natural Resources Department** (dnr.sc.gov) has tips on catching, cleaning, and cooking blue crabs.

CRAFTS South Carolina Artisans Center (843-549-0011; scartisanscenter.com), 318 Wichman Street, Walterboro. Open 10–6 Monday through Saturday, 1–6 Sunday. Artists displaying their work here have to pass two

courses located inside state parks. Most of the state's 46 parks have some form of camping, and most of the sites include electric and water hookups. Trailside and backcountry camping also are available for the more sturdy camper.

CANOEING/KAYAKING South Carolina Paddlesports Industry Association (843-928-3316; paddlesouthcarolina.org), 1107 State Street, Cayce. This website offers information on tours, rentals, and lessons as well as retail outlets in the state.

CERTIFIED SC GROWN In an effort to encourage people to eat locally grown foods, the South Carolina Agriculture Department has created the Certified SC Grown (certifiedscgrown.com) program. Growers must pass an application process to be able to put the CERTIFIED SC GROWN stickers on their products. Restaurants are participating in a companion program called Fresh on the Menu. Chefs agree to use at least

auditions. More than 250 artists are represented in all kinds of media, including clay, metal, glass, wood, and film. Live demonstrations 11–3 on the third Saturday of every month.

DECLARATION OF INDEPENDENCE

Four South Carolinians signed the Declaration of Independence: Thomas Heyward Jr., Thomas Lynch Jr., Arthur Middleton, and Edward Rutledge. Each man's homesite has been preserved.

The Heyward-Washington House (charlestonmuseum.org), 87 Church Street, Charleston. This home was built in 1772 by rice planter Daniel Heyward for his son Thomas Jr. (1746–1809) to use as a town house. The younger Heyward had returned the year before from studying law in England and traveling in Europe. He was elected to the provincial assembly in 1772 and three years later was sent to the Continental Congress to fill in for John Rutledge, who had been called home

THE DIARIES OF MARY CHESNUT

Mary Boykin Chesnut was not the only Southern woman to keep a diary of the Civil War era, she's simply the best known. She writes of her feelings and sentiments and the view from the top of the social and political ladder of the events of the war, from the first shots in Charleston Harbor to the assassination of President Lincoln and the surrender of the Confederates at Appomattox Court House in Virginia.

This is an entry from April 21, 1865, while Chesnut was in the small South Carolina town of Chester and her husband was at war:

> While the Preston girls are here, my dining-room is given up to them, and we camp on the landing, with our one table and six chairs. Beds are made on the dining-room floor. Otherwise there is no furniture, except buckets of water and bath-tubs in their improvised chamber. Night and day this landing and these steps are crowded with the élite of the Confederacy, going and coming, and when night comes, or rather, bedtime, more beds are made on the floor of the landing-place for the war-worn soldiers to rest upon. The whole house is a bivouac.

Born in 1823 in a small community just west of what is now Shaw Air Force Base in Sumter, Mary Boykin Miller was the daughter of a U.S. congressman and governor of South Carolina. She married James to help defend against a possible invasion. Heyward was just 30 years old when he signed the Declaration of Independence and became a judge back in South Carolina. He was captured along with fellow patriot Edward Rutledge when the British took Charleston in 1780 and sent to prison for a year in St. Augustine, Florida. In 1790 he was a member of the state constitutional convention and soon after retired from public life. Heyward died on his South Carolina plantation on March 6, 1809. The family's downtown Charleston home was rented to the city in May 1791 for President George Washington's weeklong stay during his Southern tour—thus the *Washington* part of the home's name. The home is located within the original walled city of Charleston and was Heyward's home until 1794. The museum bought the house in 1929, and it became the city's first historic house museum.

Thomas Lynch Jr. was born at **Hopsewee Plantation** (843-546-

Chesnut Jr. in 1840, and the couple moved in the circles of high-society South Carolina until James was elected to the U.S. Senate in 1858. After Lincoln's election in 1860, the Chesnuts left Washington for South Carolina, where the Ordinance of Secession was signed in December 1860. James became a brigadier general in the Confederate Army and was an aide to President Jefferson Davis.

Davis's last speech in Columbia was given from the steps of the Chesnuts' wartime home, which is now a bed & breakfast in downtown Columbia.

Mary Chesnut crossed paths with the leaders of the Confederacy on a regular basis as she traveled with her husband and others from Charleston to Montgomery, Alabama, the capital of the Confederacy in Richmond, Virginia, and other points inside South Carolina. She knew the players intimately, and her observations and quotes from them give readers a unique glimpse behind the scenes of the ill-fated effort.

Although the diaries were not published until after her death, Mary Chesnut had tried to get them published in the 1870s and worked for years, editing them as well as writing three novels. When she died in 1889, she was working on the diaries and several manuscripts.

Many sites in South Carolina claim a connection to the Chesnuts, who lived in several locations around the state before settling near Camden after the war.

7891; hopsewee.com), 494 Hopsewee Road, Georgetown, in 1749. His family was already quite wealthy and he—like others of his generation and class—was sent to England to be educated. Like Thomas Heyward Jr., he studied law in England and returned to South Carolina in the 1770s, when tensions between the colonists and the British were heating up. He was serving as a captain in South Carolina's provincial regiment when his father suffered a paralyzing stroke while representing the state at the Constitutional Convention in Philadelphia. The younger Lynch was elected as his replacement. Lynch Jr. was not yet 27 when he signed the Declaration. The elder Lynch died from his stroke on his way back to South Carolina; the younger Lynch was not well, either, having contracted malaria during his service in the military. He left South Carolina in 1779 first for the West Indies with an ultimate destination of France. But the ship was lost at sea, and he and his wife as well as all the passengers and crew were presumed drowned. Lynch was just 30 years old when he died.

Arthur Middleton was born in 1742 at his family's plantation, **Middleton Place** (843-556-6020; middletonplace.org), 4300 Ashley River Road, Charleston, on the banks of the Ashley River. He, too, was educated in England and traveled through Europe before returning to South Carolina in the early 1770s. Like the others, he worked

to help write a state constitution and was elected to the provincial congress in Philadelphia, where he signed the Declaration. Milddleton soon returned to South Carolina, where he helped defend Charleston from British invasion after his family's plantation home had been ransacked. Middleton was captured in 1780 and sent to St. Augustine for a year. After the war, he declined a seat in the national congress, but did hold a seat in the state legislature. He died in 1787 from a fever.

Edward Rutledge was born in Charleston in 1749 and was the youngest of Dr. John Rutledge's seven children. At age 27, he was one of the youngest people to sign the Declaration of Independence. Like the other signers, he was educated in England and became a lawyer. He married a sister of Arthur Middleton and was captured along with his brother-in-law when Charleston was taken over by the British. After a year imprisoned in St. Augustine, he returned to South Carolina. He served as a state lawmaker and state senator before being elected governor of South Carolina in 1798. But he died in Charleston two years later, unable to finish his term. Edward Rutledge's house is on the National Register of Historic Places and is now the **Governor's House Inn** (843-720-2070; governorshouse.com), 117 Broad Street, Charleston.

FERRIES All of South Carolina's islands are reachable by bridge save one: Daufuskie Island off Hilton Head Island in the Lowcountry. Two ferries, **Haig Point Ferry Co.** (843-301-3723) and **Daufuskie Island Cruises & Tours,** take passengers over for the day trip.

FILM South Carolina has been the backdrop for films dating back to D. W. Griffith's controversial epic *Birth of a Nation.* Though that movie was filmed in California, it was set in South Carolina.

At least three films based on novels by South Carolina native Pat Conroy were set in the state and filmed here: *The Prince of Tides* (1991), *The Lords of Discipline* (1983), and *The Great Santini* (1979).

The most popular location is Beaufort, which retains the look of an old Southern downtown and has some antebellum mansions still gracefully sitting by the river behind moss-draped oaks.

The Big Chill (1983) was set and filmed in Beaufort. One of the stars of that movie, Tom Berenger, liked the location so much he started living there between films.

Forrest Gump (1994) was set in several Southern locations, including Alabama and Savannah, Georgia. Many of its scenes, including those set in the jungles of Vietnam, were filmed in Lowcountry locations, including Beaufort, Fripp Island, Pritchardvill, Varnville, Walterboro, and Yemassee.

The Legend of Bagger Vance (2000) was filmed in Bluffton and Kiawah Island in South Carolina and Jekyll Island and Savannah in Georgia.

Forces of Nature (1999) was filmed in several South Carolina locations as the main characters had to wind their way down the East Coast from New York to Savannah, Georgia, including stops at South Carolina's South of the Border. Scenes also were filmed in Beaufort.

Here is a sample of some of the other movies filmed in South Carolina, according to SCIWAY, the South Carolina Information Highway:

The Abyss (1989), Gaffney

Ace Ventura: When Nature Calls (1995), Edisto Island, Green Pond

Cold Mountain (2003), Charleston

Days of Thunder (1990), Darlington

Dear John (2010), Edisto Island, Charleston, Folly Beach, Harleyville, Isle of Palms, James Island, Sullivans Island

Death Sentence (2007), Columbia

Deliverance (1972), Chatooga River, Lake Jocassee

Die Hard: With a Vengeance (1995), Berkeley County, Dorchester, Charleston

For the Boys (1991), The Citadel

The Fugitive (1993), Beaufort

Full Metal Jacket (1987), Parris Island (Beaufort County)

GI Jane (1997), Beaufort

The Jungle Book (1994), Beaufort, Fripp Island

Leatherheads (2008), Anderson, Greenwood, Greenville

The Longest Yard (1974), Hilton Head

Modern Love (1990), Columbia

Night of the Living Dead (1990), Berkeley County, Charleston County

The Notebook (2004), Georgetown County, Mount Pleasant, Charleston, Moncks Corner, Edisto Island, North Charleston, Wadmalaw Island

Nutty Professor II: The Klumps (2000), Lake City

Paradise (1991), Charleston, Georgetown, McClellanville

The Patriot (2000), Edisto Island, Brattonsville, Charleston, Moncks Corner, Chester County, Fort Lawn, Georgetown County, Dorchester County, Rock Hill

A Perfect World (1993), Beaufort

The Philadelphia Experiment (1984), Charleston

The Program (1993), Columbia

Radio (2003), Anderson, Walterboro

Renaissance Man (1994), Columbia

Shag (1989), Florence, Georgetown, Myrtle Beach

Sleeping with the Enemy (1991), Abbeville, Clinton, Spartanburg

Something to Talk About (1995), Columbia

Swamp Thing (1982), Charleston area

That Darn Cat (1997), Aiken, Edgefield

Wild Hearts Can't Be Broken (1991), Elloree, Myrtle Beach, Orangeburg

FISHING South Carolina is an angler's dream. Hundreds of freshwater lakes, ponds, and streams throughout the state all lead to the Atlantic Ocean, with dozens of piers, charter boats, and miles of beach and inlet from which to cast a line.

Like many states, South Carolina has an issue with mercury found in the fatty tissue of large fish in the state's waters. Mercury warning signs are posted at water bodies where fish should not be eaten or where fish consumption should be limited. The state **Department of Health and Environmental Control** keeps an updated list of these waterbodies at scdhec.gov/environment/water/fish.

The state **Department of Natural Resources** (dnr.sc.gov/fishing) has everything you need to know about fishing in the state, including what fish are biting where and coastal tide charts. For $11, out-of-state visitors can get a freshwater fishing license good for one week or a saltwater license good for two weeks. If you plan to visit the state for fishing several times during the year, an annual license for either fresh or salt water is $35. DNR administers the annual Governor's Cup Billfishing Series. For guidelines for each year's series, visit govcup.dnr.sc.gov.

SC Department of Parks, Recreation & Tourism, DiscoverSouthCarolina.com

FLOUR **Adluh Flour** (803-779-2460; adluh.com), 804½ Gervais Street, Columbia. Open Monday through Thursday 7:30–5, Fri 7:30–noon. You cannot miss the building that houses this mill in downtown Columbia. It's as much a part of the city's skyline as the Statehouse, and it's on the National Register of Historic Places. You can get Adluh flour in most South Carolina grocery stores. But if you go by their mill store, you can get their special biscuit mix. Take it from someone who loves to eat biscuits, but cannot bake a good one from scratch, their mix is impossible to mess up. I recommend using buttermilk for your liquid.

FORTS South Carolina's coastal forts have played significant roles in U.S. history from the Revolutionary War. Very little remains of

FORT SUMTER NATIONAL MONUMENT

Fort Sumter was built largely by slave labor over a 30-year period. Its location at the mouth of Charleston Harbor between Sullivans and James Islands made it ideal for defending the city from attack, in conjunction with guns at Fort Moultrie on Sullivans Island on the northern lip of the harbor.

Other installations designed to protect Charleston included Castle Pinckney on an island in the Cooper River. Built in 1810, the site was designed for defense of the inner harbor. Fort Johnson was built on James Island in 1708 to defend Charleston, but three forts were built and destroyed by storms over the next century and a half. In 1861 South Carolina troops began rebuilding the fort. Fort Moultrie had been the site of a key battle of the American Revolution and was built in 1776 of palmetto logs and sand. A second fort was built in 1798, but that was destroyed in a hurricane. The third Fort Moultrie was completed in 1809 with its 50 cannons and served as the primary defense of Charleston Harbor until the Civil War.

When South Carolina withdrew from the United States in December 1860, federal troops were consolidated at Fort Sumter from Fort Moultrie on Sullivans Island and other installations around Charleston Harbor. South Carolina's militia and Confederate soldiers began to bolster those forts as they took them over.

Again, slave labor was used for these construction projects. Jacob Stroyer described his experience working for Confederate soldiers in his autobiography: "Our work was to repair forts, build batteries, mount guns, and arrange them . . . the boys my age, namely, thirteen, and some older, waited on officers and carried water for the men at work, and in general acted as messengers . . . although we knew that our work in the Confederate service was against our liberty, yet we were delighted to be in military service."

inland forts, just the occasional historical marker. But coastal forts, some of which remained in use until after World War II, have been preserved.

GOLF South Carolina has more than 360 golf courses, about a third of which are in Myrtle Beach, and is one of the nation's top golfing destinations. Eleven of

The first shot of the Civil War was fired from Fort Johnson and exploded over the fort at 4:30 AM on April 12, 1861. It was a signal to those manning the Morris Island battery and Fort Moultrie across the harbor to begin firing. U.S. troops surrendered 34 hours later.

Mary Chesnut, whose diaries and writings from the era became famous, wrote in the hours before shelling began: "I do not pretend to go to sleep. How can I?" After the shelling started and she and others went to the roof of her Charleston home to watch, she wrote: "Prayers from the women and imprecations from the men; and then a shell would light up the scene." Once the shelling ended, Chestnut wrote: "After all that noise, and our tears and prayers, nobody has been hurt. Sound and fury signifying nothing! A delusion and a snare!"

When U.S. soldiers retook control of Morris Island in 1863, including the charge of the all-black 54th of Massachusetts made famous by the movie *Glory*, they began a bombardment of the fort and Charleston that lasted nearly 18 months. The city surrendered in February 1865. The siege of Charleston was the longest siege in U.S. military history—lasting 587 days.

On April 14, 1865, Major General Robert Anderson, who had surrendered Fort Sumter to the Confederates, came out of retirement and returned to the fort to raise the same U.S. flag he had lowered four years earlier.

Today Fort Sumter is a relic, no longer an imposing structure with walls reaching 50 feet above sea level. Work began to repair war damage in the 1870s, but money ran out and it was turned into a lighthouse station for decades. It was modernized at the turn of the 20th century and was manned as a protective fortress through World War II. It became a national monument in 1948.

Fort Sumter (843-883-3123; nps.gov/fosu/index.htm), 340 Concord Street, Charleston; tours run three to six times a day, depending on the season. The trip takes at least two and a half hours, so don't plan many other activities on the day you visit the monument.

Golf Digest's top 100 public golf courses are in the state, starting with **The Ocean Course** (800-576-1570; kiawahresort.com) on Kiawah Island, which will be home to the 2012 PGA Championship and hosted the 2007 Senior PGA Championship and the 1991 Ryder Cup. The state **Parks Recreation and Tourism Department** has

the most comprehensive list of courses at golf.discoversouthcarolina.com. Also available are myrtlebeachgolf.com, hiltonheadgolf.com, and charlestongolfguide.com.

GRITS The most Southern thing in the world has to be grits. It is a rare person who was not raised on grits who actually will eat them later in life. Grits are quite simply ground corn. There's grits with hominy flavoring added while they're being ground. My mother doesn't like hominy, but a lot of people do. I don't know if I can really tell the difference. I just like grits. Even the machine-ground white grits that you find in the grocery store. I cook them for hours, sometimes in chicken broth and cream, sometimes just salty water. There are as many ways to make grits as there are cooks. The

grits tend to taste like whatever you add to them—say, shrimp and gravy, or cheese. Columbia's **Anson Mills** (803-467-4122; ansonmills.com) stone-grinds grits and other grains like in the old days. Grits are kept whole with the germ attached. A lot of restaurants that specialize in Southern cuisine buy these grits. If you want to give them a try on your own, you can order them off Anson Mills website. They cost a good bit more than grocery store grits, but they taste a lot better. Make sure to follow their cooking instructions to the letter. You can't just throw these grits in a pot of salty water and boil them; they need to soak first. Another Columbia miller, **Allen Brothers Milling Co. Inc.** (800-692-3584; adluh.com), owners of Adluh Flour, also has stone-ground grits from white corn or South Carolina–grown yellow corn.

HIKING The Appalachian Trail skirts the northwestern edge of South Carolina without ever entering the state. But in 1994 a group of conservation-minded outdoorsy types decided we could have a statewide trail from the mountains to the sea. **The Palmetto Trail** will be 425 miles long when it's finished. As of spring 2011 about 300 miles of the trail were completed in a series of passages that can be hiked, biked, and/or camped. **Palmetto Conservation** (803-771-0870; palmettoconservation.org) has all the maps and info you will need to hike any or all of the trail. There is even a way to track your miles online. In the interest of full disclosure, I must tell you that I am an honorary owner of $\frac{1}{100}$ of a mile of the trail—the most beautiful 52 feet of the whole thing. My

section is located in the Fort Jackson passage at UTM17S 515797E 3761867 N.

HISTORY South Carolina Department of Archives and History (803-896-6100; scdah .sc.gov), 8301 Parklane Road, Columbia. Reference room is open 8:30–5 Monday through Friday. The agency is the keeper of the past and administers the state's historical marker program. Many people come here to do genealogical research. Free.

South Carolina Confederate Relic Room and Military Museum (803-737-8095; crr.sc.gov), 301 Gervais Street, Columbia. Open 10–5 Tuesday through Saturday. This museum chronicles the state's military history from the Revolutionary War to the most recent wars in Afghanistan and Iraq and includes an exhibit on the all-black 371st Infantry Regiment that fought in World War I. Admission:

Christy Watts Gentry

$5 adults ages 18–61, $4 seniors and active-duty and retired military, $2 for ages 13–17, free for younger children. The Relic Room is located in the same building as the South Carolina State Museum, and joint tickets are available at a discount.

HORSE RACING One of the state's earliest draws for outside visitors was horse racing in Aiken and Camden. The **Aiken Thoroughbred Racing Hall of Fame and Museum** (803-642-7650; aikenracinghalloffame.com) showcases Aiken's contribution to thoroughbred racing from 1900 to the present. Free, donations welcome.

The **Carolina Cup** (803-432-6513; carolina-cup.org), in the spring and **The Colonial Cup** in the fall are held at Springdale Racecourse in Camden. The spring races are held in late March or early April and are watched by the state's largest outdoor cocktail party as thousands flock to the sometimes muddy field. The event is a bit pricey: General admission tickets are $30 apiece and parking is $10–20 a car; infield parking is by reservation and costs more than $200 with two admission tickets included. The fall races are more family-oriented with Jack Russell terrier races in addition to the steeplechase. It's less expensive, too, with $20 advance tickets and $10 parking. Infield parking is less than $150 with two tickets included.

The **Aiken Steeplechase** (803-648-9641; aikensteeplechase .com) has spring and fall races as well, usually March and October. Advance tickets are $10, with more expensive parking packages available as well.

ICE CREAM '55 Exchange (864-656-2155; clemson.edu/ice cream), Hendrix Student Center— East End at Cherry and McMillan Roads, Clemson. Open 11:30–6

Monday through Friday, 1–6 Saturday through Sunday. This is some of the best ice cream you will ever eat. The exchange was established in 2005 by Clemson University's class of 1955 (hence, the name). The shop is staffed by students, and the ice cream comes from the college's dairy program.

ISLANDS South Carolina has several barrier islands and some slightly larger islands that draw thousands of visitors each year. The land on these islands is some of the most expensive and desired in the state. Barrier islands—like Pawleys, Sullivans, and Kiawah and the Outer Banks of North Carolina—are thin strips of land than run parallel to the mainland and help protect delicate marsh ecosystems from tides and storms. Longshore currents will typically cause the north end of an island to erode, while those same currents will drop sand at the south end of the island. But people who own land near the shifting sand don't want to lose their property to the sea, so they tend to put up structures like groins and seawalls and dredge sand up from the ocean floor to deposit on the beaches. It's all temporary and simply delays the inevitable shift of the sand.

KUDZU More than a comic strip written by the late Doug Marlette, kudzu is the pervasive vine that blankets the South. As ground cover, it can help with erosion. Cows and other grazing animals love it. It is used in some cultures as a treatment for hangovers and to help control alcohol cravings. Around these parts, Upstate artist **Nancy Basket** (864-718-8864; nancybasket.com), 1105 East Main Street, Walhalla, weaves baskets and makes paper and other products from the vine.

LAKES Most of South Carolina's major lakes are man-made, from Lake Jocassee in the northwest to the state's largest—Lake Marion—southeast of Columbia. Many of the lakes were formed by dams for hydroelectric power. Most have a state park on them; in some cases the park is the only public access point.

Lake Jocassee was formed in the 1970s by a dam on the Toxaway River. It's a deep-water lake surrounded by mountains and is largely maintained by the state and Duke Energy Co. as a wilderness area. It spills over a dam and 300 feet down into Lake Keowee, which is also operated by Duke Energy. Lake Keowee has many private homes and many access points. Farther south is Hartwell Lake on the Savannah River. This is the first of three lakes on the river, followed by Lake Russell and Lake Thurmond. They are all operated by the U.S. Army Corps of Engineers and have many public boat ramps and recreation areas. Lake Thurmond is home to Hickory Knob State Park with a lodge, cabins, and golf course. To the east is Lake Greenwood, also operated by Duke Energy through a lease from Greenwood County. In the center of the state are Lake Wateree, also operated by Duke Energy, and Lake Murray operated by South Carolina Electric & Gas. Wateree is the state's oldest man-made lake, formed by a dam on the Catawba River. Lake Murray is just west of Columbia and was created by a dam on the Saluda River. Those lakes' downstream rivers, Congaree and Wateree, meet up and pour into the 110,000-acre Lake Marion, which is operated by state-owned utility Santee Cooper along with Lake Moultrie to the south. The lakes and surrounding area draw thousands of boaters, anglers, and golfers every year. Boaters can travel through a system of locks between Marion and Moultrie and then into the Cooper River, which leads to the Atlantic Ocean at Charleston.

LAZY RIVERS Most rivers in South Carolina would qualify as lazy. They all meander from the mountains to the sea, occasionally traveling through dam spillways. But the best lazy rivers have cement bottoms. They're like skinny, winding swimming pools with all the water jets pointing in one direction to give you enough "current" to float around in circles all day. Many hotels along the coast have their own lazy rivers—and they're staples at water parks, giving Grandma something to do while the kids shoot down the rapids rides.

LIGHTHOUSES There are 10 lighthouses, including 8 historic ones, in South Carolina, with the one at Morris Island dangerously close to falling into the sea. Other lighthouses that need attention include those at Georgetown, Hunting Island, and Cape Romain. The U.S. Coast Guard operates lights at Georgetown, where the state's first lighthouse was built, and Sullivans Island, which is on the north flank of Charleston Harbor. The first lighthouse built of cypress wood on North Island at the entrance to Winyah Bay was destroyed by a storm shortly after it was built in 1801. In 1811 the lighthouse was rebuilt with bricks and is still standing today. The newest lighthouse—at Harbour Town in the Sea Pines Resort on Hilton Head Island—was never meant to help sea captains navigate in the dark or bad weather or to warn of dangerous shoals. It was built in 1970 as an advertising beacon to get boaters on the Intracoastal Waterway to dock at the marina and enjoy the nightlife at Sea Pines. Its beam can be seen for 15 miles. **Save the Light Inc.** (savethelight.org) has raised more than $5 million in the past 10 years to stabilize and protect the Morris Island Lighthouse.

MARSH TACKY This is the official state heritage horse, and its bloodlines are being protected by the **Carolina Marsh Tacky Association** (marshtack.org). Experts think the breed originated with the horses brought to the new world by Spanish explorers. The Marsh Tacky is a little shorter and stouter than your average horse, making it an excellent worker in the swampy marshes along the Carolina coast where it was predominant until the 20th century and the car. It was thought to be extinct in the 1980s and 1990s; the preservation group has counted fewer than 200. The group is working with the American Livestock Breeds Conservancy to try to increase the tackies' population.

MAYONNAISE Duke's Mayonnaise is made in Greenville, or more precisely Mauldin, as it has been for nearly 100 years. The mayo was the secret ingredient in spread sandwiches that Eugenia Duke sold to soldiers at Camp Sevier near Greenville during World War I. She started selling them in 1917; by the spring of 1919, just before the war's end, she sold more than 10,000 sandwiches in one day, according to the Duke Sandwich Co.'s website.

In 1929 Mrs. Duke sold the recipe for her mayonnaise to the C. F. Sauer Co., which continues to follow that recipe as it blends the savory spread in the same factory it built more than 80 years ago. Mrs. Duke sold the recipes for her spreads to her bookkeeper Alan Hart, who created a wholesale market for the sandwiches and sold to company stores at textile mills and local drugstores. The sandwich company has changed hands a couple of times, always staying close to the same family. It now operates a few sandwich shops in South Carolina as well as selling wrapped sandwiches to retailers.

Eugenia Duke moved to California to be near her daughter and lived out her days there, selling sandwiches to workers in shipyards during World War II. She eventually sold that sandwich company as well. Eugenia Duke died in 1968 at the age of 90.

MUSEUMS The South Carolina State Museum (803-898-4921; museum.state.sc.us), 301 Gervais Street, Columbia. Located in an old textile mill in the capital city's Vista area, the State Museum has tens of thousands of artifacts revealing the state's cultural and natural history. **EdVenture** (803-779-3100; edventure.org) children's museum is located next door. Both sit on the historic Columbia Canal once used to ferry supplies into the city. Greenville's Heritage Green brings together several museums and other attractions in one area. It is now home to the **Greenville County Museum of Art** (864-271-7570; greenvillemuseum.org), 420 College Street; a satellite gallery of **Bob Jones University's Museum & Gallery** (864-770-1331; bjumg.org), 25 Heritage Green Place; **the Upcountry History Museum** (864-467-3100; upcountryhistory.org), 540 Buncombe Street, located in the old Coca-Cola bottling building; and **The Children's Museum** (864-233-7755; www.tcmupstate.org),

300 College Street, which opened in summer 2009. Charleston practically is a museum of its own and its **Museum Mile** (charlestons museummile.org) includes a dozen museums, historical houses, and other places of interest along a 1-mile stretch of Meeting Street.

NATIONAL PARKS/FORESTS

The Congaree National Park (803-776-4396; nps.gov/cong /index.htm), 100 National Park Road, Hopkins. Open 8:30–5 daily; till 7 on summer weekends. Free admission. Congaree is South Carolina's only true national park and preserves the largest old-growth floodplain forest in North America. Towering trees shelter canoers and kayakers in the swamp. The park also includes 20 miles of backcountry hiking trails and a 2-mile boardwalk trail. It offers guided tours on land and boat throughout the year. The park is also a popular birding spot. The swamp is prone to flooding in heavy rains; check conditions before heading out.

Sumter and Francis Marion National Forests. The Sumter National Forest is split among three noncontiguous areas and takes up 371,000 acres in the northwestern portion of the state. The Francis Marion National Forest is northwest of Charleston and spans nearly 260,000 acres. A third of the forest was leveled in 1989 by Hurricane Hugo, creating an enormous fire hazard that the Forest Service has worked to reduce over the past 20 years.

The forest boasts a wide range of wildlife, including the endangered red-cockaded woodpecker.

Cowpens National Battlefield (864-461-2828; nps.gov/cowp /index.htm), 4001 Chesnee Highway, Gaffney. Open 9–5 daily. Free admission. This park preserves the scene of a key victory for the Americans during the Revolutionary War and offers visitors a walking trail, marked road tour, picnic ground, and visitors center.

NATURE South Carolina Nature-Based Tourism Association
(800-673-0679; scnature adventures.com/index.html) has information on nature-based eco-tourism companies throughout the state.

PALMETTO FLAG The South
Carolina flag is a navy-blue banner with a palmetto tree in the center and a crescent moon—the emblem worn by Revolutionary War soldiers based in Charleston—in the left corner. This image has been co-opted it seems by almost every

T-shirt seller in the state. There is no one brand that is the official maker of these clothes; the designs can range from some that genuinely look like that state flag to ones that look like a big old broccoli spear with a crescent moon. The tree is the thing that makes the difference, so as you shop, make note of the way it looks and then decide which one you like best.

PLANTATIONS The best-preserved plantations are in Charleston and Georgetown. An 11-mile stretch of Ashley River Road (SC 61) west of Charleston takes you past three of the best-known Lowcountry plantations: **Middleton Place Plantation** (843-556-6020; middletonplace .org), **Magnolia Plantation** (800-367-3517; magnoliaplantation .com), and **Drayton Hall** (843-769-2600; draytonhall.org), all of which sit on the Ashley River.

Another popular plantation in the Charleston area sits across the Cooper River from downtown: **Boone Hall Plantation** (843-216-1032; boonehallplantation .com), 1235 Long Point Road, Mount Pleasant. For a list of all the plantations in South Carolina, check out south-carolina -plantations.com.

POLITICIANS John C. Calhoun died 10 years before South Carolina seceded from the United States, but his words as much as anyone's were part of the reasoning for the state withdrawing. A superior speaker and staunch defender of slavery, Calhoun was vice president under John Quincy Adams and fellow South Carolinian Andrew Jackson. Calhoun also served in the U.S. House, the U.S. Senate, and as secretary of state.

He began his political career as a supporter of protective tariffs and a strong federal government,

SC Department of Parks, Recreation & Tourism, DiscoverSouthCarolina.com

but soon changed his position when it became clear that as more free states were added to the United States, the South would lose a vote on slavery. Calhoun said states could nullify a federal law they disagreed with, and South Carolina did just that in 1832—nullifying federal tariffs. That led to a new law giving the president power to use troops to force states to obey federal law. President Jackson sent warships to Charleston Harbor as South Carolina lawmakers nullified that law. A compromise was brokered by Senator Henry Clay of Kentucky, but the seeds of secession had been planted.

Calhoun died in 1850. The home and surrounding land where he lived eventually went to his son-in-law, Thomas Clemson, who left the property to the state to create a university. **Fort Hill** (clemson.edu/about/history/properties/fort-hill/) was completely restored in 2003 and is filled with many Calhoun and Clemson family artifacts. It is open Monday through Saturday 10–noon and 1–4:30, Sunday 2–4:30.

James F. Byrnes was a political jack of all trades, holding positions in the legislative, executive, and judicial branch of government in the first half of the 20th century. He was President Franklin Roosevelt's right-hand man, running the nation's war effort with an unusual amount of freedom. He was named *Time* magazine's man of the year in 1946.

Byrnes was born in Charleston in 1882; his father died before the future statesman's birth. His mother was a dressmaker, and as a teenager Byrnes became a court reporter/stenographer. Although he never went to college or law school, Byrnes apprenticed for a lawyer and was admitted to the bar to practice law in 1903. Just seven years later he was elected to the U.S. House when he was 28 years old and served 14 years. He then lost his first bid for the U.S. Senate, but used the time off from public service to become a wealthy man in the late 1920s. He returned to politics in 1930 and won the U.S. Senate seat from the man who had beaten him six years earlier. He served as senator for 10 years and was very close to President Roosevelt, who appointed Byrnes to the U.S. Supreme Court in 1941. But Byrnes served just 15 months on the court before joining the Roosevelt administration as head of the economic stabilization office, then the War Department. Some referred to Byrnes as the "assistant president" and thought he might become Roosevelt's choice as vice president for his final reelection bid. Instead that job went to Harry Truman, who took over as president when Roosevelt died just a few months into his fourth term. Truman appointed Byrnes Secretary of State after World War II was over—a position he held for just two years and was replaced by George Marshall. Byrnes then returned to South Carolina.

In 1950 at age 68, when most

people are thinking about retiring, Byrnes became the oldest person elected governor of South Carolina. In this position, he followed another of the state's major 20th-century politicians, Strom Thurmond. Although Thurmond, whose career continued for decades after Byrnes's death, and John C. Calhoun, who preceded him by a century, are remembered more by most South Carolinians today, James Byrnes is considered one of the most influential South Carolinians ever. He wrote two books, *Speaking Frankly* (1947) and *All in One Lifetime* (1958). He died in 1972. A statue of Byrnes sits on the Statehouse grounds at the corner of Sumter and Gervais Streets. On the statue is a different birth date, May 2, 1879. It's not clear why some official sources list his birthday as 1879 instead of the correct 1882. Some sources say it's because he needed to be at least 21 years old to hold a court reporter position, and was only 18 at the time.

Two schools are named after him—one a public high school in the Upstate town of Duncan, the other a private school in the small town of Quinby, near Florence. A building named for him at the University of South Carolina houses the college's international programs. A dormitory at Clemson University is named for him as well; he served on the board of trustees there. A scholarship program established by Byrnes and his wife, who did not have any children of their own, provides

scholarships to South Carolinians who have lost one or both parents. His papers are in the special collections of Clemson's Cooper Library (864-656-3027; clemson.edu). The James F. Byrnes Room there was dedicated in 1966. The room is open to the public and includes displays about Byrnes's life and career. The library is open daily between 10 AM and 8 PM.

POPULATION South Carolina has about 4.6 million people living on 30,000 square miles. Geographically, the state is larger than only 10 other states, but population-wise we are right smack in the middle at number 25. Columbia is not only the geographic center of the state, but also the population center as well as the largest city with 120,000 residents; next come Charleston (108,000), North Charleston (90,000), Rock Hill (61,000), and Greenville (60,000). It's just the in-city population of Greenville that is small. Nearly half a million people live in the county, making it the state's most populated.

RICE Rice was one of the most important staples of South Carolina farming for more than a century. Known as Carolina Gold, the rice was famous around the world for its quality, and is the basis for the Carolina rice cuisine. Most dishes here are served with a side order of rice rather than a potato. Several dishes are made all in one pot with meat, vegetables, and rice. Carolina Gold smells like

STROM THURMOND

As a teenager, I worked for Strom Thurmond in his U.S. Senate office in Washington, DC. He was an old man by that time, but it was still a very exciting experience for me. Looking back now, I'd say Thurmond embodied 20th-century South Carolina more than any other politician or person. He clung to segregationist policies—even though he had secretly fathered a child with his family's black maid in the 1920s. Then when all the battles were fought and lost, he changed along with everyone else and rarely mentioned his obstructionist ways. It's like when South Carolinians wax poetic about the Civil War and the Old South, and seem to forget the unpleasant fact of slavery.

Born in 1902 in very rural Edgefield County on the western edge of the state, Thurmond headed off to Clemson College at the age of 15. Degree in hand, he became a teacher and coach and was elected school superintendent back home in Edgefield. During that time, he studied law with his attorney father and was admitted to the South Carolina Bar in 1930 without going to law school. Three years later he was elected to the state senate; five years after that he became a judge.

After the attack on Pearl Harbor drew the United States into World War II, Thurmond volunteered for the U.S. Army at nearly 40 years old. He was one of the oldest participants in the D-Day invasion of Normandy and won five battle stars and more than a dozen other medals for his service in the war.

Still a bachelor, but now a war hero, Thurmond was elected governor of South Carolina in 1946 and the next year married a woman half his age. He split with the Democratic Party over racial issues during the 1948 convention and ran for president as a Dixiecrat. He was the only third-party candidate in the 20th century to win electoral votes, carrying four Southern states. He lost his first bid for the U.S. Senate in 1950, but four years later he won a write-in campaign to finish out the term of Burnet Maybank, who died in office. Thurmond resigned from the seat to run for reelection—as he had promised to do—and won in 1956. He held on to that seat until retiring in 2003 at age 100.

He still holds the record as the oldest person to serve in the Senate, though Robert Byrd of West Virginia surpassed him as longest serving.

But Thurmond also still holds the filibuster record in the U.S. Senate, attempting to block the 1957 Civil Rights Act, which he called "race mixing." In 1964 Thurmond was among the first wave of Southerners to switch from the Democratic Party to support Republican Barry Goldwater against Lyndon Johnson. By the 1970s, when schools and institutions across the South finally dropped their policies of segregation, Thurmond became one of the first Southern senators to hire a black staffer.

By the time I met the senator, he was almost 80 years old and president pro tem of the U.S. Senate, making him third in the line of succession to the presidency. His attention to constituent services had made him enormously popular back home. Even though there is very little federal legislation with his name on it, you are hard-pressed to visit any town in South Carolina and not find something named for him: the Strom Thurmond Institute of Government and Public Affairs at Clemson University, Strom Thurmond Federal Building in Columbia, Strom Thurmond High School in Aiken, J. Strom Thurmond Dam and Lake (folks on the Georgia side still call it Clarks Hill Lake). There is a statue of him on the south side of the Statehouse grounds that lists his many accomplishments and the names of his children.

His first wife died childless in 1960, but he remarried in 1968, this time to a woman a third his age. They had four children, one of whom was killed in a traffic accident in 1993. After Thurmond's death in 2003, a California woman in her 70s, Essie Mae Williams, came forward to announce that Strom Thurmond was her father. Thurmond's other children—who are roughly the same age as Williams's grandchildren—accepted their sister, and her name was added to the Thurmond monument on Statehouse grounds. Williams tells her story of growing up as Thurmond's secret biracial daughter in the book *Dear Senator*.

Thurmond's papers are kept at Clemson University's Special Collections library (clemson.edu), which is open weekdays 8–5.

TEXTILES

Almost every small town in South Carolina's Upstate has—or had—at least one textile mill. From the early 1900s up until today, textile mills drove the economy of small towns that had a water source.

Now as in much of the United States, South Carolina's textile industry is a shell of its former self, employing fewer than 30,000 workers when it had employed more than 200,000 at its peak.

Textile mills moved to South Carolina about the time that cotton prices were bottoming out. Farmers moved into the towns to find work milling the cotton they could no longer afford to grow. An abundance of water access in the Upstate made it a prime location for the plants—many of which were relocating from the Northeast, where unions drove up the price of labor. The poor populations in rural South Carolina were prime candidates for employees.

The mills would build homes that they rented to workers, stores where the workers could get credit, schools for the children, and hospitals for the sick. Sometimes workers were paid in "script"—money that was good only in the grocery, clothing, hardware, and other stores owned by the company. There were very few diversions for these hardworking folks, except church and textile league baseball teams that produced major-league stars, such as Shoeless Joe Jackson from Greenville and Red Barbary from nearby Simpsonville.

It was a hard life, and families were rarely able to build any wealth because they didn't own the homes they lived in. There was very little movement up the ranks at the mills. Supervisors lived in a different part of the village, and the company owners lived on grand estates outside of town.

Jan Hogan

green tea while it's being processed and is known for its long grain and flavor. The Carolina Gold Rice Foundation (carolina goldricefoundation.org) is in the business of restoring and maintaining the crop that is so important to

Families sent young children to work in the mills, "helping" Mom or Dad.

One mill in Honea Path, South Carolina, was the scene of the worst violence during the General Textile Strike of 1934, which involved workers across the United States. Specially commissioned deputies fired on a crowd of picketers outside the Chiquola Mill, killing six and wounding a dozen more. A mass funeral held for those killed drew 10,000 people from all across the country.

The strike soon came to an end with little immediate change in working conditions. But eventual changes in labor laws required all workers to be at least 16 years old.

Even with the law change, teenagers in these small towns would frequently drop out of high school to work in the mill . . . and spend the next 50 years of their lives there, often working next to their parents and grandparents, then their own children.

This tradition lasted for much of the 20th century, until cheap imports reduced the price of textiles and other woven goods. Mills began closing in South Carolina in the 1980s and moving to other countries with cheaper labor. They left behind a troop of brick elephants—large, sometimes toxic, buildings—sitting empty in the center of small towns and along the banks of scenic rivers.

Some towns have made good use of their abandoned mills.

In Columbia, for example, one former mill is home to the South Carolina State Museum. Another was converted into apartments inhabited mostly by students at the nearby University of South Carolina.

In Greenville old mills have been converted into shops, restaurants, galleries, and music venues along the Reedy River, which runs through the town.

There still are plenty of mills still in operation, especially in the Upstate. But these modern facilities are located for easy access to interstates.

the state's economy and heritage. A periodic newsletter on the foundation's website includes recipes, a little science, and a bit of history.

STATE PARKS South Carolina Parks, Recreation and Tourism

(803-734-1312; southcarolina parks.com), 1205 Pendleton Street, Columbia. SC PRT manages the state's parks and provides a one-stop shop for making reservations for campsites, cabins, golf courses, meeting spaces,

SC Department of Parks, Recreation & Tourism, DiscoverSouthCarolina.com

and picnic shelters located in those parks.

WEDDINGS There are hundreds of picturesque locations for getting married in South Carolina. Most people look to the beach for the big day. There is a 24-hour wait period between applying for the license and getting one. So take your shoes off and stay a night. Wedding licenses are handled by county offices, but the laws governing matrimony are statewide (scstatehouse.gov/code /t20c001.htm). Two of the best outdoor weddings I've been to in South Carolina: Cypress Gardens, where the bride made her entrance by boat, and on the beach where the groom was barefoot.

WILDLIFE South Carolina has an abundance of wildlife, from black bears to bobcats and coyotes. The **South Carolina Wildlife Federation** (803-256-0670; scwf.org), 215 Pickens Street, Columbia, keeps track of the animals and manages land for hunting.

ZOO Riverbanks Zoo and Garden (803-779-8717; riverbanks .org), 500 Wildlife Parkway, Columbia, is South Carolina's premiere zoo and one of the finest zoos in the Southeast. The zoo has more than 2,000 animals and lets the public get up close and personal with as many as possible, including feeding giraffes and birds and walking among the wallabies.

The Grand Strand, Georgetown, and Pee Dee

1

THE GRAND STRAND:
Little River, Cherry Grove, Ocean Drive,
North Myrtle Beach, Atlantic Beach,
Myrtle Beach, Surfside, Garden City,
Murrells Inlet, Litchfield, Pawleys Island

GEORGETOWN

THE PEE DEE

SUGGESTED ITINERARIES

INTRODUCTION

It's no accident that the first chapter encompasses Myrtle Beach. It has been *the* tourist destination for South Carolina since the Great Depression.

With 60 miles of flat sandy beaches, South Carolina's Grand Strand has historically drawn visitors from the Midwest and Northeast—where either there are no beaches or you have to pay to use them—and from neighboring Georgia and North Carolina, where the beaches are smaller and more difficult to reach by car.

Myrtle Beach has been called many names, and not all of them flattering. I myself have called it Myrtle Vegas on occasion, but that was more in the days when South Carolina allowed video gambling and folks would stream into Myrtle Beach and all points along the state lines with Georgia and North Carolina to try their luck. Now the name simply indicates that Myrtle Beach is a place where there are neon lights, bawdy entertainments, and the action never stops.

But Myrtle has settled down over the years. The city has taken steps to try to drive away the hundreds of thousands of bikers who used to gather a couple of times a year at the beach for motorcycle rallies. Noise ordinances quieted their hogs, and an attempt to require them to wear helmets in the city limits took the wind out of their hair. They still come, just not in as great a number.

Some parts of Myrtle have maintained their old-school attitudes and appearances, but bit by bit nationally known names have cropped up where local businesses used to be.

Gone are the Pavilion and amusement park. They were torn down to make way for new developments, but none has materialized. As a child, I mourned the loss of my favorite pier amusement park at Surfside Beach. It was cleared out for a chain hotel and parking lot.

Some of the biggest shopping draws are the Tanger Outlets and Bass Pro Shops that you can find in any large city. The biggest resorts have familiar names, like Hilton and Marriott. And what was supposed to take-the place of the Pavilion amusement park was the $400 million Hard Rock Park built on the west side of the Intracoastal Waterway, but it had the misfortune of opening during the worst recession since the 1930s and never had a successful year. It still sits there along US 501—the primary east–west route into Myrtle Beach—its brightly colored rides teasing young children.

Myrtle Beach has modernized since I used to go there several times a year with my family in the 1970s—in many ways for the better. You no longer have to save up your milk jugs to take your own fresh water for drinking. (The well water at the beach did make tasty coffee, tea, and grits; it just stained and ruined whatever appliances it went into.) And you no longer have to pack a car full of food and beverages, as there are plenty of grocery stores within a few minutes' drive of most beachside hotels. Phone service also was spotty at the beach. It was the first—and only—time I ever crossed paths with a party line; most people just didn't have a phone at their beach houses.

Back in our day, Krispy Kreme would recruit youngsters to sell doughnuts door-to-door around breakfast time. My brother did it for a few years, earning money that he would leave at the arcade and getting him out of the house early on vacation mornings.

The beach as it was holds so many memories for me—and those memories are still there to be made for young families. With more and more building along the coast, places to stay are as affordable as they ever were. The resorts may be out of reach for the average family of four, but there are plenty of mom-and-pop spots to stay that are clean and safe and have kitchens to help save money on eating out. Many have washers and dryers so you don't have to take all that sand back home with you.

Some things have stayed the same. Ocean Boulevard still has Peaches Corner and The Bowery, where the country band Alabama played in its early years.

Chapter 1 is also where I grew up. Florence was a good stopping point for folks driving long distances from the north to stop. It boasts being halfway between New York City and Miami on Interstate 95 (and before that, US 301, which ran from Delaware to Florida). Families who planned to check in at coastal hotels and rental houses on Saturday afternoons would arrive in Florence late Friday night to be fresh for that last traffic-jammed 80 miles to the coast. My grandparents operated one of those stopover motels on the main beach route for more than 20 years.

Florence also has played hotel/motel host for more than 50 years to the hordes of race fans who descended on Darlington Raceway. At one time, the "track too tough to tame" hosted two annual NASCAR races—the Rebel 400 in the spring and the Southern 500 on Labor Day. With the expansion of NASCAR across the nation, Darlington has been whittled down to one race held the Saturday before Mother's Day.

For most of the 20th century, the Pee Dee—named for the Indians who used to call it home and the two rivers that run through it—was home to most of the state's tobacco farms, curing barns, warehouses, and auctions. With the decline in tobacco production over the years, many farmers have turned to soybeans. The warehouses with their fast-talking auctioneers have disappeared; prices now are set by individual contracts with cigarette companies. The landscape is still dotted with two-story lean-tos once used as curing shacks.

Although tourism along the coast and the rise of medical-related industries in Florence have brought some prosperity to the Pee Dee, it still is one of the state's poorest regions, with high unemployment rates in the rural areas and low-performing schools, highlighted in a documentary called *Corridor of Shame*. The film shows the deplorable conditions of rural schools along I-95 throughout the Pee Dee. The story of one such school became a national issue during the 2008 presidential campaign, and a student in one of those schools was invited to attend President Obama's State of the Union address.

THE GRAND STRAND

LITTLE RIVER, CHERRY GROVE, OCEAN DRIVE, NORTH MYRTLE BEACH, ATLANTIC BEACH, MYRTLE BEACH, SURFSIDE, GARDEN CITY, MURRELLS INLET, LITCHFIELD, PAWLEYS ISLAND

I t's hard to imagine that anyone hasn't heard of South Carolina's Grand Strand or at least its largest and most famous component, Myrtle Beach. The area has been an inexpensive family vacation destination for more than 60 years. More recently, the explosion of golf course development and the recruitment of businesses that cater to an older snowbird crowd has made South Carolina's coast a year-round destination.

The 60 miles of gently sloping sandy beaches offer visitors ideal beach-going opportunities. The weather allows for walking on the beach almost year-round, while the best weather is usually from Easter to Halloween. Anyone traveling without children or with those too young or too old to be in school will enjoy the lower cost and smaller crowds in the so-called shoulder seasons before Memorial Day and after Labor Day each year.

There are hundreds of places to stay along the beach, from private homes for rent by the week, to condos with weekly and daily rentals, to nationwide-chain hotels and resorts and old-school family-owned motels. Costs vary widely. While some of the older motels are quaint, they will be unlikely to have to latest amenities. Almost every place to stay has a pool or easy beach access. And although beachfront in the heart of Myrtle Beach seems like the ideal spot, remember that summertime traffic will make leaving and returning to your hotel by car more difficult.

There are also dozens of campgrounds in the area, including two state parks, that offer RVers many choices. Many families return to the same spot year after year, developing lifelong friendships with other travelers.

From Little River on the state line with North Carolina to Georgetown,

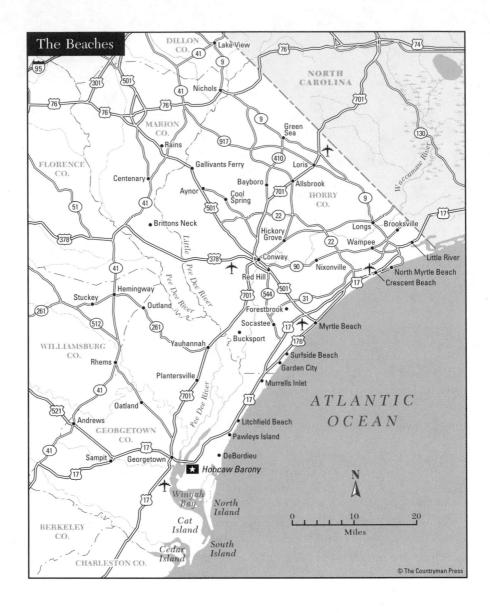

The Beaches

there are plenty of fishing piers that jut out into the water, providing anglers with an inexpensive chance to go for larger fish than can be had from the surf. Charter boats also are available mostly in Little River, Murrells Inlet, and Georgetown to take out the more ambitious fisherman. Murrells Inlet boasts a compact restaurant row, with more than a dozen affordable family-friendly seafood eateries along a 3-mile stretch of road that runs along the marsh. Murrells Inlet also is home to Brookgreen Gardens, one of the country's finest sculpture gardens courtesy of Anna Hyatt Huntington, who along with her husband created an artists' colony in what is now Huntington Beach State Park.

Farther south are the beaches of Litchfield, Pawleys Island, and Debordieu (pronounced *DEB-ah-doo*). Litchfield and the mainland side of Pawleys have restaurants, shops, and plenty of history. Litchfield has condos and private homes for rent as well as an inn. Pawleys, once a summertime getaway for plantation owners looking to escape the heat and malaria-carrying mosquitoes farther inland, boasts of being "arrogantly shabby" and has private homes for rent.

In the cooler months, the Myrtle Beach area's 120 golf courses fill with golfers from colder climates looking for more opportunities to hit the links. It is these itinerant duffers that keep Myrtle Beach's airport so busy year-round. The best way to choose a course is at myrtlebeachgolf.com. Most hotels and resorts offer golfing getaway packages and match the savings up with other attractions in the area.

Even more abundant are the area's miniature golf courses, which offer young and old the chance to putt like a pro while staring down pirates, dinosaurs, or jungle cats. The area also has several amusement parks, from the 1960s-era **Family Kingdom Amusement Park & Oceanfront Water Park** (843-626-3447; familykingdomfun.com) to a nostalgia park at **Broadway at the Beach,** with some attractions saved from the old Myrtle Beach Pavilion.

Myrtle Beach also is known for its restaurants, ranging from the glorified burger stand at **Peaches Corner** (843-448-7424; peaches-corner .com), 900 North Ocean Boulevard, to the upscale **Thoroughbreds Restaurant** (843-497-2636; thoroughbredsrestaurant.com), 9706 North Kings Highway. And there are dozens of seafood buffets and pancake houses in between.

Since the 1980s, one of Myrtle Beach's nicknames has been Branson by the Sea, referring to number of music theaters that dot the coast. These were some of the earliest year-round entertainment venues in the area. After 20 years, one of the oldest of these theaters, Dolly Parton's Dixie Stampede changed its name and show to the **Pirates Voyage** (800-433-4401; piratesvoyage.com), which opened in mid-2011.

GUIDANCE Myrtle Beach Area Convention & Visitors Bureau Welcome Center (843-626-7444; visitmyrtlebeach.com), 1200 North Oak Street, Myrtle Beach. Open 8:30–5 Monday through Friday year-round. Weekend hours vary by season.

Airport Welcome Center, Myrtle Beach International Airport (843-626-7444), 1100 Jetport Road, Myrtle Beach. Open 8–7 daily.

South Strand Welcome Center (843-651-1010), 3401 US 17 Business South, Murrells Inlet. Open 8:30–5 Monday through Friday year-round. Weekend hours vary by season.

GETTING THERE The US 17 Bypass runs along the western edge of the Grand Strand from the North Carolina state line down to Georgetown. US 501 is the main east–west route bringing travelers to the beach. At the beach, the 28-mile Veterans Highway (SC 22) links US 501 west of Conway and US 17 north of Myrtle Beach. The Carolina Bays Parkway (SC 31) runs from SC 9 to US 544; it will eventually extend to US 17 south of Myrtle Beach.

Myrtle Beach International Airport (843-448-1589; flymyrtlebeach .com) offers direct and connecting flights through U.S. carriers Allegiant Airlines (702-505-8888; allegiantair.com), Continental Airlines (800-525-0280; continental.com), Delta Air Lines (800-221-1212; delta.com), Northwest Airlines (800-225-2525; nwa.com), Myrtle Beach Direct Air (877-432-3473; visitdirectair.com), Spirit Airlines (800-772-7117; spiritair .com), United Express (800-241-6522; united.com), US Airways (800-428-4322; usairways.com).

Myrtle Beach Greyhound Station (843-448-2471; greyhound.com), 511 7th Avenue North. Greyhound offers passenger service from most U.S. cities. The station is centrally located in downtown and within walking distance of several attractions, restaurants, and hotels. Open seven days a week, 9–5. Closed on holidays.

There is no passenger train service to Myrtle Beach. The closest Amtrak station is in Florence, but there is no direct bus service from there to the beaches. There is a train stop in North Charleston, which is farther away, but a direct bus ride is just two to three hours away.

GETTING AROUND Most people get around by car or walking. Within campgrounds, bikes and golf carts are the preferred mode of transport. The Coast Regional Transportation Authority provides bus service along major thoroughfares and to and from beaches and neighboring towns. It operates year-round. Schedules are available at all Myrtle Beach Area Convention and Visitors Bureau offices.

WHEN TO COME Myrtle Beach is a year-round destination with plenty to do at all times. Some attractions close during the winter or have limited operating hours, but most restaurants and shopping outlets are open year-round. Summer is the most popular visiting time—kids are out of school and the weather is best for playing and sunning on the beach—but it's very crowded all along the coast. For travelers without children, the shoulder seasons between Easter and Memorial Day in the spring and between

Labor Day and Halloween in the fall offer excellent beach weather, and most businesses offer discounts on lodging and dining. Myrtle Beach is susceptible to hurricanes, which occur in the Atlantic Ocean between June and November. For South Carolina, the most active part of hurricane season is September and October. Be flexible when making plans to stay in those months. The live-performance theaters all offer holiday-themed shows in November and December, making those prime visiting months for long-weekend stays. January and February are the beaches' dead season, with some attractions closing to prepare for the spring. Weatherwise, these are typically the least desirable months, with the occasional nor'easter bringing cold winds and rain or sometimes snow. However, for those who can travel on short notice, a sunny weather forecast can mean excellent golf or nice quiet walks on the beach with no crowds. Businesses typically offer their best deals during these months, and all those restaurants that are crowded in summer will welcome you with open arms. Also, the farther south you go on South Carolina's beaches, the less important the seasons are and the more likely you are to find open businesses.

✳ To See

ANIMALS ♂ **Ripley's Aquarium** (843-916-0888; myrtlebeach.ripley aquariums.com), 1110 Celebrity Circle, Myrtle Beach. Open daily 9–10. Admission: $19 for adults; $10 for ages 6–11, and $4 for ages 2–5. Exhibits include a 750,000-gallon tank and Ray Bay, which lets visitors see stingrays from all angles and even touch some. Freshwater exhibits highlight life in the Amazon rain forest, and a 10-foot cylindrical exhibit shows species native to South Carolina coastal waters.

♂ **Alligator Adventure** (843-361-0789; alligatoradventure.com), 4604 US 17 at Barefoot Landing, North Myrtle Beach. Open daily 9–7. Showtimes vary. Admission: $18 for adults 13 and older, $16 for seniors, and $11 for youngsters. Kids 3 and younger are admitted free. This 15-acre habitat and serpentarium has alligators, turtles, crocodiles, and snakes, snakes, snakes, including pythons, boas, anacondas, and king cobras. Live shows include alligator feedings and talks on handling reptiles. There are exhibits where guests can touch some of the creatures. I personally spend my life avoiding such. This is best for those with youngsters who qualify for the reduced price, although some teens may enjoy it as well.

♂ **Waccatee Zoological Farm** (843-650-8500; waccateezoo.com), 8500 Enterprise Road, Myrtle Beach. Open daily 10–5. Admission: $7 for adults 13 and older; $4 for kids. This zoo is located on 500 acres in Socastee and has a wide range of animals, from chimpanzees to tigers, bears, and zebras. There is a petting area with goats and rabbits. The zoo also is a wildlife sanctuary and breeds several species of migratory birds and alligators.

MUSEUMS ✐ **The Children's Museum of South Carolina** (843-946-9469; cmsckids.org), 2501 North Kings Highway, Myrtle Beach. Open 10–4 Monday through Saturday. Admission $8. The museum invites kids to touch and explore exhibits from fossils to making their own pizza.

✐ **Ripley's Believe it or Not! Museum** (843-448-2331; myrtlebeach .ripleys.com), 917 North Ocean Boulevard, Myrtle Beach. Open daily 10–6. Cost: $14 adults (12 and older); $8 for children 6–11, and free for children younger than 5. This self-guided museum offers the weird, odd, and borderline disgusting, including a ceremonial Tibetan skull mask and a shrunken head. This museum with its 14 separate galleries is definitely the place to take 9-year-old boys on a rainy afternoon. The museum was Ripley's first exhibit at Myrtle Beach. In addition to the Aquarium, the company has added **Ripley's Haunted Adventure** (843-916-8971; ripleys.com) just next door at 915 North Ocean Boulevard. Hours vary depending on season. This attraction has more creepy stuff, with live actors and high-tech animation all designed to get the biggest screams, laughs, and reactions from your typical 9-year-old boy. Admission is $14 for ages 12 and older, and $8 for children 6–11. Younger children not admitted. **Ripley's Marvelous Mirror Maze** (843-448-2331; myrtlebeach .ripleys.com) is at the same address with hundreds of mirrors, lights, and digital sound. Open daily noon–6. One $10 ticket will let you go through as many times as you like; you can compete for the fastest time. **Ripley's Moving Theater** (843-626-0069; ripleys.com), 917 North Ocean Boulevard, combines a movie with a ride. Open daily noon–6. Children need to

RIPLEY'S BELIEVE IT OR NOT! MUSEUM, MYRTLE BEACH

be at least 43 inches tall to sit in one of the hydraulic seats that move in conjunction with the action in the 70mm film. There are still seats for smaller kids if an adult sits with them. $14 for adults and $8 for children up to age 11.

Franklin G. Burroughs–Simeon B. Chapin Art Museum (843-238-2510; myrtlebeachartmuseum .org), 3100 South Ocean Boulevard, Myrtle Beach. Open Tuesday through Saturday 10–4, Sunday 1–4. Named for the men who were the lead developers of Myrtle Beach, this museum offers half a dozen contemporary art exhibits each year. There also is a permanent collection of local art. The tea porch, where refreshments are served, overlooks the ocean. Admission is free, but donations are requested.

RIPLEY'S MOVING THEATER

PARKS & **Myrtle Beach Boardwalk** (843-626-7444; visitmyrtle beach.com/boardwalk), Oceanfront between 2nd and 14th Avenues. The

MYRTLE BEACH BOARDWALK

1.2-mile boardwalk opened in spring 2010 and provides visitors—especially those who have difficulty or are unable to walk in the sand—an unblocked view of the ocean and beach. There are shops and restaurants along the way, reminiscent of the boardwalk at Ocean City Beach, New Jersey. In the spring of 2011, the 200-foot **SkyWheel** (843-839-9200; themyrtlebeach skywheel.com), 1110 North Ocean Boulevard, opened at the boardwalk with 42 glass gondolas that let you see the sights in air-conditioned comfort. Rides—or, as the operators call them, flights—last about 12 minutes. Tickets are $12 for adults ages 12 and older and $8 for children ages 3–11. Discounts for older adults and military; free for younger children. The gondolas are handicapped accessible, and hours of operation depend on the season and the weather.

Brookgreen Gardens (843-235-6000; brookgreen.org), 1931 Brookgreen Gardens Drive, Murrells Inlet. Open daily 9:30–5. Gardens open until 9 Wednesday through Friday in summer. Created in 1931 by Archer and Anna Hyatt Huntington, Brookgreen Gardens seeks to preserve the native plant life in the Waccamaw Neck area of the South Carolina coast and provide a setting for the first public sculpture garden in the United States. More than 1,200 works by 350 sculptors are on display, including many pieces by Anna Hyatt Huntington who laid out the walkways throughout the gardens. Brookgreen Gardens is a National Historical Landmark. Admission is $12 for ages 13–64; $10 for 65 and older; $5 for children 4–12; and free for younger children and Brookgreen Gardens members. Tickets are good for seven consecutive days from purchase, so plan to make Brookgreen one

HORSE STATUE AT ENTRANCE TO BROOKGREEN GARDENS, MURRELLS INLET

Jan Hogan

of your first stops during your stay and come back often. From March through November, Brookgreen offers Lowcountry Excursions on a 48-foot pontoon boat and overland in the Trekker. Excursions cost $7 for adults and $4 for children in addition to gardens admission. Trekker excursions are not recommended for children younger than 6.

Hobcaw Barony (843-546-4623; hobcawbarony.org), 22 Hobcaw Road, Georgetown. Discovery Center is open 9–5 Monday through Friday and admission is free, although donations are appreciated. Van tours of the 17,500-acre wildlife refuge are offered year-round Tuesday through Friday and cost $20. Tour times vary depending on reservations; call for details. Hobcaw was part of a royal land grant in 1718 that was divided into 14 plantations. It became the winter home of Wall Street baron and South Carolina native Bernard Baruch. His daughter Belle left the land to the state for teaching and research of forestry and marine life by South Carolina colleges. Clemson and the University of South Carolina have research laboratories here. Exhibits in the Discovery Center focus on the property's history, from American Indian inhabitants through the rice plantations of the 18th and 19th centuries.

La Belle Amie Vineyard (843-399-9463; labelleamie.com), 1120 St. Joseph Road, Little River. Open Monday through Saturday 10–6. You can tour this operating vineyard and winery built on an old tobacco farm. The land has been owned by the same family since the 19th century. The name means "good friend," and the owners invite guests to sample the vineyard's wines and a variety of gourmet foods. The gift shop offers wine accessories and other gifts. Special events are held each month.

Freewoods Farm (843-650-9139; freewoodsfarm.com), 9515 Freewoods Road, Myrtle Beach. Open 8–5 Monday through Friday. Tours are conducted by appointment. The produce market here is open 2–6 Tuesday and 9–1 Saturday in-season. Visitors can see how the first freed black farmers worked their land from 1865 until 1900. Workers use mules and plows to plant, woodstoves to cook and make soap, and use their hands to harvest crops. Buildings on this 40-acre site include a farmhouse, smokehouse, blacksmith shed, and tobacco and storage barns. In-season, fresh produce from the farm is sold in a market on site.

✳ To Do

FISHING There are abundant piers along the Grand Strand where you can drop in a line. Some of the more popular locations are:

14 Avenue Pier (843-448-6500; pier14.com/shop.php), 1304 N. Ocean Boulevard, Myrtle Beach. Open 6 AM–1 AM in the summer; closed November through February. Free to walk the pier. Fishing pass $6 a day; weekly and yearly passes available. Rods available for rent. This pier is at

THE 14TH AVENUE PIER, MYRTLE BEACH

one end of the Myrtle Beach Boardwalk, which runs south to the **Second Avenue Pier** (843-626-8480; secondavenuepier.com), 110 North Ocean Boulevard, Myrtle Beach.

Apache Campground Pier (843-497-6486; apachefamilycampground .com/pier.php), Lake Arrowhead Road, Myrtle Beach. Open daily 6 AM– 11 PM in the summer, 8–8 in the winter. Located inside the Apache Campground. $2 for pier parking, $1 to walk on the pier. Children walk for free. Fishing pass is $8.50; rods available for rent. Crab nets for sale, not for rent, but you can bring your own. Guests at the campground get a discount.

Cherry Grove Beach Pier (843-249-1625; cherrygrovepier.com), 3500 North Ocean Boulevard, North Myrtle Beach. Open 6 AM–2 AM seven days a week in summer; 6 AM–10 PM Sunday through Thursday and until midnight Friday through Saturday rest of the year. Closed December and January. $1 to walk the pier; fishing pass is $7 for the first rod and $6.50 for additional rods if you bring your own equipment. Rods, crab nets available for rent.

The Pier at Garden City (843-651-9700; pieratgardencity.com), 110 South Waccamaw Drive, Garden City Beach. Open 6 AM–9 PM year-round.

Open till 11 PM during the summer. Free to walk on pier. Fishing pass is $8 for adults, $4 for children. Weekly and season passes available. Rods available for rent.

Surfside Pier (843-238-0121; surfsidepier.com), 11 South Ocean Boulevard, Surfside Beach. Open 6 AM–11 PM daily. $1 to walk the pier; fishing passes range $9–12.50 daily. Rods available for rent.

CHARTER BOATS Those looking for opportunities at larger fish should check out the offerings of charter boats out of Murrells Inlet and Little River. Because of the temperate weather, inshore fishing in the salt marsh and tidal creeks can be done most of the year. Spring is especially good for flounder while summer is best for Spanish mackerel. Fall is an excellent time to fish the inlets for spot.

Capt. Dick's (843-651-3676 or 866-557-3474; captdicks.com), 4123 US 17 Business, Murrells Inlet. Open 6 AM–10 PM daily March through November. Closed December through February. Capt. Dick's has everything you could possibly want or need for fishing or getting into the water along the Grand Strand, from kayak and fishing boat rentals to parasailing, WaveRunner rentals, deep-sea fishing excursions, and saltwater marsh tours. You can charter a whole boat or simply sign up for one of their regular trips and pay per person. If you have 6 to 12 people in your party, the charter is probably the best way to go. If you have fewer, you will want to take regularly scheduled trips that charge per person. If you have more than 12, give them a call and see what they can work out for you. A half-day trip is about $50 per adult. Charters start around $800 for a half day. Personal watercraft rentals are about $80 an hour, two-seater sea kayaks about $60 a day, pontoon boats are less than $300 a day, and flat-bottomed inlet fishing boats about $150 a day.

Capt. Smiley's Inshore Fishing (843-361-7445; captainsmileyfishing charters.com), Historic Waterfront Drive, Little River. Open daily for trips by reservation only. Capt. Smiley offers full- and half-day charters in the inlets and near shore wrecks. Tours include bait, tackle, and guide. Sightseeing tours also are offered.

FAMILY-FRIENDLY ACTIVITIES ❧ **Myrtle Waves Water Park** (843-918-8725; myrtlewaves.com), 3000 10th Avenue North, Myrtle Beach. There are 30 water rides here, ranging from the 3-mile-per-hour LayZee River that winds its way around the 20-acre park to the Turbo Twisters—fully enclosed tube slides that start 10 stories up and drop you at crazy high speeds. Some slides are restricted to riders more than 42 inches tall. But there are plenty of middle-speed rides for the whole family. If you're bringing a group, check out their cabana rentals. It will give you a shaded place to hang out, plus the weekday package includes meal deals for four.

Admission: $33 for adults; $30 for seniors 55 and older; $25 for shorties; children 2 and under are free.

✇ **Carolina Safari Jeep Tours** (843-497-5330; carolinasafari.com). Open daily 8 AM–9 PM. These folks know the South Carolina coast and have designed a three-and-a-half-hour tour to show it off. Sights include a former plantation, slave cabins, rice fields, graveyards, wildlife, and ecosystems from the river to the ocean. The tours are pricey—$40 for adults and $25 for kids—but for those visiting the area for the first time or who have never taken time to see anything off the beach or golf course, this is a great way to get the lay of the land. Carolina Safari offers group discounts for 14 or more people.

Also see *Mini Golf* and *Amusement Parks*, below.

MINI GOLF It's hard to miss mini golf opportunities at Myrtle Beach. They are about 50 along the Grand Strand, and for one stretch of US 17, it feels like there is one on every corner. They all offer very similar thrills of running water eager to swallow an errant ball and at least one hole in a cave. Each has its own specialized theme, like pirates or dinosaurs or volcanoes. It's a great way to wind down the little ones after dinner—or a fun way to figure out who buys the first round of adult beverages if you don't have kids. Prices vary a little among courses, but in general a round is $10 or less, and you can play all day for just a few dollars more. Most places have two courses. In the summer mini golf locations open early in the day and frequently don't close till midnight. Look for coupons in area hotels and restaurants.

Here are just a few of the favorites:

✇ **Hawiian Rumble Golf** (843-272-7812; prominigolf.com), 33rd Avenue South at US 17, North Myrtle Beach. Believe it or not, *Golf Digest* ranked this as the top mini golf location in the United States. Built around a 40-foot volcano that "erupts" every 20 minutes or so, it's a deceptive course where the easiest-looking holes are often the hardest. Bring your A-game.

✇ **Mount Atlanticus Minotaur Goff** (843-444-1008), 707 North Kings Highway, Myrtle Beach. In a world of the same, this place is different. There may be some wear in the carpet and the Minotaur course is better than the Conch, but this unique mini golf course in a former retail store is worth a try. The course twists through the building's three floors and up to the roof for great views of the amusement park and beach. The 18th hole is a doozy, but if you get a hole in one, you could play free for a year.

✇ **Jungle Lagoon Miniature Golf** (843-626-7894; junglelagoon.com), 5th Avenue South at US 17, Myrtle Beach. Both courses offer great views from the hole atop the lookout mountain. Withers Swash, a natural ocean inlet, forms the facility's rear boundary with real wildlife such as herons and other large ocean birds. The fake wildlife around the course will please the kids, though.

GROWN-UP GOLF With 120 golf courses, Myrtle Beach is a golfer's paradise. The best way to plan your golf getaway is to go to myrtlebeach golf.com. The site offers tee times, course evaluations, and countless packages. If golf is just a sideline of your visit, pick your hotel or resort first, then see what package deals they have to offer. Often, hotels also have discounts on several area attractions as well as golf packages. Courses are open year-round, sunup to sundown, and typically offer discounts for afternoon starts. Prices vary widely from course to course, day of the week, and time of year. Here are some of the top courses and some recommendations from my golfing buddy Steve Johnson:

The Heritage Club (843-237-3424; legendsgolf.com), 378 Heritage Drive, Pawleys Island. A part of the Legends Golf and Resort group, this course is one of *Golf Digest's* best buys on the South Carolina coast. Rates for this 7,040-yard, par-71 course range from $65 in January to $125 in prime fall and spring playing seasons.

Barefoot Resort and Golf (843-390-3200; barefootgolf.com), 4980 Barefoot Resort Bridge Road, North Myrtle Beach. Barefoot has courses designed by Tom Fazio, Pete Dye, Greg Norman, and Davis Love III. You cannot lose on any of these, but the Love course was ranked among the 50 best in Myrtle Beach. Fees: $110–185.

Caledonia Golf & Fish Club (843-237-3675; fishclub.com), 369 Caledonia Drive, Pawleys Island. Built on a working rice plantation, Caledonia has an old-world Southern feel and is one of *Golf Digest's* "America's 100 Greatest Public Courses." Fees: $100–170, depending on season and tee time.

Tidewater Golf Club (843-913-2424; tidewatergolf.com), 1400 Tidewater Drive, North Myrtle Beach. This course offers a variety of terrains, as holes are alongside a saltwater marsh, an ocean inlet, and the Intracoastal Waterway. Steve says this course is extremely challenging and is probably one of the nicest you'll play in the Southeast. Fees: $94–150.

Pawleys Plantation (843-237-6000; pawleysplantation.com), 70 Tanglewood Drive, Pawleys Island. Steve loves the backwater, and this course is set on the backwater of Murrells Inlet. The course is challenging, but not too much for weekend duffers. The price is fairly reasonable considering it is a Jack Nicklaus–designed course. Rates: $63–124.

Wachesaw East (888-922-0027; wachesaweast.biz), 911 Riverwood Drive, US 17, Myrtle Beach. This public companion to the private Wachesaw Plantation course is built on an old plantation and filled with old oaks and wonderful views. Steve says this course is challenging enough to host major tournament play. Rates: $59–96. Packages are available.

SC Department of Parks, Recreation & Tourism, DiscoverSouthCarolina.com

PAWLEYS PLANTATION GOLF AND COUNTRY CLUB

Prestwick (843-293-4100; prestwickcountryclub.com), 1001 Links Road, Myrtle Beach. The Surfside Beach course is lined with homes, which drives Steve crazy, but he says each hole will challenge your shot-making ability and that makes up for the lack of view. Rates: $69–121.

TENNIS Tennis Club at Grande Dunes (843-449-4486; grandedunes .com), 1000 Grande Dunes Boulevard, Myrtle Beach. A 5,000-square-foot facility that includes pool, fitness room, and 10 lighted Har-Tru courts. Lessons by USTA-certified pros are available. Morning and evening lessons starting at $20 for non-club–members; private lessons $55 an hour; court rentals $30 for all day.

PAWLEYS PLANTATION
SC Department of Parks, Recreation & Tourism, DiscoverSouthCarolina.com

AMUSEMENT PARKS ✏ Family Kingdom Amusement Park & Oceanfront Water Park (843-626-3447; familykingdomfun.com), 300 South Ocean Boulevard, Myrtle Beach. Open March–September 4 PM–midnight. The water park is open Memorial Day to Labor Day at 10 AM. Admission to the park is

THE ARCADE ON OCEAN DRIVE HAS OLD-STYLE BASEBALL AND SKEE BALL GAMES THAT STILL COST JUST A QUARTER.

$23.50; water park wristband is $18.95. Combo deals are available, and they are your best bet if you're traveling with kids. Myrtle Beach's oldest operating amusement park is located on 16 acres by the ocean and has more than 30 rides, including the historic Swamp Fox wooden roller coaster. The water park includes a 400-foot lazy river as well as speed slides and flume rides. The kids will want to stay here all day.

✒ **The Fun Plaza** (843-448-5141), 902 North Ocean Boulevard, Myrtle Beach. Open 10 AM–midnight weekends and during summer; closes around 5 PM on winter weekdays. The name says it all. This is a fun place with an entrance off the Boardwalk or off Ocean Boulevard. The games here range from old-school baseball to an electronic version of the television show *Deal*

or No Deal. Most of the games take quarters, not tokens, and actually only cost 25 cents to play. The skee ball machines and several other games give tickets depending on the score. The tickets can be redeemed for trinkets. One year we got a very respectable combination bottle opener/Myrtle Beach souvenir magnet. It has made it through years of parties and sticks very nicely to our old-school metal Pepsi cooler. The baseball game is my favorite, though I must confess I have never seen anyone get 28 runs and thus win one of the incredible shrinking stuffed animal prizes. Visitors over 40 will remember many of these games, but youngsters who haven't yet slipped into the world of Wii will enjoy their simplicity as well.

ℰ **The Pavilion Nostalgia Park** (843-913-9400; pavilionnostalgiapark .com), 1325 Celebrity Circle, Myrtle Beach. Open daily at 11 AM. Admission is free, but rides cost $3 each. The park has a sampling of rides from the former Myrtle Beach Pavilion, which was the mainstay of the beachfront for decades.

ℰ **NASCAR SpeedPark** (843-918-8725; nascarspeedpark.com), 1820 21st Avenue North Extension, Myrtle Beach. Hours vary slightly by season, but the park is typically open daily 10–10. Admission to the park is free. An all-day ride pass is $30 if you buy it online. This is the place for all those who think they could be a NASCAR driver, but have absolutely no way to take a spin around a real track. The SpeedPark offers racing-style mini cars with a variety of tracks, including a tight oval with high banks and side-by-side racing called the Competitor. There also is a road course and courses designed more for youngsters and family-style driving. The park has a super-slick bumper car track and—if the heat's getting to you—a pool for bumper boats. And it's not all cars. A rock-climbing wall, arcade, and mini golf course round out the attracations. The pass seems a little pricey, but you've saved yourself money after just three spins around one of the tracks. This is better for older kids, as most of the fun tracks require you to be at least 4 feet tall. Drivers on the Competitor track have to be at least 5 feet tall.

ℰ **MagiQuest** (843-916-1800; magiquest.com), 1185 Celebrity Circle, Myrtle Beach. Open daily 10–10. MagiQuest is kind of like being inside a video game or in a 3-D Dungeons and Dragons. Players choose their own adventure or quest and navigate this fantasy world with a magic wand that records progress for subsequent visits. There are castles and magic powers, princesses in distress, and, of course, dragons to be slayed. The wand costs about $15 and an hour of play, about $10. Nonplayers can come in for $5; it's free for seniors and nonplaying children younger than 4. Kids can take their MagiQuest wands to any of the company's dozen U.S. locations and pick up where they left off.

✸ Green Space

PARKS 🐾 🐎 **Myrtle Beach State Park** (843-238-5325; southcarolina
parks.com), 4401 South Kings Highway, Myrtle Beach. Open daily 6 AM–
10 PM, March through November; 6 AM–8 PM, December through February. The 312-acre park was created in the 1930s as part of the Civilian Conservation Corps, a government jobs program during the Great Depression.
Five cabins and two apartments are just 200 yards from the beach. The
park also has a fishing pier and ample camping in woods along South
Carolina's most popular beach. Pets are not allowed in the cabins, apartments, or cabin areas and cannot go on the beach during summer. They
are allowed in other areas on a leash. Park admission is $4 for adults,
$2.50 for South Carolina seniors, $1.50 for children 6–15. Children 5 and
younger are admitted free. Horses are allowed in the park and on the
beach from late November through February for a $25-per-horse fee, but
they are not allowed to stay overnight. The park has many programs all
year long to teach people about conservation and the wildlife and plant
life they will see at the park. The Sculptured Oak Nature Trail gives visitors a glimpse at one of the last maritime forests in South Carolina.

🐾 **Huntington Beach State Park** (843-237-4440; southcarolinaparks
.com), 16148 Ocean Highway, Murrells Inlet. This park is open 6–6 Saturday through Thursday, until 8 PM on Fridays, and extended to 10 PM during
Daylight Saving Time. Atalaya is open 9–5. This park includes access to
3 miles of undeveloped beach, camping, fishing, and excellent bird-
watching. The occasional alligator can be spotted in the park's freshwater

ATALAYA, HUNTINGTON BEACH

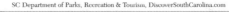
SC Department of Parks, Recreation & Tourism, DiscoverSouthCarolina.com

lake. Atalaya, built in the Spanish Moors style, was the summer home of Anna Hyatt and Archer Huntington. She was a sculptor and he, a supporter of the arts. The home is a National Historic Landmark. Brookgreen Gardens, which sits across US 17 from the park, is a tribute to Anna Huntington's artistry. An arts and crafts festival is held here at Atalaya every fall. The state bought the 2,500-acre park from Brookgreen Trustees in 1960. Pets are allowed if kept on a leash. Coastal exploration tours are offered from March through November. Birders can be seen year-round and have recorded more than 300 species in the park. Much of the park's marsh is registered under the South Carolina Heritage Trust Program, helping to preserve its pristine nature.

Heritage Shores Nature Preserve (843-280-5570; parks.nmb.us), 5611 Heritage Drive, North Myrtle Beach. This relatively new city park is on an island that juts into the Cherry Grove Marsh. A series of boardwalks and observations docks lets visitors stroll through the natural area as well as a more primitive walking path. This park gives visitors a glimpse of what the area looked like before it became the state's number one tourist destination. This also is a great way to see the backwater of the beach if you don't have a boat or a tee time. The park is free, and visitors can park at 53rd Avenue North. From there, it's about a four-block walk to the entrance of the preserve. If you are arriving by boat, there is a stationary dock at the preserve where you can pull up and take a stroll.

BEACHES Pawleys Island is the southernmost of the Grand Strand's beaches along 60 miles of gently sloping sandy shore. Along with **Litchfield Beach** and **Murrells Inlet,** it makes up what's been called the Hammock Coast, based on Pawleys's famed Island Rope Hammocks. With plenty of shops, restaurants, golf courses, tennis courts, and beach access, visitors to Litchfield, Pawleys, and Murrells Inlet rarely venture the nearly 30 miles north to the attractions of Myrtle Beach.

North of there are **Garden City** and **Surfside** beaches, which like the more southerly beaches were mostly where native South Carolinians spent their summer vacations—close enough to go see the sights of Myrtle, but not in the midst of them. However, large-scale building after Hurricane Hugo washed away many of the smaller private homes in 1989 made these areas virtually indistinguishable from their northern neighbor.

North Myrtle Beach and **Myrtle Beach** are where most of the hotels and restaurants are located; Myrtle was once home to the beachfront Pavilion, which has since been torn down. A new 1.2-mile boardwalk does keep the beach in touch with its past by providing a place for people to gather between the ocean and the street.

Between the two Myrtles is **Atlantic Beach,** nicknamed the Black Pearl because during the days of segregation in the South, it was the beach

THE GRAY MAN

Few ghost stories feature such a kind spook at their heart as the tale of Pawleys Island's Gray Man. Legend has it he shows up before major hurricanes to alert homeowners to approaching danger—a shadowy mist along the beach in a rumpled suit and hat.

Before the days of Doppler radar, South Carolina's beach residents wouldn't know about a hurricane until just hours before its arrival on shore—or sometimes not until the morning after, as in the case of 1954's Hurricane Hazel, which hit Myrtle Beach.

Many storms have washed away homes, roads, and bridges along the coast, but a heeded warning from the Gray Man would guarantee that not only would families have time to evacuate to safety, but their homes were usually spared as well.

The most popular version of the legend is that a young man in the early 19th century was riding on horseback from Georgetown to see his fiancée on Pawleys Island. He took a shortcut across the marsh, fell into quicksand, and died. His forlorn girlfriend was walking along the beach days later when she recognized him in the distance. When she approached, he told her to leave the island. The girl and her family moved inland, and the next day a hurricane hit the island, destroying almost everyone's home . . . except that of the Gray Man's fiancée.

Reported sightings preceded the Storm of 1893, which struck just north of Pawleys and was one of the most devastating storms ever to hit South Carolina's coast. There was even a reported sighting in the days before 1989's Hurricane Hugo made landfall well south of Pawleys at the fishing village of McClellenville. The massive storm was the most expensive ever to hit South Carolina, causing billions of dollars in damage and leaving few homes standing on the beachfront from Charleston to Myrtle Beach.

where black visitors were welcome. The small area was home to black-owned hotels, restaurants, and nightclubs. Atlantic Beach is still a separate town, but there is very little there.

Cherry Grove and **Ocean Drive** near the North Carolina state line were classic old beach towns and still retain some of that 1950s flavor. This is where the state dance the Shag got its start and where beach music got its name. Both have hotels, restaurants, golf courses, and nightclubs.

SWIMMING The whole 60-mile stretch of the Grand Strand is free and open for swimming. There are a few areas, such as Withers Swash in Myrtle Beach, where stormwater runoff makes swimming undesirable. The state **Department of Health and Environmental Control** (800-360-5655; scdhec.gov/environment/water/swim_map.htm) posts warnings when conditions are considered hazardous for swimming. The toll-free hotline and website offer information statewide. The towns contract with about half a dozen private companies to provide lifeguard services along the water. The certified lifeguards who staff these areas also have umbrellas and chairs for rent and sell refreshments. Service is during summer daylight hours and is dependent on staffing. Guard areas are well marked and usually near the largest hotels.

SURFING Village Surf Shoppe (843-651-6396; villagesurf.com), 500 Atlantic Avenue, Murrells Inlet. Open 9–8 Monday through Saturday, 10–6 Sunday. For more than 40 years, the Village Surf Shoppe has been selling boards, wax, and clothing. It's a small store with people who know what they're doing, and their branded T-shirts have been must-haves for Grand Strand visitors for decades. The website includes wave data for Garden City.

Surf City Surf Shop (843-626-5412; surfcitysurfshop), 3001 North Kings Highway, Myrtle Beach. Open 9–9. Surf City has been in Myrtle Beach since 1978 and in 2010 opened a second location a little farther north at 6303 North Kings Highway. Owner Mark Allison will give you the skinny on all the latest board trends, and the shop offers rentals ($25 a day) and lessons ($60 for 90-minute private session) as well as sales. Surf conditions are available on the website.

KAYAKING/PARASAILING/SCUBA Express Water Sports (866-566-9338; exprersswatersports.com), 4042 US 17 Business, Murrells Inlet. Open 9–7 Monday through Saturday, 10–5 Sunday. If you're looking for a way to play in the water, this is the place. You can fly above the water on a parasailing excursion or search under the water on a scuba diving expedition. They have dolphin-watching and sightseeing tours ($25 for adults, $20 for children younger than 12; reservations required), and banana boat rides ($25 for a 35-minute ride, up to six passengers). For the more active, there are paddleboard ($25 for the first hour, $15 for each additional hour; lessons $45) and kayak rentals ($60 a day for a single; $75 for a double) and tours ($30 per person, reservations required), surfing lessons ($50 for 90 minutes) and camps ($100 a day). Dive sites include man-made and natural reefs and wrecks. Different sites available for different skill levels, up to 115 feet. Trips start at $50; add another $40 if you need to use their gear. Parasailing is $55 per person.

Great American Riverboat Co. (843-650-6600 or 800-685-6601; mbriverboat.com), 8201 Marina Parkway, Myrtle Beach. Cruise times are set about a month in advance, so check the website or call for times. The *Barefoot Princess* departs from Barefoot Landing Marina and offers sightseeing, dinner, and sunset cruises on the Intracoastal Waterway. Adult ticket prices range $20–40 depending on the cruise taken.

RECREATION AREAS Waccamaw National Wildlife Refuge (843-527-8069; fws.gov/waccamaw), 21424 North Fraser Street, Georgetown. Visitors center open 8–4 Monday through Friday; the Cox Ferry Lake Recreation Area adjacent to the Waccamaw River in Conway is open sunrise to sunset. Admission is free. Activities include boating, canoeing, and kayaking the refuge's rivers and creeks; birding and other wildlife observation opportunities; and hiking along the Great Pee Dee River and Bull Creek. More than 200 species of birds pass through the refuge during the year. Fishing and hunting also are allowed in the refuge with proper state licenses. A recent archaeological dig in the refuge found remains of what may have been a cabin. The site was used by American Indians until the mid-1600s when European settlers began to arrive. Then it was a ferry crossing and a plantation.

HORSEBACK RIDING Horseback Riding of Myrtle Beach (843-294-1712; myrtlebeachhorserides.com), Myrtle Beach. Open 9 AM–6 PM seven days a week, 90-minute rides, $50 for the nature preserve, $75 for beach. All rides are by reservation only with a 48-hour cancellation policy. You don't have to have any experience on horseback to be able to enjoy the rides. The horses are used to a variety of riders and are well trained. You do have to be able to physically get on the horse, and all riders need to be more than 6 years old. Because of crowded beaches during the summers, rides are held in and around natural areas from March through September. Beachfront rides are offered from September to March and are in Garden City, Litchfield, and Myrtle Beach.

BIKING Waccamaw Neck Bikeway (843-545-3325), Morse Park Landing, US 17 Business at Swale Avenue, Murrells Inlet. This bike trail is open daily from dawn to dusk and gives bikers a chance to ride from Murrells Inlet to Pawleys Island. The path parallels US 17 Business and makes use of share-the-ride lanes with cars through Huntington Beach State Park. There are 6 miles of continuous trail and two sections of about 4 miles. The trail is free, and shaded portions through the marsh make it enjoyable even on hot summer days. Helmets are not required, but are recommended—especially if you're riding anywhere near US 17.

✳ Lodging

PRIVATE HOME/CONDO RENTALS Oceanfront Vacation Rentals Inc. (843-448-1700; oceanfrontvac.com), 1551 21st Avenue North, Suite 12, Myrtle Beach. Open 9–5 Monday through Saturday. This agency offers more than 100 home and condo rentals within four blocks of the ocean. Summer prices vary widely, from $800 a week for a one-bedroom oceanfront condo to $8,800 a week for an eight-bedroom ocean-front home. Off-season and homes off the water are less expensive.

Pawleys Island Realty Co. (843-237-2431; pawleysislandrealty .com), 88 North Causeway, Pawleys Island. This agency has almost 300 vacation properties for rent in both beach and golf communities south of Myrtle Beach. Prices vary widely, depending on location, size, and season.

🐾 **Litchfield Real Estate** (843-237-4241; litchfieldrealestate .com), 12980 Ocean Highway, Pawleys Island. This company has been in business for decades and offers rentals for less than a week as well as pet-friendly homes.

INNS AND BED & BREAKFASTS
Sea View Inn (843-237-4253; seaviewinn.com), 414 Myrtle Avenue, Pawleys Island. A unique oceanfront inn on Pawleys Island has guest rooms with no air-conditioning, private half bath, and showers in the main house. An adjacent cottage offers six rooms, some with porch; all have air-conditioning. The inn serves three meals a day: breakfast $12; lunch and dinner $20 each. Room rates: $215–285 a night. This place harks back to an earlier time and is probably not well suited for those traveling with children.

MOTELS The Grand Strand has large chain motels and resorts, but also is home to a large collection of mom-and-pop family-owned motels that have been operated by the same owners for years. These motels generally are inexpensive; some can be less than $100 a night even in summer. But they generally have a little more wear and tear to show for their years. They don't have restaurants, but some offer rooms with kitchens. Almost all of them have pools. Parking can be limited or in a lot located away from the motel. Be aware that posted rates usually don't include taxes, and some motels may throw in a few-dollar "fee" with some official-sounding name. Make sure you are quoted the full cost of the room when you book, so you'll know exactly what you're paying. Pets are not allowed and most won't rent to people younger than 25 or to singles, preferring families and couples. Married couples younger than 25 should ask about the age policy when booking a room. I would recommend these more restrictive motels so you won't feel like you're vacationing next to a frat house. On that note, it's best to avoid these Ocean Boulevard motels during spring break or the first few weeks of June. Come in early May or after

Labor Day when the teens and young adults are in school, the weather is still great for the beach, and the already low rates will be even lower.

Here are a few options:

Roxanne Towers (843-448-9486; roxannetowers.com), 1604 North Ocean Boulevard, Myrtle Beach. The Roxanne is centrally located just north of the 14th Avenue Pier. All the rooms come with balcony; most are suites with a kitchen. In-season rates range from $130 a night for a studio without a kitchen to $300 a night for the penthouse two-bedroom suite on the July 4 weekend. In the winter, an oceanfront one-bedroom suite goes for less than $70, taxes included. In winter, you can do a long-term rental for about $1,200 a month. The hotel has two pools, a lazy river, and a hot tub. Every suite has a washer-dryer unit.

Twilight Surf Motel (843-448-4477; twilightsurfmotel.com), 1703 South Ocean Boulevard, Myrtle Beach. The Twlight has oceanfront balconies available, and all rooms come with a full kitchen. They have a heated pool and coin-operated washers and dryers on site. Rooms are restricted to families or couples. Rates range from $40 a night in the off-season to $120 for the July 4 week. Rates are for two people; extra people, including children, are $5 a night. Rates discounted 5 percent for a weekly stay, but stays of more than three days require a deposit.

The Cherry Tree Inn (843-449-6425; cherrytree-mb.com), 5400 North Ocean Boulevard, Myrtle Beach. This motel is oceanfront, but all the rooms have side views of the beach. A two-room efficiency can sleep six. All guests must be at least 25 years old or accompanied by a parent. Rates range from $40 a night in the off-season to $120 a night for the July 4 week.

Court Capri (800-533-1338; courtcapri.com), 2610 North Ocean Boulevard, Myrtle Beach. This is one of the few "high-rise" mom-and-pop hotels. The Court Capri has an oceanfront outdoor pool and a heated indoor pool, each with a hot tub. All rooms come with refrigerator and microwave. Rates range from $40 a night in the off-season to $128 for the July 4 week. Minimum stays required. Single guests under 25 will be charged a deposit.

Hurl Rock Motel (843-626-3531; hurlrockmyrtlebeach.com), 2010 S. Ocean Boulevard, Myrtle Beach. This hotel is a block off the beach, but offers rooms that start at $20 a night in the off-season up to $100 a night for a two-room efficiency in the summer. This place is perfect for off-season golfers who may not be interested in the beach, which is just across the street. Singles must be at least 25 years old, couples at least 21.

RESORTS Grande Shores Ocean Resort (877-798-4074;

grandeshores.com), 201 77th Avenue North, Myrtle Beach. This oceanfront resort offers a variety of accommodations, from classic hotel rooms and suites to two- and three-bedroom condos with full kitchen. The resort has three pools, two lazy rivers, and five hot tubs, and it's centrally located among Myrtle Beach's attractions. It partners with many of the area's golf courses to offer discounted greens fees as well as specials with a nearby spa. Monthly rentals also available. Condos $100–300 a night in summer; hotel rooms start at $90 a night.

♪ **Grande Dunes Resort** (843-692-2323; grandedunes.com), 1000 Grande Dunes Boulevard, Myrtle Beach. One of the area's newest resorts, Grand Dunes is located on the Intracoastal Waterway and offers vacation home and condo rentals as well as hotel rooms and up to a four-bedroom suites at the Marina Inn. The resort includes a residential section and extends from the beachfront to the waterway. Prices vary by rental type and season. Hotel rooms are around $200 a night in summer. The inn offers a free summer children's program, and kids eat free in the resort's Waterscapes restaurant. The resort has a golf course and offers lessons at its golf academy.

Prince Resort (866-503-9518; princeresortonline.com), 3500 North Ocean Boulevard, North Myrtle Beach. This all-suite resort is located at the Cherry Grove Pier a little north of all the hub-

bub that is Myrtle Beach. It's just a quick drive to some of the area's premier dining and entertainment districts, and for peace and quiet, you can't beat this location. Two golf courses and the Heritage Shores Nature Preserve are within 5 miles. The resort has a rooftop lazy river in its building across the street from the ocean and a total of two pools, four hot tubs, and two restaurants (3500 Ocean Grill and the Boardwalk Beach Café). All the rooms are bigger than 500 square feet and have updated kitchens, balconies, and garden tubs. The staff are known for hospitality. Prices vary widely depending on season and day of the week; they start at $60 a night for a one-bedroom in winter and range up to $250 a night for a three-bedroom in summer.

♪ **Kingston Plantation** (800-876-0010; kingstonplantation.com), 9800 Queensway Boulevard, Myrtle Beach. This resort sits on 145 acres and has more than 1,100 accommodation options, from hotel rooms to town homes to condos. Amenities include tennis, golf, a health spa, a dozen restaurants, two bars, and a coffee shop. The hotel offers several packages whether you're on your honeymoon or want to play a little golf. The resort includes a Hilton and an Embassy Suites as well as villas and condos. There is a day spa and a wide range of golf package options. If you're staying in one of the hotels, you have plenty of pools to choose from. There's a small water park for the kids, a

Jan Hogan

POOLS AT KINGSTON PLANTATION, MYRTLE BEACH

boardwalk to take you between all the amenities, and miles of beach. The resort also provides complimentary shuttle service to nearby shopping—the Tanger Outlet is less than a mile away—and restaurants.

✍ **Landmark Resort Hotel** (843-448-9441; landmarkresort.com), 1501 South Ocean Boulevard, Myrtle Beach. This place has been, well, a landmark on the south end of Myrtle Beach for decades. It's just a 30-minute stroll south to the Springmaid Pier or about a 15-minute stroll north to the Family Kingdom Amusement Park. The Landmark has indoor and outdoor pools, including a lap pool and lazy river. The resort has a covered walkway over Ocean Boulevard to its lavish water park with a nine-hole mini golf course. There is a full-service restaurant if you don't want to venture out as well as a pub with bar food and drinks. The Landmark has standard hotel rooms and efficiencies with a kitchen area. There also are several different suites with a larger kitchen. Rooms and suites are right around $200 a night during summer and are less than $100 a night during the off-season. It's a little pricier than nearby places, but for the location and all the amenities, you can't beat it.

Anderson Ocean Club and Spa (866-578-8494; andersonocean club.com), 2600 North Ocean Boulevard, Myrtle Beach. This relatively new hotel is part of

Oceana Resorts, which operates eight hotels in the Myrtle Beach area. The Anderson Ocean Club is on the waterfront and just a mile from Broadway at the Beach. Guests have access to the Awakening Spa, a pool and fitness center. The spa treatments range from $15 for facial waxing to a daylong package for $400 and include facials, wraps, massages, and other treatments. The resort has two outdoor pools and a lazy river as well as enclosed heated pools for the cooler months. There isn't a restaurant on site, but the hotel has partnered with nearby **Magnolias** (843-839-3993; magnoliasat26th.com), 2605 North Ocean Boulevard, which offers a tasty Southern-style breakfast and lunch buffet for less than $10 a person. Rooms range from studios to three-bedroom suites, starting around $200 a night in-season and $100 a night in the off-season.

DeBordieu (800-753-5597; debordieu.com), 129 Luvan Boulevard, Georgetown. Between Georgetown and Pawleys Island is an isolated 6-mile stretch of beach called DeBordieu, which translates from the French into "borderland of God." Locally, it's lost any resemblance to French and is pronounced *DEB-ah-doo*. The resort is 2,700 acres with a Pete and P. B. Dye–designed golf course, eight Har-Tru tennis courts, and on-site pros. A health and fitness center and day spa are also on the resort. Renters' ability to use club facilities depends on the level of membership the owner of your rental property has. Prices vary widely ($4,000–9,000) depending on house size, location, and season. A quick word about the golf. My buddy Steve Johnson says, "If you are lucky enough to get a round of golf here, you won't want to ever tee it up anywhere else." The course is surrounded by beautiful homes and the marsh, with spectacular views. Because it is a private club, there are fewer golfers out; you can play a round without ever bumping into another foursome. If golf is your reason for traveling, it might be worth spending the extra dollars on your accommodations to get a tee time here.

CABINS/CAMPGROUNDS

⚓ **Pirateland Family Camping Resort** (800-443-CAMP; pirateland.com), 5401 South Kings Highway, Myrtle Beach. This is one of the area's oldest campgrounds. Families return here year after year, developing lifelong friendships with fellow campers. The campground has a store, miniature golf course, outdoor pool and lazy river, snack bar, chapel with Sunday services, kiddie pool, beach lifeguard, paddleboat and beach chair and umbrella rentals, and an arcade. Rates vary by season, from $27 for an inland area off-season to $73 for a seascape with pad in summer.

⚓ **Ocean Lakes Family Campground** (843-238-5636; oceanlakes.com), 6001 South Kings Highway, Myrtle Beach. This is another of the great old camp-grounds along the beach. There are almost 900 campsites available here, with large, pull-through sites for RVs and paved roads. Every site includes a 20–30–50 amp electrical hookup, water, sewer, and a cable-TV hookup. WiFi is available for an extra charge. Prices range $28–62 depending on season.

Myrtle Beach State Park (843-238-5325; southcarolinaparks.com), 4401 South Kings Highway, Myrtle Beach. Open daily 6 AM–10 PM March through November; 6 AM–8 PM December through February. Campers arriving after hours can get a combination to the gate. Five cabins and two apartments are just 200 yards from the beach. Cabins and apartments rent for $80–125 a night. The park has 300 campsites with electrical and water hookups for $25 a night (less in the off-season); 45 tent-only campsites are available during the summer for less than $20 a night. This is a favorite spot for RVers, so be sure to call well in advance and be aware that a minimum stay might be required during the busy season.

✳ Where to Eat

There are so many restaurants on the Grand Strand that US 17 has several stretches known as "Restaurant Row." Local chains have sprung up to provide 24-hour breakfasts and all-you-can-eat seafood buffets. It would be impossible to list all the good places to eat, so—like a good seafood buffet—here is a sampling of offerings:

DINING OUT Frank's and **Frank's Outback** (843-237-3030; franksandoutback.com), 10434 Ocean Highway, Pawleys Island. Open for dinner only 5:30–9:30, daily except Sunday. Outback is also closed Monday. Twenty years ago former grocery bag boy Salters McClary turned Marlow's General Store into Frank's, named for Mr. Marlow. The renovation was so complete that diners would never know they were in a former grocery except for the unclaimed ham hanging from the ceiling near the bar. (It's been there over 40 years.) A few years after opening, the McClarys converted an old house behind the store into Outback, with a less expensive menu and outdoor seating. The food and service are wonderful here and the atmosphere is laid-back, just like Pawleys. Dinner entrées range $17–30.

✐ **Cagney's** (843-449-3824; cagneysoldplace.com), 9911 US 17, Myrtle Beach. Open at 4:15 PM Monday through Saturday. Appetizers $5–10, entrées $15–30. Opened in 1976 by two Myrtle Beach natives named Dino, Cagney's specializes in steaks, seafood, and Italian dishes. A landmark on Restaurant Row for more than 30 years, the restaurant features antiques, woodwork, and other items from local estates, antiques dealers, and long-ago demolished Grand Strand locations. The menu also has burgers and kids' selections.

Waterscapes Restaurant (843-913-2845; marinainnatgrandedunes.com/dining/din_waterscapes.aspx), 8121 Amalfi Place, Myrtle Beach. Open daily for breakfast, lunch, and dinner starting at 6:30 AM. Located at the Marina Inn, Waterscapes is run by executive chef James Clark. Clark is as passionate about minimizing his carbon footprint as he is about fresh seafood, which he gets daily off fishing boats in nearby Murrells Inlet. Nightly selections vary, but include snapper, triggerfish, black bass, and amberjack. His specialty is crispy oysters with a country ham and leek sauce. The menu includes duck, pork tenderloin, and steaks. Almost all of Clark's food is provided by South Carolina and North Carolina farmers and fishermen, with his beef coming from Oregon. Meals are topped off with homemade dessert by pastry chef Tina Spaltro. The food is high-end with entrées up to $30, but the atmosphere is casual and beachy.

Bistro 217 (843-235-8217; bistro0217.com), 10707 Ocean Highway, Pawleys Island. Open Monday through Saturday for lunch and dinner, starting at 11 AM. Owners Anne Hardee and chef and local fisherman Adam Kirby have created a diverse menu with items ranging from blue-cheese-stuffed New York strip to a pan-seared salmon served with an edamame crabcake and tempura

fried green beans. Kirby puts an Asian spin on barbecue ribs and serves his snapper with a wasabi pea sauce. Entrées range $20–30. This small but popular restaurant fills up fast in-season, so reservations are recommended.

✐ **Flamingo Grill** (843-449-5388; flamingogrill.com), 7050 North Kings Highway, Myrtle Beach. Open from 4:15 PM Monday through Saturday. Appetizers $5–10, entrées $15–30. Opened in 1986 by two Myrtle Beach natives named Dino, The Flamingo Grill offers a similar menu to its sister restaurant Cagney's with a little more emphasis on seafood. The menu includes sandwiches, and there are special items for young diners.

Divine Fish House (843-651-5800; divinefishhouse.com), 3993 US 17 Business, Murrells Inlet. Open daily at 5. Diners can see shrimp boats coming and going through the inlet from the Divine Fish House. The restaurant serves fresh seafood with a Far East influence, such as the Thai Hot Pot—shrimp, scallops, fish, and veggies in a red curry sauce. Entrées $20–30. Reservations recommended.

Roz's Rice Mill Café (843-235-0196; rozsricemillcafe.com). Open for lunch 11–3 Monday through Saturday, and dinner 5–9:30 Tuesday through Saturday. Roz's is the only restaurant I have ever seen that serves up lobster with the Southern staple grits. It is one of many unique creations on the menu, including a seafood pie and salmon cakes. Dinner entrées are $16–24.

Thoroughbreds Restaurant (843-497-2636; thoroughbreds restaurant.com), 9706 North Kings Highway, Myrtle Beach. Open daily for dinner at 4:30. Despite the unfortunate use of a horse theme for a meat-centric restaurant, Thouroughbred's is one of South Carolina's finest dining experiences, with a wonderful variety of specialty martinis and wines and a new spin on classic appetizers such as beef carpaccio, duck confit, and a tableside-prepared Caesar salad for two. Steaks range from $30 to $40 for a 22-ounce rib eye; the rest of the à la carte menu ranges from seafood to calf's liver and is priced under $30.

Bove (843-237-7200 ; bovesc .com), 11359 Ocean Highway, Pawleys Island. Open daily at 4 for happy hour; dinner starts at 6. Chef Peter Bove Ryan is carrying on a family tradition at this elegant restaurant that fuses old-world Italian with New Age Southern cuisine. The menu includes about half a dozen dishes, such as pasta Bolognese, linguine with clams, and mac and cheese with shrimp or sausage. Entrées range from $12 to $28. Bove also offers small plates and daily specials.

Drunken Jack's Restaurant (843-651-2004; drunkenjacks .com), 4031 US 17 Business, Murrells Inlet. Open daily for lunch 11:30–2:30, dinner 4–10. The restaurant got its name from a legend of a pirate named Jack who was left behind with a case of rum when his ship sailed off. When the ship returned, all that was left were Jack's bones and empty bottles. People come to Drunken Jack's for the live entertainment on the deck overlooking Snug Harbor Marina. The restaurant has standard seafood fare and steaks for the landlubber. It gets crowded in high season, but they don't take reservations, so go early and plan to stay late. Lunch dishes $8–15; dinner entrées $18–40.

GulfStream Café (843-651-8808; centraarchy.com), 1536 South Waccamaw Drive, Garden City. Open daily for dinner 4–9, Sunday brunch 10:30–2:30. Owned by South Carolina–based Centra Archy Restaurant Management Group, GulfStream is one of the few restaurants on the Grand Strand where you can see both the ocean and the inlet. The deck is great for watching the sunset over Murrells Inlet. Entrées $20–30. GulfStream offers an early-evening menu with smaller portions and all dishes under $15.

Martini's Continental Cuisine and Piano Bar (843-249-1134; martinisfinedining.com), 98 US 17 South, Myrtle Beach. Open daily at 4:30. Martini's is known for its prime rib and the Ocean View Lounge. Locals swear by it. Appetizers $8–12, entrées $23–32.

Joe's Crab Shack (joescrabshack
.com), 1219 Celebrity Circle, Myrtle Beach (843-626-4490); 4846
US 17 South, North Myrtle Beach
(843-272-5900). Hours for both
locations: 11–11 Sunday through
Thursday, 11AM–midnight Friday
through Saturday. This is part of a
South Florida–based chain, but
everyone seems to love it. The
specialty is steam pots with some
combination of shellfish, corn,
potatoes, and sausage. The menu
includes fried and broiled seafood
as well as steaks, burgers, and
fries. Entrées about $20.

SEAFOOD BUFFETS

The seafood buffets along the
northern coast of South Carolina,
like mini golf, are everywhere,
with varying degrees of success. If
you go early, you can get a reasonably good seafood dinner at a reasonable price, but don't expect
fine dining. By and large, you get
a wide selection of fried and
broiled seafood, some landlubber
options, a salad bar, a hot sides
bar, dessert, and drink for about
$20–25 per person. Most places
have crab legs, but they usually
cost $5–10 extra. There are dis-
counts for early diners (3–6 PM);
most hotels have coupons for the
buffet restaurants, and the ones
with websites let you print out
coupons on your computer. If you
don't have a big appetite, this is
probably not the best deal for you.
But if you've been out on the
beach or golf course all day, it's a
good way to get your fill.

A quick word here about Calabash-style seafood that so many
of these restaurants serve. Calabash is a small fishing village in
North Carolina about half an hour
from Myrtle Beach. Some people
say Calabash-style means plenty of
food. Some say it means fresh-off-
the-boat. My mom says it refers to
a type of breading, very light and
crunchy—more like cornflakes
than cornmeal. So ask if you must,
but you will get a different answer
wherever you go—even if you
venture north to Calabash.

Here are a few of the favorite buffets at Myrtle Beach:

**The Original Capt. Benjamin's
Calabash Seafood Buffet** (843-
449-0821; originalbenjamins.com),
9593 North Kings Highway, Myrtle Beach. If you can't find something to eat at Benjamin's, you just
aren't hungry. There are nearly
200 items on this intricate buffet
spread around a pirate ship. The
outdoor deck overlooking a tidal
creek has plenty of rocking chairs
and is the perfect place for a cold
beer while you're waiting for a
table.

**Bennett's Calabash Seafood
Restaurant** (843-361-9743;
bennettscalabash.net), 1010 US 17
South, North Myrtle Beach; 9701
North Kings Highway, Myrtle
Beach; and 2900 North Kings
Highway, Myrtle Beach. Bennett's
specialty is crab legs, which are
typically included in the full buffet
price of about $22. With three
locations, it's fairly easy to find one.

Jan Hogan

CAPTAIN BENJAMIN GREETS DINERS IN MYRTLE BEACH.

EATING OUT Sea Captains House (843-448-8082; seacaptains.com), 3002 North Ocean Boulevard, Myrtle Beach. Open daily for breakfast, lunch, and dinner. This is one of the few oceanside restaurants you will find at Myrtle that is not inside a hotel. Dinner entrées include locally caught shrimp, a fresh catch of the day, and a selection of steaks with a chicken and pork dish. For lunch, the shrimp salad is a must, and breakfast offers a seafood twist on a classic: crabcakes Benedict.

Sara J's (843-651-1657; sarajs.com), 314 Atlantic Avenue, Garden City. Open daily at 4 PM. The crew at Sara J's are proud of their fishing prowess and show it off with stuffed sportfish on the walls. The blue marlin is the prize, weighing in at more than 500 pounds when it was caught about 70 miles off the South Carolina coast in 2004. Entrées range $9–23.

Peaches Corner (843-448-7424; peaches-corner.com), 900 North Ocean Boulevard, Myrtle Beach. Open seven days a week from 11 AM. This place has been open since 1937 serving beer, foot-long hot dogs, and its famous double cheeseburger baskets with fries. It used to be open 24 hours a day in-season, and it's next to the site of the old Pavilion. One of the legends around Peaches is that young airmen would get a little surprise with their order—money, usually enough to catch a cab back to the nearby air base. The place is still run by the same family that bought it way back in 1943, and it looks pretty much the same. Sandwiches $8–10.

PEACHES CORNER HAS BEEN A MYRTLE BEACH INSTITUTION FOR MORE THAN 40 YEARS.

Sam's Corner (843-651-3233), 101 Atlantic Avenue, Garden City. Open when the beach is crowded, closed when it's not. This is a great place to get a deep-fried hot dog and cold beer.

Island Café & Deli (843-237-9527; islandcafeanddeli.com), 10683 Ocean Highway, Pawleys Island. Open daily for lunch and dinner starting at 11. This is one of the oldest restaurants in Pawleys Island, serving soups, salads, and sandwiches, including a Strom Thurmond (hot pastrami and turkey on rye) and a PB&J for lunch, and more substantial fare such as steak and seafood for dinner. Lunch items are mostly less than $10, with dinner entrées under $20.

Pawleys Island Tavern (843-237-8465; pawleysislandtavern.com), 10635 Ocean Highway, Pawleys Island. Open every day but Monday for lunch and dinner. The PIT serves up $6 Blue Plate specials for lunch based on what's in-season. Dinner focuses on fresh seafood from nearby fishermen, but also offers steaks, burgers, and other fare for landlubbers. But mainly this is the place to come out for a beer and listen to live music, either on the large back porch or at the tiki bar out front.

Island Bar & Grill (843-235-3399; islandbarandgrill.com), 10744 Ocean Highway, Pawleys Island. Open daily 11 AM–2 AM for lunch, dinner, and late night. Just down the street from the tavern is another local music favorite. From April through August you can hear live music on the deck. Year-round there is an upstairs sports bar with pool tables, dartboards, shuffle-board, and other bar games. All menu items are under $20.

PANCAKE HOUSES Like the local seafood buffets, there seems to be an endless stream of pancake houses along the Grand Strand, and most of them have *Omega* in the name. You can get standard breakfast fare, along the lines of national chains IHOP and Waffle House. Prices are about $10 per person with coffee. Many are open 24 hours, but most are open before anyone on vacation could possibly want breakfast.

Omega Pancake & Omelet House (843-626-9949), 2800 North Kings Highway, Myrtle Beach. This is the one many people think of as "the original." Omega has great service and tasty food.

Dino's Pancake House (843-272-5411), 2120 US 17, North Myrtle Beach. Dino will give you a smile from the register at this place on the north end of Ocean Drive.

Plantation Pancake House (843-238-1690), 1003 US 17 North, Surfside Beach. This long-time fixture on the south end of the beach offers 61 different omelets.

✳ Entertainment

MUSIC VENUES Broadway at the Beach (800-386-4662; broadwayatthebeach.com), 1325 Celebrity Circle, Myrtle Beach.

Open daily 10–11 in summer; closes earlier in the offseason. This entertainment complex is home to about 20 restaurants, 100 shops, two movie theater complexes, a nightclub district, and live-show theaters.

THEATERS *⌀* **The Carolina Opry** (843-913-4000; cgp.net), 8901-A Business 17 North, Myrtle Beach. One of the oldest of the beach's music theaters, the Carolina Opry has 2,220 seats and a cast of 36 singers, dancers, comedians, and musicians. The two-hour show ranges from rock and roll to Broadway, country, and pop. Carolina Opry has a Christmas show in November and December and offers *Good Vibrations*—a 90-minute, no-intermission retrospective of the '60s, '70s, and '80s. Ticket prices vary by seat and season and max out at $52 for the best seats to the Christmas show. The lowest price is $16 for children 16 and younger.

⌀ **Legends in Concert** (843-238-STAR; legendsinconcert.com), 301 US 17 Business, Surfside Beach. Performers look and act like celebrities Buddy Holly, Elvis Presley, Michael Jackson, Martina McBride, and the Beatles, but sing in their own voices. They are backed by live musicians, backup singers, and dancers. Tickets top out at $40 for best adult seating and $15 for a child's regular seat.

Medieval Times Dinner & Tournament (843-236-8080; medievaltimes.com), 2904 Fantasy

Way, Myrtle Beach. Diners are transported back to the era of knights and ladies in this theater with dozens of locations throughout North America. Prices vary depending on packages, but start at $50 for adults and include dinner.

Palace Theatre (843-448-9224; palacetheatremyrtlebeach.com), 1420 Celebrity Circle, Myrtle Beach. Located in the Broadway at the Beach entertainment complex, the Palace offers a variety of shows including musicals, a Michael Jackson tribute show, and a summer series that includes *Alice in Wonderland*, *Narnia*, and *The Great American Trailer Park Musical* in its King Suite Showroom. The main auditorium has more than 2,600 seats while the showroom seats 140. Ticket prices vary by show, seat, and season, but max out at $45 for the theater's Le Grand Cirque—Adrenaline, a music, lighting, and acrobat performance akin to Cirque du Soleil.

♪ **Alabama Theatre** (843-272-1111; alabama-theatre.com), 4750 US 17, North Myrtle Beach. Named for the country music band that used to play at the Bowery near the Pavilion in its early years, this theater offers occasional guest shows, but its primary offering is its one show that mixes country, gospel, pop, and rock music with family comedy. Kids get in free all summer with paid adult admission. Prices vary depending on seat, show, and season.

♪ **Pirates Voyage** (800-433-4401; piratesvoyage.com), 8901-B North Kings Highway, Myrtle Beach. Shows at 6 PM Saturday through Sunday, 6 and 8 PM Monday through Friday, with a 4 PM show on Wednesday. This theater was formerly home to Dolly Parton's *Dixie Stampede*. The new show is still owned by Parton, but the theater has undergone $11 million in renovations and upgrades. The new show starts diners in the Pirate Village, where they are divided into two teams, Crimson and Sapphire, as their crews compete for the treasure of Davy Jones. Actors do several stunts underwater as well as sword fighting and acrobatics on dry land. Tickets include a five-course meal and are $45–50 for adults 12 and older; $25–30 for children ages 3–11. Younger children admitted free if they don't get a separate meal.

♪ **IMAX 3D Theatre Myrtle Beach** (843-448-4629; imax3d myrtlebeach.com), 1195 Celebrity Circle, Myrtle Beach. Open daily starting at 10:30 AM. Tickets range $10–15. The drawback here is the limited number of films that are able to fill the 60-by-80-foot screen. It's not much more expensive than just going to a regular movie, though, so I say give it a whirl. All of the offerings typically have stunning visuals. The seats are sharply tiered so everyone should have a clear view of the screen. The curve in the expansive screen will put part of the image in your peripheral field, making you feel like you are part of the action.

MUSIC VENUES House of Blues (843-272–3000; houseof blues.com), 4640 US 17, North Myrtle Beach. Open daily for dinner starting at 4, with breakfast and lunch on Saturday 8–4 and a gospel brunch on Sunday 9–2. Although there are many House of Blues locations around the country, the Myrtle Beach site tries to blend in with the area's history. It looks like an old farmhouse with a tobacco barn. Set back off the road, the venue is great if the performer plays raucous music. If the music is subtle—think Norah Jones—it can be difficult to hear with chatty crowds at the bar. The concerts are general admission standing tickets, so House of Blues gives preference to diners at the restaurant. The restaurant here is not the best. The food is a little pricey—about $20 an entrée—and what you get is standard chain-restaurant food. I recommend that if you are coming to a show and you do want to take advantage of the head-of-the-line offer by eating at the restaurant, just have a few appetizers or maybe split an entrée and have a couple of beers. Doors open at 8 and music starts around 9.

✴ Selective Shopping

The Hammocks Shops Village (thehammockshops.com), 10880 US 17, Pawleys Island. Hours:

10–6 Monday through Saturday, 1–6 Sunday. This is hands-down the best shopping along the Grand Strand. Interesting and fun shops mix in with restaurants in a shaded complex that feels more like a beach village than a shopping center. A must-see is **The Original Hammock Shop** (800-332-3490; hammockshop.com), where they have made rope hammocks since 1889. The hammocks are still handwoven of cotton. They were designed by South Carolina riverboat captain Joshua John Ward as a way to be cool and comfortable while trying to sleep on a boat on a steamy South Carolina summer night. You can even watch as the hammocks are made. Another favorite is **She Sells Sea Shells** (843-237-0118; shesellsseashells sc.com). This store offers seashells like you've never seen them before, locally harvested as well as imported arts and crafts with seashells. Take a break from shopping for lunch or dinner at **Roz's Rice Mill Café** (843-235-0196; rozsricemillcafe.com). Open for lunch 11–3 Monday through Saturday and dinner 5–9:30 Tuesday through Saturday. Other shops include: **Pawleys Island Mercantile** (843-235-0507; pawleys islandmercantile.com), open Monday through Saturday 10–6, Sunday 1–5. This store has all the beach clothing and accessories you will need. **The Candy Cottage** (843-237-8083; thecandy cottage.net), open Monday through Saturday 10–6, Sunday 1–5. Everyone feels like a kid in a candy store at this shop. The have everything from a gourmet chocolate section, to Mary Janes and Squirrel Nut Zippers, to a line of sugar-free selections.

Gay Dolphin Gift Cove (843-448-6550; gaydolphin.com), 916 North Ocean Boulevard, Myrtle Beach. Open daily 9:30–6:30. The oldest and most delightful souvenir shop on the beach, the Gay Dolphin has been open for more than 60 years and has the most distinctive building on Ocean Boulevard with its glass observation deck and spiral staircase. Named for dolphins the owners saw frolicking in the water one day, this shop has sharks' teeth, dried sea creatures of all kinds, as well as your standard shells and other kitschy souvenir items. Even if you're not buying, you need to stop in to see this place—it's a tourist attraction in its own right.

Barefoot Landing (843-272-8349 or 800-272-2320; barefootlanding .com), 4898 US 17, North Myrtle Beach. Open daily at 10 AM. This shopping complex on the Intracoastal Waterway has more than 100 shops and 14 restaurants along a boardwalk around a 27-acre lake. The House of Blues is here, as are the Alabama Theatre and Carolina Vineyards Winery.

Bass Pro Shops Outdoor World (843-361-4800; bassproshops .com), 10177 North Kings Highway, Myrtle Beach. Open Monday through Saturday 9 AM–10 PM, Sunday 10 AM–9 PM. I know you

can find these all over the world, but I find it irresistible—and I don't fish. If you're out shopping anyway, just swing by here; it's like free entertainment. Who knew there were so many products made to improve your enjoyment of the great outdoors?

Broadway at the Beach (843-444-3200 or 800-386-4662; broadwayatthebeach.com), 1324 Celebrity Circle, Myrtle Beach. Open daily at 10 AM; closing at 6 PM in the off-season, 10 PM in summer. Among the more than 100 stores in this shopping, dining, and entertainment complex are the Silver Shack with jewelry and other accessories made of silver; the Cat Store with, as you would imagine, everything for the cat fancier; in addition to nationally known brand-name stores like Birkenstock and Yankee Candle. There's also plenty for everyone to do here while you shop with more than two dozen restaurants and nightclubs, the Myrtle Beach Waves Water Park, and the IMAX 3D Theatre.

Myrtle Beach has a few typical indoor shopping malls with nationally known anchors, such as JCPenney and Sears and regional stores, like Belk and Dillard. The malls open daily at 10 AM: **Coastal Grand Mall—Myrtle Beach** (843-839-9100; CoastalGrand .com), 2000 Coastal Grand Circle, Myrtle Beach. **Inlet Square Mall** (843-651-6990 inletsquaremall .com), 10125 US 17 Bypass, Murrells Inlet. **Myrtle Beach Mall**

(843-272-4040; mymallmyrtle
beach.com), 10177 North Kings
Highway, Myrtle Beach.

The Tanger Outlet (843-449-
0491 or 843-236-5100; tanger
outlet.com) has two shopping centers in the Myrtle Beach area:
10835 King's Road and 4635 Factory Stores Boulevard. The oulets
are very similar with national
brand factory stores such as Nike,
Eddie Bauer, Coach, Liz Clai-
borne, Skechers, and Perry Ellis.

✳ Special Events

SPRING *March:* ✪ **Can-Am
Days Festival** (843-626-7444;
grandstrandevents.com/CanAm
Days), various locations. This is
one of the area's oldest festivals,
dating back to 1961, and it celebrates our neighbors to the north,
who so kindly come to visit in
early spring and entertain us by
swimming in the very cold ocean.
You can tell the Canadians from
the Americans (at least the Southerners) at this festival by what
they're wearing. Locals will be in
jeans and sweaters while the out-
of-towners will be in swimsuits.
The weeklong celebration is kid-
friendly and includes live music
and food at various locations along
the beach.

April: **Spring Flounder Tournament** (843-450-8218; gssaa.org),
4123 US 17 Business, Murrells
Inlet. This annual tournament
welcomes all anglers and includes
youth and women's categories.

Top prize is $1,500 for the largest
legal flounder. Participants meet
at Capt. Dick's the evening before
the tournament starts at sunrise
the next morning. The cost is $40
for adults 14 and older; $20 for
the youngsters.

May: **Coastal Uncorked Food
and Wine Festival** (843-839-
8818; coastaluncorked.com). This
weeklong event features beer and
wine tastings around Myrtle
Beach, live music, and cooking
demonstrations. A festival favorite
is the tasting trolley that takes you
to event locations. On the closing
night, six chefs compete in an *Iron
Chef*–style cooking competition at
the Marina Inn.

✪ **Mayfest** (843-626-7444; myrtle
beachmayfest.com), Ocean Boulevard between 8th and 9th Avenue
North. This family-oriented parade
and festival celebrates the Memorial Day weekend and the traditional kickoff of beach season.
Myrtle Beach has historically been
home to motorcycle rallies around
this time, but the city has tried to
discourage those events because
of the traffic and noise.

SUMMER *June:* **Sun Fun Festival**
(843-626-7444; sunfunfestival
.com), Grand Park at Market
Common. This is the beach's oldest event and has been drawing
visitors from points north for more
than 60 years. Held over a weekend in June, the festival includes
concerts, arts and crafts shows, a
Jet Ski competition, and fireworks.

FALL *September:* ✿ **Beach, Boogie & Barbeque Festival** (843-626-7444; sunfunfestival.com /beachboogiebbq). Just as the Sun Fun Festival kicks off summer, this one says good-bye to summer. Family-friendly entertainment and events are available as well as barbecue samples from regional teams. There are wakeboard demonstrations, beer gardens, arts and crafts vendors, and fireworks.

Annual Atalaya Arts & Crafts Festival (atalayafestival.com), 16148 Ocean Highway. Admission is $6 ages 15 and older. More than 100 artists turn out for this festival at the site of a onetime artist colony. Located on the grounds of the Huntington Beach State Park at the Moors-style castle built by Anna Hyatt and Archer Huntington. In addition to the artists' displays, local restaurants bring their best Lowcountry cuisine and area musicians perform.

GEORGETOWN

Georgtown lives in the tourism shadow of Myrtle Beach, but it's a great place to get out of the heat, sun, and crowds for a day to visit rice plantations and walk along the old port city's riverwalk.

Georgetown sits on Winyah Bay, where four South Carolina rivers dump into the Atlantic Ocean. The city has a port feel, but on a much smaller scale than Charleston. The port used to take rice, known as Carolina Gold Rice, from the countless plantations in the area and send it around the world. The city's rice museum is a must-see on any trip to the South Carolina coast.

Georgetown is the state's third-oldest settlement, dating back more than 300 years. The historic district is on the National Register of Historic Places and includes the Fyffe House, Prince George Episcopal Church, Bethel African Methodist Church, and Robert Stewart House. The city has revitalized its downtown along Front Street with museums, shops, and restaurants.

The city's longtime steelworks has recently reopened and International Paper's mill still operates, giving the air an occasional acrid sulfur scent, but providing hundreds of jobs to locals.

The nearby small town of Andrews was the birthplace of singer Chubby Checker.

GUIDANCE Georgetown Chamber of Commerce (843-546-8436; georgetownchamber.com), 531 Front Street. The chamber has information on all businesses and is home to the **Georgetown County Tourism Management Commission** (visitgeorgetowncountysc.com), whose Hammock Coast website is full of good information.

GETTING THERE *By air:* **Myrtle Beach International Airport** (843-448-1589; flymyrtlebeach.com), offering direct and connecting flights through U.S. carriers. The airport is about an hour away in heavy traffic.

By train: The nearest Amtrak stop is in Kingstree, about 40 miles west of the city.

By bus: **Greyhound** (843-546-4535; greyhound.com), 2014 Highmarket Street.

By car: US Highways 17, 521, and 701 pass through Georgetown.

GETTING AROUND The best way to get around Georgetown is by walking once you've parked your car at your lodging. You will need your car if you want to hit any of the beach attractions.

✳ To See

MUSEUMS The Rice Museum (843-546-7423; ricemuseum.org), 633 Front Street. Open 10–4:30 Monday through Saturday. The museum is located in the Old Market Building at the Town Clock and traces Georgetown's history from the mid-1700s when the city was the center of rice production for the colony through the mid-1800s when the county produced about half of the country's total rice crop. The museum tour includes a 17-minute film titled *The Garden of Gold.* Admission: adults $7; seniors 60 and older $5; students 21 and younger $3; children younger than 6 are free.

Kaminski House Museum (843-546-7706; kaminskihousemuseum.org), 1003 Front Street. Open 10–4 Monday through Saturday, 1–3 Sunday. Guided tours are available on the hour for $7 for ages 13 and older; $3 for ages 6–12; children younger than 5 are free. This is one of more than 60 antebellum homes in the city. It's located on a bluff overlooking the Sampit River and is built in a Charleston style—it appears very narrow from the street, with its main entryway along one side of the house.

HISTORIC SITES Hopsewee Plantation (843-546-7891; hopsewee .com), 494 Hopsewee Road. Open 10–4 Tuesday through Friday and noon–4 Saturday. Closed December and January. Admission is $15 for ages 18 and older, and $7.50 for children. This historic home was the birthplace of Declaration of Independence signer Thomas Lynch Jr. The plantation home was built in 1740, and Lynch was born in 1749. The home is privately owned, but is open to the public and is furnished with 18th- and 19th-century antiques. The grounds include two original slave cabins. Lynch Jr. was serving as a captain in South Carolina's provincial regiment when his father suffered a paralyzing stroke while representing the state at the Constitutional Convention in Philadelphia. The younger Lynch was elected as his replacement and signed the Declaration at the age of 26. The elder Lynch died from his stroke on his way back to South Carolina. Lynch Jr. left South Carolina in 1779 first

for the West Indies; he was lost at sea along with his wife. The plantation has stunning views of the Santee River, especially from the **River
Oak Cottage,** where they serve traditional English tea and lunch from
10 to 3:30 Tuesday through Friday and noon to 3:30 on Saturday. Reservations are recommended.

HISTORIC CHURCHES Bethel AME Church, Duke at Broad Streets.
The first separate African American congregation in Georgetown was
established in 1865. The current sanctuary was built in 1882 and remod-
eled in 1908.

Prince George Winyah Episcopal Church (843-546-4358; pgwinyah
.com), 300 Broad Street. Open 11:30–4:30 weekdays from March through
October. Year-round worship services held Sunday at 8, 9, and 11 AM.
Organized in 1721, this is one of the oldest parishes in South Carolina.
The building dates to about 1750 and includes the old-style enclosed
pews. The church was occupied twice by troops—first by the British during the Revolutionary War, then by U.S. soldiers during the Civil War. The
church is listed on the National Register of Historic Places.

✳ To Do

FISHING Delta Guide Service (843-546-3645; deltaguideservice.com),
803 Second Avenue. Delta offers onshore fishing trips of five hours ($350)
or eight hours ($450). Prices include two anglers. One additional adult is
$50. Children 14 and younger are free. They provide everything you need
for catching fish; you provide your own food and drinks.

Captain Sandy's Tours (843-527-4106; captsandy2002@yahoo.com), 343
Ida Drive. Tours of Winyah Bay and nearby rivers by reservation only.
Captain Sandy is a wonderful storyteller and will take you on a one-of-a-
kind tour or shell-hunting excursion. The tours are about $40 for adults 13
and older and $30 for children.

FAMILY-FRIENDLY ACTIVITIES ✐ **The Carolina Rover Boat
Tours** (843-546-8822; roverboattours.com), 735 Front Street. Cost: $30
for ages 12 and older; $20 for children. Departure times vary depending
on tides and are set about a week in advance. Tours aim to put you out on
the beaches by the Winyah Bay Lighthouse at prime shell-picking time.
Tours come with captain, a naturalist who can answer your questions, and
soft drinks. You provide the sunscreen.

✐ **Black River Outdoors Center** (843-546-4840; blackriveroutdoors
.com), 21 Garden Avenue. Open 9–5:30 daily. This outfitter offers guided
kayak ecotours of the state's tidelands. Tour prices range $35–55. Boat
rentals are $35–50 a day with discounts for extended rentals.

GOLF Wedgefield Plantation Country Club (843-448-2124; wedge field.com), 129 Clubhouse Lane. Depending on the time of year, rates range $25–60.

✳ Green Space

Tom Yawkey Wildlife Center (843-546-6814; dnr.sc.gov), 1 Yawkey Way. Open for guided tours by reservation only, usually four to six months in advance. Tours are available September through May on Tuesday and Wednesday only 2–5 PM. This 20,000-acre wildlife habitat is composed of 31 square miles of marsh, managed wetlands, ocean beach, and pine forest. It was a gift from former Boston Red Sox owner Tom Yawkey to the state of South Carolina. There is no hunting allowed on the land that Yawkey inherited from an uncle and where he and his wife spent winters. The beaches are considered excellent nesting locations for the threatened loggerhead sea turtle.

✳ Lodging

INNS AND BED & BREAKFASTS

Mansfield Plantation (866-717-1776; mansfieldplantation.com), 1776 Mansfield Road. Built in the 1700s, Mansfield Plantation was once one of the state's largest rice plantations. Today its 1,000 acres and home are on the National Register of Historic Places; the property is owned by the descendants of the original Parker family that built the home. Rates are $150–200, and rooms come with a warm breakfast. There's lots of room to roam here and plenty of bird-watching opportunities on the Black River.

Harbor House Bed and Breakfast (843-546-6532; harborhouse bb.com), 15 Cannon Street. This home was built on the water in the mid-18th century. There are four rooms, each with a fireplace, private bath, and some modern amenities such as hair dryers, cable TV, and an open beverage bar. Rates are $160–190. No children.

✐ **Shaw House** (843-546-9663), 613 Cypress Court. This inn is located on the grounds of Willowbank Plantation and has wonderful views of rice fields and the marsh. It's just a short walk to Georgetown's historic district. Three rooms are available, each with private bath. Breakfast is included in the rates: $100 a night. Children are welcome.

✳ Where to Eat

DINING OUT Rice Paddy Restaurant (843-546-2021; rice paddyrestaurant.com), 732 Front Street. Open Monday through Saturday 11:30–2:30 and 6–10. The building that houses this restaurant in downtown has been a bank and a barbershop. It has been home of the Rice Paddy since 2001. Lunch items include an open-faced hot crab sandwich with a house salad ($12) and a jalapeño pimiento cheese-burger ($10). Dinner entrées range from $22 for snapper and grits to $35 for roast rack of lamb.

Portafino's on the Wharf (843-485-4210; portofinosonthewharf.com), 815 Front Street. Open 11–10 Tuesday through Saturday, 5–9 Monday; closed Sunday. Portofino's offers classic Italian dishes in a waterfront location. Dishes include veal piccata, saltimbocco, and a touch of France with a duck confit. A small deck allows some outdoor dining in temperate months. This place is a favorite of locals and people who visit the area frequently. The fried calamari appetizer has a kick after being tossed with hot cherry peppers, olives, garlic, and capers. Dinner entrées range $12–25.

✎ **Goat Island Grill** (843-527-3500; goatislandgrill.com), 719 Front Street. Open daily for lunch and dinner starting at 11 AM; opens at noon on Sunday. G.I.G.—as this restaurant calls itself—is family-friendly with a fair number of kids' options and several vegetarian selections. A favorite creation on the menu is Grouper Gumbolaya: shrimp, smoked sausage, okra, tomato, and onion in a gumbo-style broth with white rice, topped with grilled grouper. Entrées range $18–22.

EATING OUT Thomas Café (843-546-7776; thomascafe.net), 703 Front Street. Open 7 AM–2 PM Monday through Saturday. This 75-year-old diner hasn't changed

much over the years, except maybe the prices. A meat-and-three-side Southern lunch comes with corn-bread or biscuit and a beverage for less than $10. Chef Ernest Brunson, a native of nearby Florence, bought the place three years ago and is adding a little more culinary spice to the menu. But the old standards of chicken-fried steak, macaroni and cheese, and fried okra are still there.

Harvest Moon (843-527-4110), 801 Front Street. Open 10–7 Monday through Thursday, 10–10 Friday through Saturday, 11–7 Sunday. This is a great place to stop on the water for hot dogs, yogurt, and ice cream.

✳ Selective Shopping

Joyfilled Garden & Gifts and Prena Knit Shop (843-545-5344; joyfilledgifts.com), 701 Front Street. Open 10–5:30 Monday through Saturday. The name here pretty much says it all. The gifts include religious-themed jewelry, and the knit shop includes a teaching studio.

Harborwalk Books (843-546-8212), 723 Front Street. Open 10–5 Monday through Saturday, noon–3 Sunday. This locally owned bookstore along the Sampit River specializes in regional history and Civil War books.

Georgetown Art Gallery (843-527-7711), 732 Front Street. Open 10–5 Monday through Saturday. This cooperative gallery shows the work of 20 member artists who work in a variety of media, including painting, sculpture, and photography.

Tomlinson Sales Co. (843-546-7571; tomlinsonsales.com/Georgetown-sc), 806 Front Street. Open 9:30–6 Monday through Saturday. Take a step back in time in this old-school department store that once was the place where everyone got the necessities of life, from clothes to outdoor gear.

Carolina Charm (843-520-1846), 1410 Highmarket Street. Open 8:30–5:30 Monday through Friday, 8:30–noon Saturday. This eclectic gift shop offers regional products such as Gullah Gourmet items, as well as Palmetto logo clothing and other merchandise.

✴ Special Events

SPRING *March:* **Plantation Tours** (843-545-8291; pgwinyah .com/PlantationTours.htm), 301 Screven Street. Held 9:30–5 on a Friday and Saturday in late March, this tour offers glimpses of

THE SWAMP FOX

Francis Marion is probably one of South Carolina's most famous warriors. Battling the British throughout the swamps of the Pee Dee and Lowcountry during the Revolutionary War, Marion—known as the Swamp Fox—used his knowledge of the terrain, and his enemy's lack of that knowledge, to help his outnumbered band of guerrillas inflict serious pain on the more regimented Royal Army.

Marion's life has inspired legends—mostly true—and even movies—not even close to true. Mel Gibson's character in *The Patriot* was inspired by Marion, though the real man did not have a plantation full of children.

Two things helped set Marion's legend. One was when British Lieutenant Colonel Banastre Tarleton unsuccessfully chased Marion and his men for hours through more than 20 miles of cypress swamps. Tarleton supposedly said of Marion, "As for this damned old fox, the Devil himself could not catch him"—thus the nickname.

Another incident was captured in an oil-on-canvas painting by John Blake White that now hangs in the U.S. Senate. White grew up next door to Marion's Pond Bluff plantation and painted the general from memory. According to the story, Marion and a British officer were discussing a prisoner exchange one morning while the militia was encamped on Snow's Island. Sweet potatoes were roasting in the fire, the city's old plantation houses, most of which are privately owned. Visitors have to drive themselves to the homes, and there's a different lineup each day. Histories and suggested routes are provided with tickets. The Episcopal Church Women of Prince George, Winyah Parish, sponsor the event and recommend planning to spend the whole day on the tour. Cost: $35 a day or $60 for a two-day pass.

WINTER *January:* ♪ **Winyah Bay Heritage Festival** (843-833-9919; winyahbayfestival.org), 632 Prince Street. The festival takes place in various locations around the county. Events include a statewide duck-calling championship, children's decoy painting, fishing guide presentations, and other traditions surrounding the outdoor life. Proceeds benefit the Georgetown County Historical Society and the Georgetown County Museum. Tickets are $10 daily or $15 for a two-day ticket.

and Marion invited the officer to have some breakfast. The legend has it that the British officer was so taken by Marion's offer that he joined the fight for independence. This may be one of the earliest examples of Southern hospitality.

Jan Hogan

FRANCIS MARION'S GRAVE MARKER

After the war, Marion participated in the writing of the South Carolina constitution and early government. He retired to his plantation and died in 1795 in his early 60s. His plantation is now under Lake Marion.

Although Marion is remembered as a hero, he was a man of his times. He owned slaves, including a personal servant named Oscar, who is thought to have fought alongside Marion as well as tend to the cooking and other menial duties. In Decmeber 2006 Oscar Marion was honored by a presidential proclamation for his service to the United States.

Also, Marion learned his swamp-fighting ways battling Indians during the French and Indian War in the mid-1700s.

The **Francis Marion Trail** (departments.fmarion.edu/fmutrailcommission /index.htm) is under development in eastern South Carolina. Archaeologists and historians are in the process of identifying locations that were significant in Marion's life to highlight on the trail. Most of those locations are in and around Georgetown, the Pee Dee, Lake Marion, and Berkeley and Charleston Counties.

THE PEE DEE

The Pee Dee area grew up around farming—namely tobacco and cotton—and the railroad. Neither of these is as important to the area as they once were; they've been replaced by the medical services industry. There still are some farmers who earn a good living in the area, but most now grow soybeans and other cash crops.

Florence is the largest town in the area and is where Interstates 20 and 95 cross. If you're trying to get to Myrtle Beach from points west and north, you almost have to drive through Florence. We natives secretly think that's why Interstate 20 has never been extended to the beach. No one would have to stop here anymore.

The area has a handful of famous natives. Federal Reserve Board chairman Ben Bernanke grew up in Dillon, *Antiques Roadshow* host Mark Walberg was born in Florence, and country music star Teddy Pendergrass was born in Kingstree.

The black-water rivers that run through the Pee Dee—named for the Indians that used to live here—are excellent for canoeing, kayaking, and fishing, but it is recommended that you don't eat too much of your catch—evidence of mercury has been found in larger fish in the rivers. Mercury warning signs are posted at water bodies where fish should not be eaten or where fish consumption should be limited. The state **Department of Health and Environmental Control** keeps an updated list of these water bodies at scdhec.gov/environment/water/fish.

Unverified monster alert: You may have heard of a creature that some say lives in this area—Bishopville, to be more exact. It's a 7-foot half lizard half man, aptly named the Lizard Man. I put no stock in this legend, obviously born in the mind of someone with a lot of T-shirts he needed to sell, but as crazy as it sounds, it actually made the news one sleepy summer in the late 1980s. Legend has it, the Lizard Man was fond of butterbeans—known as lima beans outside the South—and may have died in 1989 when the real-life Hurricane Hugo swept across the state.

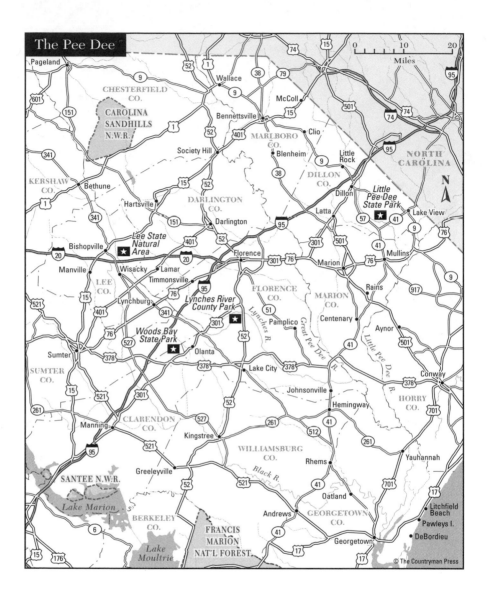

But the legend lives on T-shirts and other memorabilia that you may see in stores around Bishopville.

GUIDANCE **Pee Dee Country South Carolina** (843-669-0950; peedee tourism.com), 3290 West Radio Drive, Florence. The website, sponsored by the Pee Dee Tourism Commission, includes links to all the area chambers of commerce.

GETTING THERE *By air:* **Florence Regional Airport** (843-669-5001, florencescairport.com) offers daily flights to Atlanta, Georgia, through

Atlantic Southeast Airlines (800-221-1212; flyasa.com), and Charlotte, North Carolina, through US Airways Express (800-428-4322; usairways .com).

By train: As befitting the area's railroad heritage, two **Amtrak** (800-872-7245; amtrak.com) trains make a total of four stops in Florence and Kingstree each day. Dillon gets two stops a day. The stations are located at 805 East Day Street, Florence; 101 East Main Street, Kingstree; and 100 North Railroad Avenue, Dillon.

By bus: **Greyhound** (843-662-8407; greyhound.com), 611 South Irby Street, Florence. There are at about a dozen buses a day in and out of Florence.

By car: Interstates 95 and 20 cross in Florence, and most of the region's major cities and towns are an easy jaunt from those two roads. U.S. Highways 52, 76, and 301 also pass through Florence and can get you to those places where the interstates don't go.

GETTING AROUND You will really need a private car to get around in the Pee Dee. The area's attractions are widespread.

✴ To See

MUSEUMS Darlington Raceway Stock Car Museum & Pit Shop (843-395-8821; darlingtonraceway.com), 1301 Harry Byrd Highway, Darlington. Open 10–5 Monday through Friday, 10–4 Saturday. Admission: $5 for ages 12 and older, free for younger children. This museum houses everything anyone ever wanted to know about racing at Darlington. The track is known as the Lady in Black and the Track Too Tough to Tame. Drivers talk about getting their "Darlington stripe"—when their cars brush against a wall around the track and some of the paint gets on the car. The museum includes a line of classic race cars from the days when Darlington hosted two NASCAR races every year.

Florence Museum (843-662-3351; florencemuseum.org), 558 Spruce Street, Florence. Open 10–5 Tuesday through Saturday, 2–5 Sunday. The museum has an eclectic collection ranging from the Pueblo pottery that made up the first pieces bought for the museum, to the work of Florence native William H. Johnson, who began creating black folk art in the 1930s.

The South Carolina Cotton Museum (803-484-4497; sccotton.org), 121 West Cedar Lane, Bishopville. Open 10–4 Monday through Saturday. Admission is $6 adults, $4 for seniors, $3 for students, and free for children 5 and younger. The museum salutes all things cotton in this small town, which is the hub of the state's cotton growing area.

South Carolina Tobacco Museum (843-464-8194 or 800-207-7967; mullinssc.us/sctobaccomuseumindex.html), 104 Northeast Front Street,

Mullins. Open 9–5 Monday through Friday. This is the state's official museum dedicated to its number one (legal) cash crop. The museum shows what life was like on a tobacco farm before 1950, including displays on the plant's life cycle and a variety of equipment such as wagons, tools, and a reconstructed pole barn. The entire Pee Dee region is dotted with these structures. The museum is located in an early-20th-century train depot. Admission is $2 for adults and $1 for children and seniors.

The National Bean Market Museum (843-374-1500; lakecitysc.org), 111 Henry Street, Lake City. Open Monday through Thursday 8–4. Free admission. Built by the Public Works Administration in the 1930s, this building served as the local truck auction bean market. Displays depict early-20th-century farm life in the Pee Dee region and include the ubiquitous pole tobacco barn. The building is listed on the National Register of Historic Places. It's no world's biggest ball of yarn museum, but if you're in the area, check it out.

OTHER PLACES OF INTEREST Ronald E. McNair Memorial (843-374-8611), East Main Street, Lake City. This memorial celebrates the life of astronaut and Lake City native Ronald E. McNair, who was among those killed when the space shuttle *Challenger* exploded in 1986. There is a memorial statue and eternal flame at the site.

Fryar's Topiary Garden (803-484-5581; fryarstopiaries.com), 145 Broad Acres Road, Bishopville. Open 10–4 Tuesday through Saturday. Free, but donations appreciated. You may have seen Pearl Fryar on a network morning show or even on a John Deere tractor commercial. He is famous for the stunning topiary designs on his 3-acre plot of land. This is well worth the short drive.

✳ To Do

River Rat's Canoe Rentals (843-389-4656; riverratscanoerentals.com), 2740 Indigo Landing Road, Scranton. Tours are by reservation only and can range from one hour to eight hours. Groups are welcome, and overnight camping tours are available.

✐ **L. W. Paul Living History Farm** (843-365-3596; horrycountymuseum .org), 2279 Harris Shortcut Road, Conway. Open 9–4 Tuesday through Saturday. The family farm is such a strange concept these days that it has become a tourist attraction. Businessman Larry Paul built this working farm and museum to show what life was like on an Horry County farm in the first half of the 20th century. Visitors can not only see, but also take part in the chores that kept small farmers busy from sunup to sundown. Activities include plowing a field with mules, making soap, grinding grits, blacksmithing, curing meat, milking cows, and harvesting the crops. Different events are available during different seasons, so if you've got a hankering to plow, come in early spring. If you can build in some time for a side trip during a visit to the beach, this would be a great chance to show your children how easy they've got it compared with the kids who grew up on farms like this.

GOLF The Traces Golf Club (843-662-7775; thetracesgolfclub.com), 4322 West Southborough Road, Florence. The club offers three 9-hole courses, and you can choose which two you will play to make your 18 holes. Greens fees $24–30.

✳ Green Space

PARKS Lee State Natural Area (803-428-5307; southcarolinaparks .com), 487 Loop Road (Exit 123 off I-20), Bishopville. Open daily 8–5 (extended to 9 during DaylightSaving Time). Free admission. As a former lifeguard here, I can tell you that this area is best for RV and camping travelers. It's a wonderfully quiet spot for fishing or hiking along the cold-water artesian springs that feed the little pond here.

♿ **Lynches River County Park** (843-389-2785; lynchesriverpark.com), 1110 Ben Gause Road, Coward. Open daily 9–sunset. Free admission to the park, but there is a fee for the pool and special concerts. Located along the banks of Lynches River, this park is a great put-in spot for canoeing and kayaking. There are nature trails and a handicapped-accessible riverwalk. You could put in here and paddle all the way to the Great Pee Dee River near Johnsonville—in about 36 hours. But it is recommended that beginning boaters use a guide, as the Lynches River has a pretty significant current and many spots where boaters have to get around fallen trees and logs. Water levels are highest in late winter and spring. Boaters will want to wear bright colors, preferably orange, during hunting season from late August through May 1. There are two options for two-hour paddles, one ending at the park and one beginning at the park. A great river navigation guide can be found at dnr.sc.gov.

✳ Lodging

INNS The Cypress Inn (843-248-8199; acypressinn.com), 16 Elm Street, Conway. Just a little inland from the beaches is this inn, where you can get away from the hustle and bustle of the vacation set. But you're just half an hour away from the restaurants and nightlife. Guests can stroll from the inn to downtown shops in Conway or stroll along the Riverwalk. Rates: $145–235, maximum of two people per room.

CYPRESS INN, CONWAY

BED & BREAKFASTS

Abingdon Manor (843-752-5090; abingdonmanor.com), 307 Church Street, Latta. Tucked away in a tiny little town, Abingdon Manor just oozes luxury. There are eight guest rooms from $180 to $210 a night. A monthly cooking class is $400 per person and includes two nights' stay, dinner Friday and Saturday night, breakfast Saturday and Sunday, and co-owner and chief chef Patty Griffey's recipe book.

Breeden Inn (843-479-3665; breedeninn.com), 404 East Main Street, Bennettsville. This inn is listed on the National Register of Historic Places and is certified as a Backyard Wildlife Habitat. The main house has common rooms for relaxing and visiting. There are 13 guest rooms in four separate buildings. There is a swimming pool, bicycles are available for touring the area, or you can just take a walk in the woods. Room rates range $120–180.

Ambrias Garden Manor Bed and Breakfast (843-412-2632; ambriasgardenmanor.com), 111 Kuker Street, Florence. This B&B is located in a beautiful old home near downtown Florence. Four rooms are available at $135 a night with full or continental breakfast. Children older than 14 welcome.

Rosewood Manor Bed & Breakfast Inn (843-423-5407; rosewoodmanor.com), 900 North Main Street, Marion. This beautiful five-room B&B was built around the turn of the 20th century and takes up an entire city block in the historic district of Marion. The grounds are filled with beautiful blooming trees and plants along with a meditation fountain. Rooms are $120–150 a night and come with a full breakfast. No pets, but children 12 and older are allowed.

The Grove—The Inn on Harlee (843-423-5220; montgomerysgrove inn.com), 408 Harlee Street, Marion. Innkeepers Denley and Ann Caughman have created this retreat in a stunningly beautiful Victorian manor that sits on 5 acres in downtown Marion. The inn is filled with antiques, some original to the home. But all rooms have been recently renovated and most come with a whirlpool tub, giving guests a taste of the 19th century with the comforts of the 21st. Rates are $100–150 per night for the rooms; the suite is $200 a night. All rooms have a private bath and come with a three-course breakfast. The inn is just a short walk from Marion's historic downtown district. No children and no pets.

CAMPGROUNDS/CABINS
🐾 ♂ **Lee State Natural Area** (803-428-5307; southcarolinaparks .com), 487 Loop Road (Exit 123 off I-20), Bishopville. This park has water and electrical hookups at each of its campsites and can handle some RVs up to 36 feet. The park has central restrooms and hot showers. Half the nearly 50 campsites are for family camping and the rest are designated for equestrian campers. Campsites are about $15 a night. There also is a primitive camping area for

large groups up to 100 people at about $1 per camper with a minimum of $10. This area includes water and a bathroom.

✳ Where to Eat
DINING OUT The Dining Room at Abingdon Manor (843-752-5090; abingdonmanor.com), 307 Church Street, Latta. Open daily for dinner at 6 PM. Reservations required. Limited seating is available for those not staying at the inn. The six-course meal is $50 per person, and the menu changes daily. Guests at the inn can request a specific entrée in advance to be included in the options.

Victor's PA Bistro & Garden (843-665-0846; victorsbisto.com), 1247 South Irby Street, Florence. Open 5–10 Monday through Saturday. This is a favorite place of the locals and probably the best restaurant in Florence. Reservations are recommended. Victor's offer a variety of entrée dishes, but beef is the specialty. A wonderful tapas menu gives you the chance to sample several dishes with a smaller serving size. Entrées range $18–32, tapas dishes are $2–11.

Percy and Willie's (843-669-1620), 2401 David H. Mcleod Boulevard, Florence. Opens at 11 for lunch and dinner. This restaurant offers a wide variety of American dishes, specializing in beef and chicken. The marinated ribeye steak is one of the most popular items on the menu and is delicious. Entrées range $15–20.

This is another local favorite, so reservations are recommended.

Redbone Alley (843-673-0035; redbonealley.com), 1903 West Palmetto Street, Florence. Open 11:30–midnight Monday through Saturday, 11:30–9 Sunday. This interesting restaurant is located in an old retail store at the original open-air Florence mall. Its two floors offer an indoor sidewalk café feel. The second floor has balconies that overlook the main restaurant and has a game room with pool tables. This place is kid-friendly. The menu includes twists on classic Southern fare, like pimiento cheese grits and a macaroni and cheese dish with chicken and mushrooms. Dinner entrées $10–18.

BARBECUE JOINTS Buffets are usually all you can eat and run about $10–15 per person and include beverage (sweet tea) and dessert (banana pudding). Unless otherwise noted, restaurants are open Thursday through Saturday for lunch and dinner and Sunday for lunch only. Keep in mind that most of these places do not serve alcohol, but they do pour a lot of the house wine of the South: sweet tea.

Chucki's (843-493-0038), 625 South Walnut Street, Pamplico. This is the best barbecue and liver hash you will find. The buffet includes fried chicken so good you may only have one plate of barbecue, along with Southern vegetables (that means everything is cooked with a little bit of fatback or other pork for seasoning), coleslaw, mac and cheese, biscuits, and hush puppies. Don't forget the banana pudding for dessert.

CHUCKI'S COUNTRY BUFFET, PAMPLICO

Brown's Bar-Be-Que (843-382-2753), 809 Williamsburg County Highway, Kingstree. Open daily 11–2, till 9 PM Wednesday through Saturday. People go out of their way on their way to the beach to get this fine barbecue. The large, plain dining room lets you know the food's gotta be good because they're not wasting any money on the ambience. The buffet has all the usual suspects, including a particularly spicy red gravy that they call hash.

Scott's Bar-B-Que (843-558-0134; thescottsbbq.com), 2734 Hemingway Highway, Hemingway. Scott's isn't open on Sunday, but it has been famous for its spicy vinegar-and-pepper-style barbecue for more than 30 years. Scott's slow-cooks the whole hog over a wood-burning pit overnight and serves it with a secret family recipe sauce and a side of skins. Don't forget your slice of white bread.

Schoolhouse BBQ (843-389-2020; schoolhousebbq.com), 2252 US 52, Scranton. Located in a former schoolhouse, this restaurant has one of the best buffets going—there are so many items, you might forget about the barbecue. It gets crowded on Friday and Saturday nights, so come early. If you have to wait, there are plenty of rockers on the porch.

✴ Selective Shopping

Young's Pecans (843-662-8591; youngpecan.com), 1200 Pecan Street, Florence. Founded in the 1920s by T. B. Young, the company was sold in 2006 to a Texas agribusiness company. But it is still headquartered in Florence and still sells its shelled, chocolated-covered and toasted pecans. This place is definitely worth a stop, especially around the holidays.

✑ **Freeman's Bakery** (843-662-3903; bakingtheworldabetterplace.com), 1307 Second Loop Road, Florence. Open 7–6 Tuesday through Saturday. Maybe this is my favorite place because my dad used to bring me here for a gingerbread man after a doctor's visit; maybe it's because this is where we got our holiday desserts when I was a kid. Or maybe it's because they make the best butterscotch brownies I have ever tasted. Whatever it is, you've got to give them a try.

Russell Stover Candy Outlet (843-423-7408; russellstover.com), 2106 US 76, Marion. Open 9–6 Monday through Friday, 1–6 Saturday. There used to be a factory with this outlet store. The company closed the factory, but the store is still open with lots of chocolate.

The Cabbage Patch (843-355-8473; thecabbagepatch.org), 311 North Longstreet Street, Kingstree. Open 8–5:30 Monday through Friday. The Cabbage Patch is your typical small-town gift shop. But it's a great place to while away some time or walk off that big barbecue dinner from Brown's.

BARBECUE

The Pee Dee chapter, in my opinion, is the most appropriate place to discuss the issue of barbecue.

Barbecue, along with college football, is a religion in South Carolina, and like most major religions it has its different sects. But there are some general basics. *Barbecue* is a noun, meaning slow-cooked pulled or chopped pork. Some restaurants use the whole hog, some just Boston butts. Ribs can be cooked barbecue-style with a sauce or rub, but they are not barbecue.

The pork can be cooked in a smoker, a grill, or even an oven, but true adherents to the faith use a smokehouse and cook over smoldering coals, pit-style. In many locations, old-school restaurants are open Thursday through Saturday only. Modern times being what they are, some restaurants have started a Sunday buffet and open as early in the week as Wednesday. There are some—in the larger cities—that are open seven days a week.

The Pee Dee in my opinion as a native serves the best barbecue. (This statement alienates half my friends but strengthens the familial bonds.) The barbecue here is seasoned with vinegar and pepper, and there are as many recipes for that seasoning as there are cooks. It can be mild to almost Cajun hot. Usually the sauce is swabbed on the meat during the later stages of cooking. (I personally marinate my meat in a vinegar pepper mixture before cooking, then let it cool in another batch when it really absorbs the flavor.) Examples of this type of barbecue (also known as eastern Carolina or eastern North Carolina–style) can be found throughout the Pee Dee. My favorite place is wherever Jakie Calcutt is cooking. As of this writing, that was at **Chucki's** in Pamplico, just east of Florence. There is a little place in Hemingway called **Scott's Variety Store** that has been dishing up pulled pork for decades and is well worth the side trip.

In the Midlands, where I live now, is my least favorite sauce, but the one often referred to as South Carolina style. It is mustard-based and again can vary widely in intensity and flavor. The "twin cities" of Batesburg and Leesville just west of Columbia are home to some of the finest examples of this type of barbecue with **Hite's** and **Shealy's** (chapter 4).

The third style is a tomato-based sauce. Some people swear there is so much variation in this sauce that it's actually two separate styles: a light, fresh-tomato sauce and a heavy ketchup-style. Again, risking alienation of my few remaining friends, I have to say these are basically the same, though I prefer the lighter sauce to the ketchup. The best for this style can be found in Orangeburg south of Columbia or a little town called Trenton between Columbia and the Georgia state line.

SC Department of Parks, Recreation & Tourism, DiscoverSouthCarolina.com

This also seems to be the predominant sauce of the Upstate, though they tend to offer a little bit of everything up there.

A final note on eating at barbecue restaurants. They almost always offer a buffet, and that's what I recommend, because these restaurants also tend to have excellent fried chicken and home-style sides, such as macaroni and cheese, coleslaw, and collard greens.

Two other dishes likely will be available, but they may be a little foreign to those not from around here.

One is called chicken bog. It's a form of pilau (pronounced around these parts as *PER-low*). Basically it's chicken and rice, sometimes with spicy sausage thrown in, or onions and garlic, or all of the above. Traditionally, the bog was cooked with the broken leftover grains of rice rather than the long grains intended for sale and export around the world. It was typically made by the poorer classes, as that was deemed the inferior rice. But the broken grains gives the rice more surface area, meaning it can absorb more flavors. It also tends to be stickier than long-grain rice, giving it a thick "bog" consistency. Cooking dishes this way also helped hide the fact that there was little meat available. One small chicken—about 3 pounds—and a pound of sausage can flavor enough bog to feed a dozen people.

The other dish is called hash or liver hash, and it can vary as widely as does barbecue. My preferred type is liver hash. It is black in color and more solid than liquid. It is served over rice. I have been in some barbecue joints where the hash was so different, I didn't even recognize it. I won't go into detail about the historical preparation of hash because I think everyone should try it, but let's just say that little hog was wasted back in the day. Hash is simply a gravy made of ground pork and whatever sauce or spice is prevalent at that particular restaurant. My favorite definitely is heavily peppered and has a grayish color. In mustard country, hash tends to be yellow; it's red in tomato land. Whatever color it is, I recommend at least a taste over white rice.

Sparky's Fireworks and Gifts (843-423-2217), 2416 South Highway 501, Marion. Open daily 7–7. I wouldn't tell you to go out of your way to get to Sparky's, but if you pass it, you gotta stop. Go ahead and get some gas, it might be a penny or two cheaper than the beach. They have a huge selection of fireworks, but remember that fireworks are dangerous and should never be put inside the car of a smoker. What Sparky's does have is some fantastic fudge (including some sugar-free) and just about everything else you could want in a convenience store: T-shirts, beach memorabilia, moccasins, sandwiches, clean restrooms.

✳ Special Events

SPRING *March:* **Art Sculpture Welding Rodeo** (843-661-8003; fdtc.edu/weldingrodeo), Southeastern Institute of Manufacturing and Technology, 1951 Pisgah Road, Florence. This-one-of-a-kind event benefits the welding program at Florence-Darlington Technical College and brings together teams that will turn scrap metal into a sculpture during the daylong event. Teams compete for judges, and then all artwork is available for public auction at the end of the day. Admission is free, but bring your checkbook; you just might want to buy something.

SPARKY'S GIFT SHOP, MARION

May: **NASCAR Dodge Charger 500** and **Diamond Hill Plywood 200**, Darlington. The Dodge Charger 500 is usually held the Saturday evening before Mother's Day. The Diamond Hill Plywood 200 is held the day before.

FALL *September:* **Lee County Cotton Festival** (803-484-5090; leecountychamber.sc), Bishopville.

This festival used to be called the Cotton-Pickin' Festival. I don't know why they changed the name, but they still celebrate the fluffy white crop that is still grown in Bishopville.

November: **Pecan Festival** (florencedowntown.com/pecan -festival.aspx), downtown Florence. This festival celebrates the nut that makes Florence famous.

SUGGESTED ITINERARIES

Myrtle Beach Itineraries

If you're heading to Myrtle Beach, the first thing you have to do is decide whether you want to play golf, shop, hit the beach, ride the rides, or see a show. Of course, you can do it all, but that will take some time.

GOLF Let's start with golf. You really cannot go wrong with any of the courses down here; they are all fairly reasonably priced and open year-round. Start at myrtlebeachgolf.com. Some favorite courses are: **The Heritage Club** (843-237-3424; legendsgolf.com), 378 Heritage Drive, Pawleys Island; and **Tidewater Golf Club** (843-913-2424; tidewater golf.com), 1400 Tidewater Drive, North Myrtle Beach.

If you play at The Heritage Club, plan on dinner at **Frank's** or **Frank's Outback** (843-237-3030; franksandoutback.com), 10434 Ocean Highway, Pawleys Island. They have a great bar at Frank's, and there are lots of hearty dishes on both menus. If you play Tidewater, try dinner at **Thoroughbreds Restaurant** (843-497-2636; thoroughbredsrestaurant.com), 9706 North Kings Highway, Myrtle Beach. Thoroughbreds has great steaks and a selection of specialty martinis to help ease the painful memories of water hazards.

For a purely golfing excursion, look for the best hotel–golf packages. These save you money and give you discounts for area restaurants. You can save a little more by booking a hotel away from the water. For those flying in from colder climes for off-season golf, most packages include shuttles to and from the airport, area courses, and restaurants.

One great option is **Grande Dunes Resort** (843-692-2323; grandedunes .com), 1000 Grande Dunes Boulevard, Myrtle Beach. It's one of the newest resorts at Myrtle and has its own golf course and golf academy. The rates are reasonable in the shoulder seasons (spring and fall), when golf is at its best down here. They also have **Waterscapes Restaurant** (843-913-2845; marinainnatgrandedunes.com/dining/din_waterscapes.aspx),

8121 Amalfi Place, Myrtle Beach, which serves breakfast, lunch, and dinner.

SHOP If all you want to do is shop at Myrtle Beach, you have a wide variety of options. There are two **Tanger Outlets** (843-449-0491 or 843-236-5100; tangeroutlet.com), 10835 King's Road (off US 17) and 4635 Factory Stores Boulevard (off US 501), which both carry just about every available brand name of clothing, shoes, sunglasses, and other accessories. Broadway at the Beach and Barefoot Landing, both in Myrtle Beach, also have some high-end national chain shops. For more local flavor, Georgetown has a wonderful shopping district along its riverfront, and Pawleys Island's Original Hammock Shops should not be missed. For these excursions, I recommend locating in the middle—say, Garden City or Surfside Beach—if it's not the height of summer, and doing your southern shopping one day, the northern shopping another. I say *if it's not the height of summer* because north–south traffic at the beach can be a beast, especially US 17, whether Business or Bypass. In that case, you may want to pick where you think you might do your most shopping and stay there, possibly venturing out once to the other area. You can stay in hotels off the beach and save yourself some driving and money for shopping.

A good tour would start in Georgetown with breakfast at **Thomas Café** (843-546-7776; thomascafe.net), 703 Front Street. Once you start touring all the shops on Front Street, don't miss **Harborwalk Books** (843-546-8212), 723 Front Street, which specializes in regional history and Civil War books, or **Georgetown Art Gallery** (843-527-7711), 732 Front Street, with the work of 20 member-artists on display. On your way out of town, hit **Carolina Charm** (843-520-1846), 1410 Highmarket Street, for some Gullah Gourmet items. From there, it's a short drive (20 or so minutes) to Pawleys Island, lunch, and the **Original Hammock Shops,** where you can on occasion still see a cotton-rope hammock being made. If you don't have one, get one; you'll thank me. The shop will even ship it home for you so you don't have to try to find room for it in your already overstuffed vacation car. Among the stores at the Hammock Shops are **She Sells Sea Shells** (843-237-0118; shesellsseashellssc.com) for just about anything and everything that can be made with a seashell, and **Pawleys Island Mercantile** (843-235-0507; pawleysislandmercantile.com), home of the **Candy Cottage** (thecandycottage.com) for all your classic beachwear, souvenirs, and some tasty treats. There are a couple of places nearby for lunch. At the Hammock Shops is **Roz's Rice Mill Café** (843-235-0196; rozsricemillcafe.com), which serves up Southern fare with a twist—think grits with lobster instead of shrimp. One of my favorites is the **Island Bar & Grill** (843-235-3399; islandbarandgrill.com), 10744 Ocean Highway just a little north of the Hammock Shops. The tasty food, especially the steak salad, is reasonably priced, and the atmosphere is relaxed. You can stop in for a sandwich or salad, or you can sit awhile on their back deck sipping whatever beverage makes you happy.

Your second shopping day will start at one of the many pancake houses between Garden City and Myrtle Beach. Try **Plantation Pancake House** (843-238-1690), 1003 US 17 North, Surfside Beach. Then head to **Gay Dolphin Gift Cove** (843-448-6550; gaydolphin.com), 916 North Ocean Boulevard, Myrtle Beach, for a little souvenir shopping. It's just one of those places you have to go. From there, head north and west to **Broadway at the Beach** (843-444-3200 or 800-386-4662; broadwayatthebeach .com), 1324 Celebrity Circle, Myrtle Beach. There are more than 100 shops here and plenty of places to grab some lunch. After lunch, head north on Kings Highway to the **Tanger Outlet** (843-449-0491 or 843-236-5100; tangeroutlet.com) at 10835 King's Road, off US 17 Bypass where it meets SC 22, and **Bass Pro Shops Outdoor World** (843-361-4800; bass proshops.com), 10177 North Kings Highway, Myrtle Beach. If you have any money left, check out **Waterscapes Restaurant** (843-913-2845; marinainnatgrandedunes.com/dining/din_waterscapes.aspx), 8121 Amalfi Place inside the Grande Dunes resort for dinner.

BEACH If the beach is your goal—and for most people it is—South Carolina's Grand Strand is aptly named. Its 60 miles of sandy beaches stretch from the Little River Inlet along the North Carolina state line to Winyah Bay in Georgetown. Most of the beaches are great for swimming, playing on a raft or boogie board, or ocean kayaking. The waves are typically a little small for surfing, though that doesn't stop the folks from trying to hang 10 near the piers. I have even seen some trying sailboarding, though that fad never really caught on around here (it's too hard to lift the sail back up after it gets wet).

For those interested exclusively in the beach, I recommend staying oceanfront in a private home, condo, or resort hotel in North Myrtle Beach or the south Strand beaches of Surfside, Garden City, Litchfield, and Pawleys Island. It's worth the extra cost of staying oceanfront because of the short trip you will have to make back and forth between your room and the beach. Also, the resort hotels have activities for the kids so Mom and Dad can enjoy some grown-up time, golf, or spa treatments. And you will have plenty of time when the sun goes down to enjoy all the entertainment Myrtle Beach has to offer, from amusement park rides to dinner theater shows to fancy restaurants and nightclubs.

I prefer a condo or beach house rental, but that's not very economical for a family of four—and you typically have to rent them for a whole week. If you can get some friends and family to join you, however, a small beach house rental may be cheaper than a hotel room. Check out **Oceanfront Vacation Rentals Inc.** (843-448-1700; oceanfrontvac.com), 1551 21st

Avenue North, Suite 12, Myrtle Beach, or **Pawleys Island Realty Co.** (843-237-2431; pawleysislandrealty.com), 88 North Causeway, Pawleys Island, for some options here. You will miss out on hotel pools, bars, and restaurants, but you won't mind because of the easy access and less crowded beach. Also note that the area between 3rd and 5th Avenues South in Myrtle Beach is known as Withers Swash. It's where rainwater runs off parking lots, ultimately dumping into the ocean. During very rainy summer months, this area is prone to being closed to swimming because of contaminants in that runoff.

Pawleys Island has some of the nicest beaches, but the fewest places to stay and things to do, while Garden City's beach sometimes disappears at high tide. Myrtle Beach proper has good beaches, which is why they are fairly crowded with all those hotels filled to the gills during summer. But if a crowd is what you are looking for, this is the place. Once you arrive at your oceanfront hotel, everything you need will be right there: ocean swimming with lifeguards and rentals for chairs, umbrellas, and all manner of water toys. And if the surf is too rough, almost all of the oceanfront hotels have pools and many have lazy rivers (shallow, narrow waterways that have enough "current" to propel a floater on an inner tube around the watercourse with no effort). The hotels frequently have their own restaurants and are within walking distance of dozens of places to eat, drink, shop, and play arcade games. Most of the hotels are efficiencies—that is, they come with kitchens if you're feeding young kids and are on a budget. Most have laundry facilities on site if not in your room so you don't have to take all that beach sand back home with you.

Roxanne Towers (843-448-9486; roxannetowers.com), 1604 North Ocean Boulevard, Myrtle Beach, is a great bargain at less than $200 a night in season. The one-bedroom units are spacious with a sitting area with fold-out sofa and a king bedroom, two televisions, washer and dryer, and full kitchen with a fold-out "Murphy bed" type dining table that also could sleep a youngster. It is located just north of the 14th Avenue Pier for the anglers and the beach's newest attraction—the 1.2-mile **Myrtle Beach Boardwalk** (843-626-7444; visitmyrtlebeach.com/boardwalk) that runs between the 14th Avenue Pier and the 2nd Avenue Pier. Along the Boardwalk and Ocean Boulevard are the **Gay Dolphin Gift Cove** (843-448-6550; gaydolphin.com), 916 North Ocean Boulevard, for all the beach souvenirs you will ever need; **Peaches Corner** (843-448-7424; peaches -corner.com), 900 North Ocean Boulevard, for the best burgers and dogs on the beach; and the **Fun Plaza arcade** (843-448-5141), 902 North Ocean Boulevard, with its classic baseball and skee ball games. **Ripley's Believe It or Not! Museum** (843-448-2331; myrtlebeach.ripleys.com), 917 North Ocean Boulevard, is across the street from Peaches and that big vacant lot you see from that corner, which used to be an amusement park. The only oceanside amusement park left at the beach is about a mile south from the hotel at **Family Kingdom Amusement Park & Oceanfront Water Park** (843-626-3447; familykingdomfun.com), 300 South Ocean Boulevard, with its water park, Ferris wheel, and roller coaster. Also about a mile south of the hotel and a little off the front row is **Mount Atlanticus Minotaur Goff** (843-444-1008), 707 North Kings Highway. This is my favorite miniature golf on the beach, though kids might not enjoy it as much as adults.

Less than a 3-mile drive from the Roxanne is Broadway at the Beach with all its shopping and restaurants. **Ripley's Aquarium** (843-916-0888; myrtlebeach.ripleyaquariums.com) makes a perfect rainy-day visit for youngsters.

If you're traveling with kids, the dinner theater shows might not be as exciting for them as **Medieval Times Dinner & Tournament** (843-236-8080; medievaltimes.com), 2904 Fantasy Way, Myrtle Beach. Dolly Parton has changed her Dixie Stampede theater to a **Pirates Voyage** (800-433-4401 or visit piratesvoyage.com), 8901-B North Kings Highway, Myrtle Beach, that is sure to be a hit with the kids.

There also is live music at **Broadway at the Beach** (843-444-3200 or 800-386-4662; broadwayatthebeach.com), 1324 Celebrity Circle, Myrtle Beach, either in their little town square or in various clubs along the strip. There is a **House of Blues** (843-272–3000; houseofblues.com), 4640 Highway 17, North Myrtle Beach, with a wide variety of live acts and a Sunday gospel brunch.

Pee Dee Itineraries

Most people visit the Pee Dee on their way to or from somewhere else, and that is okay. But if you find yourself staying in the area for one reason or another, I recommend one of the B&Bs: **Ambrias Garden Manor Bed and Breakfast** (843-412-2632; ambriasgardenmanor.com), 111 Kuker Street, Florence; or **The Grove—The Inn on Harlee** (843-423-5220; montgomerysgroveinn.com), 408 Harlee Street, Marion.

From any of these locations, you can enjoy some of the sights and restaurants in the Pee Dee, including a day at **Lynches River County Park** (843-389-2785; lynchesriverpark.com), 1110 Ben Gause Road, Coward. This is a great spot for putting in a canoe or kayak on one of the state's scenic rivers and one of the few rivers that is free-flowing for its whole length in the state. Try **River Rat's Canoe Rentals** (843-389-4656; riverratscanoerentals.com), 2740 Indigo Landing Road, Scranton, to set up a guided tour. When you're finished paddling, you will have an appetite big enough for any of the area's barbecue buffets. From the park it's only 10 miles to my brother's favorite place, **Schoolhouse BBQ** (843-389-2020; schoolhousebbq.com), 2252 Highway 52, Scranton. My favorite lunch spot—**Chucki's** (843-493-0038), 625 South Walnut Street, Pamplico—is about 20 miles away.

For fine dining in the area, you simply cannot beat **The Dining Room at Abingdon Manor** (843-752-5090; abingdonmanor.com), 307 Church Street, Latta.

Charleston 2

THE PENINSULA

THE ISLANDS AND BEACHES:
Isle of Palms, Sullivans, Folly, Johns
and James Islands, Kiawah Island

INLAND AREAS:
Mount Pleasant, West Ashley,
Summerville, Moncks Corner

SUGGESTED ITINERARIES

THE PENINSULA

The prominence of church steeples dotting Charleston's low-rise skyline has earned South Carolina's oldest city the nickname "the Holy City." Charleston also was an early welcomer of different faiths, including French protestants (Huguenots) and Jews. But it's a mecca of sorts for natives who dutifully visit and swear someday we are going to live there . . . if only we can afford to live there the way we vacation there.

Charleston has no season. There are times when it is more crowded than others, but the only "bad time" I have ever found to visit the actual city of Charleston is when the temperatures reach the triple digits. Then you just go to the beaches during the day and hit downtown at night. The ocean breezes keep Charleston's weather a little more temperate than many inland parts of the state.

The city has survived occupations by "foreign" armies, earthquakes, hurricanes, and the occasional disruption caused by moviemaking. The city's Battery is a must-see and is best seen by boat if you can. Otherwise, a carriage ride or the old-fashioned foot tour are excellent choices.

Fort Sumter, built by slave labor over 30 years and the object of the first shots of the Civil War, sits in Charleston Harbor. A visit to the national monument is a wonderful excuse to get on a boat in the harbor. If you are driving to the boat, your best bet is to drive over the new Arthur Ravenel Jr. bridge—the nation's largest cable-stayed bridge—to Mount Pleasant, where parking at the privately run ferry service is ample. If you're staying downtown and walking, you can leave from the pier at the South Carolina Aquarium.

Overlooking the harbor from upriver, the aquarium is one of the city's newer attractions. Look for any coupons or bargains you can find on this one. It is great for the kids, especially the part where they get to touch some aquatic life, but it can be a bit pricey.

In spring the city is inundated with thousands of visitors from around the world for the Spoleto Festival USA. One of the nation's premier arts festivals, Spoleto provides world-class opera, dance, theater, and street

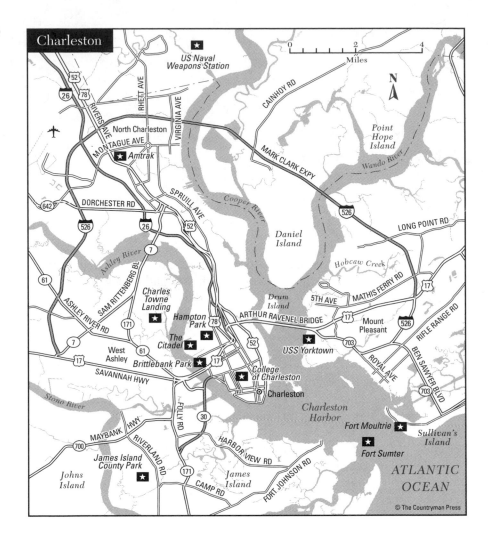

Charleston

performers. Piccolo Spoleto runs concurrently and offers many free venues to see artists from the southeastern United States. Closing ceremonies at Middleton Place Plantation on the Ashley River draw many locals as well as a throng of guests.

Middleton Place is just one of several antebellum plantations that have been preserved along the Ashley River. Many of the original homesteads were burned by U.S. troops, freed slaves, or a combination of the two during the Civil War.

The Market district is where you will find vendors of every kind. Similar to a large covered flea market, it takes up several city blocks. One of the most popular features is the sweetgrass baskets being woven by

THE ARTHUR RAVENEL BRIDGE OVER THE COOPER RIVER

women—and a few men—at edges of the buildings. The baskets are expensive, but after a few minutes of watching the intricate detail of their work, you will find they are well worth the price.

It is in the Market area that visitors will find the carriage tours. If you have more than half a dozen in your group, call ahead and book your own carriage. It will cost a little more per person than standing in line for a tour, but you get the VIP treatment.

The one quirk is you can't pick your tour area. Each morning a lottery system assigns certain carriages to certain areas of town. The idea is to give all carriage operators an equal shot at the very popular Battery area, without bringing car traffic to a standstill. All the tours are designed to give visitors a taste of the city's beautiful historic homes without overly taxing the nerves of the people who live in those homes.

GUIDANCE The Charleston Visitor Reception and Transportation Center (843-853-8000; discovercharleston.com), 375 Meeting Street. The center is open daily 8:30–5:30. This is a must-stop for the first-time visitor. Located in a restored railroad warehouse, the center is one of the few places on the peninsula with ample parking, so it's an excellent spot to store your car while you tour the city. Maps, brochures, and tickets for most attractions and events are available.

GETTING THERE Charleston sits at the eastern end of Interstate 26. You can also take U.S. Highways 52 or 17 to get there from north or south

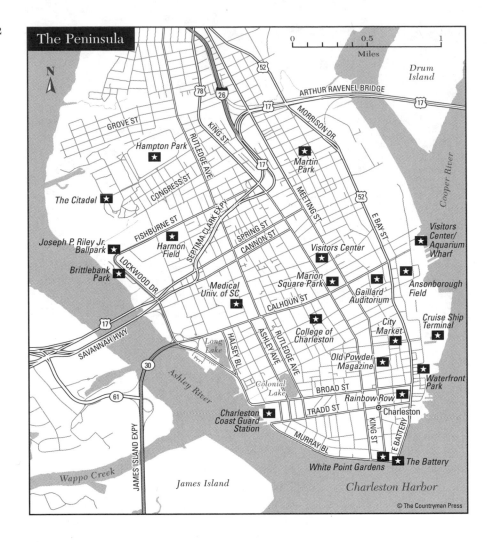

The Peninsula

locations. Interstate 95 crosses 26 about an hour north of Charleston for East Coast travelers.

By air: **Charleston International Airport** (843-767-7007; chs-airport .com) offers connections to several major U.S. airports and is served by carriers **Air Tran** (800-247-8726 or 678-254-7999; airtran.com), **American Eagle** (800-433-7300; aa.com), Continental Airlines (800-525-0280; continental.com), **Delta Air Lines** (800-221-1212; delta.com), **Northwest Airlines** (800-225-2525; nwa.com), **United Express** (800-241-6522; united.com), **US Airways** (800-428-4322; usairways.com).

By bus: **Charleston Greyhound Station** (843-744-4247; greyhound .com), 3610 Dorchester Road. Open seven days a week, 7:30 AM–10 PM.

Greyhound offers passenger service from most U.S. cities. The bus station is 6 miles north of the visitors center in the heart of downtown. You will have to take a taxi or a city bus to get there.

By train: **Amtrak** (800-872-7245; amtrak.com), 4565 Gaynor Avenue, North Charleston. Open 4 AM–noon and 4–11:30 PM daily. Trains from the northeast stop in Charleston at 7 and 9:30 PM daily; from the south, they stop at 5 and 10 AM.

GETTING AROUND Downtown Area Shuttle—DASH (843-724-7420; ridecarta.com), 375 Meeting Street. Hours: 7 AM–9 PM. The historic district's shuttle system provides air-conditioned rides to most of the city's major attractions: the South Carolina Aquarium, the Market and Waterfront areas, and the museums and shopping of Meeting and King Streets. Single rides $1; multiple-day passes are available.

WHEN TO COME Charleston is a year-round destination. Spring and fall are the most pleasant times to visit weather-wise. They also are the most crowded. Summer temperatures can easily top 90 degrees with high humidity, but virtually every facility has air-conditioning. Hurricane season (June 1 through November 30) can add some uncertainty to your trip, but residents can have as much as a week's notice before a storm hits. Unless otherwise noted, all establishments are open year-round.

✴ To See

MUSEUMS Charleston's Museum Mile (charlestonsmuseummile.org) includes a dozen museums, historical houses, and other places of interest along a 1-mile stretch of Meeting Street. The website offers discounts to several of the attractions.

✐ **The South Carolina Aquarium** (843-720-1990; scaquarium.org), 100 Aquarium Wharf. Open daily 9–5 March through August, closes at 4 September through February. Opened in 2000 on Charleston Harbor, the South Carolina Aquarium has more than 60 exhibits including the Great Ocean Tank with 385,000 gallons of water and more than 450 animals. Special programs include behind-the-scenes tours of the tank and the aquarium's sea turtle hospital. Admission: adults $18; seniors $17 (62-plus); $11 for children 11 and under. Toddlers are free.

The Gibbes Museum of Art (843-722-2706, gibbesmuseum.org), 135 Meeting Street. Open 10–5 Tuesday through Saturday, 1–5 Sunday. Funded by a bequest from James S. Gibbes, the museum has been open since 1905 with the goal of preserving and promoting the art of Charleston and the South. The museum offers docent-led tours at 2:30 PM Friday; a free audio tour can be accessed on visitors' cell phones. Several special tours that include visits to other museums and galleries are available for additional cost. Photography is not allowed inside the museum. Admission: adults $9; seniors/students/military $7; children 6–12 $5; museum members and children 5 and younger free.

The Charleston Museum (843-722-2996; charlestonmuseum.org), 360 Meeting Street. Open 9–5 Monday through Saturday and 1–5 Sunday. Located across from the Charleston Visitors Center, the museum tells the story of early Charleston from settlement through the late 19th century. The museum also operates two historic houses: the Joseph Manigault House (across the street from the museum) at 350 Meeting Street and the Heyward-Washington House at 87 Church Street. The museum offers something you will rarely find in Charleston—free parking. Admission: $10 per museum; $22 for a pass for all three sites; $5 per site for ages 3–12; 2 and younger free.

& **Children's Museum of the Lowcountry** (843-853-8962; explorecml .org), 25 Ann Street. Open 9–5 Tuesday through Saturday, 1–5 Sunday. Eight self-guided exhibits focus on family interaction. Museum staffers recommend starting in the art room so your little Picasso's work can dry before you leave. Admission: $7.

Frances R. Edmunds Center for Historic Preservation (843-724-8484; historiccharleston.org), 108 Meeting Street. Open 10–5 Monday through Saturday, 2–5 Sunday. For visitors interested in delving into the culture and architecture of the city, the center's staff can answer questions and suggest places to go. Reference material and tickets to the Nathaniel Russell House and the Edmondston-Alston House are available.

The Preservation Society of Charleston (843-722-4630; preservation society.org), 147 King Street. Open 10–5 Monday through Saturday. From the last week in September through October each year, the society offers three-hour Candlelight Tours of Homes and Gardens. Admission: $45 per person per tour or $120 for a four-day (Thursday through Sunday) or three-day (Friday through Sunday) pass. The society also operates a bookstore and visitors center.

The Charleston Artist Guild Gallery (843-722-2425; charlestonartist guild.com), 160 East Bay Street. The gallery offers free lectures, presentations, and access to 50 exhibiting artists. Annual juried shows give South Carolina artists a chance to show their work. The gallery also hosts sidewalk shows in the spring and fall.

Halsey Institute of Contemporary Art (843-953-5680; halsey.cofc.edu), 161 Calhoun Street. Operated by the College of Charleston, this gallery focuses on contemporary art in all media.

H. L. Hunley (843-743-4865, ext. 32, or 877-448-6539; hunley.org), 1250 Supply Street. Open Saturday 10–5, Sunday noon–5. Cost about $15. The

Hunley was a devastating weapon for the Confederacy. A submarine made of old locomotives, the *Hunley* killed three crews of sailors, sinking twice before its successful mission of ramming a spar into the U.S. ship *Housatonic* in Charleston Harbor. The *Housatonic* sank, but so did the *Hunley*, this time taking its crew to the bottom of the ocean off the coast of Sullivans Island, where it stayed for more than 130 years. The vessel was discovered in the late 20th century and raised from its watery grave in 2000. The submarine has been under conservation since with scientists carefully removing the remains of the eight crewmen, which were buried in a ceremony in 2004, and attempting to clean up a century of wear and tear from the vessel's exterior. Visitors can see the sub in its conservation tank and some of the artifacts found on board. For any fan of naval warfare history, this is a must-see.

PARKS Waterfront Park (843-762-2172; ci.charleston.sc.us), Concord Street. This lovely little park provides pleasant access to the Cooper River. A pier, garden, and water sprays make it a great spot to cool off in the hot summer months. It's also a great place to sit and watch the huge boats go by from swings along the waterfront.

HISTORIC SITES Fort Sumter (843-883-3123; nps.gov/fosu/index .htm), 340 Concord Street. Admission: adults $16; seniors $14.50; ages 6–11 $10; children 5 and younger free. Tours run three to six times a day,

THE FORT SUMTER VISITORS CENTER, DOWNTOWN CHARLESTON

depending on the season. The last tour from the city side leaves at 2:30 PM. Located at the mouth of Charleston Harbor, Fort Sumter took more than 30 years of slave labor to build and was the object of fire from cadets at South Carolina's military college, The Citadel, to start the Civil War. You can get to Fort Sumter from downtown Charleston or Mount Pleasant. The National Park Service recommends leaving from Patriots Point in Mount Pleasant if you need to park a car. That site is not operated by the Park Service. The trip takes at least two and a half hours, so don't plan many other activities on the day you visit the monument.

Old Slave Mart Museum (843-958-6467; oldslavemart.org), 6 Chalmers Street. Open 9–5 Monday through Saturday. Admission: $7 adults 18 and older; $5 seniors and children. This is probably the only building in South Carolina known to have been used as a slave auction site that's still in existence. The complex here included a slave jail, a morgue, and a kitchen. The last slave auction was held in November 1863. The museum tells of Charleston's role in the slave trade.

Aiken-Rhett House (843-723-1159; historiccharleston.org), 48 Elizabeth Street. Open Monday through Saturday 10–5, Sunday 2–5. Cost is $10 for adults ages 17 and older, $5 for children. This antebellum home was built in 1820 by Governor William Aiken Jr. Many of the objects collected by the governor and his wife on their European travels are still with the home. The grounds include the home's kitchens, slave quarters, stables, and outhouses. This is one of the city's best examples of life during they heyday of the Old South.

Edmondston-Alston House (843-722-7171; middletonplace.org), 21 East Battery Street. Open Sunday through Monday 1:30–4:30, Tuesday through Saturday 10–4:30. This beautiful historic home on Charleston's Battery has a wonderful view of the harbor and Fort Sumter. It is the location where General P. T. Beauregard watched the bombing of the fort by Citadel cadets in 1861, starting the Civil War. The home also provided a safe haven for Confederate General Robert E. Lee later that year when his hotel was threatened by a fire in the city. The house is operated by the Middleton Place Foundation, and package deals with Middleton Place Plantation are available.

Rainbow Row, 83–107 East Bay Street. This stretch of 14 privately owned homes along East Bay Street is known as Rainbow Row because of the beautiful pastel colors on the exterior of the homes. This section of town was built in the early 18th century and was the hub of the city's waterfront district in its day. Most walking tours, several carriage tours, and even a few boat tours include this area. The best way to get a good photo is from the water, but if you go on your own, you can scope out excellent vantage points and create your own Rainbow Row photo album. Well worth the walk as this is one area that is truly Charleston.

Battery & White Point Gardens, East Battery and Murray Boulevard. White Point was first opened as a city garden in 1837; it became a fortification point for the city during the Civil War. Today the gardens display mortars and cannons from the era and a monument to Confederate soldiers. In the early 18th century White Point was the site of the hanging of the pirate Stede Bonnet and several other outlaws. An epitaph to Bonnet is in the park. This is a great place to stop and take pictures. There is plenty of street-side parking here and it's a wonderful spot to leave your vehicle for a walk along the Battery, through the gardens, and among the beautiful old homes on the waterfront.

The Citadel (843-225-3294 or 800-868-3294; citadel.edu), 171 Moultrie Street. Open Monday through Friday 8–6. Museum open Sunday through Friday 2–5 and Saturday noon–5. Archives open Monday through Friday 9–5. South Carolina's military college was originally located on Francis Marion Square, but has been at its current home along the Ashley River since 1922. Citadel cadets played a key role in the start of the Civil War, firing first on the U.S. supply ship *Star of the West* and then on Fort Sumter. Of the 224 Citadel alumni at the start of the Civil War, 209 joined the Confederate Army and four became generals. Parades are held on Summerall Field most Fridays during the school year and are open to the public. The complete schedule is available on the website. Visitors should plan to arrive about 30 minutes before the start of the parade because of parking issues.

HISTORIC CHURCHES St. Philip's Episcopal Church (843-722-7734; stphilipschurchsc.org), 146 Church Street. One of the most recognizable churches in Charleston, the current building was completed in 1838 after a fire. In its churchyard are the graves of Vice President John C. Calhoun, signer of the Declaration of Independence Edward Rutledge, and Dubose Heyward, author of *Porgy*—on which the Gershwin opera *Porgy and Bess* was based. Sunday services at 8:15 and 10:30.

Circular Congregation Church (843-577-6400; circularchurch.org), 150 Meeting Street. Open to visitors when tour guides are available. This church was organized in 1681 and in 1806 began meeting in a Robert Mills–designed circular building that gave the congregation its unique name. The building was destroyed by fire in 1861 and damaged by the 1886 earthquake. The present building opened in 1891. Sunday services at 8:45 and 11.

Emanuel African Methodist Episcopal Church (843-722-2561; emanuelamechurch.org), 110 Calhoun Street. The congregation in 1791 was made up of freedmen and slaves. Led by Morris Brown, the black Methodists became an independent organization in 1818, and a small church was built. Four years later Denmark Vessey plotted a slave rebellion in the church, and it was closed. The congregation was reorganized at the end of the Civil War, and the current building was constructed in 1891. Sunday services at 7:30 and 11.

Congregation Beth Elohim (843-723-1090; kkbe.org), 90 Hasell Street. Open to the public 10–noon, Monday through Friday. This is the second-oldest synagogue in the United States and the birthplace of American Reform Judaism in 1824. The original structure was destroyed by fire in 1838. The current building was completed in 1840. Services at 8 PM Friday and 10 AM Saturday.

First Baptist Church (843-722-3896), 48 Meeting Street. Located near the Battery, this is the oldest Baptist church in the South. Founded in 1682, the present church building was designed by Robert Mills and completed in 1822. Sunday services at 8:45 and 11 AM. Vespers at 6:30 PM.

St. John's Lutheran Church (843-723-2426; stjohnscharleston.org), 5 Clifford Street. Founded by German immigrants in 1742, this is the church from which all South Carolina Lutheran churches sprang. The present building was completed in 1817. Sunday services at 8:30 and 11.

The French Protestant (Huguenot) Church (843-722-4385; french huguenotchurch.org), 136 Church Street. This church was completed in 1845, but its congregation goes back to 1687 as French Protestants fled persecution at home. Sunday services at 10:30.

✴ To Do

Walking Tours (843-568-0473; oldcharlestontours.com), Washington Park, Meeting at Broad Street. There are five different tours each day, and the schedule changes frequently depending on weather and guide availability. Most tours are two hours long and focus on one theme, such as an art tour in conjunction with the Gibbes Museum, or the South of Broad tour, based on the best-selling book by South Carolina author Pat Conroy. Prices range from $15 to $25. Children are about half the price.

🐚 **Anna's House & Garden Tour/Ghostwalk** (843-720-8687; ghostwalk .net), 74-A N. Market Street Garden tours begin at Charleston Gardens, 61 Queen Street, Monday through Saturday at 9:45 AM and 2 PM. Ghost tours are offered nightly at 8. Reservations are required. This tour is particularly good for the little ones. Cost is $15 for adults 13 and older; $10 for children 4 and older.

Chai Y'all and More Tours (843-556-0664), 316 Confederate Circle. This company specializes in tours that focus on the city's Jewish heritage. Charleston was the birthplace of American Reform Judaism—the first Reform group being created by individuals splitting from Congregation Beth Elohim. Chai Tours are by reservation only. Guides can provide walking or car tours or can step onto tour buses. Pricing depends on the tour.

CARRIAGE RIDES Several companies offer carriage tours of different parts of historic Charleston. You cannot select your route; tour medallions are doled out in a lottery system after the carriage is loaded. This helps minimize traffic congestion, as not everyone in Charleston is on vacation. Most tours start at 9 and run throughout the day; they cost about $20 per person. If you have a large party (at least six people), call ahead to rent an entire carriage for your group. You may pay a little more per person, but you won't be packed in and uncomfortable especially in the scorching hot summer months. The carriages are open air, but are covered to protect you from the sun. In warm-weather months, try to go early in the day for cooler temperatures and to avoid crowds. Tours are led by licensed guides—all of whom are very knowledgeable about the city, its architecture, and its history, and most of whom are quite entertaining.

Old South Carriage Co. (843-723-9712; oldsouthcarriagetours .com), 14 Anson Street.

Olde Towne Carriage Co. (843-722-1315; oldetownecarriage.com), 20 Anson Street.

Palmetto Carriage Works (843-723-8145; palmettocarriage.com), 40 North Market Street.

Classic Carriage Tours (843-853-3747; classiccarriage.com), 10 Guignard Street.

Carolina Polo & Carriage Co. (843-577-6767; cpcc.com), 102 North Market.

Gullah Tours (843-763-7551; gullahtours.com), 43 John Street. Tours offered Monday through Saturday 11 AM and 1 PM. Also at 3 PM on Saturday. Cost is about $20 for adults 18 and older, with discounts for children. Reservations required. There are many different tours of Charleston, but there is only one Gullah Tour and only one Alphonso Brown. The former schoolteacher and band leader

CHARLESTON CARRIAGE RIDE
South Carolina Department of Parks, Recreation and Tourism/Perry Baker

SC Department of Parks, Recreation & Tourism, DiscoverSouthCarolina.com

THE CHARLESTON BATTERY FROM THE WATER

weaves the story of African Americans' role in making Charleston the city it is today. He can tell his story in the singsong Gullah language of his youth, or—as most often happens—plain-spoken Southern English when the translations get too tough. The highlights of his tour are "Cabbage Row"—the inspiration for "Catfish Row" in the George Gershwin opera *Porgy and Bess*—and the many wrought-iron gates fashioned by noted Charleston blacksmith Philip Simmons, who died in 2009 at the age of 97. Brown directs his tour from the driver's seat of a 20-passenger air-conditioned bus that can be a welcome sight on hot summer days.

HARBOR TOURS Charleston Harbor Tours (843-722-1112 or 800-344-4483; charlestonharbortours.com), 10 Wharfside Street. Tours daily in season at 11:30, 1:30, and 3:30; 11:30 and 1:30 in winter. The harbor tour is about $20 for adults, with discounts for children and seniors. The company also sells package tickets with Boone Hall Plantation and Palmetto Carriage Works. Tours do not have to be taken on the same day. The 90-minute harbor tour is a great way to see Charleston Harbor without leaving the boat. The 250-passenger *Carolina Belle* has an enclosed climate-controlled bottom deck and an open-air top deck. There are refreshments and cocktails available at the on-board snack bar. Restrooms are available on the top deck. The tour passes by Fort Sumter in the middle of the harbor with swings past Fort Moultrie on Sullivans Island and Fort Johnson on the opposite side of the harbor. Viewers can get a real sense of the distance between the battlements where the first shots of the

Civil War were fired. The *Belle* also swings by the famed Charleston Battery and Rainbow Row with its brightly colored mansions overlooking the Ashley River and the harbor. The tour gives visitors a good look from the water of the new Arthur Ravenel Bridge and the USS *Yorktown* at Patriots Point. While you're out in the water, you likely will see many commercial shipping boats, which are stunning in that they are so big, so full of cargo—and still they float. If they weather is nice, I recommend the top deck. If it's too hot or cold, the downstairs with its floor-to-ceiling windows can provide a comfortable view. Visitors who rely on a wheelchair should check with tour operators in advance because there is no handicapped access between decks and on-board restrooms are not handicapped accessible.

Charleston *Schooner Pride* (843-722-1112 or 800-344-4483; schooner pride.com), 360 Concord Street. Sails by reservation only March through October. Daytime sails $30 for adults with discounts for children; sunset sails $40; moonlight sails are adults-only for $45. This 84-foot, three-masted schooner offers two-hour scenic tours of Charleston Harbor, traveling the way our ancestors would have centuries ago. Guests can be mates onboard if they wish by raising and trimming sails or even taking a turn at the wheel. This tour is a little more expensive than your basic harbor ride, but for those who have never sailed, this would be an excellent place to start.

Sandlapper Water Tours (843-849-8687; sandlappertours.com), 10 Wharfside Street. Open Tuesday through Sunday for tours at 11 AM, 2 PM, and 7 PM. Several different tours are offered on a 49-foot motorized catamaran. Tours range from a sunset cruise with a cash bar to a nature tour with a touch tank and net casting. There is a history tour and a ghost tour after dark. Costs range from $20 to $35 per person depending on the tour. Reservations are recommended. Guests can book online or by phone.

THE USS *YORKTOWN* AT PATRIOTS POINT IN MOUNT PLEASANT

GOLF Coosaw Creek Country Club (843-767-9000; coosawcreek.com), 4110 Club Course Drive, North Charleston. Designed by Arthur Hills, this par-71 semi-private course is 6,600 yards and open for public play. Rates vary ($50–70) with season, day of the week, and time of day.

Crowfield Golf & Country Club (843-764-4618; crowfieldgolf.com), 300 Hamlet Circle, Goose Creek. Designed by Robert Spence (7,003 yards, par 72). Rates vary ($27–48) depending on day of the week and time of day.

✱ Lodging

INNS Ansonborough Inn (843-723-1655; ansonboroughinn.com), 21 Hasell Street. This area of historic downtown Charleston was named after Lord Anson of England who was sent to Charleston to protect the South Carolina coast from pirates. Legend has it he won the property in a poker game with Charlestonian Thomas Gadsden. The farmlands were divided into a borough of 25 lots in 1746. The rooms of the inn are large— between 450 and 750 square feet. It underwent a complete remodel by owners George and Sandra Fennell in 1999. The inn offers guests almost a dozen different types of rooms and stays come with continental breakfast and afternoon wine and cheese. Rates start at $169 depending on season, length of stay, and room type.

Meeting Street Inn (843-723-1882; meetingstreetinn.com), 173 Meeting Street. This inn is located in the Market area. Done up in 19th century decor, the inn's 56 guest rooms overlook the garden courtyard with heated spa. Sister properties are **Indigo Inn** (843-577-5900; indigoinn.com), 1 Maiden Lane, with 40 rooms; and

Jasmine House (843-577-5900; jasminehouseinn.com), 64 Hasell Street, with six rooms in the main house and four rooms in the carriage house. Queen/two double $130–140. Prices vary by season.

BED & BREAKFASTS Ashley Inn (843-723-1848 or 800-581-6658; charleston-sc-inns.com), 201 Ashley Avenue. Along with its sister hotel, the **Cannonborough Inn** (800-235-8039; charleston-sc -inns.com), 184 Ashley Avenue, the Ashley offers guests the feeling of antebellum Charleston. The Ashley was built in 1832 and offers six guest rooms and one suite. A two-bedroom carriage house also is available. The Cannonborough was built in 1853 and offers six guest rooms and one suite. All rooms come with a private bath, air-conditioning, and cable TV. A wide shaded veranda at the Cannonborough is the perfect spot for the gourmet breakfast that hotel manager and onetime chef Jan Dolber cooks up, or for afternoon wine and snacks. The inns are filled with four-poster beds, antique furniture, sideboards, and tables. Complimentary bicycles are available for touring the

PORCH AT THE ASHLEY INN, CHARLESTON

city. Rooms are $200–240 in-season, as low as $99 off-season, and include breakfast and afternoon wine. Smoking is allowed only on the porches. Children older than 10 are welcome but pets are not.

Vendue Inn (843-577-7970; vendueinn.com), 19 Vendue Range. Located in historic Charleston, the Vendue Inn offers an eclectic mix of rooms at some of the best prices on the peninsula. Small touches, such as bikes for guests to tour the waterfront, full breakfast, and evening milk and cookies make the Vendue stand out. The hotel spans two buildings. The smaller one is sometimes rented out by whole wedding parties. The rooftop bar provides a great view of the Cooper River and the city. Rates range from $125 for a queen room to $255 for a suite.

HOTELS Mills House Hotel (843-577-2400; millshouse.com), 115 Meeting Street. The Mills House has been part of the Charleston hotel scene since 1853. It was completely renovated in 2008 and retains its 19th-century charm while providing some 21st-century

A BEDROOM AT THE CANNONBOROUGH INN, CHARLESTON

THE VENDUE INN KEEPS A STABLE OF BICYCLES FOR GUESTS.

convenience. The hotel is part of the Holiday Inn chain, but you would never know it by the decor—or the prices, which start around $200 a night. If it's luxury you're after, you will get it here. The service is fantastic and the location is right in the heart of downtown.

Charleston Place Hotel (843-722-4900; charlestonplace.com), 205 Meeting Street. This is one of the most luxurious hotels in downtown Charleston—and it comes with the most luxurious price tag. Rooms start around $300 a night, a little less in the off-season—January and February. The hotel has a full-service European spa, a private concierge level, and a rooftop pool. It probably is the best located hotel in town, just steps from the Market or from King

Street shopping. If the price is a little steep, you can get a glimpse of the elegance at the Thorough-bred Club, stop in around 4 for a great seat for cocktails, or make a reservation for afternoon tea.

Wentworth Mansion (843-853-1886; wentworthmansion.com), 149 Wentworth Street. This is truly a one-of-a-kind property with exquisite rooms. This hotel sits a few blocks away from the high-lights of downtown, but the hotel's restaurant, Circa 1886, is one of the best in the city. Rooms start around $300 a night and come with breakfast and an afternoon reception. Parking is included and that, like the Wentworth Mansion, is something very rare.

Market Pavilion Hotel (877-440-2250, marketpavilion.com),

225 East Bay Street. Located on the corner of Market Street and East Bay in the historic district, the Market Pavilion is one of the newest additions to the Charleston skyline. The rooftop bar with cascading pool is one of the best places to watch ships come and go on the Cooper River. Warmed by heaters in the winter and cooled by fans in the summer, the rooftop is a year-round treat. The hotel's Grill 225 with its dark wood decor is an elegant steak house that also offers a selection of seafood and other dishes. The hotel's 61 rooms are elegantly decorated and have oversized marble bathrooms. The concierge level offers private floor access, hot breakfast, afternoon tea, and cocktail-hour hors d'oeuvres. King/queen/two-queen rooms start $220; add about $100 for the concierge level. Suites $550 a night and include access to the concierge-level amenities.

Francis Marion Hotel (843-722-0600, francismarionhotel.com), 387 King Street. Opened in 1924, the Francis Marion is one of the tallest buildings on the peninsula of Charleston. The 12-story hotel underwent a $12 million renovation in 1996. The rooms are larger than typical modern hotel rooms, but the bathrooms are smaller. Named for South Carolina's most famous Revolutionary War hero (see the sidebar in chapter 1), the hotel is located across the street from one of the city's largest parks—Marion Square—and just a half-mile walk down the city's main shopping district (King

Street) from the City Market. The Swamp Fox Restaurant and Bar is known for its shrimp and grits and uses locally grown and raised produce and meats in its daily specials. The hotel also has a full-service day spa offering massages, facials, spa treatments, and nail care. Rates are $140–335, depending on room style. The hotel offers a variety of packages that couple with its restaurant and spa.

✳ Where to Eat

DINING OUT Cypress (843-727-0111; magnolias-blossom-cypress.com), 167 East Bay Street. Open seven days a week for dinner only. Bar opens at 5. The newest offering from the founders of Magnolia's, Cypress feels like a hip, elegant restaurant while maintaining its Southern twang. The menu has plenty of seafood and beef dishes. Cypress offers an extensive wine list and displays bottles in a three-story wall of wine. This is really one of my favorite places in Charleston. It has a very sophisticated feel, like you are in a big city, but the hospitality is all small-town Southern. I would recommend an oyster appetizer and the Charleston snapper when they are available. If you're not into seafood, get the steak Diane. Entrées are $26–36, and Cypress offers a three-course dinner with some great options for $39.

Muse (843-577-1102; charlestonmuse.com), 82 Society Street. Lunch Tuesday through Sunday from 11. Bar opens at 5 PM. A late-night menu is available until midnight Friday and Saturday. Located in a former home in the city's historic district, Muse serves Mediterranean fare and sells a wide selection of wine by the glass. Guests feel like they have been invited to someone's home for dinner with intimate dining rooms and attentive service. Starters include mussels, tuna tartare, and a platter of hummus, baba ghanoush, cucumber salad, and assorted Spanish olives. Entrées include vegetarian options and plenty of shellfish and seafood. Entrées $16–39. This is a small place, so reservations are recommended.

Husk (843-577-2500; husk restaurant.com), 76 Queen Street. Open Monday through Saturday for lunch 11:30–2:30; Sunday brunch 10–2:30; and dinner daily starting at 5:30. The bar, which is located in a separate building next door, is open daily at 4 PM and is one of the coolest features of Husk. The bar seems small when you first walk in, but the upstairs sitting area is decorated with fun brightly colored chairs and sofas. The vaulted ceiling is the exposed roof boards, and occasionally a sprig or two of something green has worked its way inside. The building had been a residence and at one time was used by an art museum to house a firing kiln. The restaurant itself is done in muted colors with splashes of whimsy and color. The service here is impeccable, and I doubt you will find better anywhere in the city. The staff know the menu as well as if they had made it up themselves—but that task is done by James Beard Award–winning chef Sean Brock.

Appetizers include fried chicken skins, which are as good as they sound, and dirty rice, a mix of middlins rice with duck confit and mushrooms. When you walk into Husk, you see a huge chalkboard listing all the farms and suppliers where Brock and chef de cuisine Travis Grimes get their food. Brock says that if it doesn't come from the South, it isn't going on a Husk plate. The menu changes daily, but some favorites are the Southern-fried chicken skins, the roasted butternut squash soup, tilefish with brussels sprouts, golden beets, and bacon jam, and the lamb terrine. Entrées are in the $20s, appetizers are $10–20, and desserts are $7, but there's no sharing these tiny treats.

Peninsula Grill (843-723-0700; peninsulagrill.com), 112 North Market Street. Bar opens daily at 4. Dinner 5:30–10 Sunday through Thursday. Open until 11 Friday and Saturday. This is one of the city's most luxurious dining experiences. Signature dishes include wild mushroom grits with Lowcountry oyster stew, and bourbon grilled shrimp with Lowcountry hoppin' John, creamed corn, and lobster-basil hushpuppies. Entrées are $25–35. If you want to try the Peninsula Grill, make your reservations about the same time you book a room, just to be sure.

39 Rue De Jean (843-722-8881; 39ruedejean.com), 39 John Street. Open 11:30–1 AM Monday through Saturday; bar open until 2 AM. Sunday brunch served 10–3. Sunday dinner 5:30–11 with bar open until midnight. Rue De Jean (pronounced *roo de jon*) serves wonderful French cuisine in a very Parisian setting. The mussels appetizer and duck confit salad are excellent at lunch, while the dinner menu features bouillabaisse (Sunday special), grilled porterhouse steak (Saturday), and duck à l'orange (Wednesday). Rue De Jean also serves sushi and maki rolls. The restaurant sits between King and Meeting Streets near the visitors center. There is street parking, or you can park at the visitors center garage. Entrées are $19–32. Lunch prices are about half the cost of dinner.

Slightly North of Broad (843-723-3424; hmavericksouthern kitchens.com), 192 East Bay Street. Lunch 11:30–3 Monday through Friday, dinner all week 5:30. Another in the Maverick Southern Kitchens collection, SNOB is great fun with great food. There is not a bad seat in the house, but the best seat is a raised banquette near the kitchen where you can see everyone coming and going in the restaurant. Entrées are $10–29. SNOB offers small dishes for the light appetite at about half the price of entrées.

Most regular entrées also can be ordered in small portions.

FIG (843-805-5900; eatatfig.com), 232 Meeting Street. Open for dinner at 5:30, Monday through Saturday. High-end foodies will not want to miss a chance to sample chef Mike Lata's FIG (Food Is Good). Lata works with local growers to put South Carolina produce on the menu. Entrées generally are under $30. Menus change weekly.

High Cotton (843-724-3815; high-cotton.net), 199 East Bay Street. The Southern phrase *steppin' in high cotton* means living luxuriously. Part of the Maverick Southern Kitchens Group, High Cotton offers elegant dining in a classic but fun atmosphere. The restaurant buys most of its ingredients from South Carolina farmers and fishermen. Saturday lunch or Sunday brunch at the bar is very popular. Offerings include a lobster crêpe, burgers, and omelets; everything is less than $20. Nightly dinner offerings include squab, shrimp and grits, and a vegetable plate. Entrées $18–36.

Magnolia's (843-577-7771; magnolias-blossom-cypress.com), 185 East Bay Street. Open 11:30 lunch, 3:30 dinner, 10 Sunday brunch. This is the original restaurant that many say kicked off Charleston's culinary renaissance in the 1990s, adding some New Age flair to down-home Southern recipes. Collard green eggrolls, pan-fried chicken livers, and fried green tomatoes anchor the appetizer menu. Magnolia's has an offering of small plates for the light appetite. Grilled salmon, tuna, and blackened catfish round out the menu. Entrées $19–32.

Blossom (843-722-9200; magnolias-blossom-cypress.com), 171 East Bay Street. Open seven days at week; lunch starts at 11, dinner at 4. This sister restaurant to Magnolia's and Cypress offers a variety of seafood and has one of the city's few outdoor dining areas in a small courtyard. Blossom also has pizza—individual-sized pies with toppings like lamb sausage, shrimp, and house-made chorizo. All entrées under $30.

Garibaldi (843-723-7153), 49 South Market Street. Open seven days a week for dinner only. Garibaldi has locations in Charleston, Columbia, and Savannah, but it is far from a chain. Its Italian menu has plenty of seafood, but one item stands above the rest—the crispy flounder, scored to the bone and served with apricot sauce. If you like fish, don't miss this dish. Garibaldi Charleston is located in the Market area. Entrées $25–30.

Hank's Seafood Restaurant (843-723-FISH; hanksseafood restaurant.com), Church at Hayne Street. Open daily for dinner at 5. Located in the Market area, Hank's re-creates a classic Charleston fish house with high-end seafood dishes. Entrées $25–32.

McCrady's (843-577-0025; mccradysrestaurant.com), 2 United Alley. Open daily for dinner starting at 5. McCrady's is located in an 18th-century four-story mansion that was built by Edward McCrady after he was released from imprisonment during the Revolutionary War. McCrady's Tavern connected to the home by a second-story double piazza. After McCrady died in 1801, the house passed through many owners before being abandoned. It has been resurrected by James Beard Award–winning chef Sean Brock, whose dishes are made from locally grown and caught meat, vegetables, and seafood. The bar offers pre-Prohibition drinks such as a Side Car (Christian Brothers Brandy VS, Cointreau, and lemon) and Sazerac (Wild Turkey Rye Whiskey, Absente, Peychaud's Bitters). The dinner menu changes daily with the chef offering a tastings menu for the entire table ($85 per person), or a three-course special ($40 per person)—or you can simply order à la carte.

Anson Restaurant (843-577-0551; ansonrestaurant.com), 12 Anson Street. Dinner only. Bar opens at 5. This sister restaurant to Garibaldi is located in the Market area and offers Southern fare such as fried okra, cornmeal-fried oysters, and a pork chop plate that comes with collards and mac and cheese. Also on the menu are several seafood dishes including a whole crispy flounder and appetizers that include pork belly and beef carpaccio. Entrées are $18–39.

Circa 1886 (843-853-7828; circa 1886.com), 149 Wentworth Street. In the shadow of the Wentworth Mansion, this small restaurant is open for dinner Monday through Saturday and has outdoor seating. Reservations are required, and dress is a little less casual than most Charleston restaurants—no shorts or T-shirts. Chef Marc Collins offers a five-course tasting meal for $75 per person ($110 with paired wines). Entrées $25–40.

Grill 225 (843-266-4222; grill 225.com), 225 East Bay Street. Open for lunch, dinner, and Sunday brunch. Located in the Market Pavilion Hotel, Grill 225 is a classic white-tablecloth steak house, featuring large booths in a rich mahogany decor. Entrées are $26–68. Lunch prices are about half as much as dinner.

Library Restaurant at Vendue Inn (800-577-7900; vendueinn .com), 19 Vendue Range. Dinner Tuesday through Saturday from 5:30. A small, intimate dining experience, so reservations are a must. Chef Sara Carter serves up lamb, duck, and short ribs as well as classic Southern fare including crabcakes, fried green tomatoes, and shrimp and grits. Entrées are $24–32.

Pavilion Bar (843-723-0500; marketpavilion.com), 225 East Bay Street. Opens daily at 11:30.

The best view of the harbor, river, and city can be had from this rooftop bar at the Market Pavilion Hotel. This is a great place for early drinks to map out evening plans or for the last stop of the night before heading to bed. Entrées are $16–24.

EATING OUT Sermet's Corner (843-853-7775), 276 King Street. Open daily at 11 for lunch. Dinner menu kicks in at 4. Owned by an artist and chef, Sermet's (pronounced *sur-MET*) has a wide-ranging menu from simple grilled salmon salads to pecan-encrusted tilapia on a bed of vegetables and butternut squash agnolotti. They also have a pork tenderloin that's been marinated in lavender, and daily fish specials that may make it hard to order off the menu. The food has a Mediterranean flair, and every table gets warm bread with flavored dipping oil. Sermet's

THE PERFECT TABLE AT SERMET'S CORNER

Jestine's Kitchen (843-722-7224), 251 Meeting Street. This is the restaurant I never miss when I come to Charleston.

Owner Dana Berlin named her place after Jestine Matthews, who had worked for her family for generations, and many of the recipes were inspired by her. Ms. Matthews was the granddaughter of a freedman; her mother was an American Indian. While she passed in 1997 at the age of 112, you can imagine that she smiles at the large crowds that gather to eat at her namesake restaurant.

When I can pull myself away from the fantastic fried chicken, the shrimp and grits (Sunday's special) are excellent, as are the oyster po' boy, fried pork chop, and meat loaf. The vegetables are cooked "Southern-style," meaning they're seasoned with animal fat or sometimes chunks of ham. If you don't eat meat, they can accommodate you: Three side dishes can easily make a meal. Even if you've never had them, order the collards and ask for pepper vinegar to add a little kick to them. Don't forget the corn bread, and you will find the sweet pickled cucumbers that they bring to your table when you sit down irresistible. Wash it all down with Jestine's "house wine"—sweet tea. The macaroni and cheese alone is worth the wait in line, which can be considerable at high noon in the high season.

My recommendation is that you either skip breakfast and get to Jestine's no later than 11:30 AM, or eat a big breakfast and wait until 2 PM. Use the same tactic for dinner, early or late, but not 7 PM.

If the line is still long, go over one block to King Street for a little shopping until things clear out. Take your time while you are there, read the many reviews of the restaurant posted on the walls, get a good look at the salt- and pepper-shaker collection, and do not skip dessert. Their

is very casual and intimate, despite the large feel you get because of the high ceilings and all the light from the windows. The walls are exposed brick, and you get a view of the kitchen on your way to the bathroom. At night, the dessert case is lit like a beacon behind the bar, reminding you to save room for something sweet. Sermet's helps with that by offering the option to order smaller portions at a smaller price. But the main reason to go to Sermet's is the corner. The restaurant is located at King and Wentworth Streets (just down

JESTINE'S, CHARLESTON

berry cobbler with ice cream and Coca-Cola cake are among the favorites, but I love the lemon cream pie, so smooth and creamy, but so light. If you are stuffed, you can step around the corner to **Jestine's Sweet Shop** (843-720-7437; 54½ Wentworth Street) and get something to go.

Jestine's Kitchen is closed on Monday, but serves lunch, dinner, supper, whatever you call it the rest of the week. The Sweet Shop is closed on Sunday.

Lunch or dinner for two, with fried green tomato appetizer, two dinner plates, corn bread, dessert, and sweet tea plus tax and tip can run over $50. But you will not leave hungry.

the street from Jestine's) and has huge windows looking out on both streets where a sea of humanity walks by in all seasons and all kinds of weather. If the people sitting in the corner window look like they are finishing up, tell the hostess you will wait for that table and enjoy a drink in the bar. It really is worth a 10- or 15-minute wait to get that table. Entrées are less than $20.

Hominy Grill (843-937-0934; hominygrill.com), 207 Rutledge Avenue. Open 7:30 AM–9 PM Monday through Friday, 9–9 Saturday,

9–3 Sunday. Dinner reservations are accepted, but breakfast, lunch, and brunch are served on a first-come, first-served basis. Hominy Grill is very casual dining with classic Southern specialties. All meals are prepared from scratch with fresh, locally raised ingredients. Entrées range from $7 to $16.

Gaulart and Maliclet (843-577-9797; fastandfrench.org), 98 Broad Street. Serving 8–4 Monday; until 10 Tuesday through Thursday; until 10:30 Friday through Saturday. This is a wonderful place to drop in for a quick bite. Sit at the bar and sample French cheeses or pâté, or have a sandwich. Thursday is fondue night, and G&M has a large selection of vegetarian dishes. Breakfast can be had for less than $5, lunch less than $10, and dinner about $15.

Kaminsky's (843-853-8270; kaminskys.com), 78 North Market Street. Open Monday through Thursday from 4 PM, Friday through Saturday at noon. Kaminsky's beckons all who walk by its Market Street storefront by putting their tantalizing dessert case right in the front window. Huge slabs of chocolate and red velvet cake, 4-inch-thick slices of cheesecake, bourbon-pecan pie, and other sugary delights call to passersby from the lighted case. Inside, Kaminsky's feels part Irish pub, part ice cream shop. The bar specializes in coffee and dessert drinks, such as a vanilla kiss martini or adult milk shakes with brandy or Frangelico. Don't worry, there are plenty of nonalcoholic options for the kids and nondrinkers. Kaminsky's packs a calorie punch, so make sure you have a good walk planned for after.

Bocci's (843-720-2121; boccis .com), 158 Church Street. Open daily for lunch and dinner starting

OUTDOOR DINING AT THE HOMINY GRILL, CHARLESTON

at 11:30. Most dishes here are under $20. The Tuscan duck and veal marsala are favorites. Bocci actually looks like a restaurant you would find in Italy—stucco walls with murals, heavy dark wood furniture. The dishes are hearty and large so if you're not starving, order the small size and save room for one of their great desserts, including tiramisu and cannoli. The bar is a little small, but the service is excellent.

⚓ **Joe Pasta** (843-965-5252; joe pasta.com), 428 King Street. Open daily for lunch and dinner starting at 11 AM. Bar open nightly as late as 2 AM. Joe Pasta has been at the north end of King Street for more than 10 years and finally the attractions of that shopping artery have come out to meet him. This is a great family-friendly place for inexpensive pasta dishes and wonderful pizza, all of which are less than $15. If you're driving, park at the visitors center on Meeting Street and walk down John Street to King.

Caviar and Bananas (843-577-7757; caviarandbananas.com), 51 George Street. Open daily 7 AM– 9 PM for breakfast, lunch, and dinner. I stumbled on this place on a recent trip to Charleston and at first thought it was a chain, but no, says Kris Furniss, half of the husband-and-wife team that opened the place in 2008. Located near the College of Charleston campus, it's like a locally owned Dean & DeLuca with high-end coffees, sandwiches, and prepared foods to go like black truffle macaroni and cheese and edamame hummus. Furniss and his wife, Margaret, a graduate of C of C, want the place to become a one-stop shop for the students and other neighborhood folks. You know, a place where you could find something special like caviar or something everyday like bananas. Prices are reasonable: breakfast for $5 or less, lunch for $10; dinner ranges widely depending on the daily selection of specials. Sushi rolls are all around $10 or less.

Fleet Landing Restaurant (843-722-8100; fleetlanding.net), 186 Concord Street. Open 11–4 for lunch, 4–10 for dinner, 11–3 for brunch Saturday and Sunday. This restaurant sits on the harbor in an old Navy building. Fleet Landing offers casual dining for lunch, dinner, and weekend brunch. In addition to classic fried seafood platters, the restaurant also has burgers and sandwiches. Reservations are accepted. Most lunch items are under $10, while dinner entrées are $15–25.

✳ Entertainment

MUSIC VENUES/THEATERS

Music Farm (843-577-6989; musicfarm.com), 32 Ann Street. The Music Farm books acts three or four nights week, usually between Wednesday and Sunday. Prices vary from $10 to $30 or more depending on the show. They usually open the doors around 7:30 or 8 PM, but the music doesn't start until much later. So you have plenty of time to grab a bite. The club is located near the visitors center on Meeting Street, so it's walking distance to almost all the great restaurants downtown. East Bay Street might be a bit of a haul, but there are dozens of pedicabs that can get you to the Music Farm from the Market in less than 30 minutes. Music Farm posts its lineup several months in advance, and tickets for some shows are available online. This place has become the venue for local, regional, and national acts. The crowd can be on the young side for many shows, but I have seen regional stars the Blue Dogs and David Clayton-Thomas of Blood Sweat & Tears fame there. So they do occasionally book acts for folks over 30. This place is not for sitting and listening to music, it's for drinking, dancing, and standing while you listen. It's a club that has great live music more than a music hall that sells beer. So if you find an act you like, grab your hottest, hippest jeans and head on over.

Dock Street Theatre (843-720-3968; charlestonstage.com), 135 Church Street. Renovated in 2010 in time for the Spoleto Festival's performance of *Flora*, which was the first opera performed in the American colonies when it played at the Dock Street Theatre on February 12, 1736. The original theater burned down in the Great Fire of 1740. The theater was replaced in the 19th century by the Planters Hotel. The hotel was a center of tourism for the city. One of its waiters, Robert Smalls, became an American hero of the Civil War when he stole a steamboat in the harbor and sailed it past the Confederate-held Fort Sumter to the U.S. fleet that was blockading the harbor. The hotel also was the birthplace of the city's famed Planter's Punch, but it was heavily damaged during the Civil War and left empty for decades. In the mid-1930s the restoration of the hotel was a Works Progress Administration project. It was turned back into a theater, and 201 years after its first opening, the Dock Street held its second grand opening. The theater is home to the Charleston Stage Company, which performs at there year-round. Other productions make stops here, and the Dock Street is a major venue for the annual Spoleto Festival. Check out the theater's website for show dates.

✳ Selective Shopping

The Old City Market (843-853-8000), Market Street. Open 9:30–6 daily. This three-block-long open-air market has a little bit of everything, from silver and jewelry to sweetgrass baskets and Charleston foodstuffs and souvenirs. No trip to the city is complete without a stop at the Market, which splits Market Street into two one-way avenues. It's where you'll find the horse-drawn carriage rides, and plenty of air-conditioned stores and restaurants line both sides of the street. You can spend a whole day down here, but note that weekends are very crowded. The building also has public restrooms and houses the Daughters of the Confederacy Museum.

King Street offers everything from antiques to designer shoes to discounted clothing seconds. Many are national chains such as Laura Ashley, Abercrombie & Fitch, Pottery Barn, and Urban Outfitters, but there are many unique shops mixed in. Most stores are open 10–6.

Raymond Clark Gallery (843-723-7555), 429 King Street. Unique furniture and home accessories, especially unique glassware.

Geo. C. Birlant & Company (843-722-3842; birlant.com), 191 King Street. This shop was founded in the 1920s by George Birlant. In addition to antiques, the company has made Charleston Battery Benches for more than 50 years after buying the original mold pattern and rights to the iconic outdoor furniture originally made by Riley Iron Works in the 1800s.

Croghan's Jewel Box (843-723-3594; croghansjewelbox.com), 308 King Street. Open 9:30–5:30 weekdays, 10–5 Saturdays. This jewelry and gift shop has been open for more than 100 years.

The Silver Vault (843-722-0631; silvervaultcharleston.com), 195 King Street. Open 10–5:30 Monday through Saturday. For more than 50 years, the Silver Vault has specialized in silverware and jewelry.

M Dumas & Sons (843-723-8603; mdumasandsons.com), 294 King Street. Pronounced *doo-MAHS*, the store has been known for decades for its South Carolina–themed men's and women's clothing and classic preppy styles—think penny loafers, khakis, and button-down shirts.

The Silver Puffin (843-723-7900, silverpuffin.com), 29 King Street. Open 10–6 Sunday through Monday, 10–8 Tuesday through Saturday. This shop has a wide range of gift options, from local artwork and glassware to chocolates.

The Audubon Gallery (843-853-1100; audubonart.com), 190 King Street. Affiliated with the Joel Oppenheimer Gallery in Chicago, The Audubon Gallery specializes in natural history and sporting art of the past 300 years. Collection includes selections from John J. Audubon's *Birds of America*.

Oops! (843-722-7768; theoopsco.com), 326 King Street. Oops! first opened in Charleston in 1982 offering sportswear from name-brand catalog merchants. Some of the clothes may have a slight flaw or may be an odd color, but they are always on sale. This is a great place to get South Carolina–themed clothing and accessories. I just love going into this tiny shop stuffed to the gills with clothes and digging until I find the perfect thing I didn't know I needed. Oops! also has a Mount Pleasant store as well as stores in Greenville, Spartanburg, and Columbia.

Gallery Chuma (843-722-7568; gallerychuma.com), 43 John Street. Open 10–6 Monday through Saturday. This gallery is located just off the main shopping of King Street and specializes in Gullah and African American art. The collection includes work of Jonathan Green and John W. Jones. Chuma frequently has special performances during Spoleto and offers books and other information on the Gullah culture of South Carolina.

Broad Street and surrounding areas offer a variety of antiques shops and art galleries as well as restaurants and bars and a few historic sites.

Moore House American Antiques (843-722-8065; moorehouseantiques.com), 105 Broad Street. This store specializes in American furniture made between 1700 and 1820 and offers to take back previously bought pieces in trade on other items.

Carolina Galleries (843-720-8622, carolinagalleries.com), 106-A Church Street. Open 11–6 Monday through Saturday. Carolina Galleries has specialized in work by Southern artists and about subjects in South Carolina and Charleston in particular. Located just South of Broad on historic Church Street.

Courtyard Art Gallery (843-723-9172; courtyardartgallery.com), 149½ East Bay Street.

Open 10–5 Monday through Saturday. Courtyard Art Gallery showcases the work of Lowcountry artists in a variety of media, including pottery, jewelry, and photography.

Spencer Art Galleries I & II (843-722-6854; spencerartgallery.com), 55 & 57 Broad Street. Open 10–5 Monday through Saturday. Spencer Galleries specialize in contemporary art, including paintings, photographs, and sculptures.

Ella Walton Richardson Fine Art (843-722-3600, ellarichardson.com), 58 Broad Street.

Hamlet Fine Art Gallery (843-722-1944; hamletgallery.com), 7 Broad Street.

Edward Dare Gallery (843-853-5002; edwarddare.com), 31 Broad Street.

OFF THE PENINSULA Terrace Oaks Antique Mall (843-795-9689; terraceoaksantiques.com), 2037 Maybank Highway (SC 700). Open 10–5:30 Monday through Saturday. This shop is off the peninsula and resembles a 90-family garage sale. An excellent place to spend a rainy afternoon looking for treasure or just wandering through the past as told in pop-culture artifacts.

Jim Booth Art Gallery (843-795-8244; jimbooth.com), 1929 Maybank Highway. Open 9–5 Tuesday through Saturday. Jim Booth is a native Charlestonian and self-taught artist who is known for his realistic paintings depicting Charleston and Lowcountry scenes.

MALLS, OUTLETS Mount Pleasant Towne Centre (843-216-9900; mtpleasanttownecentre .com), 1600 Palmetto Grande Drive, Mount Pleasant. Mall shopping outdoors.

Tanger Outlets (843-529-3095; tangeroutlet.com/charleston), 4840 Tanger Outlet Boulevard. Open 10–9 Monday through Saturday, 11–9 Sunday. This outdoor mall has brand-name stores such as Bath & Body Works, GAP Outlet, Eddie Bauer Outlet, Old Navy, and Gymboree.

✱ Special Events

SPRING *March:* **Charleston Wine and Food Festival** (843-727-9998; charlestonfoodandwine .com). Admission varies depending on individual events, but tickets can range from $50 to $150. The event offers some ticket packages at a discount. It's a pricey event, but if you are going to go to a food and wine festival, this is the one to do. You can sample some of the finest food from Charleston's best restaurants all in one place. The grand tasting tent has more than 90 vendors. There are also celebrity chef competitions throughout the weekend, and special luncheons, dinner cruises, and receptions. This is one to plan your visit around.

Annual Tea Room and Gift Shop (843-766-1541; oldstandrews .org), Old St. Andrews Episcopal Church. This is the oldest consecutively running tearoom in Charleston.

April: **Cooper River Bridge Run** (843-856-19491; bridgerun .com), 16 South Shelmore Boulevard, Suite 105, Mount Pleasant. This first 2 miles of this 10K (6.2-mile) run is in Mount Pleasant and takes runners across Shem Creek, before heading onto the Cooper River (Ravenel) Bridge for 2.5 miles; the route finishes down two of Charleston's main downtown streets before dumping participants into Marion Square for the post-run celebration. Started in 1978, the race has grown in participation every year, despite being held the same morning as the state's premier horse-racing event 100 miles inland. The event is limited to 40,000 racers and frequently sells out in advance.

Family Circle Cup (843-856-7900; familycirclecup.com), 161 Seven Farms Drive, Charleston. This Tier I WTA Tour event moved to Charleston in 2001 after 28 years at Hilton Head Island. The world's top tennis players contend every year for the title. Ticket prices vary depending on the day of the week-long event. For real fans, I recommend planning your entire trip around this event. Past winners include Martina Navratilova, Chris Evert (who has the most Family Circle Cup titles at eight), Steffi Graf, both Williams sisters, and Justine Henin. Early-round action is less expensive ($10 to watch all outer-court matches on qualifying

THE RAVENEL BRIDGE

The Ravenel Bridge (see photo page 121) is an engineering marvel—the largest cable-stayed bridge in North America when it opened to traffic in July 2005—that has become an iconic image of the city. I'm impressed every time I drive across the bridge with its seemingly effortless strength and the lines created by the cables as you pass by them. If you're driving, keep your eyes on the road, but if you are a passenger, look at everything. Heading out to Mount Pleasant you can see Charleston Harbor and the Atlantic Ocean beyond. Coming back into town, you will see the business side of the Cooper River with all its container ship traffic that fuels Charleston's other primary business.

The bridge's eight lanes of traffic and a pedestrian and bicycle lane on the harbor side are held up by 128 cables strung between the roadway and two diamond-shaped towers that bookend the 1,546-foot main span. The roadway sits 200 feet above the median high-tide mark, allowing those large container ships to access port terminals upriver from the bridge. The bicycle and pedestrian lane spans about 2.5 miles from end to end. On foot or bike, from the Patriots Point parking lot across the bridge and back would be 5 miles.

Under the bridge on the Mount Pleasant side is the Mount Pleasant Memorial Waterfront Park with a 1,250-foot pier that juts into the river. There is pay parking here for those wanting to bike or walk across the bridge or free parking is available off Patriots Point Road.

The bridge is named for longtime Lowcountry politician Arthur Ravenel, who has served as a U.S. congressman, state senator, and most recently a Charleston County school board member. He is largely credited with helping secure the federal funding needed to build the $632 million bridge.

One of the two bridges it replaced was nearly 80 years old and dangerously narrow for modern traffic. It had been closed to tractor-trailers for years. Shipping lanes were closed briefly while steel sections of the former Grace and Pearman Bridges were dynamited from their piers, pulled from the riverbed, and salvaged. More than 200,000 tons of concrete from the old bridges' demolition were used to bolster artificial reefs off the coast.

days the weekend before the event starts), and all the best players have to work their way from Day One, just like the lesser knowns. You can see players at practice and warm-ups on side courts, meet past champions during special events, and even watch as former greats take to the court in exhibition matches. Prices gradually increase throughout the event to $50 per person to watch the final on the stadium court. The event offers a variety of ticket packages. Championship weekend ($225 per person in 2011) gives average fans about all the tennis they can stand with four quarterfinal matches on Friday, two semis on Saturday, and the final on Sunday. Fans can also catch doubles action that is scheduled around the singles draw. For about twice that price, you can get a ticket to every session.

May: **Spoleto Festival USA** (843-579-3100; spoletousa.org), 14 George Street. One of the world's premier arts festivals, Spoleto Festival USA was founded in 1977 by Pulitzer Prize–winning Italian composer Gian Carlo Menotti and others looking for an American counterpart to the Festival of Two Worlds in Spoleto, Italy. The annual program includes opera, dance, musical theater, plays, concerts, and visual arts. The festival has been home to many premieres as well as professional revivals of classics. There are more than 140 events during the 17-day festival. Ticket prices range from $10 to $130, depending on the event and seating.

Piccolo Spoleto (843-724-7305; piccolospoleto.com), 180 Meeting Street. Piccolo Spoleto is the local companion to Spoleto Festival USA with a focus on artists from the southeastern United States and South Carolina. Piccolo offers many of the same types of entertainment as Spoleto and runs concurrently with the larger festival. Many events are free.

Town of Mount Pleasant Blessing of the Fleet & Seafood Festival (843-884-8517; townofmountpleasant.com). More than 11 local seafood restaurants offer a variety of local catches as the town spotlights the shrimping industry.

SUMMER ∅ **Charleston Farmers Market** (843-724-7305; charleston arts.sc), Marion Square, King at Calhoun Street. Open 8–2 Saturday in the summer and fall. Locally grown produce, plants, herbs, and fresh-baked bread and pastries are available for sale, and local musicians play. This is great free family entertainment.

WINTER *February:* **Southeastern Wildlife Exposition** (843-723-1748; sewe.com). This three-day event held in February offers art, exhibits, lectures, and other programs on wildlife and land conservation and preservation. Started in 1983, the event brings together more than 500 artists and exhibitors. A three-day pass to all events costs $40. Daily tickets also are available.

SWEETGRASS BASKETS

One of the symbols of Charleston, sweetgrass baskets are one of the most popular—and most expensive—souvenirs of a visit to the city. More than a utility, these baskets are an artform.

The baskets were made by slaves for use in harvesting rice, to separate the grain from the chaff. The bulrush and sweetgrass used to make the baskets are harvested by pulling, not cutting, and woven with leaves from the native palmetto tree or pine needles. The weaver will use a file or even the handle of a utensil to interlock the pieces. Even small baskets take hours of work.

In the 1930s when US 17 was paved through the two Carolinas and tourism came to coastal South Carolina, sweetgrass basket makers began selling their wares on the roadside.

But the same highway that brought new buyers for their product eventually made it difficult to harvest the raw materials. The growth of the road into a major urban thoroughfare also cut into the ability to sell from roadside stands.

Today, the Old City Market on the Charleston Peninsula is the best place to buy a sweetgrass basket. Small jewelry-sized baskets can start at $30 or more; prices range in the hundreds of dollars for larger pieces. Every June, just before harvesttime, the **Sweetgrass Festival** (843-856-9732; sweetgrassfestival.org) celebrates the art of basketweaving and the culture of those who made it famous. The festival is held in different locations each year and includes storytelling, basket-making demonstrations, and samples of Gullah cuisine. Admission is free.

SWEETGRASS BASKETS FOR SALE AT ANGEL OAK

ISLANDS AND BEACHES

ISLE OF PALMS, SULLIVANS, FOLLY, JOHNS AND JAMES ISLANDS, KIAWAH ISLAND

The islands and beaches surrounding Charleston range from luxurious homes and resorts around the Ocean Course golf course at **Kiawah Island** to laid-back **Folly Beach**, where young surfers change in and out of their wet suits along the road at the Washout—home to some of the best surfing in the state.

But don't be fooled by flip-flops and tattered beachwear. There isn't a square of beachfront property that goes for less than a million dollars.

To the north of Charleston are **Sullivans Island** and the **Isle of Palms**. A rumored stop for famed pirate Blackbeard, Sullivans Island was the setting for Edgar Allen Poe's "The Gold-Bug." Homes here are both elegant and relaxed. The southern end of the island is home to a former battlement used to protect the city during the Revolutionary War and from which the attack on U.S. troops at Fort Sumter started the Civil War. Sullivans has more year-round residents and fewer vacation rentals. It is home to the state's former first lady Jenny Sanford. There are a few restaurants and shops between the main highway and beach. It is well worth the 20- to 30-minute drive from downtown even if you aren't staying here.

The **Isle of Palms** (IOP to natives) to the north of Sullivans is much more of a tourist destination and home to **Wild Dunes Resort**. Built in the 1970s as a resort and tennis club, Wild Dunes now also has two golf courses. Guests can rent a hotel room, a condo, or a beach home and have access to all the resort's amenities, including pools, fitness area, and spa services. One of the area's best restaurants, The Boathouse is at Breach Inlet between IOP and Sullivans. Offering great views of the water on all sides, The Boathouse gets crowded as soon as the weather gets warm, so reservations are recommended.

Charleston Beaches

South of Charleston are Folly Beach and Kiawah and Seabrook Islands. **Folly Beach** retains a bohemian beach feel despite the large modern homes that have been built since 1989's Hurricane Hugo. Beach house rental prices vary widely, but an oceanfront home big enough to sleep 10 adults will cost more than $4,000 a week in the summer, about half that in the winter. Most have modern conveniences such as elevators and WiFi. There also is an oceanfront hotel and many condos on and off the beach. Folly has enough restaurants to keep you fed, including the Crab Shack and Taco Boy, but it's only about 15 minutes from downtown Charleston (30 minutes in heavy summer traffic). At the west end of Folly is **Morris Island**—a slight crop of land between the sea and the marsh with an endangered lighthouse on one end. It was the scene of the assault on Fort Wagner by the all-black 54th Massachusetts Regiment during the Civil

War that was highlighted in the 1989 movie *Glory*. It is worth the mile or so walk from the nearest public parking area to the end of the beach for great views of the lighthouse. From there, you can see the mouth of Charleston Harbor, the new cable-stayed bridge over the Cooper River, and **Sullivans Island** along with its famed black-and-white lighthouse on the northern mouth of the harbor. The Morris Island lighthouse base has suffered significant erosion, and the currents that swirl around it are deadly for even the strongest swimmers. Do not attempt to walk, wade, or swim to the lighthouse.

Farther south is **Kiawah Island**, home to the luxurious AAA Five Diamond resort The Sanctuary and the Ocean Course, which will host the 2012 PGA Championship. The island was named for the Indians who occupied it until European settlers arrived in the 17th century. The first owner was George Raynor, who some in the colonies suspected was a pirate and who was given title to the island in 1699 by the Lords Proprietors. The Vanderhorst family took ownership in the mid-18th century and owned the island for nearly 200 years. The first home was built in 1802 by Revolutionary War hero General Arnoldus Vanderhorst; the family successfully farmed sea island cotton until the Civil War, when the unprotected island was abandoned. After the war, Arnoldus Vanderhorst IV restarted planting, but he soon died in a hunting accident. Legend says he haunts the island and the Vanderhorst Mansion that still stands today. The family sold the island to C. C. Royal in 1951 for $125,000 in one of the best land deals in South Carolina history. Just 23 years later, Royal's family sold the island to a resort developer for $18.2 million. Development began in 1974, and the current owners bought the island in 1993. Kiawah's Beachwalker Park is ranked as the number 6 beach in America by Dr. Stephen P. Leatherman—known as Dr. Beach for his annual top-10 rankings. A boardwalk through oaks, pines, and palmetto trees leads down to an unspoiled beach. The whole island is 10 miles long, and visitors must pass through a guard gate to get to the golf courses, restaurants, and hotels.

Seabrook Island south of Kiawah is a private island community with a Robert Trent Jones–designed Crooked Oaks golf course, a dozen tennis courts, several swimming pools and restaurants, and other resort amenities. If you are renting a home or villa here, make sure the rental includes a temporary membership to the club's facilities.

Johns Island and **James Island** do not have beaches, but they have wonderful restaurants, shops, and the best dog park in the county—**James Island County Park** (843-795-7275; ccprc.com), 871 Riverland Drive.

✳ To See

HISTORIC SITES Fort Moultrie (843-883-3123; nps.gov/fosu/history culture/fort_moultrie.htm), 1214 Middle Street, Sullivans Island. Open

9–5 daily. Admission is $3 for adults ages 15–62, $1 for seniors, free for children. A quiet, windswept grassy area hidden on an island dedicated to sun and surf, Fort Moultrie offers excellent views of Charleston Harbor and lets you stand in the place of young cadets who fired the first shots of the Civil War. But the site had seen action before that fateful day in 1861. The fort was not yet finished, but won its name on June 28, 1776, when Colonel William Moultrie turned away an assault by nine British warships. Like many coastal South Carolina forts, it was neglected during times of peace; its most destructive enemy was the sea in the form of hurricanes. In the late 19th century the United States installed batteries of concrete and steel and larger weapons.

OTHER PLACES OF INTEREST Angel Oak (843-559-3496; angeloak tree.org), 3688 Angel Oak Road, Johns Island. Open 9–5 daily, free. Stepping under the twisted branches of the Angel Oak is like stepping into an ancient cathedral. Shadows and light move across the ground as sea breezes rustle the sleeping giant's leaves. The limbs are as large as many normal tree trunks and are so heavy they rest on the ground. Some even go underground before coming back up. Estimated to be as much as 1,500 years old, the tree is over 65 feet tall with a circumference of 25 feet. It casts a shadow over 17,000 square feet of land. It has survived countless hurricanes, including 1989's Hurricane Hugo, which did do some damage, and at least one major earthquake. Despite the hallowed feel of the land, the tree's name comes not from some seraphic nature of the ways the

THE ANGEL OAK, JAMES ISLAND

limbs branch out from the trunk, but from its onetime owners Martha and Justin Angel. The city now owns the tree and surrounding land. A gift shop nearby gives visitors an opportunity to donate to the cause of protecting the tree from ever-encroaching development.

The Folly Boat (follyboat.com). This local curiosity is on Folly Road between the Piggly Wiggly and the bridge over the Folly River. It's like the welcome-to-Folly sign only it's done by visitors. The story goes that the boat washed ashore in the marsh during Hurricane Hugo and no one ever claimed it, so everybody paints it. Whether it's an anniversary or a birthday, folks bring buckets of paint and splash their message on the boat for all to see. There's no guarantee how long a message will stay before some paints over it. I have never actually seen anyone painting the boat in countless treks to the beach over the past 20 years. But if you stay a week at Folly, chances are you will get to know a little bit about the other folks staying there based on the messages.

✳ To Do

FISHING IOP Marina (843-886-0209; iop.net/community/IOPMarina .aspx), 50 41st Avenue, Isle of Palms. The marina offers inshore and offshore fishing by reservation only. Trip prices include all fishing equipment, an experienced U.S. Coast Guard–licensed captain, and fishing license. Crew gratuity not included. You are responsible for your food, drink, sunglasses, and sunscreen. Rates are from $375 for a 4-hour inshore charter for two, up to $2,000 for a 12-hour offshore tour for up to six passengers.

FAMILY-FRIENDLY ACTIVITIES ⚓ **Harbor Tours, IOP Marina** (843-886-0209; iop.net/community/IOPMarina.aspx), 50 41st Avenue, Isle of Palms. The marina offers two-hour harbor tours for $250 ($100 for each additional hour) for up to six people and three-hour harbor cruises for up to 10 passengers for $1,150 (additional passengers $50 up to 49 passengers). Crews can customize any trip.

⚓ **Rosebank Farms** (843-768-9139; rosebankfarms.com), 4455 Betsy Kerrison Parkway, Johns Island. Rosebank Farms has some of the best fresh veggies and seafood in the area, but the real treat for the kids is the farm animals. Visitors can pet a miniature Brahma cow, feed the goats, and pet the pigs and bunnies. Roosters and chickens wander among shoppers, and the farm has a Marsh Tacky, South Carolina's official state horse. The Johns Island Museum is located in a one-room schoolhouse built in 1868 and takes visitors on a 4,000-year history of the island from the time of Indians through the Civil War. You'll also get a look at the important agriculture of the area, from sea island cotton to rice, indigo, and today's favorite, the Johns Island tomato.

GOLF Kiawah Island Golf Resort (843-768-2121; kiawahgolf.com), 1 Sanctuary Beach Drive, Kiawah Island. The resort offers five courses: **Cougar Point**, designed by Gary Player (6,875 yards, par 72); **Oak Point**, designed by Clyde B. Johnston (6,759 yards, par 72); **The Ocean Course**, home to the 1991 Ryder Cup, the 2007 Senior PGA Championship, and the 2012 PGA Championship, designed by Pete Dye (7,356 yards, par 72); **Osprey Point**, designed by Tom Fazio (6,932 yards, par 72); and **Turtle Point**, designed by Jack Nicklaus (7,061 yards, par 72). Greens fees vary widely and can be included in packages. The Ocean Course is the most expensive: Fees for nonguests at the resort can reach $300 for 18 holes, but include a caddy.

Seabrook Island (843-768-2529; discoverseabrook.com), 1001 Landfall Way, Kiawah Island. **Crooked Oaks Course** designed by Robert Trent Jones Sr. (6,746 yards, par 72). **Ocean Winds Course** designed by Willard Byrd (6,761 yards, par 72). Rates vary ($84–160) depending on season, day of the week, and time of day.

Wild Dunes Resort (843-886-2255; wilddunes.com), 4600 Palm Boulevard, Isle of Palms. The resort offers two Tom Fazio designs, **The Harbor Course** (6,446 yards, par 70) and **The Links Course** (6,722 yards, par 72). Harbor Course greens fees are about $60 while the Links Course is $115.

Charleston Municipal Golf Course (843-795-6517; ci.charleston.sc.us), James Island. Designed by John E. Adams (6,320 yards, par 72). Greens fees $18–24, electric carts $15, walking carts $3.

TENNIS Wild Dunes Resort (888-778-1876; wilddunes.com), 4600 Palm Boulevard, Isle of Palms. Classes start at 8 AM and are available all day. Resort guests can book courts for play from noon to 6 PM daily. Wild Dunes has seven Har-Tru courts including a stadium court; five are available after dark. The resort has a full-service pro shop and a variety of plans and programs designed to help you improve your game. Resort guests get an hour of free court time per day; additional time is $15 an hour. Lessons for all levels and ages start at $35 for half an hour.

✴ Green Space

PARKS Folly Beach County Park (843-588-2426; beachparks.com/folly beach.htm), 1100 W Ashley Avenue, Folly Beach. Open daily 9–7 in summer, 10–5 in winter. Cost is $7 per car; $10 for an RV, and $25 for a bus. This park is the perfect way to spend the day at the beach if you aren't staying on the beach. Located at the western tip of Folly, this park has views of the Folly River, the marsh, and about three-quarters of a mile of beachfront. There is a picnic area and boardwalks, but best of all, there are restrooms, showers, and dressing areas to leave the beach behind when you are done. In the summer you'll find lifeguards, chair and umbrella rentals, and a snack bar.

Isle of Palms County Park (843-886-3863; ccprc.com), 1 14th Avenue, Isle of Palms. Open daily 9–7 in summer, 10–5 in winter. Cost is $7 per car, $10 for an RV, and $25 per bus. Like the Folly Beach park, this one offers showers, dressing areas, and restrooms as well as access to about 600 feet of beachfront along with a designated swimming area with life-guards, chair and umbrella rentals, and a snack bar. There is a children's playground and a sand volleyball pit.

☙ ✐ **James Island County Park** (843-795-7275; ccprc.com), 871 River-land Drive, Charleston. This park has the best off-the-leash dog area with a designated spot for smaller dogs and a lake for plenty of wet fun on a hot summer day. Owners are responsible for their dogs and should have them under voice-command control at all times. But I recommend keep-ing a close eye on your poochie and small children as the canine crowd can get rowdy. Bring plenty of towels and plastic bags to clean up behind your best friend.

BEACHES Folly Beach (843-513-1836; follybeachsouthcarolina.org), Folly Road at Arctic Avenue. Nicknamed "the Edge of America," Folly Beach got its name from the Old English for "dense foliage" and was once a place where ships dropped off their dead, dying, and plague- and cholera-infected passengers to avoid quarantine in the city. On the way back across the ocean, the survivors were picked up and the dead were buried, earning Folly the name Coffin Island. The island sits just south of Charleston and runs east–west. The west end has a county park for day visitors with showers and restrooms; the east end has the Morris Island Lighthouse. The beaches are wide in some places, narrow in others. The beach has been renourished several times in recent years to combat the constant erosion that is inherent to barrier islands. Folly's year-round resi-dents are a laissez-faire lot that don't mind you gumming up the traffic if you're nice about it.

To me, **Sullivans Island** (843-883-3198; sullivansisland-sc.com) has the state's prettiest beach. Long expanses of white sand with little visible development make you feel like you've washed up on a deserted island. While its beaches are very wide at low tide, keep an eye on the water. You can find yourself truly stranded on a sandbar and have to wade through the incoming tide to get back to your car or house.

Where Sullivans is geared more toward full-time residents, the **Isle of Palms** (843-886-6428; iop.net) says welcome to all visitors. Wild Dunes Resort has everything to complete a beach visit: a stretch of white sand beach with water toys and chair and umbrella rentals, two golf courses, tennis courts, and three swimming pools. The resort offers boat cruises, ecotours, kayaking, sailing excursions, and spa services so guests can do as little or as much as they want. There also is a county park here.

SURFING Folly offers some of the best surfing in the state at its Washout. Paid parking is allowed along the street here on a first-come, first-serve basis. Surfers hang out here year-round—especially on sunny winter days or stormy summer days when the waves are highest. The Washout is so named because it's the area of beach that was washed out by Hurricane Hugo in 1989. The wind rolls across the ocean and the beach unimpeded to the Folly River, which is what many claim is the reason the surfing is so good here.

McKevlin's Surf Shop (843-588-2247; mckevlins.com), 8 Center Street, Folly Beach. Open daily 10–5:30. Started in 1965, McKevlin's is the oldest surf shop in the area and conveniently located near the Folly pier. A variety of surfboards and bodyboards are available for rent as well as any accessories, equipment, and even servicing for those bringing their own boards. Bodyboards go for $3 an hour or $15 a day. Surfboards are $5 an hour, $25 a day, or $75 a week.

PADDLING Coastal Expeditions Inc. (843-884-7684; coastalexpeditions .com), 2223 Folly Road, Folly Beach. Open daily 9–6. Half-day and full-day guided tours are offered from Folly Creek. The half-day tour explores the marsh side of Folly; if you hit at low tide, you can see a variety of loggerhead sea turtles, wood storks, and dolphins. Full-day tours will have you paddling through the marsh to the Morris Island Lighthouse for shelling and an up-close look at the endangered light. All the guides are trained on the water and are naturalists, so reservations are required for the tours. Prices vary depending on which tour you take. If you just want to rent a kayak for the day, it's $50 for singles and $60 for a tandem.

✳ Lodging

PRIVATE HOME RENTALS
Avocet Properties (843-588-6699; avocetproperties.net), 38 Center St., Folly Beach. Open 9–6 Monday through Saturday. Avocet offers more than 150 private homes and condos around Folly Beach. Prices vary widely depending on season, size, and location.

RESORT Quest Isle of Palms, Sullivans Island, & Wild Dunes (843-886-9704; resortquestisleof palms.com), 1517 Palm Boulevard, Suite C, Isle of Palms. Open daily 8–6. This company has more than 250 villas and homes available on the beach north of Charleston. Prices vary widely based on season, size, and location.

Seabrook Island Rentals (843-768-0880; resortquestseabrook .com), 115 Planted Row, Johns Island.

Kiawah Island Golf Resort (800-654-2924; kiawahresort.com), 1 Sanctuary Beach Drive, Kiawah Island. The official owner and operator of all the resort amenities at Kiawah Island offers hundreds of rental properties, from private homes to condos and villas. Rentals include access to resort pools, preferred golf and tennis times, as well as complimentary transportation on the island.

INNS The Boardwalk Inn (888-778-1876; wilddunes.com), 4600 Palm Boulevard, Isle of Palms. This oceanfront inn has 93 guest rooms. Guests have access to all Wild Dunes' resort amenities, including three pools, two golf courses, and tennis courts. Rooms start at $200 night in summer, $150 a night in the off-season.

BED & BREAKFASTS Water's Edge Inn (843-588-9800; innat follybeach.com), 79 West 2nd Street, Folly Beach. Eight guest rooms and two villas are available in this relatively new property on the Folly River. The inn is walking distance to most restaurants and shops on Folly's main drag. There also is a golf cart shuttle to take guests to the beach. Breakfast is included in the room rates as well as cocktails and light hors d'oeuvres in the evening. Rooms have mini refrigerators, whirlpool tubs, and screened porches or balconies. Rooms are $230–280 a night in summer; villas are $400–500 a night. The inn is $130–230 a night in the off-season, while villas drop to $300–400.

HOTELS ☃ **The Tides** (843-588-6464; tidesoffolly.com), 1 Center Street, Folly Beach. For location, you cannot beat this hotel. Located on the water in the center of town, guests can walk to every restaurant and shop in Folly, and it's just a short stroll to a bicycle rental that will put the whole island under your wheels. The Folly Beach pier where dances are held during the summer is right outside the hotel's door. Formerly a Holiday Inn, the Tides underwent an extensive renovation with its name change that included a great new oceanfront bar and restaurant, Blu. Pets are welcome for an $85 fee. Room rates are about $200 a night in shoulder seasons and $300 a night in summer. There is a heated pool for year-round swimming.

✴ Where to Eat

DINING OUT Fat Hen (843-559-9090; thefathen.com), 140 Maybank Highway, Johns Island. Open daily for dinner 5:30–10; also 10–2:30 for Sunday brunch. Bar opens at 4 PM. The Fat Hen combines French and Lowcountry cuisines for unique flavors, such as the blue cheese bacon coleslaw; the sautéed shrimp and crab with

RESORTS

THE SANCTUARY

You can feel yourself begin to exhale as you approach **the Sanctuary** (800-576-1570; thesanctuary.com) on Kiawah Island. The luxury hotel and spa are revealed by bits through the trees as you pull up the drive. It really looks and feels like a sanctuary in the middle of nowhere.

The hotel was rated Five Diamonds by AAA/CAA in 2010 for the fourth consecutive year. It is one of the most luxurious hotels in the state and comes with an equally luxurious price: $299–750 a night, depending on room type and season. The 3,100-square-foot presidential suite is $4,500 a night.

If the price seems off-putting, there are opportunities for deals. Booking a room during the week in January or February might be the best way to sample this hotel without breaking the bank. Specials are featured on the website, or you can call to see what kind of deal the hotel is willing to make.

It's best to plan to spend all your time at the Sanctuary if you visit. The hotel is on Kiawah Island, a bit removed from the hustle and bustle of Charleston. Amenities include indoor and outdoor pools, a fitness center, spa, and salon, as well as two restaurants and a bar indoors and one restaurant and bar outside.

spicy hoppin' john (black-eyed peas with rice); or flounder Niçoise—sautéed in brown butter with fresh herbs, lemon capers, and olives and served over bacon cheese grits. Dinner entrées $14–21. Brunch is $8–15. With a wonderful wine list, this is the perfect place for a celebration. The large round table in the main dining area seats 8 to 10. I highly recommend it.

Boathouse at Breach Inlet (843-886-8000; boathouserestau rants.com), 101 Palm Boulevard, Isle of Palms. Open for lunch 11–2 Tuesday through Sunday; open daily at 5 for dinner. The Boathouse has views of the Ocean and the tidal creek leading to the Intracoastal Waterway. Arrive early for cocktails and spectacular sunset views from the rooftop Crow Bar. Dinner entrées range from $17 for a seafood pasta dish to $30 for steak and lobster.

Sea Island Grill & Lounge (843-886-2200; wilddunes.com), 4600 Palm Boulevard, Isle of Palms. Open daily at 11 for lunch,

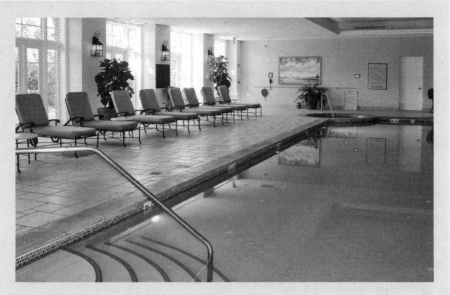

INDOOR POOL AT THE SANCTUARY, KIAWAH ISLAND

The island has two dozen tennis courts and five golf courses, including The Ocean Course by Pete Dye that was home of the 1991 Ryder Cup, the 2007 Senior PGA Championship, and will host the 2012 PGA Championship.

Of course, the best amenity of all is the Atlantic Ocean and a gently sloping white sand beach perfect for strolling year-round.

dinner 6–10 Tuesday through Saturday. Located in the Boardwalk Inn at Wild Dunes Resort, the Sea Island Grill offers Lowcountry specialties and local seafood dishes. Small dinner plates from $8 for beef carpaccio to $15 for a crabcake and large plates up to $26 for tempura softshell crab.

EATING OUT Crab Shack (843-588-3080; crabshacks.com), 26 Center Street, Folly Beach. Open daily 11 AM–2 AM year-round. My favorite place to eat at Folly, the

Crab Shack advertises that it's "shacktacular"—and I don't think they overstate. Their classic fried seafood plates are enough for two to share, as are their Lowcountry boils. The raw bar provides all the cold boiled shrimp and raw oysters you can eat. In January many menu items are $9.99 as part of their locals appreciation month. But don't worry, they won't check the address on your license to see if you're really a local; just tell them you know Ron. In-season, seafood platters can run up to $20.

CRAB SHACK, FOLLY BEACH

They also have Southern favorites like shrimp and grits and some of the best fried green tomatoes I've ever had. Oh, and have a Lowcountry lemonade. You won't regret it, but I recommend just the one.

Bowen's Island (843-795-2757; bowensislandrestaurant.com), 1870 Bowens Island Road, James Island. Open 5–10 Tuesday through Saturday. This unassuming pile of cinder blocks has been drawing people to its simply prepared, simply delicious seafood since the end of World War II. A fire in 2006 swept through the old place, doing thousands of dollars of damage (or improvements, depending on your impression of the large stack of broken television sets that filled one wall). The place soon reopened, and the oyster cook is still dumping shovels full of roasted goodness on newspaper-covered tables. Eat all you can for $22. The shrimp are off nearby boats and are lightly breaded and fried, $11 for a quarter pound, $15 for a half pound. Fried fish is $10.

Taco Boy (843-588-9761; taco boy.net), 15 Center Street, Folly Beach. Open daily 11 AM–2 AM. This recent addition to Folly's restaurant row has inexpensive seafood tacos for $3–4 each, super margaritas, and an overall fun, loud music atmosphere.

Lost Dog Café (843-588-9669; lostdogfollybeach.com), 106 West Huron Avenue, Folly Beach. Open daily at 6:30 AM for breakfast and lunch. This is the best cup of coffee you will have at Folly Beach. The breakfast here is fantastic, especially the fresh-baked muffins and cinnamon rolls. The creamy shrimp and grits is the most expensive breakfast item at $10. Most lunch dishes are also less than $10, with the best selection of vegetarian options you will find at Folly.

Planet Follywood (843-588-7380), 32-A Center Street, Folly Beach. Opens at 11 AM Wednesday through Monday. They start at 8 AM on weekends with a fantastic breakfast, but don't open till 3 PM on Tuesday. It seems like I always hit this place on the way out of town as sort of a good-bye to the beach. But if I'm staying a whole week, I usually get take-out burgers from them at least once. All menu items are less than $10.

The Mustard Seed (843-762-0072; dinewithsal.com/mustard), 1970 Maybank Highway, Charleston. Open Monday through Saturday 11–2:30 for lunch and 5–10 for dinner. The Mustard Seed is the kind of place where you feel like they are looking out for you. All the menu items come with a healthy helping of fresh veggies, and many options are vegetarian. There are no fewer than a dozen entrée salad options. When I eat here, I think flavor. The black bean cakes are fantastic, and the fettuccine carbonara has bacon and sweet peas. If you are looking for a unique sandwich, try the fried green tomato and salmon BLT. Most lunch items are $10 or less, while dinner goes up to $20 for a filet.

✎ **The Lettered Olive** (843-886-2200; wilddunes.com), 4600 Palm Boulevard, Isle of Palms. Open daily for breakfast 6:30–11 AM and dinner 6–10 PM. This family-friendly restaurant has an extensive children's menu that includes the standard grilled cheese and chicken tenders, but also offers a pasta dish and a seafood dish for more sophisticated palates with small stomachs. Breakfast buffet is $15. All children's dinner items under $10, all adult items under $20.

✳ Entertainment

MUSIC VENUES Sand Dollar Social Club (843-588-9498), 7 Center Street, Folly Beach. Open noon–2 AM Monday through Saturday, 1 PM–2 AM Sunday. This place is also known as "The Dollar" and purports to be a private club, but it's only $1 to join. Inside you will find cold beer, coin-operated pool tables, live music, and an odd collection of tourists, locals, and college students. Open your mind and your wallet, drinks are cash-only.

✳ Selective Shopping

Freshfields Village (843-768-6491; freshfieldsvillage.com), Village Green Lane, Johns Island. Most stores are open 10–6 Monday through Saturday, with limited hours or closed on Sunday. Shops include: **Aubergine Home Collection Inc.** (843-768-5554; auberginehome.com). Aubergine makes custom bedding and home accessories. **Carolina Clay Gallery** (843-243-0043; carolinaclaygallery.com). Owners Adi and Janet Sbihli retired to Seabrook

Island in 2000 and opened their gallery when Freshfields Village opened in 2004. Born out of their love of collecting pottery, the gallery offers great selections of gifts and art for your collection. **Indigo Books** (843-768-2255; freshfieldsvillage.com/shop/indigo -books). This popular independent bookstore specializes in books on local history and culture as well as stocking recent releases, children's books, games, cards, and gifts. If you are unsure of what to read during your vacation, owners Linda and Nat Malcolm also specialize in recommendations. **Sea-Coast Sports and Outfitters** (843-768-8486; seacoastsports .com). SeaCoast sells all the clothes and much of the equipment you will need to play golf and tennis, fish, paddle, bike, and surf during your vacation. **Newton Farms** (843-243-3276; newtonfarms.net). Open daily 7 AM–11 PM. This gourmet grocery store has the ambience of an open-air market with pastries and breads, full-service meat and seafood counters, made-to-order sandwiches, and fresh flowers. The store also offers catering services.

Rosebank Farms (843-768-9139; rosebankfarms.com), 4455 Betsy Kerrison Parkway, Johns Island. Open daily. Rosebank Farms has some of the best fresh veggies and seafood in the area. Get here early for the best selection. They usually open around 9 and have more limited hours as the seasons change. Gretchen says it's best to call ahead to see if the veggie stand is open.

Bohicket Marina (843-768-1280; bohicket.com), 1880 Andell Bluff Boulevard, Johns Island. The Village at Bohicket Marina has restaurants and shops, including **Doin' the Charleston** (843-243-9292; dointhecharleston.net), open 10–6 Monday through Wednesday and Saturday; until 9 PM on Thursday and Friday; noon–5 on Sunday. Hours limited in January and February. The shop sells coffees, grits, rice, and other Southern foods. They also make gift baskets and ship anywhere.

Crosby's Seafood (795-4049), 2223 Folly Road, Folly Beach. Open daily 6 AM–7 PM. This is the freshest shrimp and oysters you will find anywhere. I also love their clams and mussels. Just give the store a call to make sure they have enough for your party or maybe call a day in advance if you have something special you want.

✳ Special Events

SPRING *April:* **Lowcountry Cajun Festival** (843-795-4386; ccprc.com), 861 Riverland Drive, Charleston. This festival is held every year at James Island County Park to celebrate Louisiana Lowcountry living. Zydeco music blasts through the park as restaurants break out their best Cajun and Creole cooking.

SUMMER *June–October:* **Shaggin' on the Pier**. (843-795-4386; ccprc.com), Folly Beach pier. Selected dates over the summer, 7–11 PM. The Folly Beach pier offers visitors a glimpse back in time when beach music ruled the beach and everyone was doing the state dance, the Shag. Admission is $8 for locals and $10 for visitors. Eats and drinks are available at a restaurant and shop on the pier.

WINTER *January:* **A Taste of Folly Beach Festival** (843-513-1836; cityoffollybeach.com), Center Street, Folly Beach. All the restaurants put their best food offerings on the street for visitors get a taste. There's a chili competition where anyone with a spoon can be a judge, a hot-dog-eating contest at Bert's Market, and live music. It's worth the drive out—and if you're lucky like me, they hold it the week you are at the beach anyway.

INLAND AREAS

MOUNT PLEASANT, WEST ASHLEY, SUMMERVILLE, MONCKS CORNER

The other side of Charleston encompasses where most of the people of Charleston live and conduct their daily lives. Not everyone can afford to live at the beaches or downtown. But this backside of the city, if you will, really has some down-home flavor and is a little more laid-back than you might find in the city proper.

It also has much of the area's history, from Plantation Row—SC 61, also known as Ashley River Road—to the original settlement where Europeans dropped anchor at Charles Towne Landing.

Mount Pleasant is home to much of the area's shrimping fleet, and Summerville is home to one of the winningest football coaches ever. Summerville High School's John McKissick opens the 2011 season with 586 career victories—the most by any football coach in any venue—and he's still on the sidelines in his 80s. The next winningest high school coach has about 100 fewer wins than McKissick, and the winningest active NCAA football coach, Joe Paterno, got his 401st win in the 2010–11 season.

Summerville also is home to the Flowertown Festival and has a rare Five Diamond inn and Five Diamond restaurant in the Woodlands. Open for weekend stays and dining, the peaceful resort is just one way to recharge your batteries here. The other is with a Trappist order of Roman Catholic monks, who invite you to come share their solitude and silence. While I cannot imagine an hour, much less a weekend or week without speaking, those who have done it say, very quietly, that it was a spiritual experience.

GUIDANCE Summerville Visitors Center (843-873-8535; visitsummer ville.com), 402 North Main Street, Summerville.

Mount Pleasant (843-884-8517; townofmountpleasant.com), 100 Ann Edwards Lane, Mount Pleasant. Open 8–4:30 Monday through Friday.

Berkeley County Chamber of Commerce (843-761-8238; berkeleysc .org), 1004 Old Highway 52, Moncks Corner.

Walterboro-Colleton Chamber of Commerce (843-549-9595; walter boro.org), 109 Benson Street, Walterboro. Open 9–5 Monday through Friday. The chamber is located in the "Old Jail," which looks like a miniature castle and is on the National Register of Historic Places.

GETTING HERE *By car:* These inland towns are all connected by Interstate 26 or 526, U.S. Highways 17 and 52, and SC 61.

By air: **Charleston International Airport** (843-767-7007; chs-airport .com) offers connections to several major U.S. airports and is served by carriers **Air Tran** (800-247-8726 or 678-254-7999; airtran.com), **American Eagle** (800-433-7300; aa.com), Continental Airlines (800-525-0280; continental.com), **Delta Air Lines** (800-221-1212; delta.com), **Northwest Airlines** (800-225-2525; nwa.com), **United Express** (800-241-6522; united.com), **US Airways** (800-428-4322; usairways.com).

By bus: **Charleston Greyhound Station** (843-744-4247; greyhound .com), 3610 Dorchester Road. Open seven days a week, 7:30 AM–10 PM. Greyhound offers passenger service from most U.S. cities. The bus station is 6 miles north of the visitors center in the heart of downtown. You will have to take a taxi or a city bus to get there.

By train: **Amtrak** (800-872-7245; amtrak.com), 4565 Gaynor Avenue, North Charleston. Open 4 AM–noon and 4–11:30 PM daily. Trains from the northeast stop in Charleston at 7 and 9:30 PM daily; from the south, they stop at 5 and 10 AM.

GETTING AROUND Generally speaking, a private car is the best way to go.

WHEN TO COME This area won't get the ocean breezes that make Charleston's beaches so bearable in summertime. If you must come in August, bring plenty of patience and drink lots of water, because it will be hot, sticky, and all the other people visiting in August will be driving next to you. These areas are very busy just from the hustle and bustle of daily lives that includes a lot of truck traffic in and out of the ports, so high tourist season can overload the roads. The spring is beautiful when the azaleas pop out and temperatures are still cool in the evenings. Early summer also is good. The fall, likewise, is very pleasant. In the winter, some places may have limited hours.

MUSEUMS Slave Relic Museum (843-549-9130; slaverelics.org), 208 Carn Street, Walterboro. Open 9:30–5 Monday through Thursday, 10–6 Saturday. Admission is $6 for adults and $5 for children. Former New York antiques collector Danny Drain has spent more than a decade building his collection of 2,000 artifacts used by enslaved Africans. The museum he has created in an antebellum house also serves as a repository of historical documents and photographs for researchers. His collection is so big, it doesn't all fit in his displays, so he loans out pieces to other museums in the area and rotates his displays.

Patriots Point (866-831-1720; patriotspoint.org), 40 Patriots Point Road, Mount Pleasant. Open daily 9–6:30. Patriots Point is home to the Naval and Maritime Museum, the USS *Yorktown*, and the College of Charleston Sports Complex. It's also the best place to park for a walk over the Ravenel Bridge. The complex has a hotel, a golf course, and a marina, where you can rent a boat or take sailing lessons. The new Waterfront Park includes a Sweetgrass Cultural Arts Pavilion, a fishing pier, and a children's playground. Admission: adults $16; children ages 6–11 $9; retired/active-duty military $13; active-duty military in uniform get in for free.

HISTORIC SITES 𝄢 **Charles Towne Landing** (843-852-4200; charlestowne.org), 1500 Old Towne Road, Charleston. Open 9–5 daily. Admission: $5 adults; $3.25 seniors; $3 for ages 6–15; children 5 and

CHARLES TOWNE LANDING

SC Department of Parks, Recreation & Tourism, DiscoverSouthCarolina.com

under are free. Step back in time to South Carolina's first settlement, dating to 1670. The park opened in 1970 and was rebuilt in 2006. The 12-room interactive visitors center includes a digital dig; self-guided history trail tours come with audio. An ongoing archaeological dig at the site is open to the public, and replica 17th-century sailing ship the *Adventure* is moored in the Ashley River.

✄ **Middleton Place Plantation** (843-556-6020; middletonplace.org), 4300 Ashley River Road, Charleston. Open daily at 9 AM. One of several antebellum plantations that line the Ashley River west of the peninsula, Middleton Place was granted to Jacob Waight in 1675. The land passed through daughters till Mary Williams married Henry Middleton and began laying out the garden in 1741. The family home, outbuildings, and garden were burned just months before the South surrendered in 1865. Six years later, the first "tourists" came to see the ruins of the Middleton family. In 1886, the great Charleston earthquake further damaged the gardens. Restoration wouldn't begin for another 40 years. In 1952 the gardens were opened to visitors year-round, and in 1970 the home became a museum of plantation life. Today with a hotel and restaurant on the property, Middleton Place is a very popular wedding location as well as a tourist attraction. Eliza's House, a relic of the freedmen housing built following the war, still stands. Two tours daily focus on the history of African Americans on the plantation and throughout the state and the South. For the youngsters, the stableyards feature craft demonstrations by artisans dressed in period costumes as a weaver, cooper, carpenter, and blacksmith. The stableyards also are home to the same breeds of water buffalo, sheep, goats, hogs, and chickens that were raised at Middleton Place two centuries ago. Admission: adults $25; students $15; children 6–13, $10. Admission to the house museum is extra. There is a discount for buying your tickets online. Package deals are available, including one with a two-hour guided tour of the whole property.

Magnolia Plantation and Gardens (800-367-3517; magnoliaplantation .com), 3550 Ashley River Road, Charleston. Open daily 8–5:30. Hours vary slightly in winter. Founded by the Drayton family in 1676, this plantation along the Ashley River opened its doors to tourists in 1870 to view the flowers and plants in its famous gardens. Ticket prices vary depending on which tours you want to take. Admission: adult $43; ages 6–12, $38. Visitors can get the 30-minute Plantation House Tour, 45-minute tram tour of the lakes, woodlands, and marshes, 45-minute boat ride exploring 125 acres of rice fields, and a 45-minute tour that discusses Magnolia's street of slave cabins, which were occupied well into the 20th century and have been restored to document African American life at Magnolia Plantation. **The Audubon Swamp Garden** also is available as a stand-alone tour for less than $10. The black-water cypress and tupelo swamp once was used for rice cultivation. Now the whole 60 acres is accessible by boardwalks and bridges. A self-guided walk takes about 45 minutes.

Drayton Hall (843-769-2600; draytonhall.org), 3380 Ashley River Road, Charleston. Open daily 8:30–4 with house tours every half hour. Opens an hour later in the summer. Built between 1738 and 1742, this is the oldest preserved plantation house in the United States open to the public. Drayton Hall is as it was when built with no electricity, heating, air, or plumbing and is a National Trust Historic Site. Admission is in the $10–15 range depending on whether you want to tour the house; there are discounts for teens and children. The guided house tour is one of the best in the area and includes a discussion of the influences of African Americans at Drayton Hall from the 18th to the 20th centuries.

Boone Hall Plantation (843-216-1032; boonehallplantation.com), 1235 Long Point Road, Mount Pleasant. Open 9–5 Monday through Saturday, 1–4 Sunday from Labor Day to March 21. Spring and summer 8:30–6:30 Monday through Saturday and 1–5 Sunday. Open to the public since 1956, Boone Hall is still a working plantation, growing strawberries, tomatoes, and pumpkins. Set at the end of an oak-lined drive, Boone Hall takes visitors back to another time. A new exhibit called Black History in America is set in eight of the original slave cabins at the plantation and tells about slave daily life, emancipation, the struggle for civil rights, and the present day. The exhibit is included in the price of admission to the plantation. Admission: adults $17.50; ages 6–12, $7.50; those 5 and younger are admitted free.

Mepkin Abbey (843-761-8509; mepkinabbey.org) 1098 Mepkin Abbey Road, Moncks Corner. Open for tours 9–4:30 Tuesday through Saturday, 1–4:30 Sunday. Guided tours at 11:30 and 3. Established in 1949, this community of Roman Catholic monks belongs to the Trappist order; they live in silence. The monks sell mushrooms and garden compost from their own farm as well as candies, preserves, and honey from other Trappist abbeys. The abbey also offers weeklong and weekend retreats for those seeking spiritual renewal. Guests dine with the monks, eating the same vegetarian diet and observing the silence. Rooms provided include a bed, desk, and reading chair. Most rooms have a private bath with bed linens, towels, and soap. Married couples can attend together. Advance reservations are required, as is prior notice of cancellation. Donations are accepted. The abbey can accommodate nine people at any one time.

✴ To Do

Classic Charleston Sailing (843-388-9242; classiccharlestonsailing.com), docked at the Charleston Harbor Resort Marina of Patriots Point in Mount Pleasant. By reservation only. One of the best ways to see

Charleston is from the water. These cruises can provide a dolphin-eye view of the Battery, the Ravenel Bridge, and other sites around the harbor. You can be a true cruiser or a sailor, helping out as little or as much as you want. Prices start at $375 for a three-hour tour for up to six guests; $425 for a sunset cruise and $550 for a bed & breakfast package that includes evening sail, overnight accommodations, and breakfast.

Carolina Heritage Outfitters (843-563-5051; canoesc.com), US 15, Canadys. Open daily 9–5. Reservations are required for these tours, which take paddlers on guided or self-guided trips down the Edisto River. Overnight trips include a stay in a wood tree house in a private wildlife refuge. Tree houses have a tiny kitchen and a sleeping loft 16 feet above the riverbank. There is no running water or electricity. Bathrooms are outhouses on ground level. The trip is really one of a kind and is for the nature lover. The day trip is a 10-mile paddle at $30 per person; an overnight trip is 22 miles long. Tree houses are $125 per person per night and include the cost of canoe rental and a shuttle to the put-in point. You provide your own food and drink. Primitive campsites are also available for overnight trips. Carolina Heritage can customize day or overnight excursions for large groups or even up to 10 days on the water for those really wanting to get back to nature.

Coastal Expeditions Inc. (843-884-7684; coastalexpeditions.com), 514-B Mill Street, Mount Pleasant. Open daily 9–6. Coastal Expeditions offers full- and half-day kayak tours and rentals from barrier islands to blackwater swamps. All guides are trained on the water and are naturalists. Tour rates vary. Kayak rentals $50 a day for singles, $60 for a tandem.

Nature Adventures Kayak, Canoe and Hiking Outfitters (800-673-0679; natureadventuresoutfitters.com), 1900 Iron Swamp Road, Awendaw. Open daily 7–7. This company offers everything for the outdoors person—hiking, canoes, kayaks, guides. Tours are about $40 for two hours; $90 for all day. The Shem Creek and Crab Bank tours offer the best opportunity for spotting dolphins and other wildlife. Kayak rentals are about $50 a day for singles, $60 for tandems. Paddleboards are $40 a day.

GOLF Charleston National Country Club (843-884-4653; charleston nationalgolf.com), 1360 National Drive, Mount Pleasant. Designed by Rees Jones (6,975 yards, par 72), Charleston National is open to the public year-round. Rates vary widely ($38–69) depending on the season, day of the week, and time of day.

Dunes West Golf Club (843-856-9000; golfduneswest.com), 3535 Wando Plantation Way, Mount Pleasant. Designed by Arthur Hills (6,859 yards, par 72). Rates vary ($37–95) depending on the season, day of the week, and time of day.

Patriots Point Links (843-881-0042; patriotspointlinks.com), 1 Patriots Point Road, Mount Pleasant. Designed by Willard Byrd (6,838 yards, par 72). Rates vary ($40–85) based on the season, day of the week, and time of day.

RiverTowne Country Club (843-216-3777; rivertownecountryclub .com), 1700 RiverTown Country Club Drive, Mount Pleasant. Designed by Arnold Palmer (7,244 yards, par 72). Rates vary ($50–96) based on the season, day of the week, and time of day.

The Golf Club at Wescott Plantation (843-871-2135; wescottgolf.com), 5000 Westcott Club Drive, Summerville. Designed by Michael Hurdzan (7,210 yards, par 72). Rates vary ($27–50) depending on day of the week and time of day.

Legend Oaks Plantation Golf Course (843-821-4077; legendoaks golf.com), 118 Legend Oaks Way, Summerville. Designed by Scott W. Pool (6,974 yards, par 72). Rates vary depending on the season, day of the week, and time of day.

The Links at Stono Ferry (843-763-1817; stonoferrygolf.com), 4812 Stono Links Drive, Hollywood. Designed by Ron Garl (6,701 yards, par 72). Rates vary ($54–87) depending on the season, day of the week, and time of day.

TENNIS Family Circle Tennis Center (843-856-7900; familycircle cup.com), 161 Seven Farms Drive, Charleston. Open year-round except the week of the Family Circle Cup women's tennis tournament in April. Pro shop hours: 8–8 Monday through Friday; closes at 5 PM Saturday through Sunday. You can play where the pros play on one of 13 clay courts, available at $15 an hour for nonmembers, or four hard courts at $10. Lessons are $60 an hour; ball machine rental is $25 an hour and includes court time.

✳ Green Space

PARKS ✐ **Palmetto Islands County Park & Splash Island Waterpark** (843-795-4386; ccprc.com), 444 Needlerush Parkway, Mount Pleasant. Open daily at 8 AM, closing around sunset. It's $1 to get in. Splash Island is $7 for adults and $5 for children shorter than 42 inches; $3 for seniors. This 943-acre park has plenty to offer beside the water park, which has a 200-foot slide and a Cyclone water ride. The rest of the park is built in a tropical setting with bike paths, nature trails, boardwalks, and picnic sites. There is a playground, and pedal boat and bike rentals are available.

✐ **Wannamaker County Park & Whirlin' Waters Adventure Waterpark** (843-572-7275; ccprc.com), 8888 University Boulevard, North

Charleston. Open daily at 8, closing around sunset. It's $1 to get in the park; the water park costs $20 for adults, $15 for children shorter than 48 inches, and $5 for seniors. This park has more than 1,000 acres of woodlands, wetlands, and water. A freshwater lagoon is excellent for the pedal boats and kayaks that are available for rent. Bikes are also available, and there are paved and unpaved trails for riding. The water park has an area for toddlers, a 350-foot speed slide, three tube slides, and a lazy river.

✔ **Cypress Gardens** (843-553-0515; cypressgardens.info), 3030 Cypress Gardens Road, Moncks Corner. Open daily 9–5. Admission: $10 for ages 12–65, $9 for seniors, $5 for children 6–12, and free for children younger than 5. The guided boat tour through the swamp is $5 and requires a reservation. Self-guided paddling boat tours are free with park admission. This beautiful park offers visitors an up-close look at a black-water cypress swamp. Grounds are beautifully landscaped, and don't be surprised if you see the occasional bride and groom. The Butterfly House lets the little ones see all stages of the butterfly's life from the egg laying through the hatching. There are more than 3 miles of hiking trail through the swamp, and if you don't see any in the wild, there is a reptile center to show you all the things that live in the swamp.

✔ **The Center for Birds of Prey** (843-971-7474; thecenterforbirdsof prey.org), 4872 Seewee Road, Awendaw. Open Thursday through Saturday 10–5. Guided walking tours are available at 10:30 and 2 with flight demonstrations at 11:30 and 3. Admission is $12 adults 19 and older; $10 for youths ages 6–18. Younger children admitted free. This fascinating facility provides medical care for injured raptors but also gives visitors a chance to see birds of prey in a natural setting. Located on 152 acres near the Cape Romain Wildlife Refuge and the Francis Marion National Forest, the center has nearly 30 species of birds from around the world. The flight demonstrations are truly stunning. This is a great stop for the whole family and it's just a short drive up US 17 from Mount Pleasant.

Cape Romain National Wildlife Refuge (843-928-3264; fws.gov/cape romain), 5801 US 17, Awendaw. Open Tuesday through Saturday 9–5. Free admission. A visit to this 66,000-acre refuge starts at the Sewee Visitor and Environmental Education Center, which showcases all the wildlife and ecosystems found at Cape Romain and the nearby Francis Marion National Forest. Visitors also can see live red wolves that live at the refuge and walk along nature trails both at the center and on Bulls Island.

Coastal Expeditions Inc. (843-884-7684; coastalexpeditions.com), 514-B Mill Street, Mount Pleasant, provides the ferry service to Bulls Island for the rest of the refuge. Ferries run twice a day at 9:30 and 12:30 with return trips arriving at noon and 4. The ferry is $30 for adults 13 and older; $15 for children. Visitors can take a picnic lunch and bicycles—and definitely pack your camera for all the wildlife you will see up close.

Caw Caw Interpretive Center (843-889-8898; ccprc.com), 5200 Savannah Highway, Ravenel. Open Wednesday through Sunday 9–5. Admission is $1 for everyone over 2 years old. This park has hundreds of acres of rice fields and 8 miles of walking trails that include a boardwalk and interpretive stops along the way. Morning bird walks are at 8:30 on Wednesday and Saturday. The learning center also has a picnic area.

Colleton State Park (843-538-8206; southcarolinaparks.com), 147 Wayside Lane, Canadys. Open daily 9–6 with extended hours during Daylight Saving Time. If canoeing or kayaking is your thing, this is the park you need to know. The headquarters for the Edisto River Canoe and Kayak Trail, this park also is home to Edisto Riverfest each June. The park is an excellent put-in for boating on the Edisto River, and it has a cypress swamp nature trail, campgrounds, and a ball field.

Givhans Ferry State Park (843-873-0692; southcarolinaparks.com), 746 Givhans Ferry Road, Ridgeville. Open 9–9 from April through September; closes earlier during fall and winter weekdays. Admission is $2 for adults ages 15 and older, and $1.25 for South Carolina seniors. This park—part of the 56-mile Edisto River Canoe and Kayak Trail—is an ideal location to start a paddle down the Edisto River. It is the stopping point for a very popular 21-mile paddle from the Colleton State Park. But for the landlubber, there is also a mountain bike trail and campground, and rustic cabins are available for rent.

Barnwell State Park (803-284-2212; southcarolinaparks.com), State Park Road, Blackville. Open daily 9–6, or 9–9 summer weekends. Free. This small state park boasts prime inland fishing for largemouth bass, crappie, bluegill, and catfish in its two lakes, one of them 16 acres and the other 8 acres.

FORESTS & **Audubon Center at Francis Beidler Forest** (843-462-2150; beidlerforest.com), 336 Sanctuary Road, Harleyville. Open Tuesday through Sunday 9–5. Admission is less than $10, with discounts for children, seniors, and National Audubon Society members. This forest is located in a lovely area known as Four Holes Swamp, not to be confused with its cousin Hell-Hole Swamp located some 40 miles away in the Francis Marion National Forest. Some of the trees in this 16,000-acre bald cypress, tupelo gum swamp forest are 1,000 years old. Visitors can glimpse this natural beauty from a 1.75-mile self-guided boardwalk trail that is handicapped accessible. The center also offers canoe trips and guided walks by reservation.

Francis Marion National Forest (843-928-3368; fs.fed.us.gov), 5821 US 17, Awendaw. Some areas require a $3 daily parking fee per car. The Sewee Visitor and Environmental Education Center is open Tuesday through Saturday 9–5. The center focuses on the natural and cultural history of the forestland; there is a freshwater pond for fishing as well as a mile-long trail and butterfly garden. This portion of the Francis Marion forest was devastated by Hurricane Hugo in 1989. Much of the past two decades have been spent helping the forest rebuild itself and reducing the new dense vegetation that is prone to forest fires. The forest is home to a variety of species, but most important is a haven for the endangered red-cockaded woodpecker. It is nearly 300,000 acres and offers visitors a variety of things to see and do, such as a stroll through the I'on Swamp—a 2.5-mile interpretive trail that takes hikers through an 18th-century rice field that now teems with wildlife such as the wood duck, great blue herons, and the occasional river otter. The park also has a boat launch, rifle ranges, and trails for biking and motorcycling.

✳ Lodging

INNS The Inn at Middleton Place (843-556-0500; theinnatmiddletonplace.com), 4290 Ashley River Road, Charleston. From the outside, the inn looks like a series of dorms, but on the inside, they are simple luxury. Floor-to-ceiling windows make guests feel like they are living in the woods, with beautiful views of the Ashley River and the immense grounds of Middleton Place plantation. The 55 spacious rooms have fireplace, hardwood floors, and paneled walls and sitting areas. Guests have the run of the plantation; bikes and horseback riding are available as well as kayaking and canoeing in the river. Breakfast is served each morning at the inn, and the nearby Middleton Place Restaurant serves lunch and dinner. Rooms start at $140 a

A ROOM AT MIDDLETON PLACE PLANTATION INN

night. The Ashley River Room, a suite, goes for up to $500 depending on the season.

Shem Creek Inn (843-881-1000; shemcreekinn.com), 1401 Shrimp Boat Lane, Mount Pleasant. This great hotel sits right on Shem Creek, and the large pool overlooks the waterway. The inn is surrounded by great restaurants that are an easy walk; or you can take a quick hop over the Ravenel Bridge to downtown. The hotel has a 1950s fishing village feel and just 50 rooms, some of which were renovated in 2011. All rooms have a private balcony, some overlooking the marsh, some overlooking the creek. Rooms are around $200 a night and come with a complimentary continental breakfast. The inn also offers packages with a nearby spa and kayak outfitter.

BED & BREAKFAST
The Hampton House Bed & Breakfast (843-542-9498; hampton housebandb.com), 500 Hampton Street, Walterboro. One of the area's smaller B&Bs, the Hampton House offers just three rooms at $125 or $145 a night. Guests can enjoy a full country breakfast in the dining room or poolside. The home also boasts a permanent exhibit of more than 50 dollhouses, toy kitchens, and paper and antique dolls.

CAMPGROUNDS/CABINS
Givhans Ferry State Park (843-873-0692; southcarolinaparks.com), 746 Givhans Ferry Road, Ridge-

ville. You cannot beat this deal. These two-bedroom cabins sleep six with heat, air-conditioning, bath and bed linens, cooking utensils, and television for $50–70 a night, depending on the season. A three-night minimum stay is required from April through September, and pets are not allowed. Cabins sit on a bluff overlooking the Edisto River.

Barnwell State Park (803-284-2212; southcarolinaparks.com), State Park Road, Blackville. Open daily 9–6, or 9–9 summer weekends. This small state park has five furnished cabins that have heating and air-conditioning and are supplied with linens, basic cooking and eating utensils, coffeemaker, and television. The cabins are located between the park's two lakes and can sleep six people. They rent for $48–60 a night depending on the season. (See the sidebar on state park cabin rentals.) Pets are not permitted in the cabins or cabin area.

✳ Where to Eat
DINING OUT The Dining Room at Woodlands Inn (800-774-9999; woodlandsinn.com), 125 Parsons Road, Summerville. The Dining Room is one of the finest restaurants in South Carolina and serves lunch and dinner 11–9:30 Wednesday through Saturday, breakfast starting at 7 Thursday through Sunday. Menu changes daily. Entrées $25–32, and there also are five- and six-course tasting menus.

RESORTS

THE WOODLANDS INN

Tucked away in the woods in small-town South Carolina is a gem—the **Woodlands Inn** (843-308-2115; woodlandsinn.com), 125 Parsons Road, Summerville. It is the only place in South Carolina that has earned the AAA/CAA Five Diamond designation for both its accommodations and its restaurant. Most of the Woodlands guests also are restaurant customers and visa versa.

Located in the woods of a little town northwest of Charleston, the Woodlands is a relaxed resort with pool, tennis courts, and spa rooms. Guests can choose one of several large common rooms to rock, relax, read a book, play a board game, or maybe check the insides of their eyelids.

The inn is located in a restored 1906 mansion on 42 acres that was the summer home for Robert Parsons and his family. It was sold to botanist and internationally known chess player Alan White in 1939. During World War II, White would invite soldiers and debutantes to the estate for lavish parties. White left the home to Ruth Gadsden, a prominent member of Summerville society, and she lived there the rest of her life.

The home gained life in the mid-1980s as the Gadsden Manor Inn, but closed after just three years. In 1995 it reopened as a luxury hotel and dining room and has been a Five Diamond selection almost the whole time.

WATER'S EDGE RESTAURANT AND CABANA, SHEM CREEK, MOUNT PLEASANT

Water's Edge (843-884-4074; waters-edge-restaurant.com), 1407 Shrimp Boat Lane, Mount Pleasant. Open daily at 11 AM; closes when you're done eating. There are lots of restaurants on Shem Creek, and each has its specialty. The Water's Edge is comfortable, affordable, and most important tasty. Dinner prices max out around $30 for a filet mignon. For lunch, have the shrimp salad. For dinner, any seafood dish will do, but the crabcakes are especially good.

WOODLANDS INN, SUMMERVILLE

In 2006 the inn was bought by Salamander Hospitality, and all the rooms and commons areas were refurbished and updated.

Rooms are available Wednesday through Saturday night, when the restaurant is open. The Dining Room also serves Sunday brunch. Room rates start around $200 a night, and the inn offers several packages with restaurant meals and spa treatments.

EATING OUT Red's Ice House (843-388-0008; redsicehouse .com), 98 Church Street, Mount Pleasant. Open daily 11–1 AM. Red's has fish sandwiches for less than $10 and all-you-can-eat crab legs for $25, but the real reason to come here is to sit on the deck, drink your favorite adult beverage, and watch the dolphins play in Shem Creek.

Shem Creek Bar & Grill (843-884-8102; shemcreekbarandgrill .com), 508 Mill Street, Mount Pleasant. Open daily starting at 11:30 AM. Lunch is about $10 and offers all the fried or grilled seafood you could want. Shem Creek also serves jambalaya and étouffée. You can get yourself a seafood boil from $20 for shrimp to $30 for king crab. Most dinners are less than $20. There is a wonderful view of the creek from most seats. They know their oysters here, so give them a try.

The Wreck (843-884-0052; wreck rc.com), 106 Haddrell Street,

RED'S ICE HOUSE, SHEM CREEK, MOUNT PLEASANT

Mount Pleasant. Open daily for dinner starting at 5:30. The owners of The Wreck will tell you straight up, they don't have a sign and they don't look like a restaurant. But the food tells another story. Most dishes are under $20, except the stone crab claws ($25 for a pound)—and that's what you should have. They bring you an iron pipe to use as your claw cracker. There is no frou-frou here, just good food, cold beer, and nature.

Buddy Roe's Shrimp Shack (843-388-5270; buddyroesshrimp shack.com), 1528 Ben Sawyer Boulevard, Mount Pleasant. Open daily at 11:30. This is another on a short list of local seafood dives. Like The Wreck and Bowen's Island, there is very little extra here. Buddy Roe does make a commitment to serving nothing but locally caught shrimp. That means in different seasons, the shrimp may be a little different size and taste. Buddy Roe also puts a little twist on its crustaceans by tossing them in a variety of sauces like you would get on chicken wings. The sweet bourbon and hot bacon are local favorites. Buddy Roe also has great happy-hour prices ($2 beer). Lunch shrimp baskets are less than $10 and for dinner, less than $15. The menu includes other seafood items, burgers, and you gotta try the sweet potato fries.

R. B.'s Seafood (843-881-0466), 97 Church Street, Mount Pleasant. Open daily for lunch and dinner starting at 11:30. Most dishes are under $20. If you like ample fried seafood, this is your restaurant. Ronnie Boals has been working in the restaurant business in Shem Creek for more than 30 years, and he knows what you want. His place may look new, but it was rebuilt in 2003 after a fire. This is a favorite bar/hangout for locals, especially those celebrating a birthday. Menu favorites include the raw oyster plate and a better-than-average shrimp and grits. The menu has a wide range from steaks to sashimi tuna to pastas. The view cannot be beat: over Shem Creek and pointed in the right direction for great sunsets from the deck. There is parking or you can pull up your boat or kayak right on the creek.

Duke's Barbecue (843-549-1446), 949 Robertson Boulevard, Walterboro. Open 11–9 Thursday through Saturday; Sunday for lunch only. Dukes is tucked away in the small inland town of Walter-

boro, sort of halfway to nowhere. They do the mustard-based barbecue sauce here, but you can also get four-alarm spicy red sauce. For $10 you get all you can eat at the buffet.

❋ Selective Shopping

People, Places & Quilts (843-871-8872; ppquilts.com), 129 West Richardson Avenue, Summerville. Open 10–5:30 Monday through Friday, 10–5 Saturday. In addition to supplies that you need for quilting, this shop also sells locally made folk art and old and new quilts.

Art Central Gallery (843-871-0297; artcgalleryltd.com), 130 Central Avenue, Summerville. Open 10–5 Monday through Saturday. The cooperative offers a varied selection of paintings, photography, jewelry, pottery, and woodcarving.

R. B.'S SEAFOOD, SHEM CREEK, MOUNT PLEASANT

Hometown Bath & Body (843-761-3113; htbab.com), 1008 Old Highway 52 South, Moncks Corner. Open 10–6 Monday through Friday, 10–4 Saturday. Everything from women's clothing to gifts, candles, and jewelry.

Marigolds (843-851-2828; marigoldssummerville.com), 145 Central Avenue, Summerville. Open 10–6 Monday through Friday, 10–4 Saturday. This corner shop has a mix of antique furniture, linens, art, silver, and glassware mixed in with newer merchandise.

Antiques shopping in downtown Walterboro. After lunching at Duke's, stroll through these downtown shops to work off your meal. There are 11 antiques shops, including **Albert's Attic** (843-549-9221), 545 East Washington Street, **Green Lady Gallery** (843-782-4569), 259 East Washington Street, and **Lowcountry Antiques** (843-549-2101), 251 East Washington Street.

MALLS, OUTLETS Mount Pleasant Towne Centre (843-216-9900; mtpleasanttownecentre.com), 1600 Palmetto Grande Drive, Mount Pleasant. Mall shopping outdoors.

✳ Special Events

SPRING *March:* ❧ **Flowertown Festival** (843-871-9622; flowertownfestival.com), South Main Street at West 5th Street, Sum-

merville. This family-friendly three-day festival in spring is timed with the blossoming of Azalea Park. Admission is free, and there are about 200 arts and crafts and food vendors. There is live entertainment, a tennis tournament, and a tour of historic homes and gardens. No alcohol and no pets allowed.

April: ❧ **Town of Mount Pleasant Blessing of the Fleet & Seafood Festival** (843-884-8517; townofmountpleasant.com), Memorial Waterfront Park, US 17. This event sends the shrimpers out with a blessing and a prayer for a bountiful, safe season. Free admission, free parking. Local seafood restaurants break out their best dishes, and there are loads of family-friendly events.

SUMMER *June:* **Sweetgrass Cultural Arts Festival** (843-856-9732; sweetgrassfestival.org), Mount Pleasant. This fest zeros in on the rich Gullah Geechee cultural heritage and provides a showcase of sweetgrass baskets in the Lowcountry. Enjoy gospel songs, praise dance, storytelling, drummers, and a waterslide.

Edisto Riverfest, Colleton State Park.

WINTER *January:* ❧ **Lowcountry Oyster Festival** (843-452-608; charlestonrestaurantassociation.com). This fund-raising event is held usually the last weekend in January at **Boone Hall Plantation** (843-216-1032; boone hallplantation.com), 1235 Long Point Road, Mount Pleasant. Events include oyster-shucking and -eating contests and there is live music, a kids' area with rides, and, of course, lots of food and beer from local restaurants. Tickets are usually around $10 to $15, with children younger than 10 admitted free. Pets and coolers not allowed. The annual event has raised more than $1 milion for a variety of charities in the Charleston area.

SUGGESTED ITINERARIES

W hen folks think of Charleston, they think of history and old homes, cobblestone streets and military battlements—and there is a lot of that. But Charleston also is a place of stunning natural beauty, from its beaches and tidal inlets to the wildlife refuges and national forests—all less than 30 minutes away. Then there are the areas of Charleston that combine both history and natural beauty, and those are the plantations along its rivers.

Charleston

PLANTATIONS If you're going to see Charleston's plantations, I recommend just picking one and seeing all it has to offer. Each is distinctive, but if you tried to absorb more than one on a single trip, they would tend to run together. **Middleton Place Plantation** (843-556-6020; middleton place.org), 4300 Ashley River Road, Charleston, is my favorite. It's where Spoleto wraps up each season with a band concert and fireworks. It is enormous and offers a variety of activities that would keep most kids entertained, such as kayaking and horseback riding. Plus with **Middleton Place Restaurant** (843-266-7477) and **The Inn at Middleton Place** (843-556-0500; theinnatmiddletonplace.com) on site, you could park your car and spend the whole weekend there. Guests at the hotel have the run of the plantation; bikes and horseback riding are available as well as kayaking and canoeing in the river. Breakfast is served each morning at the inn. You also are just about 45 minutes from one of the Lowcountry's best barbecue joints, **Duke's Barbecue** (843-549-1446), 949 Robertson Boulevard, Walterboro. An easy little drive due west toward Interstate 95 will bring you to Duke's. The buffet is less than $10.

The one thing that is missing from Middleton Place is that big *Gone with the Wind* Tara-looking home with the big white columns. For that, you will need to go to **Boone Hall Plantation** (843-216-1032; boonehallplantation .com), 1235 Long Point Road, Mount Pleasant. You can practically hear

Scarlett O'Hara saying "Fiddle-dee-dee" as you approach the house on a lane lined with giant 18th-century live oaks. Plan to spend several hours here with a house tour, coach tour, and strolling around the gardens. The butterfly pavilion will be a hit with the kids, and like all of the plantations, Boone Hall includes exhibits that show the harsh conditions that defined slave life and the struggle of Africans to gain their freedom.

DOWNTOWN There are a couple of ways to do downtown Charleston. There's the first-class way, which is very expensive, and then there is the trade-off way, where you choose either to sleep or to eat first-class, but for most of us, it really is difficult to do both. If you want to luxuriate in your hotel, there are: the Mills House Hotel (843-577-2400; millshouse.com), 115 Meeting Street; the Charleston Place Hotel (843-722-4900; charleston place.com), 205 Meeting Street; or the Wentworth Mansion (843-853-1886; wentworthmansion.com), 149 Wentworth Street. The Mills House is the least expensive of these three, the Charleston Place Hotel is the most ideally located, and the Wentworth Mansion is the most unique. If, however, you would rather dine in luxury, there's the Francis Marion Hotel (843-722-0600; francismarionhotel.com), 387 King Street, or the Market Pavilion Hotel (877-440-2250; marketpavilion.com), 225 East Bay Street. The Francis Marion is old but recently renovated. It sits in a slightly quieter area of downtown along the main shopping district of King Street about halfway between the market and the visitors center. The Market Pavilion is new and a bit pricier, and located where the best "action" is downtown. For romance, you could try the Ansonborough Inn (843-723-1655; ansonboroughinn.com), 21 Hasell Street, a little off the beaten path near the Market and easy walking distance to all the restaurants and bars.

Any of these would be a great jumping-off point for exploring downtown.

First things first. Check out **Charleston's Museum Mile** (charlestons museummile.org) to find a combo package of the historic sites and museums you want to see, and purchase your tickets in advance. It would be difficult to do them all in one day, so consider buying a package and spreading your visits out over a couple of days. The best package is the one dubbed **African-American Heritage**. It has the two museums you don't want to miss: the **Charleston Museum** (843-722-2996; charleston museum.org), 360 Meeting Street, and the **Gibbes Museum of Art** (843-722-2706, gibbesmuseum.org), 135 Meeting Street. You'll also find the wonderfully preserved **Aiken-Rhett House** (843-723-1159; historic charleston.org), 48 Elizabeth Street, as well as the **Old Slave Mart Museum** (843-958-6467; oldslavemart.org), 6 Chalmers Street—all for about $35.

Second, it may seem so very touristy, but try a carriage ride. **Old South Carriage Co.,** (843-723-9712; oldsouthcarriagetours.com), 14 Anson

Street. They are popular for a reason. A few years back, I had some friends on their first visit to Charleston and they wanted to do a carriage ride. We laughed, we scoffed, but we did it and enjoyed the heck out of it. Now, I do it at least every other year. It really is the best way to remind yourself of all the color and history of this amazing city that at one time was the largest in the colonies. (If air-conditioning and anti-malarial drugs had been invented earlier, Charleston would have been a rival for New York City.) If you are traveling in warm months, I recommend doing the carriage ride as early as possible in the morning. After you are done, get some water and cruise through the **City Market**. The sweetgrass ladies (and a few gentlemen) will be here. There are jewelry sellers and T-shirts at great prices, framed art, pottery, and bags of Charleston foodstuffs, like Lowcountry rice, 13-bean soups, and spices for gumbos.

Then it will be time for lunch. From the Market, turn right onto East Bay Street. **Magnolia's** (843-577-7771; magnolias-blossom-cypress.com), 185 East Bay Street, is still one of the best. It was considered the first in Charleston's restaurant renaissance in the 1990s and it still wows. The shrimp and grits are always good, as are the fried green tomatoes. After a carriage tour and the Market, this will simply continue your immersion in all things Southern.

From Magnolia's continue south on East Bay. To your left will be **Waterfront Park** (843-762-2172; ci.charleston.sc.us), Concord Street, and to your right will be the **Old Slave Mart Museum** (843-958-6467; oldslave mart.org), 6 Chalmers Street. Both are worth a look. From the Slave Mart, it's just a block to Broad Street and a series of art galleries and shops. At Meeting and Broad is a spot known as the Four Corners of the Law: city hall, the county courthouse, a federal courthouse, and St. Michael's church. You also are now on the Museum Mile, and it's time to find the locations you picked out and pay them a visit. But remember, you don't have to do them all in one day, because you are probably about ready for cocktails and dinner. If you're not staying at **Charleston Place Hotel**, now is the time to stop in there and have a drink at the Thoroughbred Club. While you are here, you can have a late-afternoon nibble and make reservations for dinner. Try **FIG** (843-805-5900; eatatfig.com), 232 Meeting Street, for probably the most interesting meal you will have in Charleston. If you have a fun-loving group, try **Slightly North of Broad** (843-723-3424; hmavericksouthernkitchens.com), 192 East Bay Street, or **Husk** (843-577-2500; huskrestaurant.com), 76 Queen Street, one of the newest additions to the city's great culinary trail. If you are not dead tired after dinner, stroll down to the Market Pavilion Hotel and check out their rooftop bar for after-dinner drinks.

Your second day of touring downtown should start with breakfast at the **Hominy Grill** (843-937-0934; hominygrill.com), 207 Rutledge Avenue,

before heading out to **Fort Sumter** (843-883-3123; nps.gov/fosu/index
.htm), 340 Concord Street, Charleston. If it's summertime, take the earliest tour out, so you can have the most time exploring the fort in the middle of Charleston Harbor. The last tour boat back to downtown leaves at
2:30. Even if you are on that late boat, you will be back downtown at a
perfect time for a late lunch at **Jestine's Kitchen** (843-722-7224), 251
Meeting Street. After eating, I recommend a rest and freshen-up at your
hotel before heading out for **Anna's Ghostwalk** (843-720-8687; ghost
walk.net), 74-A North Market Street. Anna's is by reservation only, so
make that call the day before or before you head out to Fort Sumter at
the latest. After your tour, you can grab a late supper at **Bocci's** (843-720-
2121; boccis.com), 158 Church Street, or just get dessert and drinks at
Kaminsky's (843-853-8270; kaminskys.com), 78 North Market Street,
which is open late night every night except Sunday.

On your third day downtown, you need to finish up any museums you did-
n't get to on the first day before heading over to King Street for some serious shopping. Have breakfast at **Caviar and Bananas** (843-577-7757;
caviarandbananas.com), 51 George Street, a gourmet food shop that also
serves wonderful deli-style breakfast items for about $5 along with great
coffee that you can enjoy there or take with you. After you finish your
museums have lunch at **Sermet's Corner** (843-853-7775), 276 King
Street, and try to get the window seat. It's the best people-watching in
town. Sermet's is also perfectly located to start your King Street shopping.
You can head south and hit the shops at Charleston Place and continue on
to the antiques shops and galleries on South King, then work your way
back north through the name-brand stores like Abercrombie and Fitch,
Pottery Barn, and Urban Outfitters as well as some great shoe stores and a
few local shops, such as **Oops!** (843-722-7768; theoopsco.com), 326 King
Street. If you've packed for the wrong season or forgotten something basic
to your wardrobe, this is the ideal place to pick up an inexpensive replacement. Some items are seconds, meaning they have a slight flaw, and some
are just items that didn't sell. There are bargains to be had. This is also a
great place to get souvenir clothing items. Continue north past Marion
Square and you reach **Joe Pasta** (843-965-5252; joepasta.com), 428 King
Street, for an inexpensive dinner, or **39 Rue De Jean** (843-722-8881;
39ruedejean.com), 39 John Street, for a wonderful French dinner.

Off the Peninsula
NORTH Mount Pleasant is a lovely fishing village that has played second
fiddle to Charleston since people have been able to easily cross the
Cooper River. It's less expensive and almost as fun as being downtown.
First stop is **Patriots Point** (866-831-1720; patriotspoint.org), 40 Patriots
Point Road, Mount Pleasant, home of World War II aircraft carrier the

USS *Yorktown*. From here, you can tour the *Yorktown*, take a stroll on the Ravenel Bridge, book a sail at **Classic Charleston Sailing** (843-388-9242; classiccharlestonsailing.com), or catch a ferry to **Fort Sumter** (843-883-3123; nps.gov/fosu/index.htm), which is about a three-hour tour. If you're staying on this side of the river, I recommend **Shem Creek Inn** (843-881-1000; shemcreekinn.com), 1401 Shrimp Boat Lane, Mount Pleasant. It's centrally located and a pretty good bargain. Shem Creek is surrounded by seafood restaurants. From Mount Pleasant, it's just a quick drive to **Sullivans Island**—prettiest beach in South Carolina—and the **Isle of Palms**. You also can pack the family up for a nature trip from here. The **Cape Romain National Wildlife Refuge** (843-928-3264; fws.gov/caperomain), 5801 US 17, the **Center for Birds of Prey** (843-971-7474; thecenterforbirdsofprey.org), 4872 Seewee Road, and the **Francis Marion National Forest**—all in Awendaw—are just a 30-minute drive up US 17 from Shem Creek.

SOUTH To the south of the city are Folly Beach and Kiawah and Seabrook Islands. These are each unique and very different places. Folly is for the beach bum, while Seabrook is a little fancier with resort-style amenities and Kiawah is the granddaddy of luxury with its AAA/CAA Five Diamond **Sanctuary** (800-576-1570; thesanctuary.com). Folly is my favorite because it's so laid-back, but for those who want to drink up some luxury and don't mind the expense, you simply have to try The Sanctuary. Unlike anything else in South Carolina, it will knock your socks off. Bring your clubs, tennis racket, and swimsuit, and you will never have to leave the resort. If the idea of $400 a night and $200 greens fees is overwhelming, try booking in the off-season. The Sanctuary never turns off its luxurious service and attention to detail; it just will cost you a little less in January, February, and March. Also, note that Kiawah's Ocean Course will be home to the 2012 PGA Championship in August of that year, so things will be pretty busy around that time.

If you want to stay at Folly Beach for less than a week, I recommend **The Tides** (843-588-6464; tidesoffolly.com), 1 Center Street, Folly Beach. It's in the perfect spot to enjoy all things Folly. **Island Trike Rentals** (843-879-8473; islandtrikerentals.com) has two-person three-wheelers you can rent for a day or a weeklong stay. Island Trike also rents bikes made for riding on the beach. A bike is a great way to get around the island, which is only 6 miles from end to end. You'll want to have breakfast at least once at the **Lost Dog Café** (843-588-9669; lostdogfollybeach.com), 106 West Huron Avenue. This is a great cup of coffee, and their fresh muffins and pastries are fantastic. Mornings and early afternoons will likely be spent on the beach. There are a handful of shops on the main drag, but I suggest one day, if the weather is bad or you've just had too much sun, drive the 15 or 20 minutes to check out **Terrace Oaks**

Antique Mall (843-795-9689; terraceoaksantiques.com), 2037 Maybank Highway (SC 700). You'll pass some other shopping along the way, but the Terrace Oaks is a destination worth hitting. It's like a huge garage sale with thousands of items ranging from kazoos to credenzas. It's a great way to while away the afternoon. While you're out this way, have lunch at **The Mustard Seed** (843-762-0072; dinewithsal.com/mustard), 1970 Maybank Highway. It offers great healthier fare and is the place for vegetarians—but don't worry, meat eaters, there's also chicken, beef, and pork on the menu as well as a fettuccine carbonara with real bacon. If you're preparing any of your own meals on any of the southern beaches, you have to go to **Rosebank Farms** (843-768-9139; rosebankfarms.com), 4455 Betsy Kerrison Parkway, Johns Island, for your fresh veggies and fish. If you want shrimp and shellfish, **Crosby's Seafood** (843-795-4049), 2223 Folly Road, is the place to go. There is an in-town location as well. If you prefer dinner out—and really, who doesn't—my favorite place in this area is the **Fat Hen** (843-559-9090; thefathen.com), 140 Maybank Highway, Johns Island. The food here is fantastic and the atmosphere is just plain fun. The servers are some of the best in town. The only drawback I can find is that it's located out in the middle of nowhere, so designate a driver if you plan to sample some of their adult beverages.

The Lowcountry

BEAUFORT

HILTON HEAD ISLAND

SEA ISLANDS:
Hunting, Lady's, Fripp, Daufuskie,
St. Helena, Edisto

SUGGESTED ITINERARIES

INTRODUCTION

South Carolina's Lowcountry is located on the southern tip of the state. Rivers, creeks, and tidal marshes flow through the area like pulsing blood vessels, beating the heartbeat of the ocean's tides. These waterways create a network of islands and peninsulas from Interstate 95 to the sea. It is some of the most beautiful and sought-after land in the state. Its culture and economy are a study in contrasts—from the wealth of Hilton Head and Fripp Islands to the poverty on those long stretches of rural road between developments.

Before Hilton Head Island with its golf courses, retirees, and seasonal visitors, the area was populated mostly by poor farmers and mosquitoes. It was where freed slaves built communities and schools after the Civil War. They are the Gullahs—a mix of African, Indian, and European heritage that gives the Lowcountry its flavorful food, music, art, and storytelling.

The campus of one of these early schools—the Penn Center—still stands on St. Helena Island as an education center for all things Gullah. Designated a National Historic Landmark in 1974, there are 19 buildings on the 50-acre campus, including Darrah Hall, one of the oldest buildings on St. Helena Island. It was here that civil rights leaders of the 1960s came to recharge and plan marches and actions.

The area also has a history of military service with the Parris Island Marine recruit training base and the Marine Corps Air Station. In nearby Yemassee, named for the Indians that used to live there, U.S. troops passed through near the end of the Civil War, using a local church as a hospital.

The area now is known as a high-end tourist destination, from Hilton Head's more than 75 golf courses to the Palmetto Bluff resort along the May River. Even small Daufuskie Island, whose poor schoolchildren were highlighted in the Pat Conroy book *The Water Is Wide*, has luxury home developments; undeveloped lots go for more than half a million dollars an acre. It's still reachable only by ferry, and bikes and golf carts are the only transportation on the island that measures 2.5 by 5 miles.

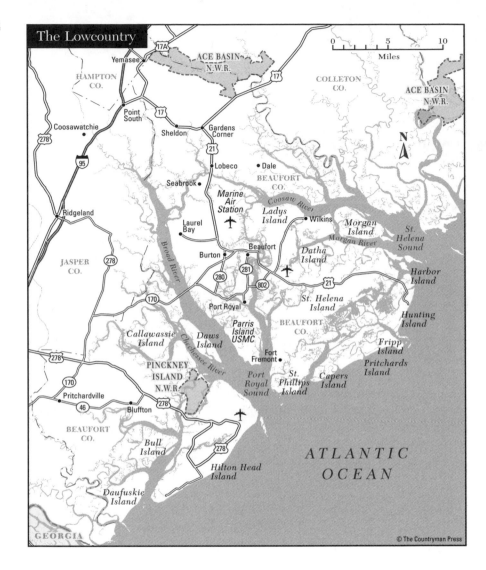

The Lowcountry

Despite all the development, the area is still home to much wildlife, including the occasional alligator on the golf course and so many deer that hunts are held periodically to thin the herds. Recently, the National Audubon Society named Harbor, Hunting, and Fripp Islands as one of the state's 49 important bird areas. The designation will help identify and protect habitats for local and migrating birds. The Fripp Island Audubon group has been asked to monitor piping plovers.

GUIDANCE Lowcountry & Resort Islands Tourism Commission
(843-717-3090; southcarolinalowcountry.com), 1 Lowcountry Lane,

Yemassee. Open daily 9–5:30. Located in a farmhouse rebuilt by John Frampton in 1868 after his previous home had been burned by U.S. troops, the commission operates a museum and gift shop as well as providing information for travelers.

WHEN TO COME Summer is the best time for fun in the ocean and on the beaches. Beaufort and the off-island areas, including the golf courses, can be a little too hot for some people, especially in August. Fall is an excellent time to get in a few rounds without melting—and there will be less traffic to contend with. Spring is excellent weather-wise, but the PGA's Heritage golf tournament in April is probably the island's most crowded time. Winters do get cold and can be rainy, but that's when the best deals can be had. The golf courses are open year-round, and you never know when a batch of sunny warm weather will break out in February.

BEAUFORT

B eaufort in South Carolina is pronounced *BEW-fort*—unlike the town of the same spelling in North Carolina, which is pronounced *BO-fort*. The South Carolina city is a throwback to another time. The downtown has been rejuvenated with new restaurants and shops, but looks and feels like it did 50 or 100 years ago. Several old plantation-style homes still stand and are private homes.

One of the nation's oldest church buildings still stands, and the ruins of another old church sit quietly in a nearby woods, beckoning all to come and take a surreal walk through time.

Home to the Marine Corps' Parris Island Training Depot for more than 60 years and the Marine Corps Air Station, Beaufort also has the feel of a military town. Marines and sailors pop up periodically, again reminding visitors of another time.

The town's seafaring history also is part of its vibrant present with an annual shrimp festival in the fall, celebrating the pink crustacean at the heart of so much Lowcountry cuisine.

In the winter, there's an international film festival that brought in a record 202 entries in 2010.

GUIDANCE Beaufort Regional Chamber of Commerce (843-525-8529; beaufortsc.org), 1106 Carteret Street, Beaufort. Open 9–5 Monday through Saturday, noon–5 Sunday. The chamber offers information on more than 900 businesses in the Lowcountry and resort island area.

Bay Street Visitor Center (843-379-6335; historicbeaufort.org), 801 Bay Street, Beaufort. Open daily 10–5:30. This center is located in the Federal-style historic John Mark Verdier House, built in the early 1800s and is something of a museum itself with much of its original architecture intact. Named for the wealthy merchant and planter who built the home, Verdier House was used as a headquarters by U.S. soldiers during the Civil War and was home of the first telephone exchange in the city.

BOAT APPROACHES SWING BRIDGE ON BEAUFORT RIVER

Beaufort County Black Chamber of Commerce (843-986-1102; bcbcc.org), 801 Bladen Street, Beaufort. Open daily 10–5. This center guides visitors to historic sites of African American and Gullah cultural interest.

GETTING THERE *By air:* **Hilton Head Island Airport** (843-689-5400; bcgov.net/Airport_HHI) has daily flights to and from Charlotte, North Carolina, and Washington, DC, through US Airways Express (800-428-4322; usairways.com), and seasonal flights through Delta Connection (800-221-1212; delta.com).

Some folks also use the larger **Charleston International Airport** (843-767-7007; chs-airport.com), about two hours to the north, or the **Savannah/Hilton Head Airport** (912-964-0514; savannahairport.com), about an hour to the south.

By car: Beaufort sits on US 21, east of Interstate 95 and east of US 17.

By train: **Amtrak** (800-872-7245; amtrak.com), 9 Main Street, Yemassee. Four trains, two heading north and two heading south, stop in Yemassee each day. Trains from the north stop around 8 PM and 6 AM; from the south they stop around 9 PM and 9 AM.

By bus: **Greyhound** (843-524-4646; greyhound.com), 3659 Trask Parkway, Beaufort. There are several buses leaving and arriving in Beaufort every day.

GETTING AROUND The best way to get around Beaufort is by foot or by bike once you have parked your car at your hotel. But to get to some attractions and restaurants or if you aren't staying right in town, you will need to drive.

✳ To See

MUSEUMS Verdier House (843-379-6335; historicbeaufort.org), 801 Bay Street, Beaufort. Open 10–4 Monday through Saturday for tours. Admission is $5, which includes guided tour. Free exhibit on the ground floor documents the Union occupation of Beaufort during the Civil War. Located in the city's National Historic Landmark District, the Verdier House is the city's only historic house regularly open to the public. The house is also the location for the historic foundation's periodic dinner and lecture series.

Parris Island Museum (843-228-2951; mcrdpi.usmc.mil/graduation /museum.asp), Marine Corps Recruit Depot, Parris Island. Open 10–4:30 daily, though access to base may be limited depending on events and security level. Admission is free. Drivers must show license, vehicle registration, and proof of insurance to get on the base. All adults should have identification. The first floor details the history of Parris Island, from the American Indian tribes who called the area home to the establishment of the Marine Corps base there at the end of the 19th century. The second floor chronicles Marine Corps history from 1900 to the present.

The Beaufort Museum (843-379-3331; beaufort-sc.com/history/bfttown /tour/wt18.htm), 713 Craven Street, Beaufort. Open 10:30–4 daily except Wednesday and Sunday. Admission: $3; ages 6 and younger admitted free. The museum is housed in a 19th-century arsenal and tells the story of Southern plantation life and the area's military history. The museum was renovated in 2002 and includes exhibits on the prehistoric settlements in the area up to the 21st century.

Milton Maxcy House ("Secession House"), 1113 Craven Street, Beaufort. This privately owned home is nonetheless a historic site as the seeds of secession were planted here, according to an inscription on the basement wall. After voting, the Beaufort County Delegation went directly to the boat landing and set off for Charleston to cast their ballots for secession. The foundation of the house represents the base of an earlier two-story home that was constructed in 1743. Around 1800 Milton Maxcy came to Beaufort from Massachusetts to open a school for boys and bought the property. He removed the tabby second floor, and added two stories of wood siding. The next owner, Edmund Rhett, rebuilt the two upper floors completely circa 1861, using modified Greek Revival architecture. The house was occupied by U.S. troops during the Civil War and served as a headquarters for General Rufus Saxton, an officers' quarters, a hospital, and for the office of paymaster.

ART GALLERIES ARTworks (843-379-2787; beaufortcountyarts.com), 2127 Boundary Street, Beaufort. Open daily 10–5. The Arts Council of Beaufort County operates this free gallery and 90-seat black box theater to showcase local artists. The organization also puts on free concerts twice a month in the spring and summer called Street Music on Paris Avenue in Port Royal.

HISTORIC SITES The Parish Church of St. Helena (Episcopal) and Cemetery (843-522-1712; sthelenas1712.org), 505 Church Street, Beaufort. Open 10–1 Monday and Saturday, 10–4 Tuesday through Friday, and 1–4 Thursday. Admission is free. The church is one of the oldest in the country in continuous service. The parish was founded in 1712, but the original church was not completed until 1724 after a break from the Yemassee War, which nearly destroyed European settlement in South Carolina. The interior of the church was gutted and turned into a hospital for U.S. troops occupying Beaufort during the Civil War. Among the famous buried in the graveyard are Declaration of Independence signer Thomas Heyward Jr., Indian fighter Colonel John Barnwell, and Confederate General Richard Anderson.

Old Sheldon Church Ruins, Old Sheldon Church Road at SC 235 between Gardens Corner and Yemassee. Open dawn to dusk. Hidden among centuries-old hardwoods, the Sheldon Church ruins are a surreal sight for the passing traveler. As you walk around the remaining brick columns and across the crumbled threshold, you will feel the need to whisper—if you speak at all. I kind of stumbled upon these ruins on a trip to Hilton Head just following a road sign. At first I thought, "How neat could it be?"—two of us raised in South Carolina had never heard of it, and it's just sitting there on the side of a minor state road. But it was fantastic. There are no souvenir stands, no people telling you how great this place is. It just is. It is impossible not to feel like you are transported to another time when survival was the thing that kept you busy all day. Loss was a part of everyday life, and yet these people built and rebuilt and rebuilt. And what they built still stands and still feels somehow hallowed ground. The fact that it was never completely annihilated or that it wasn't plowed under or bulldozed for progress is itself amazing. It just stands there and speaks to you like very little else you will ever see. It is so far removed from daily life that it's like a Stonehenge or Easter Island statue, though its origins are not nearly as mysterious. The church was built in the 1740s and stood as an early example of Greek Revival construction in the colonies. Its reputation as a storage house for gunpowder led to it being burned during the Revolutionary War. It was rebuilt in the 1820s

OLD SHELDON CHURCH RUINS

only to be torched again in 1865 by U.S. troops on their way to Columbia from Savannah. Part of me doesn't want to tell about this place for fear it will be overrun. Still, it really has something that you cannot name, but you can definitely feel.

Beaufort National Cemetery (843-524-3925; cem.va.gov/CEM/cems /nchp/beaufort.asp), 1601 Boundary Street, Beaufort. Open daily sunrise to sunset. This cemetery was established by President Lincoln during the Civil War. More than 7,500 soldiers from that war are buried there, including 117 Confederate soldiers. A monument was built in the 1870s to honor the unknown soldiers buried there. The original burials were men who died in nearby hospitals during the U.S. occupation of Beaufort during the Civil War. About 2,800 remains were removed from cemeteries in Millen and Lawton, Georgia, and reinterred in the national cemetery. In 1989 the remains of 19 soldiers were reburied at the cemetery after being located on Folly Beach near Charleston. Archaeologists determined that they were part of the 55th Regiment and the 1st North Carolina Infantry, both of which were made up of black soldiers who fought with the 54th Massachusetts Regiment that launched an assault on a Confederate fort near Charleston. The soldiers had been listed as missing since 1863. A memorial to Confederate soldiers was added to the cemetery in 1997. The cemetery is listed on the National Register of Historic Places and continues to be a burial ground for U.S. soldiers.

PARKS **Henry C. Chambers Waterfront Park** (cityofbeaufort.org), Bay Street, Beaufort. This lovely park runs along the Beaufort River as it wends its way through downtown. Lined with historic markers, the walkway is wide and welcoming. Just off it are shops and restaurants, many with outdoor seating. Swings overlook the river when you need to take a break from all the shopping and eating.

OTHER PLACES OF INTEREST **Cole-Heyward House** (843-757-6293; heywardhouse.org), 70 Boundary Street, Bluffton. Guided tours of the home are offered 10–3 Monday through Friday. The cost is $5 for adults, $2 for students, and free for children younger than 10. Guided tours of Bluffton's National Register Historic District include a 30-minute tour of the Heyward House and an hour walk through town, $15 per person. Tours are by appointment only. This West Indies–style home was built on the bluffs overlooking the May River around 1840 as a summer home for a local plantation owner.

African Village Tour (843-846-8900; oyotunjiafricanvillage.org), 56 Bryant Lane, Sheldon. Open 10 AM to dusk for tours. Admission is $10 for adults (12 and older), $5 for children 8–11, and free for children younger than 7. Discounted rates are available for groups of 20 or more. The vil-

BEAUFORT RIVERWALK

lage offers visitors a glimpse at life in an African village with an option to pitch a tent and camp on site.

✻ To Do

Carolina Buggy Tours (843-525-1300), 901 Port Republic Street, Beaufort. Tours start about 10:30 AM. Reservations required. Cost: $18 adults, $7 children ages 6–12. A slow-paced horse-and-buggy tour fits right in with the historic homes of the Old Point Neighborhood. Tour guides also can point out all the homes that have appeared in the many films made in the Beaufort area.

Ghost Tours of Beaufort (843-524-4678), departs from the West Street Extension at 8 PM daily by reservation only. The candlelight tours are led by costumed guides who know every ghost's backstory. Tours last 45 minutes to an hour and cost $10.

Lowcountry Estuarium (843-524-6600; lowcountryestuarium.org), 1404 Paris Avenue, Port Royal. Open 10–5 Wednesday through Saturday; animal feedings at 11:30 and 3. The estuarium showcases the land and water animals that live the areas where fresh water meets the sea. Admission: $5 adults ages 12 and older; $3 for children 3–11; free for children younger than 3.

The Spirit of Old Beaufort Tour Center (843-525-0459; thespiritofold beaufort.com), 1001 Bay Street, Beaufort. Reservations are required. The 1.25-mile walking tours are offered at 10:30 AM, 2 PM, and 7 PM. Guides wear 19th-century clothing and sing period songs as they lead visitors through the city's historic homes (east-side tour) or churches and historic sites along Bay Street (west-side tour). Van tours are by appointment only and take visitors to Lady's, St. Helena, and Hunting Islands. The walking tour costs $15 per person for a nearly two-hour trip, while the driving tour costs $25 for a 90-minute ride. I recommend the walking tour unless you are physically unable or it's one of those scorching South Carolina summer days.

FISHING Aqua Sports Inc.–*Sea Wolf* Charter (843-525-1174; seawolf charter.com), 1 Landing Drive, Port Royal. Offering charters daily 5 AM– 6 PM. If it involves water, Captain Waldo Phinney can do it. He earned his Eagle Scout badge as a 13-year-old for saving an even younger swimmer in distress off Hunting Island Beach. He learned the waters around Hilton Head Island while his father was stationed at Parris Island. After graduating from Clemson University, Captain Wally joined the Army and served during the Vietnam War. These days, he is "retired" to a life of taking visitors to the Lowcountry fishing aboard the *Sea Wolf VI*, a 35-foot Power-Cat. He welcomes all skill levels, but won't take anyone younger than 8.

The maximum number of anglers is six. Since it is a charter, guests and Captain Wally set the itinerary and pricing individually depending on the customers' needs. Guests bring their own food, beverages, sunscreen, and seasick remedies; Captain Wally provides the rest.

Drifter and *Gypsy* **Excursions** (843-363-2900; hiltonheadboattours .com), 232 South Sea Pines Drive, Hilton Head Island. Reservations are required for deep-sea and inshore shark fishing on one of three boats, including the *Boomerang*, which offers private sportfishing charters. Boats operate March through November out of the South Beach Marina in Sea Pines Plantation. In addition to fishing trips, the company offers dolphin-watching and educational children's cruises.

Cast Away Fishing Charters (843-322-1043; beaufortcastawaycharter .com), 1006 Bay Street (city marina), Beaufort. Reservations required. Inshore fishing excursions start at $350 for four hours and range up to $550 for eight hours. The price includes licenses, bait, rods, and light tackle.

Seas So Shallow (843-252-3882; seassoshallow.com), 1006 Bay Street (city marina), Beaufort. Reservations required. Inshore fishing tours will take you around Port Royal Sound, the Broad River, and Fripp Inlet. All trips include licenses, tackle, lures, and bait. You bring food, drink, and sunscreen. Four-hour tours for up to three people, $350. The boat can accommodate a fourth person for an additional $50.

GOLF Hilton Head has the bulk of the area's golf courses; a complete listing can be found at hiltonheadgolf.com.

May River Golf Club at Palmetto Bluff (843-706-6580; palmettobluff resort.com), 476 Mount Pelia Road, Bluffton. Set along the May River, the course requires you to dodge 300-year-old oak trees as well as some Jack Nicklaus–designed hazards. The 7,171-yard course is a par 72. Greens fees $175 in spring and summer, $260 September through December.

BOATING **Beaufort Kayak** (843-525-0810; beaufortkayaktours.com), 600 Linton Lane, Beaufort. Tour times are set by reservations. No kayak experience is necessary as these guides focus on easy in and out of the water kayaks, paddling with the tidal currant. Half-day tours are $40 for adults, $30 for children younger than 18.

Capt. Dick's Beaufort River Tours (843-524-4422; beaufortrivertours .com), 1006 Bay Street, Beaufort. The 24-passenger *Prince of Tides* departs at 2 PM Monday through Friday, 11 AM and 2 PM Saturday, and 2 PM Sunday for an 80-minute tour of the Beaufort River. The cost is $18 for adults (over 12), $12 for children. On Friday and Saturday evenings, the *Prince* turns into a restaurant shuttle, leaving at 5:30 PM with plenty of cold beer and wine and taking passengers to the Dockside restaurant for dinner. $20 per person.

✱ Lodging

INNS 🐾 **The Beaufort Inn**
(843-379-4667; beaufortinn.com),
809 Port Republic Street, Beaufort. Frequently found on travel
guides' lists of best inns, most
romantic inns, or best getaways,
the Beaufort Inn surrounds visitors with its Southern charm and
elegance. Rooms include fireplaces, cast-iron tubs, and verandas or balconies; the inn also
offers suites and private cottages,
and has recently added a two-
bedroom loft and its Residence at
Town Center for longer stays.
People frequently drive for miles
from nearby beaches for dinner at
the restaurant. The inn is walking
distance from most of Beaufort's
downtown attractions. Rooms
come with a hot traditional Southern breakfast. Rates vary widely
depending on room type and season, but typically start in the
$160s and range to more than
$400 a night for the loft or cottage
in peak season. The inn offers military and government discounts as
well as packages and specials. Pets
are allowed in some rooms; call
for more information.

The Rhett House Inn (843-524-
9030; rhetthouseinn.com), 1009
Craven Street, Beaufort. A Four
Diamond winner from AAA, the
Rhett House Inn is in a restored
antebellum home in the historic
district. A stay here includes a full
Southern breakfast, afternoon tea
and pastries, evening hors d'oeuvres, and nightly desserts. Guests
also have access to bicycles for
getting around downtown, beach
chairs, and towels, as well as
access to the pool at the nearby
Sanctuary Golf Club and complimentary tennis. The Rhett House
offers discounts for booking more
than 45 days in advance, for online
booking, and for packages. Rates
vary by room and season, but start
at $170. Guests get special rates at
The Sanctuary Golf Club for golf
and golf lessons.

Greyhound Flats (843-441-5998;
greyhoundflats.com), 210 Scott
Street, Beaufort. This truly one-
of-a-kind place to stay is located
where thousands of people probably caught some ZZZs while waiting on their bus. Located in the
old bus station, the facility has just
two rooms, but they are spacious
at 600 square feet and can accommodate up to six people each. The
flats are centrally located near the
historic neighborhoods, shops, and
restaurants. About $140 a night.

**BED & BREAKFASTS The Old
Point Inn** (843-524-3177; old
pointinn.com), 212 New Street,
Beaufort. Built by a newspaper
editor in 1898 as a gift for his new
bride, the inn is located in the historic Point neighborhood amid the
city's oldest homes, yet it's just a
block off the hustle and bustle of
downtown. Verandas offer river
views, and the inn has its own garden. Much of the original design
remains, including the porch
columns, pocket doors, and bull's-
eye window decoration. The inn
has five rooms ranging from $125

to $175 a night. A full breakfast is served in the dining room, and complimentary afternoon wine and soft drinks are provided. The inn offers discounts for seniors and members of the military. No pets are allowed, and smoking is permitted on verandas.

Twosuns Inn Bed & Breakfast (843-522-1122; twosunsinn.com), 1705 Bay Street, Beaufort. Located in the historic district with views of the bay, the Twosuns has six rooms that come with a hot breakfast, free on-site parking, and free WiFi Internet connection. There is no online reservation system.

🐾 **Cuthbert House Inn** (843-521-1315; cuthberthouseinn.com), 1203 Bay Street, Beaufort. The inn offers eight rooms, ranging from $150 to $270 a night, with coffee service, Southern breakfast, and evening hors d'oeuvres and refreshments on the veranda. Bicycles are available, and the home has a formal garden. One pet-friendly room is available.

HOTEL City Loft Hotel (843-379-5638; citylofthotel.com), 301 Carteret Street, Beaufort. This is a very modern hotel in a very old city. The hotel has 23 rooms, a coffee shop, and a fitness center. Free WiFi is available throughout the hotel. Rates start about $160 a night.

RESORT Inn at Palmetto Bluff (843-706-6500; palmettobluff resort.com), 476 Mount Pelia Road, Bluffton. The resort is located on high ground overlooking the May River and boasts that it has everything you could want during your stay, from croquet and bocce to tennis and golf on a Jack Nicklaus–designed course. The resort also offers canoe and kayak tours as well as larger boat rentals. There is an equestrian center for riding lessons and stabling of guests' horses. The resort provides daily water transport to nearby Daufuskie Island for a day at the beach. All this service comes at a pretty steep cost. Spa treatments range from a $55 manicure to a four-hour, $550 treatment designed especially for brides. Cottages start at $475 a night during summer and range up to $1,100 a night in spring and fall seasons. A four-bedroom home is available for rent at $2,500 a night or $12,500 for the week.

✳ Where to Eat

DINING OUT Saltus River Grill (843-379-3473; saltusriver grill.org), 802 Bay Street, Beaufort. Opens at 4 daily for sushi and cocktails. Dinner 5–9 Sunday through Thursday; till 10 Friday through Saturday. When you ask natives what's the best place to eat in Beaufort, this is the place they name. Its excellent patio provides wonderful views of the Intracoastal Waterway. Its seafood grill may look chic, but the food is strictly down-home with local fried shrimp ($10) and skillet crabcakes ($25). A raw bar serves oysters and local clams.

Plums (843-525-1946; plums restaurant.com), 904 Bay Street, Beaufort. Open daily at 11 for lunch; 5–9 for dinner. Plums opened in 1986 and was one of the first restaurants along the downtown waterfront park. Lunch is bustling with downtown workers mixing with tourists. In the evening fresh seafood is the highlight of the menu. Start off with Beaufort Baked Oysters with bacon, crabmeat, spinach, and Gruyère cheese for $9. Dinner entrées range $16–23.

Breakwater (843-379-0052; break watersc.com), 203 Carteret Street, Beaufort. Open for dinner 5–9:30 Tuesday through Saturday. Breakwater is part of a new Southern cuisine that focuses on local ingredients whenever possible and is lighter than the usual deep-fried fare. Try the crab stack with black-eyed pea relish ($10) to start—and save room for the pecan tart with homemade bourbon ice cream ($6.50). Entrées range $16–33.

Emily's Restaurant and Tapas Bar (843-522-1866; emilysrestau rantandtapasbar.com), 906 Port Republic Street, Beaufort. Open daily for dinner 6–10. Emily's offers a tapas menu of items $8–12. Full entrées run $18–30. Emily's has live music on the weekends.

River House at The Inn at Palmetto Bluff (843-706-6542; palmettobluffresort.com), 1 Village Park Square, Bluffton. Open daily for dinner at 6 PM; open

Sunday at 8 AM for breakfast. A light menu served daily in the bar and on the porch starting at 2 PM. This elegant restaurant offers a modern twist on Southern fare with dishes like crawfish and risotto and boiled-peanut hummus on its charcuterie platter. Entrées are in the low $30s.

EATING OUT 11th Street Dockside Restaurant (843-524-7433; 11thstreetdockside.com), 1699 11th Street West, Port Royal. Open 4:30–10 PM daily. Located on Battery Creek with wonderful views of the sunset over the water, Dockside serves seafood broiled, boiled, and Southern-style (fried). For landlubbers, there is a small selection of nonfish items. Entrées range $16–20.

Uptown Grill (843-379-3332; theuptowngrill.com), 1001 Boundary Street, Beaufort. Open Monday through Saturday for lunch and dinner starting at 11:30 AM, Sunday brunch 10–2:30. The Uptown Grill offers a variety of cuisines from traditional American dishes to Mediterranean fare. The tapas menu includes spring rolls, eggplant, shrimp scampi, calamari, and crabcakes ranging $5–10. Dinner entrées are $12–20 and include grilled meat loaf and Carolina crabcakes. The grill wants to be not just a place people come to eat, but also a place where folks like hanging out.

Paninis Café (843-379-0300; paniniscafe.net), 926 Bay Street, Beaufort. Open daily for lunch and dinner starting at 11. Located in the old Beaufort Bank building, Panini's offers a variety of Mediterranean-flavored foods from pizza to pasta and steaks. The restaurant caters to group tours with a 70-seat private dining room. Pizzas $8–17, tapas menu $8–15, and entrées $17–22.

Nippy's Fish (843-379-8555), 310 West Street, Beaufort. Open 11–3 Monday through Wednesday and Saturday; 11–9 Thursday through Friday. Nippy's is the only place to find a shrimp dog with a side of slaw and fries for $8. Fish tacos are just $3 each, and the shrimp basket is $9. Nippy's has outdoor seating.

Buffalo's at The Inn at Palmetto Bluff (843-706-6630; palmetto bluffresort.com), 11 Village Park Square, Bluffton. Open daily, except Sunday, at 7 AM for breakfast. Lunch served daily 11–3. Buffalo's is known for its sandwiches including roasted chicken salad, turkey melt, and hot dogs. Most meal choices are less than $15 per person.

❋ Entertainment

Plums (843-525-1946; plums restaurant.com), 904 Bay Street, Beaufort. Starting at 10 PM on Friday and Saturday and select nights during the week, Plums turns into a live-music venue with local and regional acts.

❋ Selective Shopping

Preston Pottery (843-757-3084), 10 Church Street, Bluffton. Open 10–5 Tuesday through Saturday. This working pottery studio is located in the old Bluffton Tabernacle church building and has been in operation since 1977. Master potter Jacob Preston, who claims to be both the oldest living potter and the tallest potter in this small enclave, often can be seen at his wheel making functional pieces such as bowls or even sinks and one-of-a-kind artworks depicting Lowcountry scenes. Preston also makes sinks to order.

Lowcountry Winery (843-379-3010; lowcountrywinery.com), 705 Bay Street, Beaufort. Open 10–6 Monday through Saturday. This winery makes traditional wines such as Merlot and Chardonnay as well as blends and wines that include raspberries and peaches. One specialty is a Sea Island elderberry wine.

221 Antiques (843-522-3049), 1001 Bay Street, Beaufort. Open 8–5 Monday through Friday, 10–5 Saturday. More than a store, 221 Antiques also offers coffee and lunch with outdoor seating.

Beaufort Art Association & Gallery (843-379-2222; beaufort artassociation.com), 905 Port Republic Street, Beaufort. Open 10–5 Monday through Friday. This gallery has 2,500 square feet filled with the works of more than 60 local and regional artists, including photographs, reproductions, and framed originals.

The Spirit Of Old Beaufort Gift Shop (843-525-0459; the spiritofoldbeaufort.com), 1001 Bay

Street, Beaufort. Open 9:30–5:15 Monday through Saturday. This shop offers the work of local artists, including sweetgrass baskets, pottery, and carved wood items as well as a variety of Civil War art, miniature soldiers, and reproduction weapons.

✳ Special Events

SPRING *May:* **Southern Comforts Quilt Show** (843-379-1940; creativestitchesbft.com/SIQ -Show.html), 110 Hamer Street, Beaufort. Held in May in odd-numbered years, the weekend show at the Brown Activity Center features more than 150 quilts, vendors, silent auction, consignments, and books for sale. Cost is $5; free for children 12 or younger.

Gullah Festival (843-525-0628; gullahfestival.org), Henry C. Chambers Waterfront Park, Beaufort. The 25-year-old festival celebrates the history, customs, culture, and language of Lowcountry African Americans. Features arts and crafts, exhibits in the Black Inventions Museum, music, dance, and, of course, food. The festival is held the weekend leading up to Memorial Day. Admission is $25 a day for adults, $10 for children 12 and younger; children 6 and younger are free.

FALL *October:* **Beaufort Shrimp Festival** (843-525-6644; down townbeaufort.com/beaufort-shrimp -festival), Henry C. Chambers Waterfront Park, Beaufort. This festival celebrating one of the key ingredients of Lowcountry cuisine kicks off with a Friday-evening concert in the park. Saturday (11–5) has a 5K run/walk, and local restaurants break out their best shrimp recipes. There's even a shrimp race for the kids. Admission is free. The festival is usually held in early October.

Fall Festival of Houses & Gardens (843-379-3331; historic beaufort.org), 208 West Street, Beaufort. This festival offers three days of touring private homes and plantations in the Beaufort National Historic Landmark District and surrounding Lowcountry. Tickets are limited, so make reservations. The event is usually in mid- to late October. Dates for 2011 are October 28–30.

Ghost Tours of Beaufort (843-524-4678; capabeaufort.org/events /ghost-tours), 714 14th Street, Port Royal. Held the last two weeks of October every year as a fund-raiser for the Child Abuse Prevention Association, the guided walks or carriage rides take visitors on a spectral tour of downtown. No strollers are allowed on the walking tour. Carriage tours, $18 for adults and $10 for children 3–11, are about 45 minutes and recommended for the very young or anyone not steady on their feet. Walking tours are about an hour and are $10 per person. Tours start at 6:30 each night.

WINTER *February:* **Beaufort International Film Festival** (843-522-3196; beaufortfilm festival.com), 1106 Carteret Street, Beaufort. Started in 2007, the festival recognizes aspiring filmmakers of almost every genre including independent film, music, animation, short and long features, documentaries, and screenwriting. The 2010 festival had a record 202 entries from 24 countries. Dates, times, and locations vary, but the festival is usually held in February.

HILTON HEAD ISLAND

Hilton Head as it is known today did not begin until the late 1960s and early 1970s. Until then, it was alternately a place where rich South Carolinians had cotton farms or where poor freed South Carolina slaves had cotton farms.

Thousands of years ago, the island was home to American Indian tribes. The evidence of their communities can be found in shell rings that are still visible in certain locations on the island.

European explorers began naming things on the island when they landed or passed by in the 16th century. A fort was built near the modern-day Port Royal, and the Spanish established a fort at St. Elena, which later became St. Helena Island.

It was not until the mid-17th century that the island got its name from English captain William Hilton, who was exploring Port Royal Sound and decided to name the high bluffs of the island after himself. He spent some time there documenting plant and animal life.

By the mid-18th century the island had a community of about two dozen families. During the Revolution, apparently the residents of Hilton Head were on the side of the colonies while neighboring Daufuskie was loyal to the Crown. Hostilities between the two islands continued even after the British had surrendered at Yorktown.

After the Revolution, farming began in earnest on the island with wealthy plantation owners who also had homes in Beaufort, Charleston, and Savannah, Georgia. The island was occupied by U.S. troops who blockaded the state's ports during the Civil War. The troops built the town of Mitchellville on the island for freed slaves who were left behind.

After the war ended and the troops left, the island was home to former slaves who farmed as much of the land as they could. This was the heyday of the Gullah culture—a mix of African, American Indian, and European DNA and cultures.

By the turn of the 20th century, whites—mostly Northerners—returned to the island to hunt and fish. Hunt clubs bought much of the land, and the U.S. government still held some. The native black population was about 300 at the time. The island was accessible only by water.

Then came World War II. Marines were training at nearby Parris Island, and the shore patrol placed guns on Hilton Head for target practice over the Atlantic.

After the war, electricity arrived on the island, then telephones. Charles Fraser and a group of Georgia natives bought much of the island and began to create residential development plans based on the old plantations. Homes and businesses are built to blend in with their natural surroundings. You won't find another McDonald's or Kentucky Fried Chicken anywhere in the world that looks like the ones on Hilton Head Island. Even the Walmart has a weathered wood facade. The resorts and developments along the islands are set behind gates that require visitors to have a purpose for visiting and reduce traffic flow through individual developments. Wildlife is still abundant, with alligators frequently seen sunning on golf courses and deer in Sea Pines so numerous that they hold special seasons for bow hunters there to help thin the herds.

HARBOURTOWN LIGHTHOUSE
South Carolina Department of Parks, Recreation and Tourism/Perry Baker

GUIDANCE Hilton Head Island Chamber of Commerce (843-785-3673; hiltonheadisland.org), 1 Chamber of Commerce Drive. Open 8:30–5:30 Monday through Friday.

GETTING THERE *By air:* **Hilton Head Island Airport** (843-689-5400; bcgov.net/Airport_HHI) has daily flights to and from Charlotte, North Carolina, and Washington, DC, through US Airways Express (800-428-4322; usairways.com) and seasonal flights through Delta Connection (800-221-1212; delta.com).

Some folks also use the larger **Charleston International Airport** (843-767-7007; chs-airport.com), about two hours to the north, or the **Savannah/Hilton Head Airport** (912-964-0514; savannahairport.com), about an hour to the south.

SC Department of Parks, Recreation & Tourism, DiscoverSouthCarolina.com

HILTON HEAD ISLAND

By car: The most direct route to Hilton Head is to take Exit 8 off Interstate 95 onto U.S. Highway 278. This road takes you by the myriad outlet shopping centers on your way to the island. US 278 is the island's main road, known as William Hilton Parkway after you cross the bridge.

By train: **Amtrak** (800-872-7245; amtrak.com), 9 Main Street, Yemassee. Four trains, two heading north and two heading south, stop in Yemassee each day. Trains from the north stop around 8 PM and 6 AM; from the south they stop around 9 PM and 9 AM.

✳ To See

MUSEUMS Coastal Discovery Museum (843-689-6767; coastaldis covery.org), 100 William Hilton Parkway (located inside the welcome center) and 70 Honey Horn Drive. Open year-round 9–4:30 Monday through Saturday, 11–3 Sunday. The welcome center location opened in 1985 and includes a small exhibit gallery and a gift shop with a variety of South Carolina products. The Coastal Discovery Museum at Honey Horn opened in 2007 at a 68-acre historic property. Visitors can step back in time to see what the island looked like before the bridge and the development came—a collection of salt marshes and centuries-old live oaks. The museum has preserved some of the oldest buildings standing on the island. Admission for walks: $10 adults, $5 children. Talks on the history of the island, its wildlife, and the Civil War era are $5 for everyone.

OTHER PLACES OF INTEREST Harbour Town Lighthouse (866-305-9814; harbourtownlighthouse.com), 149 Lighthouse Road. Open 10–sunset daily. Admission: $3 to walk to top of the lighthouse and to tour museum. The 90-foot, red-and-white-striped tower is the backdrop of the 18th green at the PGA's Heritage golf tournament. For millions of people, the lighthouse says *Hilton Head*. From the top, you get an excellent view of the island. Inside are some Civil War–era photographs and artifacts that date back thousands of years.

✳ To Do

Adventure Cruises (hiltonheadisland.com/adventure), Dock C, Shelter Cove Harbour. Cruises are offered daily at 2 PM in the off-season and at 11 AM and 3 PM during summer. Sunset cruises at 7 PM in summer. Adventure Cruises offers two options for getting out on the water. Both cruises are one hour and 45 minutes long. **Dolphin Watch Nature Cruise** (843-785-4558) is a cruise through calm water looking for the smiling dolphins. Reservations not required. Cost: $26 adults (13 and older), $12 children. **Sport Crabbing Cruise** (843-422-5110) runs from April to early September. Reservations are required. Cost: $20 adults, $15 children 3–12, and $5 for infants. The boat anchors in nearby Broad Creek, and everyone fishes for blue crab. The person who catches the most wins a T-shirt.

BOATING Commander Zodiac (843-671-3344; commanderzodiac.com), 232 South Sea Pines Drive, Hilton Head Island. Open daily 9–5 spring and fall, 8–8 in summer; closed December through February. Reservations are required for any of this company's programs. The guides here can take the whole family out for a sail or kayaking; or you can drop the kids off for the morning in the summer for beach fun. Commander Zodiac offers sailing lessons, or you can rent one of their two sailboats. Half-hour lessons are $80 on a 14-foot Hobie Wave or $70 on a Sunfish. Rentals are $45 and $35 an hour. The Hobie can carry up to four people and the Sunfish, two. All dolphin-watching tours are done on a 18-foot, hard-bottomed Zodiac raft and can take up to six passengers. Prices range from $30 per adult for an hour tour to $50 an adult for a two-hour tour.

Advanced Sail (843-686-2582; hiltonheadisland.com/sailing), 86 Helmsman Way, Hilton Head Island. This company offers daily dolphin-watching and nature excursions and sunset and fireworks tours in the summer aboard two catamarans. The boats sail daily from Palmetto Bay Marina. Sail times vary depending on season, weather, and tides. Costs are $35 for adults on the *Pau Hana*, $20 for ages 11 and younger. The *Flying*

Circus is available for two-hour private charters for six or fewer people at $225.

Vagabond Cruise (843-785-2662; vagabondcruise.com), 149 Lighthouse Road, Hilton Head Island. Open daily year-round. Cruises start at 9:30 AM. Reservations required. Costs range from $30 to $60 for adults and $10 to $25 for children. The Vagabond Cruise offers 21 different cruises aboard three different vessels. The *Vagabond* offers dolphin-watching cruises and excursions to Daufuskie Island. The *Spirit of Harbour Town* has a heated and air-conditioned cabin and offers cruises to Savannah, Georgia, and a dinner cruise. The company also offers sailing cruises in warm weather aboard the *Stars & Stripes*, one of Dennis Conner's America's Cup 12-meter racing yachts. All three vessels are available for private charters, weddings, and corporate events.

Gullah Heritage Trail Tours (843-681-7066; gullaheritage.com), 528 Spanish Wells Road, Hilton Head Island. Tours are given Sunday at noon and Wednesday through Saturday at 10 AM and 2 PM. Admission is $32 for adults 13 and older; $15 for children 12 and younger. This two-hour tour is led by fourth-generation Gullahs, who tell stories about family traditions, food, and language. There are stops at Queen Chapel AME Church, Gullah family compounds, a one-room schoolhouse, plantation ruins, and the historic marker for the first freedom village. Tours leave from the Discovery Museum of Hilton Head, 70 Honey Horn Drive.

FAMILY-FRIENDLY ACTIVITIES *𝒮* **The Sandbox** (843-842-7645; thesandbox.org), 18A Pope Avenue. Open 10–5 Tuesday through Saturday in the off-season. Also open Monday in summer. This museum is more like a sandbox in that children can touch everything and learn as they play together. There is an international bazaar that teaches about shopping and preparing meals. A challenging rock course is part of a "track the T-Rex" exhibit. There also is a "Rhythm and Hues" room for painting and instrument playing. Admission: children younger than 2 are admitted free; $6 for everyone else.

FISHING Capt. Hook Party Fishing Boat (843-785-1700), 1 Shelter Cove Lane. Capt. Hook offers five-hour deep-sea-fishing excursions year-round for $65 per adult (over 12), $55 for those 12 and younger. Night shark fishing is offered May through August. Five-hour tours are $65 and $55 for kids; four hours costs $60 and $50, and three-hour tours are $48 and $38 for kids. Prices do not include food, drinks, or gratuity, but do include rods, reels, bait tackle, fishing license, fish cleaning, and instructions. Guests can buy food and drinks on board or can bring their own small cooler.

GOLF Hilton Head Island has 20 public golf courses for visitors and is known as one of the golf capitals of the South. The area including off-island sites has about 75 courses that can be found at hiltonhead golf.com. Here are a few of the highlights:

The most famous course is **Harbour Town Golf Links** (843-842-8484; seapines.com), where the pros tee it up every April in the PGA's Heritage Tournament. Rates range $150–250 on this 6,973-yard, par-71 course. Harbour Town has two other courses that are less expensive. The **Ocean Course** ($60–120) is Hilton Head's oldest golf course and offers junior tees from 150 yards out, so the whole family can play. **Heron Point** greens fees range from $70–130.

Robert Trent Jones Oceanfront Golf Course (843-785-1136; palmetto dunes.com), 7 Trent Jones Lane. One of three courses at the Palmetto Dunes Resort, the Robert Trent Jones course is 6,100 yards, par 72. A round for two with a cart is about $200.

Shipyard Golf Club (843-689-4653; shipyardgolfclub.com), 45 Shipyard Drive. Shipyard has three courses of nine holes each that can be mixed and matched for an 18-hole round. Greens fees range $50–140.

TENNIS Van Der Meer Tennis Center (843-785-8388; vandermeer tennis.com), 19 DeAllyon Avenue. This facility named for famed instructor Dennis Van der Meer provides clinics for adult and junior players, as well as an academy for serious young players looking possibly to a career in tennis. Adult programs run three to five days. Weekend programs are $300 for 10 hours of instruction. Play is at Shipyard Racquet Club. Courtside villas available through the tennis center at vandermeertennis.com /36_courtside.htm. Rates: $105–175 per night.

HORSEBACK RIDING Lawton Stables (843-671-2586; lawtonstables hhi.com), 190 Greenwood Drive. Located inside Sea Pines Plantation, the stables provide carriage rides and pony rides for kids as well as the experience of riding horseback through the development's 600-acre Forest Preserve. Carriage rides for up to five people are $175 for the first hour and $125 for additional hours. Trail rides on horseback leave the center at 9 and 11 AM and 2 and 4 PM daily. Reservations required. Cost is $60 per person; all riders must be 8 or older.

✳ Green Space

Pinckney Island National Wildlife Refuge (843-784-2468; fws.gov /pinckneyisland). The entrance is about half a mile west of the bridge to Hilton Head Island on US 278 on the right as you leave the island. The refuge has more than 14 miles of nature trails, gravel and grass, for hiking, biking, and bird-watching. The endangered wood stork feeds on the mudflats in the estuaries. Popular spots within a 3-mile round trip include Ibis

Pond and Osprey Pond. White Point is about an 8-mile round trip from the parking lot. A public boat ramp and fishing pier are located on the southern tip of Pinckney Island at Last End Point.

Sea Pines Forest Preserve (843-363-1872; exploreseapines.com/forest -preserve.asp), entrances on Lawton Road and Greenwood Drive. Open sunrise to sunset. This 600-acre protected area located within Sea Pines Plantation is on the National Register of Historic Places. Some areas are bike-friendly, but bicycles are not allowed on the miles of nature trails. The preserve offers visitors a self-guided tour of shell ring sites that mark where American Indians used to live. These tours are at 9 AM Tuesday and Thursday and leave from the east entrance on Lawton Road. Lake Mary offers a glimpse of the bird life and wildlife that used to rule over the island. Boardwalks take strollers past rice field marshes and through Vanishing Swamp. The best picnic spot is at Fish Island in the center of the preserve.

BEACHES Hilton Head has about 14 miles of beach (hhisleinfo.com /beaches.htm). Most have mats to make them accessible to wheelchairs.

Coligny Beach with its volleyball nets and outdoor bar at the Holiday Inn is the most popular beach. It can get a little crowded here in summer, but a short walk up or down from the main access point will get you away from the crowds. The beach has lifeguards who also rent equipment for fun in the water and on the beach. The area has restrooms, changing rooms, and showers to rinse off the sand. Parking in the town lot is $4 a

BEACH AT HILTON HEAD ISLAND

day ($2 after 2 PM), and you can leave and come back on the same day as long as you keep your receipt.

Folly Field Beach is where the surfers go. There is limited parking at meters that cost $1 an hour. There are lifeguards, but swimmers beware: The currents that make good surfing waves also create dangerous conditions.

Dreissen Beach Park, located off William Hilton Parkway at Bradley Beach Road, has plenty of parking, restrooms, showers, and vending machines as well as a playground, grill, and picnic tables. You pay for your parking with quarters at machines near the restrooms, so remember your space number. It's a bit of a haul down the boardwalk to the beach, so be ready to walk.

Alder Lane is one of the island's less crowded beaches and is located beside the Marriott Grand Ocean Resort on South Forest Beach Road and Alder Lane. The park here has restrooms and vending machines. Metered parking is $1 an hour.

The locals use the **Islander's Beach Club**, where parking is limited to those with annual permits—and only Hilton Head Island property owners can buy those. But if you're riding a bike or otherwise don't have a car to park, it's fair game. There are restrooms, playgrounds, and vending machines. It's located off Folly Field Road at Sparkleberry Lane.

Fish Haul Creek Park is a small beach located on Port Royal Sound. It's a long walk from parking to the water, but you will feel like you have found your own private strand.

✳ Lodging

INNS AND BED & BREAKFASTS
Main Street Inn (843-681-3001; mainstreetinn.com), 2200 Main Street. A quiet getaway amid the hustle and bustle of Hilton Head, Main Street Inn offers 33 rooms with a formal garden. The inn's spa offers a variety of massage and other relaxation therapies. This is one of the neatest little places to stay. It has a very European feel with the rooms surrounding the garden. The luxurious rooms come with private courtyards on the first floor or balconies on upper floors. Rates start at $140.

South Beach Inn (800-367-3909; sbinn.com), 232 South Sea Pines Drive. As its name implies, this inn is on the southern tip of the island and offers weekly as well as nightly rates. Many modern amenities with the intimacy of a B&B. Rates range from a low of $65 a night in the off-season to $190 a night in peak season.

HOTELS 🐾 Park Lane Hotel and Suites
(843-686-5700; hilton headparklanehotel.com), 12 Park Lane. Located right in the middle of the island, the Park Lane is just 2 miles from Coligny Beach. All

suites come with full kitchen and private balcony, and most have fireplace. Bike rentals and laundry service are also available. Pet fee is $75 for stays of more than two nights. Rates are $120–150 a night, with discounts for extended stays.

Beachwalk Hotel & Condominium (888-843-4136; hilton headbeachwalkhotel.com), 40 Waterside Drive. This hotel is walking distance to most of the island's beaches and the shops of Coligny Plaza. All rooms have refrigerator, and some have kitchenette. The hotel was completely renovated in 2008. Rates $130–150 a night.

Fiddlers Cove Condominiums (866-899-8039), 45 Folly Field Road. This condominium complex offers rentals through hoteltravels .com. The complex has two pools and a hot tub and is two blocks from the beach at Folly Field. It also has clay tennis courts. Rates vary depending on size, but a typical unit will rent for $800 a week during summer and $1,000 a month in winter. Nightly rates are available in the off-season, but typically a two-night minimum stay is required.

RESORTS Sea Pines Resort (843-363-8100; seapines.com), 32 Greenwood Drive. Sea Pines is the island's oldest and, at 5,000 acres, largest resort. Home to Harbour Town and the Heritage golf tournament, as well as the Yacht Basin and the iconic candy-cane-striped lighthouse, Sea Pines offers visitors a variety of accommodations from private homes, condos, and villas to rooms at the **Inn at Harbour Town**. Rates at the inn range $110–190 a night. Villas and home rates vary widely depending on size and location. Amenities include a truly world-class tennis facility (Sea Pines used to host the Family Circle Cup tennis tournament) and three golf courses, including the course where the PGA plays the Heritage tournament.

Palmetto Dunes Oceanfront Resort (866-380-1778; palmetto dunes.com), 4 Queens Folly Road. The resort rents villas and homes and provides access to all amenities, including golf courses, kayak rentals, and tennis. Palmetto Dunes offers several golf packages starting at $113 per person per night. The resort also includes the **Hilton Oceanfront Resort** (843-842-8000; hiltonoceanfrontresort .com), the **Hilton Head Marriott** (843-686-8400; hiltonheadmarriott .com), and **Disney's Hilton Head Island Resort** (407-939-7828; dvc.disney.go.com) located within Palmetto Dunes across US 278 at Shelter Cove Harbor and Marina. Hotel rates range from about $160 to $400 a night, with lots of packages and specials available.

CAMPGROUNDS 🐾 ✿ **Hilton Head Harbor RV Resort** (843-681-3256; hiltonheadharbor.com /HiltonHeadRV.htm), 43A Jenkins Road. All sites at this campground

HILTON OCEANFRONT RESORT AT PALMETTO DUNES

have concrete pads and 30- and 50-amp service as well as cable television access. The campground has two swimming pools, three tennis courts, and a playground for children as well as a fishing pier, restaurant, and water sports rentals. Pet-friendly. Open year-round. Does not allow pop-up campers. Interior sites are $55 a night; waterfront, $65.

✳ Where to Eat

DINING OUT CQ's (843-671-2779; cqsrestaurant.com), 140A Lighthouse Road. Open for dinner daily 5:30–10 April through October, 5–9:30 November through March. CQ's is located in the Sea Pines Plantation and offers intimate dining with small rooms of three or four tables. Chef Eric

Sayers offers early diners a sampler's menu that includes soup or salad, an entrée, and dessert for $20 per person. The crabcake served with a winter succotash and Dijon caper rémoulade is included in the early menu options, but you must be seated before 6 to order that option. Dinner entrées range $26–37. Children's menu items are about half the size and half the price and include individual pizzas and smiley fries. Sayers also offers a chef's table with a variety of selections. Prices for that vary depending on what's cooking.

Michael Anthony's (843-785-6272; michael-anthonys.com), 37 New Orleans Road, Suite L. Open Monday through Saturday for dinner starting at 5:30. Reservations are recommended. Michael

Anthony's offers classic Italian dishes with a contemporary edge. Entrées range from about $18 for tagliatelle with a Bolognese meat sauce to $33 for a filet served on a bed of wilted spinach.

Antonio's (843-842-5505; antonios .net), 1000 William Hilton Parkway. Open nightly 5–9:30 in winter, 5–10 in spring, and 5:30–10 in summer and fall. Owned by the same group that owns CQ's, this Italian restaurant offers entrées ranging from $9 for a small portion of fettuccine carbonara to $32 for a 7-ounce filet mignon. Sides are separate and average $4.

The Old Fort Pub (843-681-2386; oldfortpub.com), 65 Skull Creek Drive. Open daily 5–10; Sunday brunch 11–2. Tucked away near the ankle of the foot-shaped island, the Old Fort Pub was named in honor of nearby Fort Mitchell. Open since 1973, it is one of the oldest restaurants on the island and has served its famed she-crab soup the whole time. Some of the more interesting dinner items are crawfish cakes and roasted quail. Early dining three-course menu available. Dinner entrées range $24–38.

The Jazz Corner (843-842-8620; thejazzcorner.com), The Village at Wexford C-1, 1000 William Hilton Parkway. Open daily at 6 PM for dinner; entertainment starts at 8. Founded in 1999 by jazz musician historian Bob Masteller and jazz lover Charles Swift, the Jazz Corner tries to blend an outstanding

venue for listening to music with equally high-quality food. Masteller books acts that specialize in New Orleans, mainstream, swing, and traditional jazz; he plays on Tuesdays. Executive chef Mark Gaylord serves up new Southern cuisine. He graduated from Johnson & Wales when it was located in Charleston. Entrées range from $20 to $40 and include calf's liver, country-fried veal loin chop, filet mignon, and a wide selection of seafood. Start with the fried green tomato salad or she-crab soup and finish with the crème brûlée or the best chocolate layer cake ever. Shows cost $5–15. It's best to plan to have dinner as that's the only way to make a reservation and the best way to guarantee you get one of the club's 100 seats.

Skull Creek Boathouse (843-681-3663; boathouserestaurant .net), 397 Squire Pope Road. Open 11:30–10. There are so many options on this menu, you will never be able to try everything. The Boathouse's Dive Bar offers chilled seafood dishes that serve two to four people. Ceviche and sushi also are on the menu. Lunch includes foot-long jumbo dogs for up to $10 for the Francheezie—a heart-stopping combination of a hot dog on a yeast roll with cheddar cheese, wrapped in bacon and deep-fried. Lunch combos—choice of entrée and side—are $9. Dinner offers seafood pots ranging up to $36 for crab legs; lobster tacos cost $18 for a double order. There are a handful of nonseafood items as well. For dessert, try the warm apple bread pudding with caramel sauce if you have room.

The Topside at the Quarterdeck (843-842-1999; seapines .com), 160 Lighthouse Road. Open daily for dinner 5–9. Fresh seafood dishes prepared simply as well as several steak dishes. Dinner entrées $16–30.

Surfside Outdoor Grill (843-842-1888; seapines.com), North Sea Pines Drive. Open for dinner 5–9 with live music in summer only. Surfside offers diners a selection of seafood, steak, and chicken plus beachfront dining.

Sunset Grille (843-689-6744), 43 Jenkins Road. Open for lunch 11:30–1:30 Tuesday through Friday and Sunday; open for dinner 6–8:30 Tuesday through Sunday. Reservations required. The location on Skull Creek provides the Sunset Grille with some of the best sunset views on the island. But it also is situated above a Laundromat, about 20 steps up. The smoked poblano Bloody Mary, the shrimp and grits, and the crabcake are all favorites. Dinner entrées start around $25.

Charlie's L'Etoile Verte (843-785-9277; charliesgreenstar.com), 8 New Orleans Road. Open for lunch 11:30–2 Monday through Friday; dinner starts at 5:30 Monday through Saturday. Reservations recommended for dinner. Charlie's has been in Hilton Head for 25 years and offers a classic French menu in a casual laid-back

atmosphere, like being in a country farmhouse. The menu includes pâté, pork with oyster sauce, and bread pudding or crème brûlée for dessert. The lunch menu is $10–15 while dinner entrées are $25–40.

EATING OUT Charley's Crab (843-342-9066; chart-house.com), 2 Hudson Road. Charley's Crab is now part of the Chart House chain of restaurants, but retains its local flavor by serving fresh seafood, like shrimp from the Benny Hudson Seafood ships and fresh trout from Hoover Farms.

✍ **Frankie Bones Restaurant & Lounge** (843-682-4455; frankie boneshhi.com), 1301 Main Street. Open daily 11–10; 11–11 Friday through Saturday. Frankie Bones specializes in sandwiches for lunch, with most dishes under $10. Dinner has a decidedly Italian theme with entrées ranging $13–24. An early-bird dinner menu is available as well as a kids' menu.

The Salty Dog Café (843-363-2198; saltydog.com), 232 South Sea Pines Drive. Open 11–10 daily. Located in Sea Pines Plantation, the Salty Dog Café may be one of the most recognizable restaurants on the island because of its iconic T-shirts feature the original salty dog, Jake. The dinner menu is all about the seafood with the occasional steak thrown in. Dinner items range from $10 for a grilled chicken sandwich to $27 for a filet. Favorites are the crabcake sandwich and the sea-food potpie.

The Harbour Town Grill (843-363-8380; seapines.com), over-looking the ninth hole of Harbour Town Golf Links in Sea Pines. Opens daily 7 AM–9 PM for break-fast, lunch, and dinner. The Grill offers a two-course dinner for $20 per person or three courses for $25 if you get there between 5 and 6.

The Harbour Town Bakery and Deli (843-363-2021; seapines .com), 140 Lighthouse Road. Open for breakfast and lunch 7–2:30. If you're looking for a quick, inexpensive meal at Har-bour Town, this place is famous for its breakfast, including French toast, pastries, and huge chocolate muffins.

It's Greek to Me (843-842-4033; itsgreektomesc.com), 11 Lagoon Road. Open daily 11–10. This is the perfect place for when you need a break from all the Southern-fried food. The menu includes all classic Greek dishes from calamari to stuffed grape leaves and mous-saka to gyros. Start with the avgolemono soup (that's chicken-rice-egg-lemon), have the spana-kopita (spinach, feta, eggs, fresh herbs wrapped in filo), and finish with the baklava (nuts and cinna-mon layered in filo and covered with honey syrup) or kataifi (shredded baklava with heavy cream). Entrée prices range from $10 to $20, but you have to save room and $5 for dessert.

✳ **Entertainment**

MUSIC VENUES The Quarter-deck (843-842-1999), 160 Light-house Road. Located at the base of the Harbour Town Lighthouse, the Quarterdeck has live enter-tainment every afternoon starting at 5 PM and Friday and Saturday nights starting at 8. Full bar with snacks and sandwiches after 4 PM. The Quarterdeck opens for lunch at 11:30.

THEATERS Arts Center of Coastal Carolina (843-842-2787; artshhi.com), 14 Shelter Cove Lane. This center includes a 350-seat theater that hosts visiting per-formers as well as producing its own shows. Also includes a gallery for visual arts. The center fre-quently hosts outdoor festivals and concerts including the Taste of Gullah festival.

✳ **Selective Shopping**

Endangered Arts Ltd. (843-785-5075; endangeredarts.com), 841 William Hilton Parkway, South Island Square. Open 10–7 Mon-day through Saturday in-season; closes at 6 PM in winter. Photogra-pher Julie Rogers opened this gallery in 1994 to highlight the work of environmental artists. Works include originals and limit-ed editions, sculptures and glass pieces.

Hilton Head Factory Stores I & II (843-837-4339; tangeroutlet .com/hiltonhead), 1414 Fording Island Road, Hilton Head Island.

Open 10–7 Monday through Saturday (until 9 in summer), 11–6 Sunday year-round. These two complexes have more than 100 outlet stores, from Skechers to Abercrombie and Fitch.

Coligny Plaza (843-842-6050), 1 North Forest Beach Drive. The plaza has 60 stores, including apparel, gifts, and accessories. Outdoor family entertainment is also provided during the summer. There are also 19 restaurants, including a bakery, sandwich shop, and bar and grill. Each store and restaurant has its own hours. There also is a theater open Monday through Saturday.

Camp Hilton Head (843-681-4101; camphiltonhead.com). Seven locations on the island including Coligny Plaza and Harbour Town. Open 10–8 Monday through Fri, 10–7 Saturday, noon–5 Sunday. The ultimate in island-branded clothes and merchandise, Camp Hilton Head offers shirts, magnets, coffee mugs, calendars, glasses, bumper stickers—anything you can put a logo on. If you can't leave a place without something to show you were there, this is the shop for you.

Loose Lucy's (843-785-8093; looselucys.com), Coligny Plaza. Open 10–7 Monday through Saturday, 11–6 Sunday. If you were ever a Deadhead or wished you could dress like one, this is the place for you. With seven stores in the Carolinas and Georgia, Loose Lucy's specializes in tie-dyed clothing, tapestries, posters, and other cool stuff.

The Mall at Shelter Cove (843-686-3090, mallatsheltercove.com), 24 Shelter Cove Lane, mid-island on US 278 near Palmetto Dunes. Open 10–9 Monday through Saturday, 12:30–5:30 Sunday. This enclosed mall has typical regional and national department stores and specialty shops.

✳ Special Events

WINTER *February:* **Hilton Head Island Gullah Celebration** (843-689-9314; gullahcelebration.com). This monthlong celebration coincides with Black History Month and features food, storytelling, and other Gullah traditions. Prices vary by event. The festival ends with the Marsh Tacky Run at Coligny Beach Park.

March: **Hilton Head International Piano Competition** (843-842-5880; hhipc.org), 32 Office Park Road, Suite 214. Twenty of the world's best young pianists (ages 18–30) compete in four rounds. The winner gets $15,000 and a chance to perform at Carnegie Hall and in concert with the Hilton Head Orchestra.

Hilton Head Island Wine & Food Festival (843-686-4944; hitonheadwineandfood.com), Sea Pines Resort and the Coastal Discovery Museum at Honey Horn. If the Charleston event is too pricey, this smaller version at Hilton Head includes wine dinners, tastings, competitions, and a wine auction. Tickets for the whole weekend are less than $100.

SPRING *April:* **The Heritage Golf Tournament** (843-671-2448 or 800-234-1107; theheritagegolf sc.com), 71 Lighthouse Road, Suite 4200. This annual stop on the PGA Tour typically has been played the week after the Masters, but in 2011 came two weeks after the first major of the season played just over the state line in Augusta, Georgia. After more than 40 years at Harbour Town, the Heritage teed up the 2011 tournament without a named sponsor. But RBC stepped in with a five-year sponsorship deal starting in 2012, and the tournament is moving back to the week after the

Masters. Past winners have included Arnold Palmer, who won the first tournament in 1969; Jack Nicklaus, who helped create the course with famed designer Pete Dye; and Davis Love III, who has won the tournament five times— more than anyone else—including in 1987 when he was just barely 23 years old. If it's still operating and you love golf, check it out. The players are more laid-back after the stress of the Masters, and since it's so close, many of them make the drive over from Augusta. Daily passes are $50–60 for the four tournament play days; $150 will get you a pass for the whole week. The Arnold Palmer Pass is $375 and includes access to entertainment tents on the grounds.

SEA ISLANDS

HUNTING, LADY'S, FRIPP, DAUFUSKIE, ST. HELENA, EDISTO

The Sea Island Parkway (US 21) winds its way like a tidal creek from downtown Beaufort across the tiny sea islands that dot the coast. Fripp Island is a private resort with rental properties and a handful of restaurants. It was once a hunting ground for visiting Northerners; it's now a wildlife refuge. But beware: Many of the animals have lost their fear of humans and can be dangerous, especially the alligators that live on golf courses. Fripp also is home to South Carolina's most famous living author, Pat Conroy.

Hunting Island is mostly a state park, while Harbor Island is a private community with a few rental options for visitors. St. Helena is the largest of the islands and is home to the historic Penn Center, the site of the first school for freed slaves in South Carolina. To the north of Beaufort is Lady's Island, and although it's just across the sound from the other islands, Edisto is about an hour away by car from downtown Beaufort. Edisto is one of the few old-school family beaches left in South Carolina. There is plenty to do, but you won't find a waterslide here.

The islands have some beautiful stretches of beaches precisely because visitors are limited. This is a great area if you're boating, either under power, sail, or paddle, as all the tidal inlets provide miles of unspoiled waterways.

GUIDANCE Edisto Chamber of Commerce (843-869-3867 or 888-333-2781; edistochamber.com), 430 SC 174, Edisto Island. Open daily 9–5.

Lady's Island online business directory (ladysisland.com). This website lists events going on at Lady's Island.

✳ To See

MUSEUMS York W. Bailey Museum (843-838-2432; penncenter.com), St. Helena Island. Open 11–4 Monday through Saturday. This museum highlights the history of the Penn Center, site of one of the first schools

HISTORIC SITES

THE PENN CENTER

One of the most significant locations in African American history in the United States is found in coastal South Carolina. **The Penn Center** (843-838-2432; penncenter.com), St. Helena Island, was the site of the first school built to educate free slaves. Founded in 1862 by Northern missionaries, the Penn School operated until after World War II, educating the black children of the sea islands. Students then began going to Beaufort County schools, but it wasn't until the early 1970s that black and white children went to the same schools in South Carolina. That delay came even though a South Carolina family's lawsuit against the state was one of the original cases lumped in with *Brown v. Board of Education* that led to the 1954 U.S. Supreme Court ruling ordering an end to segregated schools.

In the years after *Brown*, the civil rights movement took off. Many of the architects of the peaceful push for equality spent time at the Penn Center, planning strategy, writing speeches, and refueling after difficult encounters with entrenched racism across the South.

Today the Penn Center is a living testament to their struggle. In 1974 the center was designated a national historic landmark. It comprises 19 buildings, including Darrah Hall, one of the oldest buildings on St. Helena Island, and Gantt Cottage, where the Reverend Martin Luther King Jr. stayed during his visits to the center.

The Penn Center today is the keeper of that history and the history of the Gullah people—a mix of African, Indian, and European cultures along the coasts of South Carolina, Georgia, and Florida.

The Penn School and Center is open for tours, educational programs, conventions, and other group meetings. The property includes four residences, a nature trail, and Chowan Creek. Each year, the Heritage Days Celebration featuring Gullah music, dance, and art is held here. A two-week Gullah Studies Institute also is held annually.

for freed slaves. Artifacts date back to 1862, when Penn School was founded. The center is a national historic landmark. Admission is $5 for adults age 16 and older, $4 for seniors, and $2 for children up to age 16.

Edisto Island Museum (843-869-1954; edistomuseum.org), 8123 Chisolm Plantation Road. Open 1–4 Tuesday through Saturday in summer; just Tuesday, Thursday, Saturday in the winter. Admission is $4 adults, $3 seniors, and $2 students. Children 10 and younger and members are admitted free. Trace the lineage of Edisto inhabitants all the way back to the Indians that gave the place its name. Exhibits include ancient pottery, sweetgrass baskets, photographs, a diary, and furniture. This is a good stop for a rainy day.

OTHER PLACES OF INTEREST ✐ **Edisto Island Serpentarium** (843-869-1171; edistoserpentarium.com), 1374 SC 174, Edisto Island. Open 10–6 Monday through Saturday in summer, Thursday through Saturday in spring and fall; 10–3 Saturday in winter. If you're traveling with young boys or just like snakes, alligators, turtles, and lizards, this is a must-see. Admission is $13 for adults (ages 13 and up); $12 for 65 and older; $10 ages 6–12; $6 ages 4–5; free for 3 and younger. There are discounts for school, camp, church, and club groups and AAA members.

Mystery Tree of Edisto, SC 174. The mystery is who decorates it, how they get to it, and why. The tree is about 100 feet from the road. It really is nothing more than a stick tree, but it finds itself adorned with items of the season, from Christmas decorations in winter to a child's bike in summer. It's nothing to go out of your way to see, but keep an eye out for it if you're down that way.

MYSTERY TREE AT EDISTO ISLAND

Jan Hogan

✳ To Do

The Kayak Farm (843-838-2008), 1289 Sea Island Parkway, St. Helena Island. Guided tours and kayak rentals Monday through Saturday. Reservations are required. The excursions take paddlers into salt marshes and the state's three-river ACE Basin. Tours are about $55 per person; single kayaks rent for $35. Takes checks as well as credit cards.

ACE Basin Tours (843-521-3099 or 866-521-3099; acebasintours.com), 1 Coosaw River Drive, Lady's Island. Open Wednesday and Saturday at 10 AM; other days by appointment. Cost for the three-hour tour is $35 for adults 13 and older and $15 for children. Captain Stan can take up to 40 passengers on a 25-mile excursion aboard his pontoon boat. The tour covers the unique history and nature of the basin formed by the Ashepoo, Combahee, and Edisto Rivers.

Gullah-N-Geechie Mahn Tours (843-838-7516; gullahngeechietours .net), 97 Perry Road, St. Helena Island. Tours are given at 9:45 and 1:45 Monday through Saturday. Admission is $25 for adults 13 and older and $20 for children 12 and younger. This tour of St. Helena and other sea islands tells the stories of enslaved Africans and how their culture mixed with others in South Carolina to create the Gullah culture. Stops include the Penn Center and Museum, the Brick Baptist Church, and the Oaks Plantation with a praise house still standing.

THE ACE BASIN

The southern tip of South Carolina—what I like to call the first bite of the big ol' slice of pecan pie that the state is shaped like—is crisscrossed with rivers, streams, tidal pools, marshlands, and sea islands. It is what makes this area—the Lowcountry—so intriguing. It's largely undeveloped outside the major tourism area Hilton Head Island and the shrimping village and tourism town of Beaufort.

The ACE Basin is the crown jewel of this area. It's one of the largest undeveloped estuaries on the U.S. East Coast. There are more than 350,000 acres of area included in this system, which includes the Ashepoo, Combahee, and South Edisto Rivers. Because of the diversity of habitats represented in this area, from woodlands to beach, there is a wide range of plant and animal life to be found here, including several endangered and threatened species such as bald eagles, woodstorks, shortnose sturgone, and loggerhead sea turtles.

Settlers in the 18th century turned the tidal swamps into rice beds,

FISHING Captain Eddie's Fishing Charters and Sightseeing Cruises (843-838-3782; fishingcapteddie1.com), 28 Salt Wind Drive, Saint Helena Island. Open daily during daylight hours for tours. Captain Eddie offers offshore and inshore fishing charters on the 27-foot *Glory Hallelujah II* or inshore on the 17-foot *Little Glory Hallelujah*. Two-hour dolphin-watching and sightseeing cruises are available for $200 for up to six people. Fishing prices range from $300 for two passengers on a four-hour trip on the smaller boat to almost $1,000 for six anglers on an all-day trip on the big boat. Passengers need to provide their own food and beverages.

✐ **Edisto Watersports & Tackle** (843-869-0663; edistowatersports.net), 3731 Docksite Road, Edisto Beach. This shop offers fishing charters with Coast Guard–licensed captains. Bait, tackle, and licenses are included in the cost; you provide your own food, beverages, and sunscreen. Prices are for up to six people and range from $300 for a three-hour inshore trip to $800 for a seven-hour offshore trip. You can also book guided tours, kayak rentals, and a shell excursion, which is especially popular with children. Two-hour kayak guided tours cost $30 per paddler; kayak rentals are $20. Boat tours of ACE Basin and Alligator Alley run $30–35. A three-hour shell-hunters tour on a "deserted island" costs $30.

GOLF Fripp Island Resort (800-334-3022; golf.frippislandresort.com), 201 Tarpon Boulevard, Fripp Island. There are two courses available to

which lasted for about 100 years until the rice crop began to decline and the area became the hunting grounds for wealthy sportsmen. In the 20th century the land was identified as vital to waterfowl, and the former rice fields have become part of the North American Waterfowl Management Plan. Landowners came together in the 1990s to form the ACE Basin Project to maintain the natural character and to hold the land for traditional uses such as farming, recreation, fishing, and hunting.

Thousands of acres in the basin are public land and include two wild-life management areas: a National Estuarine Research Reserve and the Hollings National Wildlife Refuge.

Generally, the best time to check out this area is during the cooler months when biting insects are at a minimum. The best way to tour the area is by paddle-powered boat, and to help with this there are two dozen boat landings in the basin area.

There also are many places to camp along the way—especially on the Edisto River—making this a truly unique place.

guests at the resort or to guests at rental houses that offer club amenities with the rental. The Ocean Creek course was Davis Love III's first signature course and opened in 1995. The par-71 measures 6,613 yards and is as pretty as it is challenging with its saltwater marsh holes and freshwater lagoons. The Ocean Point course was designed by George Cobb and offers players beautiful ocean vistas on a 6,556-yard par-72 course that opened in 1964.

Lady's Island Country Club (843-524-3635; ladysislandcc.com), 139 Francis Marion Circle, Lady's Island. This is one of the oldest golf clubs in the Beaufort area and has hosted an LPGA event. This par-72 plays more than 7,000 yards from the back tees. Greens fees and cart are $30–45.

Plantation Course at Edisto (843-869-1111; theplantationcourseatedisto.com), 19 Fairway Drive, Edisto Beach. This course plays at 6,175 yards from the back tees and is a par-70. Walking players are welcome at $25–45 for greens fees; with a cart, it's $60.

✳ Green Space

PARKS (STATE AND NATIONAL) ♿ 🐾 **Edisto Island State Park** (843-869-2756; southcarolinaparks.com), 8377 State Cabin Road. Open daily 8–6. This park is famous for its shell-hunting opportunities and has two campgrounds, one along the beach, the other in the forest on the marsh side of the island. The park also has cabins and has some of the state's longest handicapped-friendly biking and hiking trails. The education center features exhibits highlighting the natural history of the island including the river basin formed by the Ashepoo, Combahee, and Edisto Rivers. The ACE Basin is one of the country's largest preserved estuaries. Admission: $5 for adults; $3.25 SC seniors; $3 children ages 6–15; free for children 5 and younger.

Hunting Island State Park (843-838-2011; southcarolinaparks.com), 2555 Sea Island Parkway, Hunting Island. Open 6–6 daily, till 9 during Daylight Saving Time. Cost: $5 adults (16+), $3.25 SC seniors, $3 children 6–15; free for those under 6. In addition to more than 4 miles of pristine undeveloped beach, visitors also have marsh areas they can explore on hiking and biking trails and by canoe or kayak. There is a fishing pier, and horse trails are available in winter. Visitors at least 44 inches tall can tour the lighthouse for $2. Be prepared, it's 185 steps to the top, but the views are worth the walk.

BEACHES Edisto, Hilton Head, Hunting, Daufuskie, and Fripp all have beaches. **Hunting Island** logs more than a million visitors a year. It also is a prime nesting ground for the threatened loggerhead turtle. In early summer, the huge turtles lay hundreds of eggs. Volunteers give nature a hand by relocating some of these nests to areas where the babies can hatch in safety. Fripp Island is a 3-mile-long beach.

South Carolina Department of Parks, Recreation and Tourism/Perry Baker

HUNTING ISLAND LIGHTHOUSE

BOTANY BAY

(803-953-9300; dnr.sc.gov). Open daily dawn to dusk, though seasonal hunting may affect the area's accessibility. This stunning 5,000-acre seaside plantation once belonged to just one family, but thanks to the generosity of Margaret Pepper, it is now a wildlife area managed by the state Natural Resources Department. Botany Bay is not a park, but it is open to the public. The beaches feature the famed boneyard of trees killed by salt water, but still standing along the surf.

Botany Bay was once two plantations that grew sea island cotton, which was noted for its long silky fibers. For about 40 years it was the preferred cotton, and Edisto Island and its plantations thrived, particularly that of John Ferrars Townsend.

But, as is so often the case in Southern history, then came the war. About six months or so after the first shots of the Civil War were fired about 50 miles north of Edisto, the island was evacuated then occupied by U.S. troops starting in February 1862. By the end of the war some three years later, Townsend had to ask for special dispensation from President Andrew Johnson to get clear title to Bleak Hall and Sea Cloud plantations.

The family returned to farming sea island cotton, which brought in handsome prices until the boll weevil's arrival in 1917. The crop never recovered, even though generations of Townsend descendants continued to hold title to the land and harvest timber there. Some of the foundations

AT BOTANY BAY WILDLIFE PRESERVE, EDISTO ISLAND

Jan Hogan

Jan Hogan

of those plantation homes remain and are accessible to visitors. In particular, a gardening shed still shows walls of tabby—a mixture of lime, mortar, sand, and oyster shells.

The plantation is also a testament to adaptability, as the live oaks in the seaside forest survive in the salt air by secreting a waxy film to protect leaves. Palmettos, loblolly pines, and hardwoods fill the forests around the plantation; wax myrtles are in abundance below. The natural landscape has been the backdrop for films such as *Ace Ventura: When Nature Calls* and *The Patriot.*

Botany Bay is an excellent birding spot, as the unspoiled terrain offers sanctuary to a wide variety of shorebirds.

All of this, of course, is even before you see the 2 miles of beach. The federally protected loggerhead sea turtle nests in abundance here as well as the least tern, a bird listed as threatened in South Carolina. Visitors will take a causeway through the salt marsh to the beach, which is accessible only by foot. Adults are asked not to take shells, while children are allowed a small quart-bucket of shells per day.

Much of the old plantation is accessible by car, and a driving tour has been mapped out by the Natural Resources Department. At one point on the drive is a spot to put in canoes or kayaks into Ocella Creek, which connects to the Edisto River and the Atlantic Ocean.

Again, this is not a park, so there are no public restrooms for visitors and no trash cans. If you bring it in, take it out with you.

✷ Lodging

PRIVATE HOMES Edisto Sales and Rentals (843-869-2527; edistorealty.com), 1405 Palmetto Boulevard, Edisto Island. Open 9–5 Monday through Saturday and 1–5 Sunday except October through December. This realty company handles more than 300 rental properties, including oceanfront homes, marsh- and deepwater-access homes, and golf villas. Prices range widely depending on location, size of home, and amenities.

Egrets Pointe Townhouses (843-869-0100; egretspointe.com), 547 SC 174, Suite 5, Edisto Island. The town houses are in a gated community and surrounded by 300 acres of woods filled with bike paths, a fishing pond, tennis courts, a swimming pool, and a golf course to keep guests busy. There is a two-night minimum stay. Rates range $200–500 a night.

Fripp Vacation (877-374-7772; frippvacation.com). This online booking website is easy to use and offers a wide variety of options from beachfront condos to private homes on the water or on the golf course.

RESORTS Wyndham Ocean Ridge (877-296-6335; wyndham oceanridge.com), 1 King Cotton Road, Edisto Island. Resort amenities are free for the entire party for the length of your stay as long as your rental balance is paid off three days in advance. Amenities include three outdoor swimming pools, golf, tennis courts, fishing, sailing, kayak tours, and bike rentals. No pets. Most units are accessible only by stairs. There is a wide range of rental sizes. A three-bedroom condo during summer rents for about $800 a week; a one-bedroom for about $600.

CAMPGROUNDS/CABINS
Edisto Island State Park (843-869-2756; southcarolinaparks .com), 8377 State Cabin Road, Edisto Island. Open daily 8–6. The cabins at Edisto are the most popular rentals in the state. There are just seven of them, so I recommend booking well in advance. They range in price from $70 a night in the off-season for a one-bedroom cabin that can comfortably sleep four to $135 a night in season for one of the three-bedroom cabins that can sleep six. The cabins overlook the marsh and are about a mile-and-a-half walk from the beach—or you can bike or drive to the beach. This is a great way to experience a South Carolina sea island at a not-so-expensive price.

Tuck in the Wood Campground (843-838-2267; tuckinthe wood.com), 22 Tuc In de Wood Lane, St. Helena Island. Office hours: 9–9 daily year-round. This campground has 80 sites with full water, electrical hookups, a bathhouse with hot showers, and a self-serve laundry. There is a freshwater pond stocked with fish as well as a playground with basketball courts and volleyball. Reservations are accepted, but not

South Carolina Department of Parks, Recreation and Tourism/Perry Baker

BEACH AT EDISTO ISLAND

required. Tents sites $26. RV sites $32–34.

Hunting Island State Park

(843-838-2011; southcarolinaparks .com), 2555 Sea Island Parkway, Hunting Island. The park has 173 campsites with electric and water hookups at $30 a night; tent sites are available on trails at $20 a night. One two-bedroom cabin that can accommodate six people is available for $120–150 a night, depending on the season.

✳ Where to Eat

DINING OUT Sweetgrass Restaurant & Bar (843-838-2151; sweetgrassdataw.com), 100 Marina Drive, Dataw Island. Open 11:30–9 Friday through Tuesday. This waterfront bistro is located at the Dataw Island Marina. Fresh seafood and local produce highlight a menu that includes an appetizer of deviled eggs, a plate of Carolina-made cheeses, and sides that include macaroni and cheese as well as greens and coleslaw. Dinner entrées: $9–22.

The Plantation Grill and Grovers Seafood Bar (843-869-0345; theplantationgrill.com), 21 Fairway Drive, Edisto Beach. Open daily 11–10. Located on the Plantation Golf Course, the grill is very casual, but tank tops and swimsuits are not allowed. The Seafood Bar serves up big steam pots full of fresh seafood with cold draft beer. Reservations not accepted. Dinner entrées range $14–21.

EATING OUT Shrimp Shack (843-838-2962; theshrimpshack .biz), 1929 Sea Island Parkway, St. Helena Island. Order at the window and eat on the porch at this laid-back island eatery. Shrimp burgers and flounder sandwiches are the favorites. Nonseafood items are available for the landlubber.

Gullah Grub (843-838-3841; gullahgrubs.com), 877 Sea Island Parkway, St. Helena Island. Restaurant open 11:30–8 PM Monday through Friday, 11:30–4 for Sunday brunch. Owner Bill Green blends his own spices and cooks with fresh local seasonal produce. Fish chowder is his specialty, along with shrimp gumbo and fried fish. For those not into seafood, there's barbecue—ribs, chicken, or chopped pork. Entrées start at $9.

The SeaCow Eatery (843-869-3222; theseacoweatery.com), 145 Jungle Road, Edisto Beach. Open 7–3 Monday, 7–9 Tuesday through Sunday. Serving breakfast, lunch, and dinner every night except Monday, the SeaCow has outdoor dining with or without the screen as well as air-conditioned comfort. Breakfast items are around $5, lunch salads and sandwiches range up to $10, and dinner entrées max out around $20.

Edisto Eats (843 869-4166; edistoeats.com), 51 Station Court, Edisto Island. Open daily 9–5. This place's primary function is to sell seafood and meats to guests staying on Edisto, but if you call ahead and tell them what you want, they will cook it for you. All meals are for take-out, and Edisto Eats also will cater meals at your vacation home or for the beach. Shrimp, oysters, crab, and other seafood available as well as steaks, lamb, pork chops, and quail. The cost is based on the market prices.

Bonito Boathouse Restaurant & Sunset Lounge (843-838-15061), Tarpon Boulevard, St. Helena Island. Open for diner at 5. Bonito Boathouse is located on top of the marina with great views. Southern fare such as shrimp Creole, catfish sandwiches, and field pea relish are on the menu. Prices are about $10. Discounts are offered for Fripp Island amenity card holders.

✴ Selective Shopping

The Red Piano Too Art Gallery (843-838-2241; redpianotoo.com), 870 Sea Island Parkway, St. Helena Island. Open 10–5 Monday through Saturday, 1–4:30 Sunday.

The gallery highlights the work of folk and craft artists as well as books and other materials focused on the Gullah culture.

Monkey Sea Island Boutique (843-869-1919; monkeysea boutique.com), 114 Jungle Road, Edisto Island. Open 10–5 Monday through Saturday. This gift shop has beachwear, home decor, and body care products.

Barefoot Bubba's (843-838-9222; barefootbubbas.com), 2135 Sea Island Parkway, Harbor Island. Open daily 9–6. This beach store offers clothes, souvenirs, and beach toys. It is loud (visually as well as aurally) and boisterous shopping for those items everyone has to have to complete a beach vacation.

What's in Store (843-838-7473), 853 Sea Island Parkway, St. Helena Island. This shop offers everything from antiques, children's toys, and collectibles to soaps.

DAUFUSKIE ISLAND

Just 2.5 miles wide by 5 miles long, Daufuskie is a unique sea island. Settled by freed slaves after the Civil War, the island remained isolated for most of the 20th century. Still accessible only by boat, Daufuskie has been developed in recent years with expensive luxury homes. Longtime residents have been displaced as skyrocketing land values increased their taxes. Unable to sell land that had been passed down through the generations without a clear title, many lost their homes and property to tax auctions.

Still, Daufuskie retains some of the charm and cultural mix that has been its heritage for hundreds of years. There are no cars on the island, just bikes and golf carts.

Two official ferry services run daily, and several Hilton Head Island resorts offer guests day cruises to the island. You can also arrive by your own boat.

After you land at Freeport Marina, there is the Old Daufuskie Crab Co., where Gullah ladies make their special Fuskie Deviled Crab. Up from there is the Freeport General Store with snacks, drinks, and the best place to buy books and memorabilia about the island.

There are several historic sites on the island. Most places are just there and you walk up or pedal by. Few have phones or websites. It's just not that kind of place.

Ferry boats are $26 per person round trip.

Haig Point Ferry Co. (843-301-3723) generally leaves from Palmetto Bay Road on Hilton Head Island on the half hour between 6:30 AM and 10:30 PM. Call for reservations; schedule subject to change.

Calibogue Cruises & Tours (843-342-8687; daufuskiefreeport.com), departs Broad Creek Marina, 18 Simmons Road, Hilton Head Island. Four departures, at 7 AM, 11 AM, noon, and 4 PM Tuesday through Friday; no noon departure on Monday. Weekend departures at 11 and 4.

Several resorts on Hilton Head offer their own ferry to Daufuskie for guests who want to take a day trip over.

✳ To See and Do

Old Daufuskie Crab Co. and **Freeport General Store**, 256 Cooper River Landing Road. The restaurant has a shaded dining gazebo complete with hammocks. The general store has cold drinks, snacks, T-shirts, and gifts, including books about the island.

Janie Hamilton School, Old Haig Point Road. An example of a typical 19th-century island schoolhouse.

Mary Fields Elementary School, School Road. Built in 1930, this is where Pat Conroy taught. His experiences were chronicled in the book *The Water Is Wide* and later the movie *Conrack*.

First Union African Baptist Church, Church Road at School Road. This church was built in 1882 and is still used today. It was restored in 1998.

Cooper River Cemetery, Cooper River Road. This early Gullah cemetery was built on the river in the belief that the souls of the dead would enter the water and be able to return to Africa.

Library, White School Lane. The island's only library is housed in the schoolhouse that was used by the island's white children until 1962.

Daufuskie Island Museum, Old Haig Point Road. Located in the old Mount Carmel Baptist Church, which was built in 1942 for the island's white residents.

Bloody Point Lighthouse, Beach Drive. Built on the ocean in 1883, this lighthouse at the site of an Indian battle during the late 1700s was moved to its current location by a team of mules dragging it over logs.

Beach nature walk. The whole point of coming here is to walk on a quiet beach, so take off your shoes and get on the sand. Golf carts are not allowed on the beach.

Haig Point Lighthouse, Haig Point. Constructed in 1873 on Daufuskie's southwestern tip, this was the first lighthouse built for the island. The light was decommissioned in 1936, but the keeper's house still stands. The lighthouse is inside the private Haig Point community and is used for guests of the community's residents.

INLAND AREAS

GUIDANCE Greater Hardeeville Chamber of Commerce (843-784-3606; hardeevillechamberofcommerce.com), 6 Argent Boulevard #A, Hardeeville. Open Monday through Friday 10–1. This center offers information on Jasper County and the city of Hardeeville, the first South Carolina exit off Interstate 95 for northbound travelers.

Hampton County Chamber of Commerce (803-943-3784; hampton countychamber.com), 1000 Pine Street, Varnville. Open Monday through Friday 9–5.

Jasper County Chamber of Commerce (843-726-8126; jaspercounty chamber.com), 403 Russell Street, Ridgeland.

✳ To See

MUSEUMS Pratt Memorial Library & Webel Museum (843-726-7744), 451-A Wilson Street East, Ridgeland. Open daily at 10:30. Closed Sunday. The library has more than 200 rare books on Lowcountry history as well as Indian artifacts, portraits, and maps. The museum also has rice culture displays as well as historical materials from the Revolutionary and Civil Wars.

Hampton County Historical Museum (803-943-5484; hamptoncounty sc.org), 702 1st Street, Hampton. Open Thursday 10–2 and 3–5. This free museum is located in the old jailhouse. The second floor includes a cell-block unchanged since 1878. The museum also includes a Confederate Room with photographs, uniforms, and memorabilia from several wars, including the War of 1812, the Civil War, and both world wars.

Hampton Museum & Visitors' Center (803-943-5318; hamptoncounty sc.org), 15 Elm Street, Hampton. Open 2–5 Tuesday, Thursday, and Saturday, and 3–5 on the first Sunday of each month. This free museum is housed in a 19th-century bank building with vault, safe, and handpainted doors intact. Exhibits range from artifacts and memorabilia from American Indians who lived in the area, to a 1930s-era beauty shop, to information about the atomic submarine USS *Hampton*.

HISTORIC SITES Thomas Heyward Jr. Tomb (843-726-8126), SC 462 at SC 336, Ridgeland. Open daily till dusk. Admission is free. A historic marker along SC 462 will show the way to the grave of Thomas Heyward Jr. (1749–1809), one of the signers of the Declaration of Independence. His family's plantation home was burned during the Civil War, but the ruins can be seen near the family graveyard. Dozens of moss-draped oaks line the drive toward the home, lending the whole site an otherworldly feel.

✳ Green Space

PARKS Savannah River National Wildlife Refuge (843-784-2468; fws.gov/savannah), 763 Alligator Alley, Hardeeville. Open daily dawn to dusk. Admission is free to this 22,940-acre refuge along the Savannah River. The refuge was established in 1927 and protects wildlife from whitetail deer to alligators. A 4-mile driving tour takes visitors by the remains of a rice levee and mills, foundations of slave quarters, and small graveyards.

✐ **Sergeant Jasper County Park** (843-784-5130; jaspercountysc.org), 1458 Red Dam Station, Hardeeville. Open 8 AM–6 PM daily. This free park is a great green space for picnicking or burning off some energy on the playground. There are fishing ponds, nature trails, an 18-hole disk-golf course, and canoe and kayak rentals.

Victoria Bluff Heritage Preserve (803-734-3886; dnr.sc.gov), Sawmill Creek Road, Daufuskie Island. Open daily dawn–dusk; closed October through December for hunting season. This 1,100-acre tract has nature trails through dense forests of palmetto and pine trees and areas for seeing white-tailed deer, foxes, and birds. Spring is the best observation time.

Blue Heron Nature Center (843-726-7611; blueheronnature.com), 321 Bailey Lane, Ridgeland. Trails are open daily during daylight hours. The Nature Center is open 9–5 Monday through Friday. This free green space has the quarter-mile Blue Heron Nature Trail, made of recycled rubber, that goes around a 3-acre pond. You'll also find a butterfly garden, picnic area, observation deck, and a Learning Center. Displays along the trail describe the plants and flowers seen around the Lowcountry.

✳ Lodging

CABINS Palm Key (843-726-6524; palmkey.com), 330 Coosaw Way, Ridgeland. Located on a 350-acre marsh island, Palm Key is a community of cottages surrounding a freshwater pond and overlooking a saltwater marsh. More than 40 cottages ranging from one to five bedrooms with full kitchen and modern appliances, but no TV or telephone, are available. Amenities include miles of forest walking trails, kayak and birding tours, an arts workshop, and fishing. One-bedroom cottages start at $165 a night; five-bedroom cottages go for $675. There are five pet-friendly units for an extra $20 a night.

✳ Where to Eat

EATING OUT Jasper's Porch (843-726-9521; jaspersporch.com), 100 James Taylor Drive, Ridgeland. Open 7 AM–9 PM Monday through Saturday; Sunday brunch 10:30–2. Diners can sit on a large screened-in porch overlooking a small lake and enjoy a good Southern breakfast, lunch, or dinner at a reasonable price. It's located just off Interstate 95 for road-weary travelers. Dinner entrées range $8–16.

✐ **The Pink Pig** (843-784-3635; the-pink-pig.com), 3508 South Okatie Highway, Hardeeville. Open Tuesday, Wednesday, and Saturday 11–3, Thursday through Friday 11–3 and 5–7. This family-owned and -oriented barbecue joint opened in 1993 and has been wowing folks in the Lowcountry with its nontraditional sauces and restaurant. There's no debate about vinegar vs. mustard vs. ketchup here. It's all original with a honey mustard, Gullah spices, and a Lowcountry fire that will have you reaching for the water glass. Most dishes here are less than $20, and they serve everything with Brunswick stew—a chicken and potato, gumbo-style stew popular along the Georgia and South Carolina coasts.

SUGGESTED ITINERARIES

M ost of the things to do and see in chapter 3 require a few nights' stay to fully appreciate. Because of traffic in the summer, I wouldn't recommend Hilton Head or any of the sea islands as day trips. It's better to plan on staying awhile, because if you're rushed, traffic is not going to work with you—and that will sort of destroy the whole point of vacation. There are so many things to see and do here, you have to decide whether you want to shop, go to the beach, golf, or tour the unique natural area known as the ACE Basin. The headwaters of the rivers that make up this unique area lie to the north and west of Beaufort and the sea islands, but because the waters all come together in this region, this is the best place to talk about all the things you can do in the basin.

GOLF Let's start with golf. Hilton Head, like Myrtle Beach, is known as a golfing mecca. Home to the PGA tour's annual Heritage Tournament, the island was built on the premise that people with money who are retired want to play golf—and play they do. When my aunt and uncle lived down here, golf was a three-times-weekly if not daily activity. Many of the courses, however, are private. There are 20 public golf courses for visitors. The best way to choose a course is hiltonheadgolf.com. But the top three are: **Harbour Town Golf Links** (843-842-8484; seapines.com), where the pros tee it up every April in the PGA's Heritage Tournament. Rates range $150–250 on this 6,973-yard, par-71 course. Set on Calibogue Sound, it's one of the most famous golf courses in the state. The **Ocean Course** at Harbour Town with rates $60–120 is the island's oldest course and probably one of the most player-friendly courses on the island. This course offers a junior tees from 150 yards away so the whole family can play.

At Palmetto Dunes, there is the **Robert Trent Jones Oceanfront Golf Course** (843-785-1136; palmettodunes.com), 7 Trent Jones Lane. This Robert Trent Jones course is 6,100 yards, par 72. A round for two with a cart is about $200. The real prize is the par-5 10th hole, where you play straight at the ocean and get remarkably close to the water before turning to the 11th tee and getting the sea breeze at your back.

For accommodations, there are several packages offered by Sea Pines Resort and Palmetto Dunes, but one of my favorite places is **Main Street Inn** (843-681-3001; mainstreetinn.com), 2200 Main Street. This quiet little getaway really feels completely different from anywhere else on the island—and with room rates that start at $140 a night, it's really quite reasonable. Its location is the one drawback for golfers: It's at the first plantation on the island and miles away from Sea Pines, Palmetto Dunes, and some of the higher-end golf courses. But it is easy access if you're playing off the island.

BEACHES If beaches are your goal, I recommend renting a private home or condo along the beach either in Hilton Head or Fripp if you're not on a budget, or a cabin at **Edisto Island State Park** (843-869-2756; south carolinaparks.com), 8377 State Cabin Road, or **Hunting Island State Park** (843-838-2011; southcarolinaparks.com), 2555 Sea Island Parkway, if you are watching your dollars. The cabins at Edisto are among the state's most popular rentals and are a great way to explore the island with the kids. Edisto and Hunting Islands have the best beaches in the area, and you can tour the ACE Basin with **ACE Basin Tours** (843-521-3099 or 866-521-3099; acebasintours.com), 1 Coosaw River Drive, Lady's Island, or rent a canoe or kayak and do your own exploration through the tidal creeks and marshes. **Edisto Watersports & Tackle** (843-869-0663; edisto watersports.net), 3731 Docksite Road, Edisto Beach, offer tours of the marsh and shelling islands. Hilton Head has about 14 miles of flat white sand beaches. I recommend renting a private home along the oceanfront or staying at one of the oceanfront resorts, such as **Palmetto Dunes Oceanfront Resort** (866-380-1778; palmettodunes.com), 4 Queens Folly Road, or **Sea Pines Resort** (843-363-8100; seapines.com), 32 Greenwood Drive, because typically the folks using those beaches are only the people staying in those resorts. It keeps the crowds down. But if you're staying at an inland hotel, the island has half a dozen public beaches. They're mostly on the Atlantic Ocean, though some are on Calibogue and Port Royal Sounds. The gentle slope makes these island beaches ideal for walking, biking, sunbathing, and swimming. A variety of water sports also are available. Most of the public beach access points have restrooms, showers, and vending machines. I recommend the nice quiet **Alder Lane** beside the Marriott Grand Ocean Resort on South Forest Beach Road and Alder Lane.

SHOPPING For shopping, Hilton Head has so many outlet stores, it's a traffic hazard in summer. The outlet stores are located on US 278 before you go over the causeway onto the island. My recommendation is to plot

out the stores you want to hit before leaving your hotel. For things you
can't get anywhere else, check out **Endangered Arts Ltd.** (843-785-
5075; endangeredarts.com), 841 William Hilton Parkway, South Island
Square, and **Camp Hilton Head** (843-681-4101; camphiltonhead.com),
which has seven locations on the island including Coligny Plaza and Harbour Town. At Endangered Arts you can find all kinds of environmental
artwork. Camp Hilton Head has proprietary souvenirs. At Edisto you will
find roadside stands selling sweetgrass baskets.

NATURE For a glimpse of the area's natural beauty, drive the Edisto
Island National Scenic Byway with its moss-draped oak trees, fields, and
marshes. Check out the ACE Basin Environmental Education Center,
which has handicapped-accessible trails through its beach forest.

BEAUFORT is a step back in time, and so your visit will be all about history. But it's more than just the dates and facts of history, it's the feel. If
there is only one thing you see in Beaufort County, make it the **Old Sheldon Church Ruins**, Old Sheldon Church Road at SC 235 between Gardens Corner and Yemassee. I cannot adequately say how awesome this
place is. There is nothing here and no T-shirt to say you visited, but you
will never forget it. Next, hit the **Parris Island Museum** (843-228-2951;
mcrdpi.usmc.mil/graduation/museum.asp), Marine Corps Recruit Depot,
Parris Island, which offers a look at this unique Marine training base and
has seen hundreds of thousands of Marines pass through since the beginning of the 20th century. Downtown Beaufort also is intriguing. You won-
der sometimes how modern commerce is carried out in this town that is
too picturesque. From there, hit downtown and walk through history at
the **Verdier House** (843-379-6335; historicbeaufort.org), 801 Bay Street,
and stroll by **Milton Maxcy House**—also known as "Secession House—
1113 Craven Street, and **The Parish Church of St. Helena (Episcopal)
& Cemetery** (843-522-1712; sthelenas1712.org), 505 Church Street.
Head back downtown for lunch at the **Uptown Grill** (843-379-3332;
theuptowngrill.com), 1001 Boundary Street, then work off lunch with a
stroll at the **Henry C. Chambers Waterfront Park** (cityofbeaufort.org),
Bay Street. For places to stay, **The Beaufort Inn** (843-379-4667; beau
fortinn.com), 809 Port Republic Street, is beautiful and will really give you
the feel for the town's history. Speaking of history, as you drive from Beaufort down the Sea Island Parkway (US 21) toward Fripp, you will hit St.
Helena Island. The Penn Center is home to the first school for freed
slaves and was a meeting place for civil rights leaders in the 1960s.
Gullah-N-Geechie Mahn Tours (843-838-7516; gullahngeechietours
.net), 97 Perry Road, St. Helena Island, can tell you everything you want
to know about the island and its history. Sticking with the Gullah theme,
grab some lunch at **Gullah Grub** (843-838-3841; gullahgrubs.com), 877

Sea Island Parkway, St. Helena Island. Then head out to Hunting Island to see the lighthouse and take a hike through the forest or even paddle in the marsh and lagoon.

The Midlands 4

Jan Hogan

INTRODUCTION

The Midlands is a wide swath of land that runs aptly across the center of the state, from the North Carolina border south to the edge of the Low-country and from the start of the sandhills in the east to Georgia state line in the west.

In between are a collection of small historic towns and the capital, which is located in the geographic center of the state. These are some of the places you might never have heard of, but that make for wonderful day trips and can provide a little insight into the psyche of South Carolina.

Clarendon and Orangeburg Counties are home to the state's largest lake, Lake Marion, at 173 square miles, and to the best inland boating and fishing sites, the Santee Cooper Lakes. This area is also known for its hunting—a woman caught and killed a 1,025-pound alligator during the monthlong gator season here in 2010.

Columbia's three rivers, the Saluda, the Broad, and the Congaree, have a few challenging rapids and provide a wonderful spot for cooling off in the heat of summer. Lake Murray, created by an early-20th-century dam on the Saluda to the west of the city, also offers excellent boating and fishing opportunities.

Camden has Lake Wateree, where the Catawba River that snakes from the North Carolina state line through much of the region is stopped at another hydroelectric dam. The Wateree River comes out the other end and meanders down to Lake Marion, which itself was formed by a hydro-electric dam.

To the west, Aiken County has been bringing visitors to South Carolina since the early 20th century, including President Franklin Roosevelt. And North Augusta, which sits on the South Carolina side of the Savannah River, offers great views of the waterway that separates the state from Georgia. Beech Island in Aiken County was home to R&B singer James Brown for much of his life.

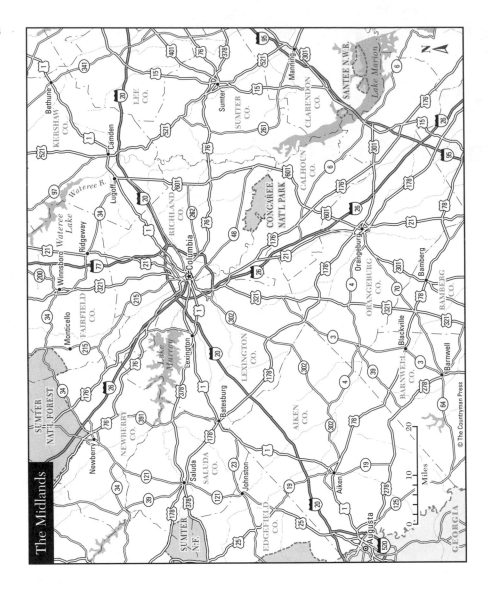

GETTING THERE Columbia is located along three interstates—20, 26, and 77—connecting most of the Midlands area from Aiken on I-20 to Rock Hill on I-77 and Orangeburg on I-26.

By air: **Columbia Metropolitan Airport** (803-822-5000 or 888-562-5002; columbiaairport.com) offers connections to several major U.S. airports and is served by carriers American Eagle (800-433-7300; aa.com), Continental Airlines (800-525-0280; continental.com), Delta Air Lines (800-221-1212; delta.com), Northwest Airlines (800-225-2525; nwa.com),

South Carolina Department of Parks, Recreation and Tourism/Perry Baker

THE BROAD RIVER PASSES BY DOWNTOWN COLUMBIA.

United (800-241-6522; united.com), US Airways (800-428-4322; usair ways.com).

By train: **Amtrak** (800-872-7245; amtrak.com), makes stops in Camden, Columbia, and the Orangeburg County town of Denmark with its Silver Star line.

By bus: **Greyhound** (803-256-6465), 2015 Gervais Street, Columbia.

By car: Most of the key cities in this area are on Interstates 20, 26, and 77, all three of which pass through Columbia.

COLUMBIA

South Carolina's capital city was the second planned city in the United States. The location was chosen for a new state capital in 1786 because it is roughly in the geographic center of the state, meaning lawmakers from the growing Upstate region would not have to make the more-than-200-mile trip to the capital in Charleston.

After 60 years in an old wooden building, the South Carolina Legislature, called the General Assembly, decided to build a more fireproof structure. Construction began in 1851 but was not completed for more than 50 years because of disagreements with architects, along with the Civil War—including the burning of the city of Columbia near the end of the war—and the subsequent poverty of the state afterward. The scars of cannon fire can still be seen on the Statehouse, and bronze stars mark where cannonballs hit.

The Statehouse went through a total renovation in the 1990s to make the building more stable in an earthquake and to restore some of the grandeur of its 19th-century design. It is one of the highlights of any visit to the city.

Columbia is also home to the University of South Carolina, which was established in 1801. The original campus of the South Carolina College, called the Horseshoe, looks much as it did when first built in the 1800s.

Columbia did not officially become an incorporated city until 1805, but its wide streets, rail and river access, and central location helped it grow quickly. Its economy was based almost entirely on cotton.

Very few buildings in Columbia survived the fire of February 1865. There is some debate about whether that fire was started by General William T. Sherman's troops seeking to punish the state and its capital for its role in starting the war. Some have said the fire was started by retreating Confederates to prevent U.S. troops from using the rail lines or ammunition stored in the city. Many of the buildings that did survive are open to the public for tours.

Columbia also is home to the U.S. Army's largest training base. Although

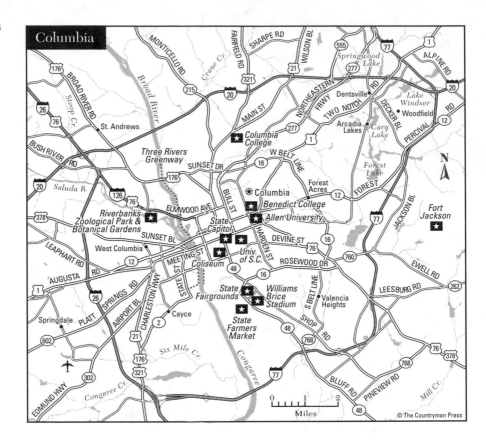

Columbia

© The Countryman Press

access to Fort Jackson has been restricted since the 2001 terrorist attacks, it is open to the public for troop graduation ceremonies and its annual Independence Day fireworks display.

Because of the influence of the university, Columbia tends to be a little more progressive than most South Carolina cities. A training facility for federal prosecutors that opened about 10 years also brings in visitors from all over the country, who help fill restaurants in several entertainment districts in town. It means that a lot of people you may meet on your travels to Columbia "ain't from around here." But don't worry, we're training them as fast as we can.

In this section, unless otherwise noted all entries are located in the city of Columbia.

GUIDANCE Lake Murray Country (803-781-5940; lakemurraycountry .com), 2184 North Lake Drive. Open 9–5 Monday through Friday, 10–4 Saturday, 1–5 Sunday. This organization provides a comprehensive listing of things to see and do in Richland, Lexington, Saluda, and Newberry Counties, which all surround Lake Murray.

Greater Columbia Chamber of Commerce (803-733-1110; columbia chamber.com), 930 Richland Street. Open 9–5 Monday through Friday. The chamber also provides visitor and lodging information for the metropolitan area.

GETTING THERE *By car:* Columbia is probably South Carolina's most accessible city, with Interstates 20, 26, and 77 passing through the city, which is roughly the geographic center of the state.

By air: **Columbia Metropolitan Airport** (803-822-5000 or 888-562-5002; columbiaairport.com) offers connections to several major U.S. airports and is served by carriers American Eagle (800-433-7300; aa.com), Continental Airlines (800-525-0280; continental.com), Delta Air Lines (800-221-1212; delta.com), Northwest Airlines (800-225-2525; nwa.com), United (800-241-6522; united.com), US Airways (800-428-4322; usair ways.com).

By train: **Amtrak** (800-872-7245; amtrak.com), 850 Pulaski Street. The Silver Star heading south stops in Columbia between 1:30 and 2 AM; heading north, it stops around 4 AM.

By bus: **Greyhound** (803-256-6465; greyhound.com), 2015 Gervais Street, Columbia.

GETTING AROUND A car is your best bet for getting around these areas. Many attractions in downtown Columbia and its two main entertainment districts are within walking distance of ample parking on the streets and in garages.

FEEDING THE GIRAFFES IS A POPULAR ATTRACTION AT RIVERBANKS ZOO IN COLUMBIA.

✳ To See

ZOOS ✐ **Riverbanks Zoo and Garden** (803-779-8717; river banks.org), 500 Wildlife Parkway. Open 9–5 daily, except Christmas and Thanksgiving. Open till 6 on Saturday and Sunday April 4 through October 4. Admission is $9.75 for adults, $8.75 for military and seniors, $7.25 for children ages 3–12, and free for younger children. This zoo is extraordinary for any city, but especially so for a medium-sized town. It is well planned and really just surprises you every time you visit with how up-close and personal you can get with the wildlife. The first time I saw it, I hated the gorilla exhibit, but over the years, I have gotten more comfortable with looking at animals that seem like they could be cousins of mine. I could never get so close to such an amazing animal without the zoo, but it is that closeness that makes me uneasy with gawking as the gorillas attempt to live their lives in odd circumstances. I am less uneasy with the giraffes, which you can feed straight from your hand—a surreal experience. The koala house looks like a boring refuge building from the '70s until you spy one of the misleadingly adorable animals in one of the trees. Again, it feels like you might be too close, but the zoo's planners and keepers seem to know exactly how to bring people and animals together without harming either.

One of my favorite things about the zoo on my annual visits as a youngster was the bird house. There were no cages. The only thing that separated me from the carrion-eating vultures with their sharp beaks was a bird's dislike for the dark. I stood in the shadows and watched the birds that had as much freedom as any of the animals at the zoo. On a recent visit, I noticed a group of vultures living at the giraffe exhibit.

SC Department of Parks, Recreation & Tourism, DiscoverSouthCarolina.com

The Walkabout lets you share a trail with wallabies. You want to reach out and touch them, they are so close, then you remember they are not pets. Amazing. Normally, I am not a big fan of captive animals, but I do believe that Riverbanks makes an enormous effort to provide the animals as much freedom as possible while providing the general public the opportunity to see and appreciate them.

Riverbanks is home to more than 2,000 animals and sits on the banks of the Saluda River just outside downtown Columbia. The zoo boasts an award-winning Aquarium and Reptile Complex and a birdhouse complete with a penguin island. The 70-acre botanical gardens have been named by HGTV as one of the 20 great public gardens across America. The zoo and garden hold several seasonal events, most notably "Boo at the Zoo" during the fall and "Lights Before Christmas," which features almost a million twinkling lights and runs from November through the end of the year. Riverbanks also offers Adventure Tours that give visitors a peek behind the scenes, including the animal hospital and kitchen as well as meeting a zoo animal. The cost is $25 for the general public, and tours are Saturdays only.

THE KOALA ARE A BIG ATTRACTION AT RIVERBANKS ZOO IN COLUMBIA.

MUSEUMS The South Carolina State Museum (803-898-4921; museum.state.sc.us), 301 Gervais Street. Open 10–5 Tuesday through Saturday, 1–5 Sunday. Open Monday in summer only. Curators like to say this museum is housed in its largest exhibit—a 19th-century textile mill that was one of the first all-electric mills with its own hydroelectric dam outside to provide power. Located along the river in the city's Congaree Vista area, the State Museum has tens of thousands of artifacts about the state's cultural and natural history. Admission: $7 adults; $5 for those ages 62 and older; $3 for children to 12; free for infants 2 and younger. Major exhibits may have an extra admission charge. The museum has a wonderful set of hands-on exhibits for kids of all ages, while the Stringer Discovery Center is especially for children 6 and younger and includes a tree house, floor puzzles, and books. One very popular annual event is the Southeastern Toy Soldier Show, typically held in late summer, which brings together dozens of exhibitors from across the South with collections of military miniatures, including tanks, planes, cannons, and vehicles, as well as soldiers. Live reenactments are held on the museum's grounds. A gift shop and café are located on site.

✒ **EdVenture** (803-779-3100; edventure.org), 211 Gervais Street. Open 9–5 Monday through Saturday, noon–5 Sunday. Admission $9.50 for adults and children; $8.50 for those 62 and older. This children's museum is located next door to the State Museum; both sit on the historic Columbia Canal once used to ferry supplies into the city. The centerpiece is Eddie, a 40-foot "boy" that kids can crawl around inside and see how he works. There are lots of things for the little ones to see and touch, so plan to stay awhile. One exhibit features a nearly life-sized figure from the board game Operation that most of today's kids have never played. But the exhibit is always full of parents using oversized salad tongs to remove the patient's breadbasket or funny bone.

McKissick Museum at the University of South Carolina (803-777-7251; cas.sc.edu/mcks), 816 Bull Street. Open Monday through Friday 8:30–5, Saturday 11–3. One of the country's largest university museums, the McKissick houses a well-known collection of gems and minerals and other natural science displays. Also on permanent display is an extensive collection of 18th- and 19th-century silver donated by the estate of early-20th-century financier Bernard Baruch. The museum also has rotating exhibits that highlight research and work by South Carolinians and others from the American South. Located at the end of the university's famed Horseshoe, the McKissick is the perfect capper to a trip down the grassy commons area that once was the center of the South Carolina College. Admission is free.

Cayce Historical Museum (803-739-5385; historysc.com), 1800 12th Street, Cayce. Open Tuesday through Friday 9–4, Saturday through Sunday 2–5. Admission: adults $2, children (ages 12 and younger) 50 cents, seniors/students $1; free admission on Sunday. This museum traces the history of the inhabitants of the area known as the backcountry in the early 1700s, from American Indians thousands of years ago to European settlers to modern times. The museum's main building is a replica of Fort Granby, a trading post that was seized by the British during the Revolutionary War and used as a fort. The Cayce family bought the building in 1817 and used it as a private residence for almost 100 years. Included in the exhibits is a display on the Civil War battle of Congaree Creek just before the U.S. Army prepared to occupy Columbia.

Columbia Museum of Art (803-799-2810; columbiamuseum.org), 1515 Main Street. Open 11–5 Tuesday through Friday, 10–5 Saturday, noon–5 Sunday. Admission: $10 adults; $8 military; $8 seniors ages 65 and older; $5 students; free for members. Sunday is free. The museum has long been a focal point of art in the Midlands, but until its move to Main Street was in cramped quarters that didn't allow for much display space. In its new home since 1998, the museum now has 25 galleries to show off its Italian Renaissance art from the Samuel H. Kress Collection, its European and American furniture, as well as contemporary art pieces including a Chihuly chandelier installed in spring 2010. The 14-foot-tall work was commissioned for the museum and includes golds, oranges, and reds reminiscent of a Carolina sunset. The museum also has added a collection of Asian art in recent years. The Museum Shop is open during museum hours.

Lexington County Museum (803-359-8369; lex-co.com/museum), 231 Fox Street, Lexington. Open 10–4, Tuesday through Saturday and 1–4

Sunday. Admission: $3 adults, $2 for children 12 and younger. This 7-acre property is centrally located in Lexington and features 36 historic buildings, including a colonial cabin circa 1771 and a schoolhouse and cotton gin from the 19th century. Several programs for schoolchildren include docents in period dress and offer youngsters a hands-on look at life in the 18th and 19th centuries. Exhibits include period furniture and textiles, including quilts. Outbuildings include a dairy, an outhouse, and a loom house. The centerpiece is the 10-room John Fox House, a plantation home built in 1832.

South Carolina Archives and History Center (803-896-6100; scdah .sc.gov), 8301 Parklane Road. Research room is open Tuesday through Saturday 8:30–5. Free. If you want to conduct genealogical research, the home of more than 325 years of South Carolina history is the place to start. In short, the center tells the story of South Carolina through historical documents, such as legislative journals, governors' papers, and land records as well as military service records from the Revolutionary and Civil Wars. The center also includes historical exhibits, a gift shop, and a reference room.

South Carolina Confederate Relic Room and Military Museum (803-737-8095; crr.sc.gov), 301 Gervais Street. Open Tuesday through Saturday 10–5 and 1–5 on the first Sunday of each month. Admission: $5 ages 18–61, $4 seniors and military, $2 ages 13–17, free for children 12 and younger. Everybody pays $1 on the first Sunday of the month. This museum was founded in 1896 as the Confederate Relic Room, but has expanded its mission to include artifacts from South Carolina's military from the Revolutionary War to the present. A popular recent exhibit is the Write from the Front program that collects emails, photographs, and other objects from South Carolinians serving in the 21st-century wars in Iraq and Afghanistan. Located in the same building as the State Museum, the relic room is home to permanent and rotating exhibits. From 2010 through 2015, the museum will focus on the 150th anniversary of the U.S. Civil War, from the signing of the articles of secession in South Carolina in December 1860 through the surrender of General Robert E. Lee at Appomattox in 1865.

HISTORIC SITES South Carolina Statehouse (803-734-2430; scstate house.gov), 1101 Gervais Street. Free guided tours are available 9–5 Monday through Friday. Note that the General Assembly is in session Tuesday through Thursday from late January through the first week of June every year. Some of the best days to visit are Mondays while they are in session or in the afternoons on days they meet, as most business is conducted in the mornings. Fridays are usually full of schoolchildren, especially in the spring. Call ahead to confirm tour times.

SOUTH CAROLINA STATEHOUSE

African-American History Monument (803-734-2430), 301 Gervais
Street, on the east side of the Statehouse. This monument was dedicated
in spring 2001 and traces the history of Africans brought to the colonies as
slaves, through the fight for freedom during the Civil War and the ensuing
struggle for civil rights, and historic achievements in the 20th century. A
dozen scenes are depicted in the sculpted work including a slave auction,
workers in the rice fields, celebrating emancipation, and modern-day
heroes from a variety of fields. The obelisk at the monument includes four
rubbing stones from the regions of Africa where slaves were captured:
Senegal, Sierra Leone, the Republic of Congo, and Ghana.

Governor's Mansion (803-737-1710; scgovernorsmansion.org), 800 Richland Street. Open Tuesday through Thursday with tours at 10, 10:30, and
11 or by appointment. Free. The building was originally constructed as a
home for military officers. Governors have been living here since 1868. A
renovation in 2001 added 5,000 square feet to the mansion. Tours are
given of the first floor of the state dining room, drawing rooms, library,
and a smaller dining room. All are furnished with 19th-century antiques.
The best time to tour is either the spring when the gardens are in bloom
or at Christmas when the house is decorated for the holidays. The Lace
House on the grounds of the mansion is frequently rented out for weddings. The gardens are open year-round.

1601 Richland Street. Open 10–3 Tuesday through Saturday, 1–4 Sunday.
Admission for one house: $6 adults ages 17–65; $5 for seniors, active-duty
military, and college students; $3 for ages 6–17; and free for children five
and younger. You save $1 per house if you buy a three-house combo tick-
et. Despite being burned almost to the ground at the end of the Civil War,
Columbia does still have a few historic homes open for touring.

Robert Mills House, 1616 Blanding Street. Robert Mills was the first
architect born and trained in the United States and designed some of the
young country's most prominent buildings, including the Washington
Monument. His 1832 home is in the Greek Revival style.

Hampton-Preston Mansion, 1615 Blanding Street. This is one of the city's
oldest homes, dating back to 1818, and was the city house of wealthy 19th-
century planter Wade Hampton I.

Woodrow Wilson Boyhood Home, 1705 Hampton Street. This Victorian
home was built after the Civil War and was where the 28th president
spent his childhood. Many of the family's original furnishings are on display at the home, including the bed Woodrow Wilson was born in.

Mann-Sims Cottage, 1403 Richland Street. Celia Mann earned her living as a midwife and purchased her freedom from slavery before the Civil
War. This was one of the few homes in the state owned by a freed slave
prior to the war. It remained in her family from 1850 until 1970. Many
family heirlooms are on display, and the cottage has been returned to how
it would have looked in the 19th century.

South Caroliniana Library (803-777-3131; sc.edu/library/socar), Senate
at College Streets on the USC Horseshoe. Open Monday through Friday
8:30–5. This library was the first freestanding academic library building in
the United States. Completed in 1840, it was designed by South Carolina
native Robert Mills. The reading room was modeled after the original
Library of Congress. The university built the larger McKissick Library 100
years later, and the Caroliniana was dedicated to house materials on the
history and culture of South Carolina; today it's a major research facility.
The library houses books, newspapers, manuscripts, maps, audio record-
ings, and visual images. In the 1970s library researchers helped retrieve a
collection of photographs from glass-plate negatives shot by black photographer Richard Samuel Roberts of Columbia. More than 3,000 images
were printed from the plates and put on display at the Columbia Museum
of Art in 1986 and put in the book *A True Likeness: The Black South of
Richard Samuel Roberts: 1920–1936*. The pictures show an economically
secure black middle class during the early 20th century.

Trinity Episcopal Cathedral & Cemetery (803-771-7300; trinitysc
.org), 1100 Sumter Street. Open daily. Free. Trinity completed an exten-

sive renovation in 2010—the first major face-lift in its more-than-160-year history. The present building was designed by Edward Brickell White and modeled on the York Cathedral in England. It was dedicated in 1847 and miraculously survived the burning of Columbia 18 years later. The sanctuary has those old box-style pews, and the graveyard is the final resting place for six former governors, including James F. Byrnes, who also was a U.S. House member, a U.S. Senator, and an associate justice on the U.S. Supreme Court.

✳ To Do

CANOE/KAYAK TOURS Adventure Carolina Inc. (803-796-4505; adventurecarolina.com), 1107 State Street, Cayce. Nothing is better on a hot summer day than a cool paddle or dip in the Congaree River. Adventure Carolina offers guided tours and boat and inner tube rentals. Trips are $30 for a 3-mile trip starting at either 6 PM on Tuesday, Thursday, and Friday nights or 2 PM Saturday through Sunday. Each Saturday at noon, there is a tube launch for $15 per tube. Adventure Carolina will shuttle you and your tube to the river for the coolest thing you can do on a hot summer day.

River Runner Outdoor Center (803-771-0353; riverrunner.us), 905 Gervais Street. Open Monday through Saturday 10–6. The folks at River Runner are known for their customer service. If you have something you want to do on the water in Columbia, just ask, they can probably help you. Located in Columbia's Congaree Vista just a few blocks from the water, the River Runner has guides who can tell you everything you need to know about getting on the water. Rentals are charged per day and since they aren't open on Sunday, that is a free day for rentals. The initial day is $40 for any recreational boat; $10 for each additional day. All equipment is included in the rental of a boat. The company also offers hourly rentals on weekends at Saluda Shoals Park just outside Columbia: $23 for an hour, $38 for three hours, and $48 for all day. Rentals available daily 10–5. These guys also do guided tours on the Broad, Saluda, and Congaree Rivers on weekends and during the week. A word, though, about paddling the Broad: She tends to paddle back. If you go on the Broad River trip, the rapids aren't big, but they are pervasive and can dump you out of your boat several times in a few hours. I suggest that everyone take his or her own boat—double kayaks tend to get caught up on the rocks more easily than single ones. And the Broad River is filled with rocks. The River Runner's guides are the best at helping you get free, but it can get tiresome getting stuck over and over again.

♧ *Southern Patriot* **Tour Boat** (803-749-8594; lakemurraytours.com), 1600 Marina Road, Irmo. This tour boat can hold up to 100 passengers and is used for weddings, anniversaries, and birthday parties as well as

PURPLE MARTINS

The purple martin is the largest North American swallow and breeds primarily in the summers of the American South; it winters along the Amazon River in South America. The first officially designated sanctuary for these beautiful songbirds is at Lake Murray, which sits northwest of Columbia. The birds that nest east of the Rockies are almost entirely dependent on man-made structures for their summer homes.

The birds return to the same nesting grounds year after year. Bird enthusiasts can use a variety of methods to lure young birds to their backyards to start their own annual tradition. I remember my grandfather set up martin gourds in his backyard in Florence and outside his beach house at Garden City. They filled his yard with music in the morning and helped reduce the number of mosquitoes at dusk.

When the birds reach a critical mass—as they do at Lake Murray every spring and early summer—their daily flights off and back onto their island in the lake are quite the show. The island is known by several names: Bomb, Doolittle, or Lunch. The first two names come from its use during World War II as a bombing range for pilots, especially those in the famed Doolittle Raider (see the sidebar in this chapter) squadron that carried out an air raid on Tokyo in April 1942—just months after the attack on Pearl Harbor.

Hundreds of thousands of birds nest on the 12-acre island, which is closed to visitors when the martins are there in the summer. The birds leave their nests in the morning to forage; their mass departures are so large, they can be measured by weather radar in the area. In the early evening, scores of boaters surround the island to watch the martins come home to roost.

community events. In July and August, the boat offers tours Sunday and Monday nights for people to watch the nightly return of hundreds of thousands of purple martins to their Lunch Island roost. The tours depart at 6:45 and 9:15 from Lake Murray Marina and cost $30 per person. A light supper is served, and your guide will tell you about the history of the area and the purple martins. The 65-foot double-deck *Southern Patriot* is also available for private charters and has a dance floor, music system, catering station, and bar. It is handicapped accessible.

Spirits and Spectres of Columbia (803-600-1328 or 877-820-5160). Tours start on the north steps of the Statehouse at 8 PM by reservation only. Cost: $15 per adult, $10 for children 5–13; free for younger children. There is a $3 discount for seniors, college students, and military with ID. This is a great tour led by guides who really know the history—real and spectral—of the capital city. The highlights of the tour are the Statehouse grounds, the Trinity Cathedral graveyard, and the University of South Carolina Horseshoe. Call or email (dbtours@sc.rr.com) at least a week in advance to make reservations. Tours can go with as few as four people. The length of the tour varies by the walkers' speed, but usually is about 90 minutes.

✍ **Harmon's Tree Farm and Christmas House** (803-359-4454), 3152 Augusta Highway, Gilbert. Open 9–6 Monday through Saturday, 1:30–6 Sunday. This 75-acre farm is known for its Christmas trees, though over the years the family has added attractions that make it a great place to visit year-round. But, first, Christmas. Harmon's has for years been the place that locals get their Christmas trees. They will take you on a tram ride with hot cider or cocoa so you can pick out just the one you want. The farm also has a grits mill and farm museum with a spray pool, jumping pillows, a candy store, miniature golf, and a 500-foot slip and slide. In spring the farm is colored with new life, flowers and baby animals. In May and June the blueberries are ripe; peaches are ready in July. That's when you can get Gerald's homemade ice cream. In the fall the farm turns to the harvest and all things Halloween with hayrides, a pumpkin patch, and a corn maze.

✳ Green Space

PARKS The Congaree National Park (803-776-4396; nps.gov/cong /index.htm), 100 National Park Road, Hopkins. Open 8:30–5 daily, open till 7 on summer weekends. Free admission. Congaree is South Carolina's only true national park and preserves the largest old-growth floodplain forest in North America. Towering trees shelter canoers and kayakers in the swamp. The park also includes 20 miles of backcountry hiking trails and a 2-mile boardwalk trail. The park offers guided tours on land and boat throughout the year. It's also a popular birding spot. The swamp is prone to flooding in heavy rains; check conditions before heading out.

🐾 **Sesquicentennial State Park** (803-788-2706; southcarolinaparks .com), 9564 Two Notch Road. Open daily 8–6 with extended hours during Daylight Saving Time. This is where people in Columbia go to play. Walking and biking trails through the Sandhills offer a chance to find a little wilderness just 15 minutes from downtown. So if you go, you are as likely to see locals on a morning jog as you are to see campers on an overnight

SC Department of Parks, Recreation & Tourism, DiscoverSouthCarolina.com

SESQUICENTENNIAL STATE PARK

stay. The park was built in the 1930s, and its name is a tribute to the 150th anniversary of the city of Columbia. A recently added dog park makes this a great location for RVers with pups. If you're just coming by Sesqui (*ses-KWEE*) for the day, it's $2 to visit with an additional $4 per pooch for the dog park. You'll also need a record that your dog has been spayed or neutered and is up-to-date on rabies, parvo, and kennel cough vaccines. For camping, there are about 84 sites with electric and water hookups at about $20 a night.

CITY PARKS 🐾 ✎ **Finlay Park** (803-545-3100; columbiasc.net), 930 Laurel Street, Columbia. Admission is free. Open daily sunrise to sunset. This is Columbia's Central Park with a waterfall, pond, and grassy area where hundreds of folks come out on Saturday in summer to hear live music. There is a great playground where the kids or puppies can burn off some energy. The park is named for a former mayor who championed development of the city's Vista area between Main Street and the river. Parking is available along Taylor Street for the easiest in and out at the park.

Three Rivers Greenway (803-765-2200; riveralliance.org), Alexander Road. Open daily dawn to dusk. Free. The Broad and Saluda Rivers come into Columbia from the north and west and meet downtown to form the Congaree, which divides Columbia from West Columbia and Cayce. The Three Rivers Greenway extends from the diversion dam on the Broad River that forms the Columbia Canal through the city to the Granby Locks south of the city. There are parts of the Greenway on both sides of the river. There are plans for dedicated walking and biking paths along the bridges that cross the river, but for now if you want to get from one end to the other, you're going to have to trek on some city streets. There are four separate parks that are part of the developed Greenway. On the Columbia side are: **Granby Park** (803-545-3100; columbiasc.net), Catawba Street. This 24-acre park offers canoe access points, fishing, and a half-mile nature trail along the Congaree River. **Riverfront Park & Historic Columbia Canal** (803-545-3100; columbiasc.net), Laurel at Huger Street, is a 167-acre park encompassing the city's original water-works that ends with the oldest operating hydroelectric plant in the state, which once provided power to the nearby textile mill that is now the State Museum. A 2.5-mile paved roadway and trail runs from the hydroelectric dam at the end of the canal up to the Diversion Dam that forms it. Parking is available at the Broad River dam as well as off Huger Street at the park's main entrance. On the West Bank are the **Cayce** and **West Columbia Riverwalks**, which connect to each other and run from Meeting Street to the Granby locks south of Knox Abbott Drive. There is fishing and a put-in for kayaks or canoes. An amphitheater in the West Columbia park is used for summer concerts and seasonal plays. This spot also offers great views of the city and the Gervais Street Bridge, which was unique for its day (1927) because it was made of reinforced concrete and was the state's widest roadway when it opened.

Memorial Park (803-545-3100; columbiasc.net), Hampton at Gadsden Streets. Open daily dawn to dusk. Free. This park contains memorials to the 980 South Carolinians killed in the Vietnam War, a Holocaust monument, and a Korean War Memorial. This park takes up a whole city block and is just a few blocks from the city's Finlay Park. Parking is available at Gadsden and Washington Streets.

Saluda Shoals Park (803-731-5208; icrc.net/saludashoals), 5605 Bush River Road. Open daily dawn to dusk. Admission $5 per personal vehicle; $7 for a 12-person-plus passenger van, $11 for buses. This beautiful 350-acre riverfront park is just 1.5 miles downstream from the Lake Murray Dam. There are miles of trails for walking, biking, and horseback riding. The park also has a canoe and kayak put-in, and rentals are available as well as a boat launch and fishing spots. A splash park is open during the summer for an extra $3 per person.

✳ Lodging

PRIVATE HOME RENTALS 🐾
Lake Murray Vacation Rentals
(803-798-8559; lakemurrayvacation
.com), 2727 US 378, Gilbert. This
company has dozens of properties
for rent from two nights to a week
or more. Prices range widely, from
one-bedroom cabins at $200 for a
two-night stay to $300 a night for
a three-bedroom home that can
sleep 14. All are on the water, and
most homes allow pets.

BED & BREAKFASTS Chesnut
Cottage Bed and Breakfast
(803-256-1718; chesnutcottage
.com), 1718 Hampton Street. Gale
Garrett has been the owner of the
B&B for 20 years. It is located
near the city's historic homes district and is itself a historic home.
Built in 1850, the cottage was the
wartime home of Confederate
general James Chesnut and his
wife, Mary Boykin Chesnut (see
the sidebar in this book's introduc-
tion). A collection of entries from
Mary Chesnut's diaries were first
published in 1905—20 years after
her death—as *Diary of Dixie*,
which later won a Pulitzer Prize
for history. First editions of the
English and U.S. versions of the
book are on display at the cottage.
The cottage has many Civil
War–era artifacts and period furnishings throughout. They serve a
full breakfast that guests can eat in
the dining room or in the comfort
of their rooms. The kitchen can
accommodate most dietary needs
and aims for healthy fare. Each of
the five guests rooms has a private
bath with whirlpool tub. All rooms
also have televisions and telephones. The cottage is a healthy
stroll away from the main food
and entertainment districts. It
might be too much for a round
trip, but you could walk to your
destination then take a very inexpensive cab ride back to the cottage. Rates are $125–225.
Well-behaved children and pets
are welcome.

INNS The Inn at Claussen's
(800-622-3382; theinnatclaussens
.com), 2003 Greene Street. Located in a former bakery, the Inn at
Claussen's is a 27-room boutique
hotel in the heart of the city's Five
Points restaurant and entertainment district. Two restaurants and
a bar are located in the same
building, but operated independ-
ently. Within a few blocks' walk
are shops, a dozen restaurants,
clubs, and the University of South
Carolina. Each room is individually furnished; beds can be four-
poster, iron, or brass. Suites have
loft bedrooms suitable for families
or longer-term guests. Fresh-
baked breakfast breads are deliv-
ered to rooms each day, and wine
and scotch are served in the lobby
each afternoon. Weekend rates
run from $129 for a queen bed to
$149 for a premium king bedroom.
Suites are $169. Some weekends
may require a minimum stay, and
weeknight rates are a little cheaper. Rates do not include an 11 percent bedding and sales tax. No

SOUTH CAROLINA AND THE DOOLITTLE RAID

Lake Murray was created to generate electricity for South Carolina Electric & Gas Co. Over the years, the lake has attracted high-end homes; people use it for fishing, swimming, and boating. But during World War II, Lake Murray was a training site for U.S. Air Force B-25 pilots stationed at what is now the Columbia Metropolitan Airport. Among those training there was a group of pilots who would pull off an unbelievable raid on Tokyo just months after the Japanese bombed Pearl Harbor and destroyed much of the U.S. Navy's Pacific fleet.

The squadron began in February 1942 with B-25 bomber crews from the Columbia Army Air Base. All the pilots knew was that they were training for a dangerous mission. They did some training runs at the lake before heading to a Florida air base.

On April 18, 80 crew members in 16 planes loaded to the hilt with fuel and bombs took off from the deck of the USS *Hornet* and bombed targets in Tokyo. Mission commander Jimmy Doolittle considered it a failure because little physical damage was done on the ground and all the U.S. planes were lost. But the primary objective was more of a morale boost, as the United States had suffered several setbacks in the Pacific following the attack on Pearl Harbor.

Three crew members died bailing out or drowned after ditching their plane. Eight were captured by the Japanese; three of those were executed, and one died of malnutrition. Four were rescued from captivity at the end of the war. One crew landed in the Soviet Union where they were held, but later escaped during the war.

The mission has been chronicled in several books and movies, including *Thirty Seconds Over Tokyo*, written by one of the raid's pilots, Ted Lawson.

pets or smoking allowed on the property.

♿ **The 1425 Inn** (803-252-7225; the1425inn.com), 1425 Richland Street. This inn is located among Columbia's historic houses, but a little off the main dining and entertainment districts. Owners

David and Karen Brown have beautifully decorated each of their five rooms, all with private bath. One room is handicapped accessible. Rates are very reasonable at $130 a night during the week and $150 for weekends, and come with a full breakfast. The inn can host weddings, receptions, and luncheons and can provide a sit-down meal for up to 40 people or on-site catering for up to 100. The inn is nonsmoking. Pets are not allowed, but children are with advance notice.

The Inn at USC (866-455-4753; innatusc.com), 1619 Pendleton Street. The inn is located on campus at the University of South Carolina with 117 guest rooms, including 31 two-room suites. Rooms start at $130 and go up to $280 for suites. Breakfast is included with the room. The nearby Black House serves as the inn's welcome center and has been restored to its 1910 grandeur.

HOTEL ☕ **The Whitney** (803-252-0845; whitneyhotel.com), 700 Woodrow Street. This hotel is in the heart of the Shandon neighborhood, near the restaurants, shops, and galleries on Devine Street and within walking distance from Five Points. Rates in the all-suite hotel start at $90 a night for a one-bedroom up to $120 for a two-bedroom. The hotel offers a full breakfast buffet with room and a limousine service that comes in handy if you want to check out the restaurants and bars of nearby Five Points. Pets are welcome here.

✳ Where to Eat

DINING OUT Mr. Friendly's (803-254-7828, mrfriendlys.com), 2001-A Greene Street. Open Monday through Friday for lunch 11:30–2; open Monday through Saturday for dinner starting at 5:30. Offering Southern cuisine with a gourmet twist, Mr. Friendly's is located in the former Claussen's Bakery building. Favorites are the fried oyster Caesar salad ($12.50), Monday-night meat loaf ($17), classic shrimp and grits ($17), and black bean cakes ($7.50 appetizer). For dessert, they make a homemade version of that Southern classic, a moon pie, but only on Monday night. The chefs will try to meet specific dietary needs, and all dishes can be made vegetarian. The café boasts an extensive wine list and holds wine tastings at least once a month. Owner Ricky Mollohan owns several restaurants in Columbia, including a wine and tapas bar, **The Cellar on Greene** (803-343-3303; cellarongreene.com), located in the same building. Ricky posts daily and weekly specials on the Web page. Dress is casual. They don't take reservations and dinner for two will cost $25–50 without alcohol; lunch, $15–25. Mr. Friendly's won my heart the night I walked in craving a white fish in a lemon sauce over pasta. That night's menu had all the pieces I wanted, but not all in one dish. So I asked if they could fix the tilapia a little differently and was rewarded with exactly what I wanted. It was the only time I have ever gone "off the menu," but it was nice to know they would accommodate a special request. Mr. Friendly's really lives up to its name.

Garibaldi's of Columbia (803-771-8888; garibaldicolumbia.com), 2013 Greene Street. Open daily at 5:30 for dinner. The art deco bar and eclectic mix of politicians and artists make Garibaldi's one of the coolest places in town for drinks at the bar or full dinner with dessert—or both. The crispy whole flounder has been the centerpiece of the menu for more than 20 years. Entrées range from linguine with marinara sauce at $8, to $24 for the flounder. Some specials may be higher.

Dianne's on Devine (803-254-3535; diannesondevine.com), 2400 Devine Street. Open daily except Sunday for dinner starting at 5. Dianne has been in the restaurant business in Columbia for at least 30 years and has been at her current location for more than 15. The menu is mostly Italian with the best crabcakes in town. Entrées range $12–33.

116 Espresso and Wine Bar (803-791-5663; 116state.com), 116 State Street, West Columbia. Open Tuesday through Friday for dinner starting at 4, Saturday 10 AM–midnight, and Sunday 10–5. This great little restaurant is part coffeehouse, part gourmet tapas and wine restaurant. It is located in the bohemian area of West Columbia commonly called "the West Bank." The food is fantastic and comes in small, shareable portions. The dishes include mussels, chimichurri, cheese plates, and a Mediterranean platter with olives, hummus, and orzo salad. There is a wonderful selection of pizzas and martinis. Most dishes are $10 or less.

Motor Supply Co. Bistro (803-256-6687; motorsupplycobistro.com), 920 Gervais Street. Open Tuesday through Sunday 11:30–2:30 for lunch, with dinner starting at 5:30. Opened in 1989, Motor Supply was the first restaurant to gamble that Columbia's old steel mill and warehouse district would turn into the restaurant and entertainment area that it is. Their handwritten menu changes nightly, but there usually are one or two seafood dishes, one chicken, one pork, and one red meat. This is a favorite place for Sunday brunch, and they have the best outdoor dining in the Vista. Lunch items are typically less than $12, and dinner entrées usually range $18–28.

Blue Marlin (803-799-3838; bluemarlincolumbia.com), 1200 Lincoln Street. Open Sunday through Friday starting at 11:30. Saturday dinner only starting at 4. Located in another old train station, the Blue Marlin was one of the early restaurants in the city's Congaree Vista area. The restaurant gained some notoriety when police reports showed that a suspected serial killer had spent an evening there buying drinks for a large bar crowd before being arrested in Augusta, Georgia, right after the Masters golf tournament. The bar is a fun place to wait for dinner or even enjoy dinner if you can't wait for a table. In temperate weather, Blue Marlin has great outdoor dining. Lunch items are $9–12, and dinner entrées range $16–25.

California Dreaming (803-254-6767; centraarchy.com/california dreaming.php), 401 Main Street. Open daily 11–10. This is the restaurant that started the California Dreaming chain, but its unique location makes it unlike any other. Located in the historic Union Station train depot in Columbia, the restaurant has been feeding students at nearby University of South Carolina and their families since 1984. They don't take reservations and there can be quite a wait on weekends, especially if there is a game or big concert in town. Go early or be prepared to wait. The Dreaming Salad—a massive bowl of lettuce, chopped egg, meats, cheeses, and toasted almonds, served with a warm honey buttered croissant—brings in the lunchtime crowds and is still under $10. Sandwiches are under $12 and dinner entrées range $12–26.

EATING OUT M Vista (803-255-8878; miyos.com), 701 Lady Street, Suite C. There are six locations around Columbia in the Miyo's family of restaurants. The menus vary slightly from place to place, and all have similar decor and prices. My favorite is M Vista, in part because the bamboo talks to you as it cools in the early evening, especially in summertime. This location also has the best bar. Menu

items include traditional Chinese dishes, sushi, and sashimi as well as very healthy vegetarian and nonfried foods. This is the best Asian food in Columbia by far. Lunch entrées are typically less than $10, with dinner entrées ranging up to $20.

Compton's Kitchen (803-791-0755; comptonskitchen.com), 1118 B Avenue, West Columbia. Open 6 AM–2 PM Monday through Friday for breakfast and lunch; breakfast only on Saturday 6–noon. One of the best bargains and friendliest staffs you will find anywhere, Compton's Kitchen has been open since 1977, and prices haven't changed much since then. For about $5, you can get two eggs, choice of meat, grits, and biscuit (or hash browns and toast for you Yankees) for breakfast, including coffee. For about the same price, you can have a lunch with a meat, two sides (I recommend the mac and cheese), biscuit, and tea. You will notice that

SUSHI PLATE AT M VISTA IN COLUMBIA

COMPTON'S KITCHEN IN WEST COLUMBIA

everyone seems to know everyone else. If you eat here more than once, chances are the waitress will remember what you're drinking, darlin'.

DiPrato's (803-779-0606; dipratos .com), 342 Pickens Street. Open daily 10–6. This is Dianne's lunch place. A gourmet deli with the best homemade pimiento cheese you will ever taste and an open-faced roast beef sandwich big enough for two. Most items under $10. Lunchtime gets very crowded with locals, so come around 11:30, then enjoy people-watching while you eat.

Yesterday's (803-799-0196; yesterdayssc.com), 2030 Devine Street. Open daily 11:30–midnight. The iconic cowboy in the bathtub sits atop this restaurant, located in a flat-iron-style building that makes up one of the points of Columbia's Five Points entertainment district. Since 1976, the MacRae brothers have served burgers, loaded nachos, and home cooking. Yesterday's bar is a gathering place for students, faculty, and alumni of the University of South Carolina. If there is a sporting event going on anywhere in the world, you'll be able to see it at Yesterday's. Favorites are El Nacho Man ($7), Confederate Fried Steak ($8), mushroom Swiss burger ($7), and the Arkansas Traveler—roast beef with gravy served over corn bread with hoppin' John ($7.50). The most expensive dish is the 11-ounce rib eye at $14.

Hunter-Gatherer (803-748-0540; huntergathererbrewery.com), 900 Main Street. Open for lunch 11–2 and dinner 4–11, Tuesday through Friday. This is a great place to meet friends for tasty brews that you won't find anywhere else. There is limited outdoor dining, but plenty of room in the two-story dining room and bar inside. The eclectic menu includes many vegetarian options. Most lunches are under $10 and include gyros and salads, individual pizzas, and a roasted chile pulled pork sandwich with coleslaw. Dinners range $7–18 and include a smoked chicken ravioli in a Gouda cream sauce. Most dishes come with a great mixed green salad. For the late-night crowd, there's live music, with Thursday reserved for jazz with a wonderful mix of local players. It's packed on Jazz Night so get here early, have dinner, and stay for some great music.

Pawleys Front Porch (803-771-8001; pawleys5pts.com), 827 Harden Street. Open Monday through Thursday 11:30–10, Friday through Saturday 11:30–11, Sunday 11:30–9:30. We love the burgers here, because the kitchen grinds its own meat, so you can get your burger cooked to any temperature. Featured on an episode of the Food Network's *Diners, Drive-Ins and Dives*, Pawleys has a great twist on a Southern staple: Fried Green Tomato Napoleon, with layers of Boursin cheese, Cajun crab dip, and sweet chipotle mayonnaise between crispy fried 'maters. In keeping with the coastal name, Pawleys also serves up fish tacos and has a wonderful deck for drinking, eating, and watching the big game. Entrées are $7–11.

 **Jake's Kickstand Café** (803-781-2590; jakeskickstandcafe.com), 7811 Broad River Road, Irmo. Open for dinner Monday

HUNTER-GATHERER BREWERY AND ALE HOUSE IN COLUMBIA

through Saturday 4:30–10. Jake does a burger every which way with more than 16 specialty toppings including banana peppers, blue cheese, and fried pickle chips. The Dixie burger has fried green tomato, pimiento cheese, bacon, and honey barbecue sauce. Sides include baked beans and sweet potato fries. Burgers start around $7; salads and kids' menu items start around $5.

Columbia has two barbecue joints that I can recommend even though I am not a fan of the mustard-based variety (see the chapter 1 sidebar on barbecue). They are located in the "Twin Cities" of Batesburg-Leesville on US 1 west of Columbia.

Shealy's Bar-B-Que (803-332-3022; shealysbbq.com), 340 East Columbia Avenue, Batesburg. Open 11–9 every day except Wednesday and Sunday. Open for breakfast Saturday only 7–9:30. For just a little more than $10, you get some of the best Midlands-style barbecue there is. The buffet includes fantastic fried chicken, and their mac and cheese will melt in your mouth.

Jackie Hite's Bar-B-Q (803-532-3354), 467 West Church Street, Batesburg-Leesville. Open Friday through Saturday for take-out only. Jackie Hite slow-cooks his barbecue in a pit, giving the meat an extra-smoky flavor, and douses it in a light mustard sauce. He also is known for his fried pork skins, extra crispy and light.

✳ Entertainment

The White Mule (803-661-8199; thewhitemule.com), 1530 Main Street. Open daily at 5 PM for dinner and music. The pizza here is fantastic, and the Mule offers a variety of live music, including an open-mike night. This is a great place to grab a late-night snack and get your groove on. Door prices vary widely, but $10 should get you in and another $10 will get you anything on the menu.

Trustus Theatre (803-254-9732; trustus.org), 520 Lady Street. Trustus has been located in Columbia's Congaree Vista shopping and restaurant district since 1985. The city's only professional theater, Trustus offers eight mainstage productions and a Late Night season of one-act plays and sketch comedy that starts at 11:15 PM on Friday. Each year the theater produces the winning play from its playwrights festival. In addition to putting on cutting-edge shows, the theater boasts recliner-style rockers for seats and free popcorn. The bar opens an hour before showtime. The box office is open 1–6 Tuesday through Saturday. Musical tickets are $25, and nonmusicals are $20 on Thursday, $22.50 on Friday and Saturday nights, and $17.50 on Sunday. Seniors, students, and military pay $15. The first Sunday matinee for all nonmusicals is "I Pay What I Can," with a minimum donation of $1. Late Night shows are $5.

Nickelodeon (803-254-8234; nickelodeon.org), 937 Main Street (moving to 1607 Main Street by 2012). The Nick—as it is called by locals—is a 75-seat theater showing art-house films and movies that you might not get to see in large chain theaters. Admission is $7.50, and the theater sells, popcorn, candy, water, soda, and beer and wine. The theater is in the process of moving to a larger location on the other side of the capitol. When the Nick makes its move, it will become the South Carolina Center for Film and Media with about 200 seats and two screens as well as the Columbia Media Education Center. If you get here before it makes its move, give it a try anyway; it really is a fun way to see a great film.

✷ Selective Shopping

FIVE POINTS (fivepointscolumbia .com), Saluda Avenue, Greene Street, Santee Avenue, Harden Street. The city's oldest neighborhood shopping and entertainment district, Five Points boasts art galleries, eclectic clothing stores, bookstores, wine shops, and a record store. Shops are open 10–6 Monday through Saturday unless otherwise noted.

Blue Sky Gallery (803-779-4242; blueskyart.com), 733 Saluda Avenue. Open 11:30–5:30 Wednesday through Saturday or by appointment. The shop features work by famed muralist and Columbia native Blue Sky. His artwork can be seen around the city, and his gallery has photographs

and smaller versions of some of his most memorable murals and installations.

Portfolio Art Gallery (803-256-2434; portfolioartgal.com), 2007 Devine Street. The gallery offers an eclectic mix of art, jewelry, and gifts including the works of Brian Andreas.

Gourmet Shop (803-799-3705; thegourmetshop.net), 724 Saluda Avenue. Open 9–6 Monday through Saturday, 10–5 Sunday. A longtime staple of Five Points, the Gourmet Shop serves brunch and lunch in addition to selling its freshly made deli salads in bulk. The store carries just about every kitchen gadget and food imaginable as well as a wide variety of beer, wine, cheese, and gourmet snacks. They also have a humidor and sell high-end cigars. If you stop here for lunch, I recommend the chicken salad.

Loose Lucy's (803-252-1390; looselucys.com), 709 Saluda Avenue. If you were ever a Deadhead or wished you could dress like one, this is the place for you. With seven stores in the Carolinas and Georgia, Loose Lucy's specializes in tie-dyed clothing, tapestries, posters, and other cool stuff.

Papa Jazz Record Shoppe (803-256-0096; papajazz.com), 2014 Greene Street. Do you miss the popping sounds of a vinyl record playing on a turntable? Then Papa Jazz is the place for you. They buy and sell old records, some still in the shrink wrap.

DEVINE STREET (doorsofdevine .net). This area just up from the Five Points area includes shopping, dining, commercial buildings, and a salon and day spa in a neighborhood setting.

Bohemian (803-256-0629), 707 Saluda Avenue. Open 10:30–6 Monday through Saturday, 1–5 Sunday. The Bohemian has been around for 35 years offering unique clothing, jewelry, and accessories as well as candles and gifts. The store also offers home furnishings that you won't find anywhere else.

Just the Thing (803-771-9969; shopjustthething.com), 2732 Devine Street. Open 10–6 Monday through Friday, 10–5 Saturday. Just the Thing is part of a small chain of three shops in Atlanta, Georgia, and High Point, North Carolina. It offers a wide selection of jewelry and handbags.

MORE SHOPPING OPPORTUNITIES ✇ **State Farmers Market** (803-737-4664; scstatefarmersmarket.com), 3483 Charleston Highway, West Columbia. Open 6 AM–9 PM Monday through Saturday, 1–6 Sunday. After decades across the street from the University of South Carolina football stadium, the State Farmers Market has moved to a new home near Interstates 26 and 77. Shoppers can find South Carolina produce as well as that shipped in from around the country. There also is an exhibition

kitchen, a specialty foods shop, and a place for the kids to play. The new market has room for RVs loading up of fresh fruits and veggies. This is a great place to stop by on your way home to see if there is anything from Columbia you would like to take home with you.

Old Mill Antique Mall (803-796-4229), 310 State Street, West Columbia. Open 10–5:30 Monday through Saturday, 1:30–5:30 Sunday. More than 75 dealers bring their antiques to this huge mall on the West Bank of Columbia's Congaree River. Everything—and I mean everything—can be found here: antiques, collectibles, furniture, jewelry, books, and even vintage clothing. This is a wonderful way to while away a couple of hours.

✳ Special Events

FALL *October:* **South Carolina State Fair** (803-799-3387, scstate fair.org), 1200 Rosewood Drive. For two weeks every October, the State Fair brings together farmers, crafters, bakers, and artists and surrounds them with amusement park rides, Italian sausages, and Fisk fries. There is a variety of entertainment during the fair as well, from country music singers to oldies groups. The fairgrounds also host several events throughout the year, including boat, RV, and home shows, 4-H competitions, and two craft shows a year, one in the spring and one for Christmas crafts held in late

November, All event dates and prices are listed on the State Fair's website.

November: **Craftsmen's Christmas Classic** (gilmoreshows.com). Event dates vary from year to year, but typically it's the first weekend in November. Ticket prices are set a few weeks before the show, and the website offers $1-off coupons. It's usually less than $10 for a three-day pass with discounts for kids. This traveling show is a big hit in the Columbia area every November with hundreds of craftsmen from across the Southeast bringing their wares to the State Fairgrounds for a three-day weekend of Christmas shopping. Everything from soups and dips for your Christmas party to works of art and furniture can be found at these shows. Friday morning is the best day to start, as most of us locals are at work. That gives you plenty of time to mull over a purchase and come back before they close on Sunday. A similar show comes by in the spring, usually the first weekend in March, with fewer seasonal items.

SPRING *March:* ✆ **St. Patrick's Day in Five Points** (stpats5 points.com), Harden Street. This daylong festival kicks off with an 8 AM road race followed by a 10 AM parade down Devine Street into the Five Points shopping and entertainment district. There is a children's carnival area, craft vendors, several stages for live music, and lots of food, beer, and green things. If you have little ones, come early for the parade and play area before the college kids wake up. If you're coming for the music—a great mix of rock, country, and alternative bands—get there around noon, have some food, and map out your stage strategy. Alcohol is allowed on streets that are part of the festival. Parking is blocks away so be prepared for the walk back after the festival wraps up. The best way to do this festival is to book at the Whitney on Devine Street or even Claussen's Inn, which is inside the festival area. The festival does have trolley pickup and drop-offs at various locations around town; check out the website to see if any are near your hotel.

REVOLUTIONARY WAR CORRIDOR

CAMDEN TO KINGS MOUNTAIN

This wide band of counties ranging north from Columbia to the North Carolina state line are all tied together by their roles in the Revolutionary War, from one of the worst defeats for the Patriots at Camden to one of the first victories in the Southern colonies at Kings Mountain. The area stretches from McBee in the east—where you will find the tastiest peaches—to Newberry in the west, where you should come for dinner on the square and a show at the Newberry Opera House.

Sumter County is named for Revolutionary War hero Thomas Sumter. His nickname "the Gamecock"—for his relentless fighting spirit—is the name for the University of South Carolina's sports teams.

Lancaster County in the north is the birthplace of the seventh president of the United States (see the sidebar), and York County is home to wonderful rivers and lakes as well as Winthrop University, which for generations has turned out many of the state's teachers.

One of this area's most famous natives is early-20th-century educator Mary McLeod Bethune, who was born in the Sumter County town of Mayesville, began her teaching career in South Carolina schools, and helped open schools for black students across the South. Bethune-Cookman College in Florida is the result of her school for women merging with Cookman College for men. There is a memorial to her in Lincoln Park in Washington, DC, and her portrait hangs in the South Carolina Statehouse.

GUIDANCE Kershaw County Chamber of Commerce (803-432-2525; kershawcountychamber.org).

York County Visitors Bureau (803-329-5200; visityorkcounty.com), 452 South Anderson Road, Rock Hill.

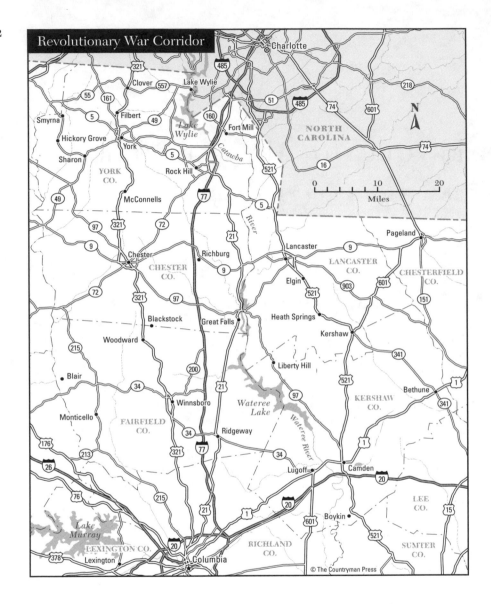

Revolutionary War Corridor

Sumter Visitors Bureau (803-436-2640; sumtersc.gov), 21 North Main Street, Sumter. Welcome Center located on Interstate 95.

Newberry County Chamber of Commerce (803-276-4274; newberry county.org), 1109 Main Street, Newberry.

GETTING THERE *By air:* **Columbia Metropolitan Airport** (803-822-5000 or 888-562-5002; columbiaairport.com) offers connections to several major U.S. airports and is served by carriers American Eagle (800-433-

7300; aa.com), Continental Airlines (800-525-0280; continental.com), Delta Air Lines (800-221-1212; delta.com), Northwest Airlines (800-225-2525; nwa.com), United (800-241-6522; united.com), US Airways (800-428-4322; usairways.com).

Charlotte-Douglas International Airport (704-359-4000; airport -charlotte.com). Most major carriers and many smaller ones pass through this airport with direct flights to most U.S. and many international cities. Since many flights to and from South Carolina cities pass through Charlotte anyway, many people find it more convenient and less expensive to fly in and out of there. It is less than an hour's drive from most locations in the Revolutionary War Corridor to Charlotte-Douglas.

By train: **Amtrak** (800-872-7245; amtrak.com), 1060 West Dekalb Street, Camden. The Silver Star heading south stops in Camden around 1 AM; heading north, it stops around 5 AM. Unless someone is coming to pick you up, this is not your best bet, as the location of the station and the lateness of the hour are not conducive to finding public transportation.

By bus: **Greyhound** (803-432-2121; greyhound.com), 907 South Broad Street, Camden. The bus stop is within walking distance of at least one B&B, the main shopping district, and several restaurants. But public transportation and taxi service are limited.

By car: Driving yourself is your best bet for visiting this region. Interstate 20 passes a little to the south of Camden and to the north of Sumter. Interstate 77 pass through York County. U.S. Highways 1, 521, and 601 run right through the middle of the region and through most towns here.

✳ To See

MUSEUMS Museum of York County (803-389-2121; chmuseums.org), 4621 Mount Gallant Boulevard, Rock Hill. Open 10–5 Monday through Saturday, 1–5 Sunday. Cost: $5 adults 18–59, $4 seniors, $3 ages 4–17; free for children 3 and younger. Free for everybody on Sunday. Exhibits include the Catawba River and Stans African galleries as well as Settlemyre Planetarium.

Southern Revolutionary War Institute (803-684-3948; chmuseums .org), 212 East Jefferson Street, York. Open 10–4 Monday through Saturday. Free. Resources include the published papers of Henry Laurens and Nathanael Greene, as well as books, microfilm, and artifacts relating to the Southern campaign of the war. Historian Michael C. Scoggins manages the institute and has written several books on the Revolutionary War in the South.

Catawba Cultural Center (803-328-2427), 1536 Tom Steven Road, Rock Hill. Open 9–5 Monday through Saturday. Admission is free (donations accepted). This museum is home to the only remaining reservation schoolhouse. Outside there is a half-mile walking trail along an 18th-century wagon trail to the Catawba River.

Mac's Pride Museum (877-789-9252; macspride.com/museum.asp), 29247 SC 151, McBee. Open daily 10–5. Free. More than 20 cars from the past 90 years, plus antique farming equipment including tractors and plows are on display. This is a nice little sidelight when you stop at Mac's Pride roadside stand to buy the best peaches you will ever taste.

HISTORIC SITES **The Kershaw-Cornwallis House** (803-432-9841; historic-camden.net), 222 Broad Street, Camden. Open 10–5 Tuesday through Saturday, 2–5 Sunday. Guided tours are offered twice a day during the week at 10:30 and 3 and most of the day on weekends. Cost: $5 adults, $4 seniors, $3 ages 6–18; free for children younger than 6. Self-guided tours are free. During the Revolutionary War, Lord Cornwallis used the home as a headquarters; it was occupied for more than a year. In the early 19th century it was used as an orphanage. During the Civil War it was a Confederate storehouse and was destroyed in 1865. The home was rebuilt in 1877. It has been restored and furnished as it would have been during the Revolutionary War era. Other things to see include log cabins from the early 1800s, a blacksmith exhibit, two walking trails, and a Quaker cemetery.

OLD CARS AT MAC'S PRIDE MUSEUM IN MCBEE

Jan Hogan

THE KERSHAW-CORNWALLIS HOUSE IN CAMDEN

Historic Camden Revolutionary War Site (803-432-9841; historic
-camden.net), Flat Rock Road off US 521, Camden. This is the site of the
worst Patriot defeat of the American Revolution.

Kings Mountain National Military Park (864-936-7921; nps.gov/kimo
/index.htm), 2625 Park Road, Blacksburg. Open daily 9–5. Free. This is
the site of the first significant Patriot win after the British destroyed the
Continental Army in Charleston and Camden. The park features a 27-
minute film exhibit and a 1.5-mile self-guided tour of the battlefield.

Kings Mountain State Park (803-222-3209; southcarolinaparks.com),
1277 Park Road, Blacksburg. Open daily 8–6 with extended hours during
Daylight Saving Time. This park is next door to the military park and has
miles of trails, equestrian facilities, a group camping barracks, two fishing
lakes, and the Living History Farm. Built to show a typical farm from this
area in the early 19th century, the farm includes a barn, a garden, cows,
chickens, and a few cats. Admission is $2 for adults 16 and older, $1 for
seniors, and free for children.

Historic Brattonsville (803-684-2327; chmuseums.org), 1444 Brattonsville Road, McConnells. Open 10–5 Monday through Saturday, 1–5 Sunday. Admission: $6 adults ages 18–59, $5 seniors, $3 children 4–17; free
for children 3 and younger. This site where Mel Gibson filmed *The Patriot*
is a 775-acre Revolutionary War site with more than 30 historic buildings.
Check the schedule for reenactments of the Battle of Huck's Defeat and
living history Saturdays. The site also has a Heritage Farm Program with
rare breeds of farm animals such as Gulf Coast sheep, Devon cattle, and

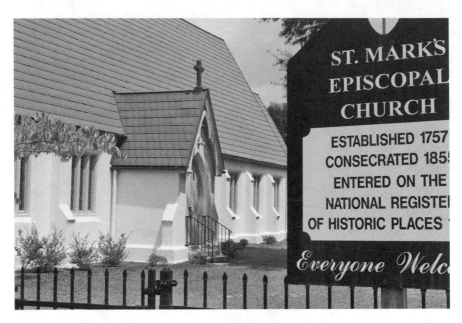

ST. MARK'S EPISCOPAL CHURCH IN SUMTER COUNTY

Ossabaw Island hogs. Constumed interpreters give demonstrations of historical farming techniques and plantation life.

St. Mark's Episcopal Church (803-452-9995; sumtersc.gov), 6205 Camp Mac Boykin Road, Pinewood. The original St. Mark's was built in 1767, but was destroyed during the Revolutionary War. The current St. Mark's was built in 1855 in the Gothic Revival architectural style. Tucked away in Sumter County where two dirt roads cross in the Manchester State Forest, this is worth the short drive off the main road.

Bonds Conway House (803-425-1123; kershawcountyhistoricalsociety .org), 811 Fair Street, Camden. Open Thursday 1–5 or by appointment. Admission is free. The house was built around 1812 and was the home of Bonds Conway—thought to be the first slave in Camden to buy his and his family's freedom, no small feat considering he had 11 children. He was an architect and lived to be 80 years old. He died in 1843. The Kershaw County Historical Society is located in the home.

✳ To Do

AMUSEMENT PARK 𝒮 **Carowinds Amusement and Water Park** (803-548-5300; carowinds.com), 14523 Carowinds Boulevard, Fort Mill. When this theme park opened in 1973, one highlight was the gold-paved North Carolina–South Carolina state line running through the middle. Over the years, the park has paid tribute to its Carolina stock car roots with ride names such as Thunder Road, White Lightning, and, new in 2010, the Intimidator, after famed NASCAR driver Dale Earnhardt. The 112-acre theme includes the 20-acre Boomerang Bay water park and offers 13 roller coasters as well as other rides, attractions, and shows. The amusement park is neither as expansive nor as expensive as Disney, but is more so on both counts than Dollywood. Open daily June through mid-August; weekends only from March through May and September through October. The park opens at 10 AM, and closing times vary. The park is closed late October through mid-March. Admission: $45.99 adults; $19.99 juniors shorting than 48 inches tall and seniors 62 and older. Children younger than 3 are admitted free.

FISHING ✐ **Cheraw Fish Hatchery** (843-537-7628), 433 Fish Hatchery Lane, Cheraw. Open Monday through Friday 7–3. Admission is free. Okay, so technically this isn't "fishing," but visitors can tour (by appointment only) this location that provides millions of sport fish each year for the state's public lakes and rivers. If you're in this area, it would be a fun and educational stop for the kids.

GOLF Cheraw State Park (843-537-9656; southcarolinaparks.com), 100 State Park Road, Cheraw. This 6,928-yard, par-72 course is located inside Cheraw State Park. Pine forests and a lake mix with Tom Jackson's man-made hazards to make this a challenging course. Rates are $30 during the week, $35 weekends.

CAROWINDS AMUSEMENT PARK NEAR FORT MILL

South Carolina Department of Parks, Recreation and Tourism/Perry Baker

Beech Creek Golf Club (803-499-4653; beechcreekgolfclub.com), 1800 Sam Gillespie Boulevard, Sumter. This 6,805-yard, par-72 course is on the site of one of the last battles of the Civil War. Rates of $30–35 include a cart. Discounts for seniors, juniors, and military.

Crystal Lakes Golf Course (803-775-1902), 1305 Clara Louise Kellogg Drive, Sumter. This par-72 is 6,236 yards from the back tees. Lessons and club rentals also are available.

✴ Green Space

PARKS Andrew Jackson State Park (803-285-3344; southcarolinaparks .com), 196 Andrew Jackson Park Road, Lancaster. Open 8–6, seven days a week; 9–9 during Daylight Saving Time; the museum is open 1–5 Saturday through Sunday, while the schoolhouse is open 1–5 Saturday and 2–5 Sunday from mid-March to November. $2 adults; $1.25 South Carolina seniors; free for children 15 and younger.

Swan Lake—Iris Gardens (803-436-2640; sumtersc.gov), 822 West Liberty Street, Sumter. Open daily 7:30–dusk. Free. In the 1920s local businessman Hamilton Bland was trying to grow Japanese irises at his home, but he failed and decided to dig the bulbs up. He ordered his gardener to dump the bulbs in a swamp he owned. The next spring, they blossomed into a beautiful accidental garden. The gardens now comprise more than 150 acres and have eight species of swans. From mid-May through June the gardens are in bloom with the stunning colors of more than 120 vari-

SCULPTURE AT SWAN LAKE IN SUMTER

Jan Hogan

ANDREW JACKSON'S BIRTHPLACE

North and South Carolina have had many disputes over the years, ranging from who has the better basketball team (North Carolina usually wins that one) to what the Tar Heel State takes from or puts into rivers and streams that eventually wend their way into South Carolina (that battle continues in federal court).

But one of the oldest disagreements is over where the seventh president of the United States was born. Each Carolina claims him as a native son.

There is no dispute that Jackson spent his early years on his uncle James Crawford's farm, which had land in both Carolinas and was in the Waxhaw area of South Carolina. Another uncle McKemey lived on a farm 3 miles up the road near the town of Waxhaw, North Carolina.

Jackson said many times during his life that he was born in South Carolina, but as one North Carolina senator put it after Jackson's death, "He was too young to remember the event of his birth."

The resulting dispute leaves the Andrew Jackson State Park with the site of the Crawford cabin in South Carolina, about 30 miles south of Charlotte, North Carolina, and a monument marking the spot of Jackson's birth in Waxhaw, North Carolina, about 27 miles south of Charlotte.

The South Carolina park is 360 acres and features a museum that details Jackson's boyhood and an equestrian statue of "Old Hickory" sculpted by Anna Hyatt Huntington of Brookgreen Gardens fame. (There's more about Huntington in chapter 1). There also is a replica of an 18th-century schoolhouse, an amphitheater that hosts an annual bluegrass festival, a fishing lake, campsites, and trails. Pets are allowed in most outdoor areas on a leash.

eties of irises. A boardwalk takes you over black waters of Swan Lake surrounded by cypress trees. This is a must-see if you are in the area.

Carolina Sandhills National Wildlife Refuge (843-335-8401; fws.gov /carolinasandhills), 23734 US 1, McBee. The refuge is open daily from sunup to sunset. Admission is free. Visitors to this 45,000-acre refuge can see the endangered red-cockaded woodpecker and brown-headed nuthatches, among many other species. There are two observation towers and an interpretive display. The refuge can be toured by car or by bike along more than 100 miles of dirt and gravel roads. There also are miles of trails exclusively designated for walking and hiking around the refuge's lakes and ponds. Maps at the refuge highlight the best areas for spotting the woodpeckers and other wildlife. This is truly a great way to spend a morning.

Lake Wateree State Recreation Area (866-345-PARK; southcarolina parks.com), 881 State Park Road, Winnsboro. Lake Wateree is a 21-mile-long, 13,700-acre reservoir that marks the end of the Catawba River.

Ebenezer Park (803-366-6620; yorkcountygov.com), 4490 Boatshore Road, Rock Hill. Open daily 6 AM–dark. Summertime fees: $3 per car for York County residents, $6 for out-of-county guests. This park sits on the shores of Lake Wylie and offers camping, picnicking, swimming, fishing, and boating.

Landsford Canal State Park (803-789-5800; southcarolinaparks.com), 2051 Park Drive, Catawba. Open daily 9–6. Admission is $2 for adults, $1.25 for South Carolina seniors, and free for children 15 and younger. This state park's claim to fame is the rocky shoals spider lily—a delicate-looking but sturdy plant that hangs on to rocks in the swiftly moving Catawba River and blooms in a beautiful blanket of white in late May and early June. Visitors plan whole trips around this annual event. Visitors also can see the remains of the canal system that once made the river that runs from Charlotte to Columbia a route of commerce. There also is plenty of fishing, picnicking, and nature-watching to be done.

Poinsett State Park (803-494-8177; southcarolinaparks.com), 6660 Poinsett Park Road, Wedgefield. Open daily 9–6, until 9 PM Friday through Saturday during Daylight Saving Time. Admission is free to this park next to Manchester State Forest. The park has plenty of fishing and swimming, but the main activity here is hiking along the Palmetto Trail through the forest. This area sort of marks the transition in topography in the state from sandhills to piedmont, which makes for unique mixes of plant life. The park also has five cabins as well as RV and tent campsites.

Mill Creek Park (803-436-2248; sumtercountysc.org), 7975 Milford Plantation Road, Pinewood. Open daily during daylight hours. Free admission. This park is an access point for the "High Hills of Santee" passage of the Palmetto Trail and has plenty of biking and horse trails as well. There is a rustic lodge with kitchen facilities, and campsites are available.

Manchester State Forest (803-494-8196; state.sc.us/forest/refman.htm), 6740 Headquarters Road, Wedgefield. Open daily dawn–dusk January 2 through September 14; open Sunday only dawn–dusk from September 15 through December 31. The forest offers public access for two sections of the Palmetto Trail—the High Hills of Santee and the Wateree. Permits are required for motorcycle and all-terrain vehicles as well as horses and bicycles. The forest also offers hunting and fishing.

✴ Lodging

INNS The Inn at Winthrop
(803-323-2300; www2.winthrop
.edu/inn), 128 Joynes Hall, Rock
Hill. This inn has 12 suites in the
center of Winthrop's campus.
Built in the 1920s, it has the look
of a historic inn with many modern conveniences. This is a wonderful way to spend a few days in
Rock Hill.

**BED & BREAKFASTS Camden
House** (803-713-1013; camden
house.us), 1502 Broad Street,
Camden. Built in 1832, this onetime mansion is in the heart of
historic downtown Camden within
easy walking distance of shops and
restaurants. Amenities include
breakfast, sitting rooms, porches,
and a pool. The house has four
rooms available at $110–150 a
night.

Bloomsbury Inn (803-432-5858;
bloomsburyinn.com), 1707 Lyttle-
ton Street, Camden. Owners
Bruce and Katherine Brown live
on site at this historic home built
in 1849 with a fireplace in every
room. Amenities include breakfast
every morning and a social hour
every evening in the ladies' parlor
or on the veranda. No children
younger than 12. Five rooms at
$150–215 a night.

Honeysuckle Acres (803-635-
7583; honeysuckleacres.com), 70
Honeysuckle Lane, Winnsboro.
This large four-column home was
built in 1927 and looks like an
antebellum mansion. It sits on 7
acres and has the original stables

and carriage stone in front. Breakfast is included in room rates, and
the owners say they can pack you
a picnic if you want. Packages start
at $130.

CAMPGROUNDS/CABINS
Cheraw State Park (843-537-
9656; southcarolinaparks.com), 100
State Park Road, Cheraw. Cabins
start at $50 a night during the week
and range up to $170 on the week-
ends. Weekly rentals are available.
These cabins aren't really what I
would call roughing it. Rentals
include bed and bath linens, cooking and eating utensils, heating and
air-conditioning, coffeemaker and
color television. But you can sit on
the screened porch and cook on
the outdoor grill to get you back to
nature. The cabins can accommodate up to four people. The park
also has two group camps that can
accommodate 90 or 120 people.
They rent for $200–300 a night
depending on season.

**Lake Wateree State Recreation
Area** (866-345-PARK; southcaro
linaparks.com), 881 State Park
Road, Winnsboro. There are 72
lakeside campsites, all with water
and electrical service. The park
also has a tackle shop and refueling dock. Camping fees $14–19 a
night, with a two-night minimum.

🐾 **Ebenezer Park** (803-366-
6620; yorkcountygov.com), 4490
Boatshore Road, Rock Hill. The
69 campsites at this park each
have electrical, water, and sewer
hookups as well as hot showers.
The fee is $15 per night with dis-

counts for York County residents and seniors; maximum 14-day stay. Campsites are available on a first-come, first-served basis. Pets are allowed, alcoholic beverages and firearms are not.

Poinsett State Park (803-494-8177; southcarolinaparks.com), 6660 Poinsett Park Road, Wedgefield. Open daily 9–6, until 9 PM Friday through Saturday during Daylight Saving Time. Five cabins are available here, sleeping four, six, or seven people and ranging in price from $50 a night for the small cabins in the off-season to $120 a night for the largest cabin in season. The park has plenty of fishing and swimming, but the main activity here is hiking along the Palmetto Trail through Manchester State Forest. Campsites also are available at $15 a night for RV sites with water and electrical hookup, or $10 a night for tent sites.

✳ Where to Eat

DINING OUT Mill Pond Steakhouse (803-425-8825; themillpondsteakhouse.com), 84 Boykin Mill Road, Rembert. Open Tuesday through Saturday at 2 for appetizers and lighter fare; dinner starts at 5. This place is out in the middle of nowhere, but just a short ride from Columbia or Camden. Steaks are the centerpiece of the menu, but Mill Pond offers a variety of American-style dishes including a cornmeal-crusted grouper. The restaurant sits on Boykin Mill Pond, and its ambience takes you back to the days of the general store. Dinner entrées $25–44.

Sam Kendall's (803-424-2005; samkendalls.com), 1042 Broad Street, Camden. Open for dinner

CHERAW STATE PARK

SC Department of Parks, Recreation & Tourism, DiscoverSouthCarolina.com

at 5 Monday through Saturday. Entrées range $15–25. This great old building on Camden's main downtown street has exposed-brick walls and a 1950s-looking decor. The menu runs from barbecue ribs to pork with a marsala sauce and is heavy on the seafood. The portions are plentiful, so sharing might be a thought if you have no way to handle leftovers. That will leave more room for one of their tasty salads and an appetizer.

EATING OUT Boykin Company Grille & Store (803-425-6724; boykinmillfarms.com/grill.asp), 73 Boykin Mill Road, Rembert. Open 11:30–2 Tuesday through Saturday, 5:30–9 Thursday through Saturday. The grill offers a variety of sandwiches as well as traditional Southern meals. Inside the old store is the old post office with items dating to 1874 and shelves filled with products from the Boykin Mill, such as grits and cornmeal.

Charleys Café and Catering (803-285-1145), 306 South Main Street, Lancaster. Open 11–2 Monday through Friday and 5–9 Wednesday through Saturday. If you are going to check out the Andrew Jackson State Park, this is a great place for lunch. The Tuscan pasta with shrimp and sausage in Asiago cheese with a side salad is great at just $10.

Delamater's (803-276-3555; delamaters.com), 1117 Boyce Street, Newberry. Open 11:30–2 and for dinner starting at 5 Monday through Saturday Located just a few doors down from the Newberry Opera House in an old bank building, Delamater's offers diners high-end taste for a low-end price. The wine cellar is located in an old vault. The crabcake sandwich for lunch is just spicy enough to make you remember it and a steal at $9. An especially nice touch is that they let you substitute a small salad for fries with all lunch sandwiches, no extra charge. All lunch items are under $15. Dinner entrées range from the Southern staple shrimp and grits to vegetable ravioli and steaks. Prices range from $15 to $26.

Brick Street Coffee Break (803-773-4433; brickstcoffee.com), 9 Caldwell Street, Sumter. Open 7–2 Tuesday through Friday. This locally owned coffee shop has muffins and bagels for breakfast and soup, salad, and sandwiches for lunch. Every third Thursday of the month, Brick Street takes a break from coffee and puts out the linen tablecloths and fine china for afternoon tea 3–6 PM. All lunch items under $10.

Hanna's Grill (803-773-9480), 541 East Liberty Street, Sumter. Open 6 AM–2 PM Monday through Friday; 5 PM–10 PM Friday through Saturday; and 10 AM–2 PM Sunday. It's like eating dinner at Grandma's house, only no seconds. Hanna's is a once-through buffet with fried chicken and other meats and veggies. Price is $7 (includes dessert and tea).

NEWBERRY OPERA HOUSE

Old Armory Steak House (803-432-3222), 514 Rutledge Street, Camden. Open Monday through Saturday 11–10 for lunch and dinner. The Old Armory has live music on Thursday, Friday, and Saturday nights. This is a great place for a lunch or dinner that tastes more expensive than it costs. The prime rib or signature steak tops out the menu at $20. The Old Armory also has a wide selection of beer, wine and other adult beverages, so it's also great to stop in when you get tired from all that antiquing on nearby Broad Street.

✳ Entertainment

Newberry Opera House (803-276-5179; newberryoperahouse .com), 1201 McKibben Street,

Newberry. This wonderful venue brings in acts from around the country, from folk music to Big Band to the Three Irish Tenors. Built in 1881, this French Gothic building has been entertaining residents of central South Carolina for more than a century, with traveling shows from New York and other large cities making stops here. In the early 1900s silent movies were shown; in the 1920s the Opera House was converted to a movie theater, which it remained for another 30 years. By 1960 there were calls for tearing the old building down, but the Newberry Historical Society saved it in 1969, and it was placed on the National Register of Historic Places the following year. The Opera House also held many city offices and meeting spaces, but as part of its renovation in the 1990s, the city vacated the building. The Opera House seats 426 people.

McCelvey Center Theater (803-684-3948; chmuseums.org), 212 East Jefferson Street, York. Open 10–4 Monday through Friday. The theater offers musical performances by local and regional acts as well as special programming for children and young adults. Ticket prices vary by event.

Sumter Opera House (803-436-2616; sumtersc.gov/visitingus /operahouse.aspx), 21 North Main Street, Sumter. This opera house was built in the 1890s after the first one was destroyed by fire. It was renovated in 1936 as a movie theater. Today it hosts live performances year-round as well as films. Shows include dance, theater, and concerts. Ticket prices vary by event, but classic film showings are $2.50.

✳ Selective Shopping

Mac's Pride (877-789-9252; macs pride.com), 29247 SC 151 South, McBee. Open daily 8:30–6. This is a summertime must-do, but still fun in the off-season. These are some of the best peaches you will ever eat. They are picked and packaged on the spot and sold out of Mac's country store. The store also offers fresh veggies, such as okra, corn, squash, and tomatoes (I know, technically a fruit), as well as jams, jellies, and other locally made foods. There also is an old-car museum at the site and

lots of food to eat while you're there. I recommend the ice cream and the fruit breads.

ANTIQUES Camden has more than 20 antiques shops and arts shops located downtown. Most are open 9–6 daily.

Springdale Antiques Inc. (803-432-0312), 951 Broad Street, Camden. Southern furniture is available at this store, which also offers furniture restoration, refinishing, and repair services.

SUMTER OPERA HOUSE

Jan Hogan

Jan Hogan

HISTORIC CAMDEN EXCHANGE

Camden Antiques Market (803-432-0818), 830 South Broad Street, Camden. Thirty dealers bring items ranging from silver to furniture and everything in between.

Heritage Antique Mall (803-425-4191), 113 East DeKalb Street, Camden.

Antiques on Broad (803-424-1338), 821 Broad Street, Camden. This is the area's largest antiques mall with a large selection from all eras. Items include furniture, silver, linens, railroad and Civil War collectibles, and jewelry.

Andries van Dam, Investment Art and Antiques (803-432-0850), 914 Market Street, Camden. Open 10–5:30 Thursday through Saturday or by appointment. This shop specializes in European and American paintings as well as Asian art and silver.

Historic Camden Exchange (803-432-9841), 222 Broad Street, Camden. Open 10–5 Tuesday through Saturday, 1–5 Sunday. On the grounds of the Kershaw Corn-wallis House, this unique gift shop is itself a historic building selling books, crafts, jewelry, and gifts.

F. D. Goodale Jeweler (803-432-3445; fdgoodalejeweler.com), 543 DeKalb Street, Camden. Founded by Dess Goodale in 1922, the store is still in the family and has a wide selection of new jewelry, silver serving pieces, and other home decor as well as antique and estate items.

Bethune Pottery (843-334-8346; bethunepottery.com), 3736 Jefferson Davis Highway, Bethune. This place started as a handmade pottery outlet that sold clay to local potters. Bethune Pottery still supplies clay to artists and classrooms across the state, but now it focuses more on ornamental concrete, such as birdbaths, benches, planters, and fountains.

Catawba Craftstore (803-328-2427; catawbaindianpottery.com), 1536 Tom Stevens Road, Rock Hill. Open 9–5 Monday through Saturday. Features Catawba pottery, including the Wedding Vase, porcelain dolls. and spiritual beadwork.

✸ Special Events

SPRING *March:* **Carolina Cup** (803-432-6513; carolina-cup.org), 200 Knights Hills Road, Camden. South Carolina's largest outdoor cocktail party—oh yeah, they have a few horse races, too—is held every year in late March or early April. Two rules: The Cup is a marathon, not a sprint; and stop drinking before the last race. If you have never been here before, you would really benefit from knowing someone who has. If that isn't possible, go to the website and try to get a designated parking space either in the infield or on the south rail. It makes life so much easier. It is expensive: $215, but that includes two general admission tickets ($30 in advance; $45 at the gate). If you don't have the money or desire for an infield parking pass, there is plenty of parking around the outside of the track for less than $20. You will still need a general admission ticket to get in. Pack plenty of food, drinks, and patience for the day, and put on your best spring duds. Leave the kids at home for this one, designate a sober driver, and buy a program; they are only $5 but come in very handy.

HORSE RACE AT THE CAROLINA CUP IN CAMDEN

May: **Iris Festival** (803-436-2640; sumtersc.gov/visitingus/festivals _iris.aspx), Swan Lake, Sumter. This three-day festival is one of the best South Carolina has to offer, with concerts, arts and crafts, a golf tournament, and of course irises in full bloom. Don't miss this one.

Flopeye Fish Festival (803-482-6029; flopeyefishfestival.com), 2534 James Baker Boulevard, Great Falls. This uniquely named festival is held in the small town of Great Falls on the Saturday of Memorial Day weekend each year. There are food vendors, bands, and a general welcome-home atmosphere even for visitors who have never been to the town. The free event started in 1983. The name does not come from a species of fish, but rather from the nickname for a "sleepy" section of the former textile mill town. The town is known for its good fishing holes. This is a classic small-town street festival.

SUMMER *July:* **Watermelon Festival** (843-672-6400; pageland watermelonfestival.com), 128 North Pearl Street, Pageland. For obvious reasons, the town of Page-land is one of my favorites, though I seldom pass through it anymore unless I am heading to North Carolina. But here in this tiny little town, they celebrate my favorite fruit—the watermelon. For 60 years, the town has celebrated that most Southern delicacy. Some folks eat it with salt; some eat it plain. I've even seen folks fry it up with some balsamic vinegar (this tastes

better than it sounds). The festival features a parade, a watermelon-eating contest (with your hands behind your back, naturally), and, of course, the seed-spitting contest. This one is worth making a special trip. It's usually around the second or third weekend in July and starts on Friday afternoon with events all day Saturday. It is a small-town festival at its best.

FALL *October:* **Apple Harvest Festival**. Sponsored by and located at the **Windy Hill Orchard and Cider Mill** (803-684-0690; windyhillorchard.com), 1860 Black Highway, York. Open Monday through Saturday 9–6 (August through December). Tours of the orchard are $6 per person and include hayrides, the Johnny Appleseed story, and cider making. Visitors can pick their own apples, and the store here sells all things apple: cider, butter, pies, wassail, and doughnuts.

November: **Colonial Cup** (803-432-6513; carolina-cup.org /colonial-cup.php), 200 Knights Hills Road, Camden. This one is for the kids. In addition to the steeplechase horse races, there are Jack Russell terrier races. The smaller crowd and typically more reliable weather make this more of a family event. It's less expensive, too, and might be a way for novices to get their feet wet before jumping into the Carolina Cup in the spring. Infield parking is $135 and includes two general admission tickets ($20 in advance; $30 at the gate). General parking is $10.

AIKEN

Aiken is like a beautiful Southern woman just a little over middle-aged, but always dignified and still a little mischievous. I am surprised every time I go to Aiken about some new thing that has opened there or about some old thing that I haven't seen in all my lifetime of previous trips.

Long a getaway for wealthy Northerners and the horsey set, Aiken was probably South Carolina's first inland tourist destination. Located near the Georgia state line, the small town now is probably known more as the home of the former nuclear weapons plant at the Savannah River Site and for a stopover President Franklin Roosevelt made on his way to Warm Springs, Georgia, for spa treatments he hoped would restore his ability to walk after a bout of polio took the use of his legs.

GETTING THERE *By air:* **Augusta Regional Airport** (706-798-3236; augustaregionalairport.com), 1501 Aviation Way, Augusta, Georgia. Carriers include Delta Connection, Atlantic Southeast Airlines, and US Airways Express. Rental cars are available from most major companies. About 30 minutes from Aiken.

By bus: **Greyhound** (803-648-6894; greyhound.com), 153 Pendleton Street, Aiken.

By car: Aiken sits on U.S. Highway 1, about 60 miles southwest of Columbia and about 20 miles east of Augusta, Georgia. It's an easy drive on US 1 from either city. For those in a hurry, take Interstate 20 from Columbia to the US 1 exit, then south to Aiken. US 78 also runs to Aiken from Charleston.

✳ To See

Aiken County Historical Museum (803-642-2015), 433 Newberry Street, Aiken. Open 10–5 Tuesday through Saturday; 2–5 Sunday. Free. This unique museum in a 1930s winter getaway mansion named Banksia sits on 3.5 acres. The grounds include an 1890s one-room schoolhouse and a log cabin built in 1808. The exhibit I Don't Live Here Anymore is a tribute to those whose homes were destroyed to make way for the Savannah River Site. Other exhibits chronicle the lives of black residents, South Carolina's most famous politician Strom Thurmond, and the days when Aiken was the asparagus capital of the United States.

Aiken Thoroughbred Racing Hall of Fame and Museum (803-642-7650; aikenracinghalloffame.com), 135 Dupree Place, Aiken. Winter hours: 2–5 Tuesday through Friday, Sunday; 10–5 Saturday. In the summer open 10–5 Saturday, 2–5 Sunday. Located inside historic Hopelands Gardens, the museum showcases Aiken's contribution to thoroughbred racing from 1900 to the present. Free, but donations are welcome.

HISTORIC SITES **Redcliffe Plantation State Historic Site** (803-827-1473), 181 Redcliffe Road, Beech Island. Open 9–5 Thursday through Monday. House tours are held on the hour at 1, 2, and 3. Free admission to the grounds. Tours are $4 for ages 16 and older, $2.50 for South Carolina seniors, and $3 for children ages 6–15. This plantation home was completed just one year before South Carolina decided to withdraw from the United States. There is a great view of the Savannah River from the top floor. The slave cabins have been preserved along with heirloom gardens. Picnicking is allowed on the lawn. The property was donated to the state in 1973 by the descendants of the original owner.

DOWNTOWN AIKEN

Jan Hogan

OTHER PLACES OF INTEREST **DuPont Planetarium at the University of South Carolina–Aiken** (803-641-3654; rpsec.usca .edu/planetarium), 471 University Parkway, Aiken. The DuPont Planetarium offers about a dozen different shows throughout the year, ranging from an explanation of the development of the telescope to a view of weather from outer space and the perspective of a raindrop. Special shows are offered on National Astronomy Day, which is actually two days: one in the fall, usually in October, the other in the spring, usually April or May. The planetarium is open every Saturday. Show listings can be found on the website. Children younger than

Jan Hogan

THOROUGHBRED RACING HALL OF FAME, AIKEN

4 are not allowed in the planetarium. Reservations can be made by calling the main number or by email: planetarium@usca.edu. Reservations are not required, but are encouraged, especially if you need any special services or assistance. Shows are typically at 7 and 8 PM, but are also put on at 4 and 5 at discounted prices. Admission is $5.50 for adults at the Digistar laser shows. General shows are $4.50 for adults; the early-bird price is $3.50. Admission prices are discounted for all shows: $1 for senior citizens and $2 for students in kindergarten through high school.

✳ To Do

FAMILY-FRIENDLY ACTIVITIES ✐ **Nine Mile Range** (803-266-4714), 4327 Williston Road, Windsor. This farm sells beef, goat meat, chickens, ducks, and rabbit. The Nine Mile Range Dark Skies Observatory is an open-air location with little light pollution that draws members of the Augusta, Georgia, Astronomy Club. Stop by and see the animals, buy some fresh fruit, and maybe take a dip in the outdoor pool.

✐ **Eudora Farms** (803-564-3305; eudorafarms.com), 219 Salem Lane, Salley. Eudora is home to exotic animals, draft horses, and Akita dogs. A horse-drawn wagon tour of the animal farm by appointment only includes a stop at the animal nursery, the petting barn, and access to a picnic area. $5 per person; a minimum of 15 people or $75 is required to book a tour.

GOLF Golf Club at Cedar Creek (803-648-4206; cedarcreek.net), 2555 Club Drive, Aiken. This par-72 course offers five distances per hole and plays 7,206 yards from the back tees. Lessons are available at the practice facility. Fees: $33–40.

The Aiken Golf Club (803-649-6029; aikengolfclub.com), 555 Highland Park Drive, Aiken. Built in 1912, this is one of the oldest courses in the country. Celebrities such as Fred Astaire and professional golfers Babe Zaharias and Patty Berg have played here. Fees: $25–34.

✳ Green Space

PARKS 🐾 **Aiken State Natural Area** (803-649-2857; southcarolinaparks .com), 1145 State Park Road, Windsor. Open 9–6, seven days a week

THEATERS

When I was a youngster, my brother and I would put on our pajamas, pack up blankets and pillows, and load into the station wagon for a trip to the drive-in movies. Even by then—the early 1970s—the movies shown at drive-ins were not the same first-run movies you would see at an indoor theater. But it wasn't so much the movie as the experience. It was the days before cable movie channels, and it was a way for the whole family to sit and watch a movie on a Friday or Saturday night. Sounds archaic, doesn't it? Well, it still exists. Only now, the movies are the biggest hits of the day and you don't have to attach one of those heavy metal speakers to your car window and listen as the sound crackles in; you can hear everything on your car stereo. Rescued from certain destruction as a junkyard in 1999, **"The Big MO" Monetta Drive-In Theatre** (803-685-7949; thebigmo.com), 5822 Columbia Highway, Monetta, is a few miles from everything and a few decades from modern life, where movies play on smartphones. On Friday, Saturday, and Sunday evenings from March through November, the Big MO runs double features on two screens off US 1 between Columbia and Aiken. The Big MO is not oblivious to modern technology—you can find out what's playing by checking out its website or Facebook page. The place fills up quickly on Friday and Saturday nights in the summer, so if you're coming then, come early—gates open about 6:30 PM, and the first feature starts at dusk. The box office is cash only—and exact change is appreciated. It's $7 for people 12 and older and $3 for those 3–11. It's free for children younger than 3. You can use your debit and credit cards at the (extended to 9 Friday through Saturday during Daylight Saving Time). Fees are $2 adults; $1.25 South Carolina seniors; free for children 15 and younger. Built during the Depression, this natural area has 1,000 acres along the South Edisto River. Canoeing, fishing, camping, and hiking trails are available. Pets are allowed in most outdoor areas on a leash.

☃ **Hitchcock Woods** (803-642-0528; hitchcockwoods.org), Dibble Road or South Boundary Road, Aiken. Open daily dawn to dusk. There are nine entrances to this wonderful urban forest. Admission is free. Open to joggers, hikers, dog walkers, and those on horseback, the woods has 65 miles of sandy trails.

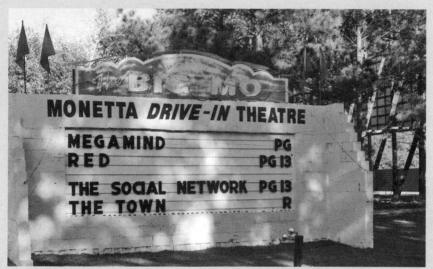

Jan Hogan

THE BIG MO': MONETTA DRIVE-IN, MONETTA

concession stand, where they sell more than popcorn. Make a night of it and come early, have a hot dog, hamburger, or barbecue sandwich from the concession stand. Let the kids burn off some energy on the playground, then sit back in your car—or folding chair—tune in your radio to the movie soundtrack, and watch a movie on a screen considerably bigger than your cell phone. Not only is it cheaper than taking the kids to a theater in the mall, but you can show them a slice of life that has all but disappeared from the American landscape. The Big MO turned 60 in 2011, and the owners plan to keep it going for many years to come.

✳ Lodging

INNS Aiken Carriage House Inn (803-644-5888; aikencarriage house.com), 139 Laurens Street, Aiken. Rates start at $110 for a deluxe queen room and range up to $145 for a king courtyard suite; they include a hot breakfast. The 16 rooms are simple but elegan, and the inn offers several golf packages.

The Guest House (800-735-4587; houndslakeguesthouse.com), 897 Houndslake Drive, Aiken. Rates $95–120. The Guest House offers 30 rooms overlooking the golf course at Houndslake Country Club. Your stay comes with access to the club's amenities, including the 27-hole golf course, eight lighted tennis courts, and swimming pool.

BED & BREAKFASTS Rose Hill Estate (803-648-1181; rose hillestate.com), 211 Greenville Street Northwest. A classic winter getaway for guests from a bygone era, Rose Hill has seven bedrooms and two suites as well as a guest-house with two kings, a queen, three sleeper sofas, three bathrooms, and a full-service kitchen. A chapel on the property seats 60 for weddings. Packages start at $180, and rooms include breakfast.

☗ ✑ Annie's Inn Bed & Breakfast (803-649-6836; anniesinnbnb .com), 3083 Charleston Highway, Montmorenci. This 19th-century home lost its head in the Civil War, literally. U.S. troops were using the home as a headquarters because of the strategic view from the third floor and the widow's walk. When a battle in nearby Aiken led back to the house, Confederate troops hit the top floor with a cannonball. When the house was rebuilt, it was changed to a two-story home with a large attic. The home also briefly served as a doctor's office and hospital before becoming the center of an asparagus operation in the early 20th century. Owners Dallas and Scottie Ruark bought the house in 1984 and completely renovated it into a B&B with 11 rooms—5 inside rooms and 6 cottages—all with private bath. The room rates range $110–135 a night, with rates higher during the Masters golf tournament held in nearby Augusta, Georgia. Rooms come with full country breakfast in the dining room. The cottages rent for $125 a night, or $600 a week; monthly rentals are available. The cottages do not come with breakfast. One cottage is pet-friendly, and families with children usually stay in the cottages. Annie's Inn has a large pool and is just 5 miles from downtown Aiken and in the center of Montmorenci's growing horse culture.

HOTELS Hotel Aiken (803-648-4265; hotelaiken.com), 235 Richland Avenue West, Aiken. This hotel was built in 1898 and has gone through many renovations since, including one in 2001 that added many modern amenities such as Internet access. The hotel's bars, the Tiki Tavern and

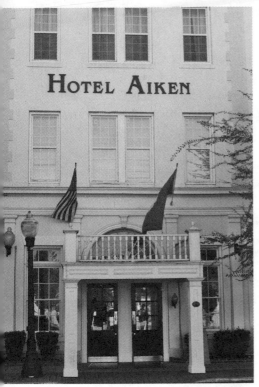

Jan Hogan

HOTEL AIKEN, AIKEN

body wraps, and aromatherapy. All suites and most guest rooms have fireplace. Rates: $185 to $525 for the Roosevelt Suite.

CAMPGROUNDS/CABINS 🐾
Deerfeathers Campground (864-443-2384), 2536 SC 283, Plum Branch. Store open daily 9–9. The campground has 80 sites with power and water. There is a dump station, two bathhouses, and clothes washer and dryers. The country store sells gasoline and ice. Pets allowed.

Aiken State Natural Area (803-649-2857; southcarolinaparks .com), 1145 State Park Road, Windsor. Open daily 9–6, extended to 9 PM Friday through Saturday, during Daylight Saving Time. The park offers 25 campsites with electricity and water for $14 a night. There also is a primitive area for group camping.

the Polo Tavern, are popular watering holes for travelers and locals alike. So if you plan to stay here, be prepared for a lively crowd. Rates start at $50 for two doubles, with king suites starting at $90.

RESORT The Willcox (803-648-1898; thewillcox.com), 100 Colleton Avenue, Aiken. This is one of the most famous hotels in Aiken and has been around since the 1920s as a stopping point for the well-heeled horsey set. This is where President Franklin Roosevelt stayed when he visited the town. The hotel offers a variety of spa treatments including facials,

THE WILLCOX, AIKEN

Jan Hogan

✴ Where to Eat

DINING OUT Davor's Cafe
(803-641-1909; davorscafe.com),
227 The Alley, Aiken. Open daily
for dinner 5–midnight; for lunch
11–2:30 Friday through Saturday,
and 9–2:30 for Sunday brunch.
Davor's serves dinner indoors or
outside on its patio. This place is
known for its Sunday brunch and
cocktails in the evening. Live
entertainment is provided Friday
and Saturday, and this is the place
where many locals stop for a cocktail before dinner. Entrées average
$30 and include black truffle sac-
chetti and pan-seared yellowfin
tuna.

The Willcox (803-648-1898;
thewillcox.com), 100 Colleton
Avenue, Aiken. Open 11:30 AM–
10 PM Monday through Saturday,
and Sunday 9 AM–10 PM. Serving
brunch, lunch, and dinner, the
Willcox is casual dining in one of
the city's oldest hotels. Dinner
entrées range from burgers ($12)
to shrimp linguine ($16) to a 12-
ounce filet ($34).

Stable Restaurant & Bar (803-
648-1181; rosehillestate.com), 211
Greenville Street Northwest,
Aiken. Open for dinner at 5 Tuesday through Saturday. The Stable
is located at Rose Hill Estate and
offers indoor and outdoor dining
with live music several nights a
week.

Linda's Bistro (803-648-4853;
lindasbistro-aiken.com), 135 York
Street Southeast, Aiken. Open for
dinner starting at 5:30 Tuesday
through Saturday. Chef-owner
Linda offers a small variety of
entrée options, from seared calf
liver to a wild mushroom ravioli
with sage butter and Asiago
cheese. The menu is definitely
Italian, and prices range from $12
for the penne Gorgonzola to $40
for a 12-ounce New York strip.
The wine list is small, but offers a
variety of wines in a wide price
range. The small dining room in a
renovated home provides an intimate atmosphere—but make
reservations, especially if there is
something big going on in town or
during Masters week.

**EATING OUT Aiken Brewing
Company** (803-502-0707; aiken
brewingcompany.com), 140 Laurens Street, Aiken. Open 11 AM–
2 AM Monday through Friday.
The restaurant offers a variety of
locally brewed and seasonal
beers, including red ale, grand
cru, pale ale, stout, wheat, blond,
and porter. Dinner entrées
$8–20.

West Side Bowery (803-648-
2900; westsidebowery.com), 151
Bee Lane, Aiken. Open 11:30–10
Tuesday through Saturday; for
lunch only on Monday, 11:30–3.
For lunch, the Bowery offers
homemade soups and salads as
well as hot and cold sandwiches.
Lunch specials start at $9. Steaks
and seafood dominate the dinner
menu. Entrées are $8–20. This
place in the heart of downtown
Aiken has a great outdoor seating
area. It's worth a stop for a least a

Jan Hogan

WEST SIDE BOWERY, AIKEN

cup of coffee or your favorite adult beverage.

✱ Selective Shopping

DOWNTOWN AIKEN (803-649-2221; downtownaiken.com), 208 A The Alley.

Aiken Center for the Arts (803-641-9094; aikencenterforthearts .org), 122 Laurens Street. Open 10–5 Monday through Saturday. It's a gallery and an art shop all in one. Three galleries rotate shows every month or so. The store has jewelry, pottery, and other art for sale.

3 Monkeys (803-648-7592; 3monkeysaiken.com), 133 Laurens Street Northwest. Open 10–6 Monday through Saturday. Shoppers can choose from antiques, home accessories, artwork, and jewelry.

Equine Divine (803-642-9772; equinedivineonline.com), 126 Laurens Street Southwest. Open 10–6 Monday through Friday, 11–6 Saturday. This store offers art, home decor, clothing, and jewelry that appeals to the horse lover.

✱ Special Events

SPRING *March:* **Aiken Steeplechase** (803-648-9641; aiken steeplechase.com), 538 Two Notch Road, Aiken. The Imperial Cup race started in 1930. Admission: $10 in advance; $15 at the gate. Limited general admission parking, $25. Railside passes $150–200 and include two to four tickets.

May: **Aiken Bluegrass Festival** (803-640-9287; aikenbluegrass festival.org), 198 Gaston Road,

Aiken. This two-day event kicks off with a barbecue dinner and open bar for $45 per person. Bluegrass bands play throughout the festival. Camping is available. Tickets for day two are $10 in advance, $15 at the gate. No coolers allowed.

FALL *October:* **Aiken Steeplechase** (803-648-9641; aiken steeplechase.com), 538 Two Notch Road. The Holiday Cup race started in 1991. Admission: $10 in advance; $15 at the gate.

WINTER *February:* **Battle of Aiken** (803-642-2500; battleof aiken.org), 1210 Powell Pond Road, Aiken. Civil War reenactors stage the fierce fighting that raged around Aiken during General Sherman's march to the sea in the waning days of the war. The event offers demonstrations on weaponry of the time and how it was used. Vendors offer period art, woodcrafts, and replica swords, uniforms, and music of the era. Food and beverages are available at the event. Coolers are not allowed. Reenactors camp out and perform several battle scenes during the three-day weekend.

ORANGEBURG

SANTEE COOPER LAKES

Orangeburg is home to South Carolina's largest lake—Lake Marion—and one of the smallest, Lake Moultrie. Together the two create the Santee Cooper Lakes and are used by the state-owned utility for electric power generation. They also make up one of the state's premier inland recreation areas, with fishing, boating, camping, and hiking available all along the lakes.

The town of Orangeburg was the scene of the bloodiest battle in the effort to integrate public facilities in the state. "The Orangeburg Massacre" (orangeburgmassacre1968.com) happened when white state troopers fired on a crowd of unarmed protestors from the all-black South Carolina State College. Three students were killed, and dozens were injured. The students had been protesting for several days over the fact that they were not allowed in the city's bowling alley because they were black.

In the years that followed, only one person was convicted of a crime, and that was civil rights activist Cleveland Sellers—a native of the area who had returned to help students in their protest efforts. Sellers was convicted of riot, while the nine members of the highway patrol who admitted firing into the crowd that February night were acquitted. Sellers received a full pardon in the 1990s. There are historical markers at South Carolina State, now a university, commemorating the protests and the three students who were killed.

✳ To See

MUSEUMS Elloree Heritage Museum & Cultural Center (803-897-2225; elloreemuseum.org), 2714 Cleveland Street, Elloree. Hours: Wednesday through Saturday 10–5. Admission is $5 for adults 18–60 years old, $4 for seniors, $3 for students ages 6–18, and free for children younger than 6. Step back in time to 1900 and let Elloree town founder William J.

Snider welcome you to a re-created Cleveland Street with stores, bank, and hotel. You can also see a cotton gin, the 18th-century Snider Cabin, and Ruby Doo, the farm mule.

Edisto Memorial Gardens (803-533-6020; orangeburg.sc.us/gardens), 200 Riverside Drive, Orangeburg. Open daily dawn to dusk. Free. A historic marker at the gardens commemorates the encampment of 600 Confederate soldiers charged with defending the Edisto River Bridge in the last throes of the Civil War. After some success in blocking the advance of the U.S. Army, the Confederates withdrew to Columbia on February 12, 1865. Sixty years later, the beginnings of the gardens took shape with azaleas on about 5 acres of land. A nursery and greenhouse were added in 1947, and roses were planted in 1951 to give the gardens a longer blooming season. The gardens now encompass 150 acres and have 4,000 plants with at least 75 varieties of roses as well as the spring-blooming azaleas. It is one of 23 official test gardens that recognizes up to five desirable hybrid roses introductions each year. Its military roots are marked with a memorial fountain honoring veterans of U.S. wars. A butterfly garden and a sensory garden are recent additions. The gardens also feature the Angel of Hope Project, which provides a place for meditation for grieving parents of young children who have died.

OTHER PLACES OF INTEREST Railroad Shrine and Museum (803-274-8820), US 21, Branchville. Open 10–2 Friday through Saturday and

EDISTO MEMORIAL GARDENS IN ORANGEBURG

2–4 Sunday, early spring through September; by appointment at other times. This museum sits at one of the oldest railroad junctions in the United States and was on a line that ran from Charleston to Aiken County. The museum includes a replica of the steam locomotive "The Best Friend of Charleston."

✳ To Do

FISHING With the state's largest lake, there are many fishing guides in the area. Here are a select few:

Santee Cooper Charters (843-899-4325; santeecoopercharters.com), 806 Bowfin Drive, Moncks Corner. Charters by reservation. Boats are $350 a day for up to three fishermen; $50 for each additional angler up to six. However, service owner Truman Lyon says if you give him enough notice, he can accommodate about 40 folks on a fishing trip. Anglers provide their own food, beverage, and license—which non–South Carolina residents can get online for about $10 for a week's worth of fishing. Truman also recommends bringing some sunscreen, sunglasses, hat, and long-sleeved shirt. Truman has been plying the waters of Santee as a guide for more than 35 years. He fell in love with the place on a fishing trip in 1970.

Santee Cooper Catfishnfool Guide Service (803-238-0596; catfishnfool.com), 12819 Old Number 6 Highway, Eutawville. This service guarantees you'll catch a fish or you won't pay. Rates: $250 for two hours, and up to $450 for six hours.

Captain Darryl's Guide Service (803-324-7912; captaindarryls.com), 3145 Long Meadow Road, Rock Hill. Open year-round. Trips start at $350 for first two guests 13 years old and older and $50 for each additional person up to six people. Captain Darryl has a 28-foot pontoon boat and can take you on any South Carolina waterway, but he specializes in the Santee Cooper Lakes.

GOLF Golf Santee (803-854-2149; golfsantee.com), 8829 Old Number 6 Highway, Santee. This is a one-stop shop for golf vacations in the Santee Cooper Lakes area.

Here is a sampling of courses available in Santee:

Santee National Golf Club (803-854-3531; santeenational.com), 8636 Old Number Six Highway, Santee. This 6,100-yard, par-72 meanders through gently rolling hills and moss-covered oaks. Greens fees average $35.

Lake Marion Golf Course (803-854-2554), 9069 SC 6, Santee. This par-72 course plays 6,670 yards from the back tees and is located on the shores of South Carolina's largest lake. Greens fees average $40.

Wyboo Golf Club (803-478-7899; wyboogolfclub.com), 2565 Players Course Drive, Manning. This Tom Jackson–designed course opened in 1999. Rates for this 6,900-yard, par-72 course range $40–50.

PARKS Santee State Park (803-854-2408; southcarolinaparks.com), 251 State Park Road, Santee. Open 6 AM–10 PM, Monday through Sunday. Admission: $2 adults; $1.25 South Carolina seniors; ages 15 and younger admitted free. The park sits on the larger of the two Santee Cooper Lakes with access to some of the best inland fishing in the state. There are 10 cabins that sit on piers over the lake. Guests can take pontoon boat tours of the lake and its swampy headwaters out of the park's marina.

Santee National Wildlife Refuge (803-478-2217; fws.gov/santee), 2125 Fort Watson Road, Summerton. Visitors center open 8–4 Tuesday through Saturday. Trails open daily 7–7 in spring and summer, 8–5 in fall and winter. This area was created in 1941 after the damming of the Santee River caused saltwater intrusion into the Santee delta, destroying some natural waterfowl habitat. The refuge is in Berkeley and Clarendon Counties. Things to see range from 3,500-year-old Indian Mound to the Wrights Bluff Nature Trail, with great birding areas. Pine Island is accessible only by foot or bicycle and provides protection for alligators and bald eagles; it's the winter home of ducks, geese, and swans.

CABINS ON A PIER AT LAKE MARION

Jan Hogan

✳ Lodging

Lake Marion Waterfront Rentals (803-433-7355; dees rentals.tripod.com), 601B Mill Street, Manning. Open 9–5 Monday through Friday. This rental company has more than 20 waterfront homes and condos available on Lake Marion, some with private piers. Weekly rental rates from $650 to $1,300.

MOTELS Clark's Inn & Restaurant (803-854-2141, clarksinnand restaurant.com), 114 Bradford Boulevard, Santee. This inn first opened in 1946 and is a classic Southern motel at a very reasonable price. The inn offers large rooms with two double beds, king rooms, two-room suites, and suites with full kitchens. Rates range $80–90 a night.

Southern Lodge (803-531-7333; southernlodge.com), 3616 St. Matthews Road, Orangeburg. This is another classic small-town motel at reasonable rates. Southern Lodge also has weekly rates and rooms with kitchenette. Rates start at $60 a night.

RESORTS Lakeside Marina & Resort (803-492-7226; lakemarion vacation.com), 107 Cypress Shores Road, Eutawville. Waterfront cottages from one to five bedrooms rent for $100–200 a night. The marina also rents houseboats for $175 a night. Pontoon boat rentals are available for up to 30 passengers at $100 a day.

CAMPGROUNDS/CABINS Rocks Pond Campground & Marina (803-492-7711; rocks pondcampground.net), 108 Campground Road, Eutawville. This facility on Lake Marion has acres of natural area available for exploring and camping. Lakefront sites are $40; pond sites are $35. Trailer rentals range from $75–110 a night.

✳ Where to Eat

DINING OUT Four Moons (803-531-1984; fourmoons.com), 1145 Orangeburg Mall Circle, Orangeburg. Open for lunch 11:30–2 Tuesday through Friday and for dinner 5:30–9 Tuesday through Saturday. The bar opens at 4:30 Tuesday through Saturday. When they hear about Four Moons, most people think you've got to be kidding. Orangeburg is known for good barbecue, good shopping, good golf, and the Santee Cooper Lakes; it is not known for its AAA Four Diamond restaurants. Yet here is Four Moons. Specialties include jumbo lump crabcakes, crispy fried whole flounder, and of course shrimp and grits. There is a full grill menu including steaks and a burger— the cheapest entrée on the menu at $9. Prices top out at $30 for the lobster. Most lunch items are under $10. The owners also operate a wine and gourmet food shop and an Internet café.

Clark's Restaurant (803-854-2101; clarksinnandrestaurant.com),

114 Bradford Boulevard, Santee. Open daily 6 AM until the evening dinner crowd leaves. Clark's is the oldest restaurant in Santee, having opened in 1946. Warm and inviting with a fireplace in the main dining room and an English-style bar, Clark's serves breakfast every morning, a weekday lunch buffet, and a sit-down dinner with specials that change nightly. Dinner entrées range $13–22.

EATING OUT Lone Star Barbeque & Mercantile (803-854-2000; lonestarbbq.net), 2212 State Park Road, Santee. Open 11–9 Thursday through Saturday; closes at 7 on Sunday. This all-you-can-eat barbecue restaurant is spread across four old buildings that served as country store, post office, and supplier to local farmers as late as 1997. The buffet here includes barbecue, fried fish, ribs, and shrimp and grits; $9–12 per person.

✳ Special Events

SPRING *April:* **Striped Bass Festival** (clarendoncounty.com /stripedbassfestival.html), Manning. For more than 30 years, this festival has saluted the fish that brings visitors to the Santee Cooper Lakes. There are golf and fishing tournaments, a parade, dance and boating events. This is a great way to kick off boating season on South Carolina's largest lake—Lake Marion.

✒ **St. George World Grits Festival** (843-563-7943; worldgrits festival.com), US 15, St. George. Since 1986, the ultimate Southern food, the grit, has been celebrated at this festival in St. George near the intersection of Interstates 95 and 26. It was founded on the

LONE STAR BARBECUE & MERCANTILE IN SANTEE

Jan Hogan

THE ARTS AND CRAFTS ALLEY AT THE ORANGEBURG FESTIVAL OF ROSES

belief—proved to the satisfaction of some—that the tiny town of St. George eats more grits per capita that anywhere else on earth. Events include food booths, grits-grinding exhibits, grits contests for children, and of course a grits-eating contest. Bring your own salt.

Late April, early May: **Orangeburg Festival of Roses** (803-534-6821; festivalofroses.com), 200 Riverside Drive, Orangeburg. The free festival held every year at Edisto Memorial Gardens marked its 40th anniversary in 2011. The weekend celebration includes beauty pageants for all ages; music, golf, and softball tourna-ments; and a road race. The gardens have 4,000 plants with at least 75 varieties of roses. It is one of 23 official test gardens that recognizes up to five desirable hybrid roses introductions each year.

WINTER *March:* **Trash to Treasures** (803-897-2821; elloree southcarolina.com), Cleveland Street, Elloree. In advance of spring cleaning, come out to the annual townwide yard sale. Local merchants and traveling craftsfolk show their wares along with food vendors. If you're going to be in the Santee area in early March anyway, it's worth a stop.

SUGGESTED ITINERARIES

Revolutionary War Corridor

To see this area, I recommend staying at a bed & breakfast in the wonderful historic town of Camden. I consider Camden to be the highlight of this area, and it's centrally located for short day trips to see the interesting things throughout the region. **Camden House** (803-713-1013; camden house.us), 1502 Broad Street, is located right on the main downtown area of Camden and is an easy walk to all the great shops and lunch places. You can head out straight down Broad Street and meander through monument park that runs on either side of the street, then hit the **Old Armory Steak House** (803-432-3222), 514 Rutledge Street, to get a hearty lunch to prepare you for your long day of shopping and walking. Head back down Broad to **Springdale Antiques Inc.** (803-432-0312), 951 Broad Street, **Camden Antiques Market** (803-432-0818), 830 South Broad Street, and **Antiques on Broad** (803-424-1338), 821 Broad Street, Camden. Then continue about half a mile to the **Historic Camden Exchange** (803-432-9841), 222 Broad Street on the grounds of the **Kershaw-Cornwallis House** (803-432-9841; historic-camden.net). This beautiful old house has seen it all in Camden, from the Revolution through the Civil War and up to the modern era. There also is a Quaker cemetery at the site. From here, you can trace your route back, and you should be ready for cocktails and dinner at **Sam Kendall's** (803-424-2005; samk-endalls.com), 1042 Broad Street. You may want to make a reservation a day in advance—more if you're planning on stopping by on a weekend. You will have worked up quite the appetite, so the plentiful portions here should not be a problem. From here, it is a short walk back to your room at the Camden House.

If you're visiting during summer, Day 2 is best started in McBee (pronounced *MACK-bee*), where you will find everything peachy. On your drive over, stop in at **Bethune Pottery** (843-334-8346; bethunepottery .com), 3736 Jefferson Davis Highway, to see the large collection of yard art and other interesting pieces before turning right onto SC 151 toward McBee and Mac's Pride peaches. At Mac's Pride, you will find some of the best peaches you have ever had, but the store also sells peach ice cream, peach chutney, peach jam, and peach cobbler. And you'll find a variety of locally grown crops from corn to cucumbers, sweets with or without sugar, and an eclectic collection of gifts. Even if you can't cart home a bushel of peaches, it's worth a stop here just to taste.

From McBee, take 151/903 to Lancaster and have lunch at **Charley's Café and Catering** (803-285-1145), 306 South Main Street. Lancaster's short Main Street has a few interesting little shops, and Charley's is a wonderful inexpensive lunch. From here, it's a short drive to **Andrew Jackson State Park** (803-285-3344; southcarolinaparks.com), 196 Andrew Jackson Park Road. There is a museum devoted to the seventh president of the United States and a replica of an 18th-century schoolhouse. There also is a fishing pond and two 1-mile trails for a gentle walk or hike.

Continue north a little way to **Landsford Canal State Park** (803-789-5800; southcarolinaparks.com), 2051 Park Drive, Catawba, to see the rocky shoals spider lily—a delicate-looking but sturdy plant that hangs on to rocks in the swiftly moving Catawba River and blooms in a beautiful blanket of white in late May and early June. After your long outdoorsy day, I recommend returning to home base and get fresh for dinner at **Mill Pond Steakhouse** (803-425-8825; themillpondsteakhouse.com), 84 Boykin Mill Road, Rembert. The food here is great, but the atmosphere is like taking a step back in time. You have cocktails in the old general store before eating in a dining room that overlooks the pond at the old mill. This is great for couples or for a large group.

On Day 3, I suggest a trek over to **Swan Lake—Iris Gardens** (803-436-2640; sumtersc.gov), 822 West Liberty Street, Sumter. The gardens host the **Iris Festival** (803-436-2640; sumtersc.gov/visitingus/festivals _iris.aspx) in May. These gardens are truly stunning from mid-May through June with more than 120 varieties of irises; the lake has eight species of swans. You are surrounded by cypress trees as you stroll along the boardwalk over the lake's dark water. After touring the gardens, drop in at **Hanna's Grill** (803-773-9480), 541 East Liberty Street, Sumter, for a wonderful home-cooked meal like Grandma used to make. After lunch, check out **St. Mark's Episcopal Church** (803-452-9995; sumtersc.gov), 6205 Camp Mac Boykin Road, Pinewood. This beautiful old church is tucked away in the woods near **Manchester State Forest** (803-494-8196; state.sc.us/forest/refman.htm), 6740 Headquarters Road, Wedgefield, and **Poinsett State Park** (803-494-8177; southcarolinaparks.com), 6660 Poinsett Park Road, Wedgefield. Both are excellent locations for some outdoor fun, including hiking along the Palmetto Trail's High Hills of Santee or Wateree passages.

If you still have time, head north up Interstate 77 and check out **Kings**

Mountain National Military Park (864-936-7921; nps.gov/kimo/index .htm), 2625 Park Road, Blacksburg, and **Historic Brattonsville** (803-684-2327; chmuseums.org), 1444 Brattonsville Road, McConnells. Historic Brattonsville was where Mel Gibson filmed much of his Francis Marion–inspired film, *The Patriot*. Rock Hill also has the **Southern Revolutionary War Institute** (803-684-3948; chmuseums.org), 212 East Jefferson Street, York. If you need a place to stay in York County, check out **The Inn at Winthrop** (803-323-2300; www2.winthrop.edu/inn), 128 Joynes Hall, Rock Hill.

Columbia

To me, Columbia is the hardest spot in South Carolina to create visitor itineraries for. I live here and every day, I drive past all the things that would be cool to see—but I never do. One of the things that amazes me the most about Columbia is the natural, outdoorsy things that are available. For your first day in Columbia, if it's a warm, summer day, I recommend starting with breakfast at my favorite breakfast joint, **Compton's Kitchen** (803-791-0755; comptonskitchen.com), 1118 B Avenue, West Columbia. It's just a short drive from there to the West Columbia entrance to the botanical gardens at **Riverbanks Zoo and Garden** (803-779-8717; riverbanks.org), 500 Wildlife Parkway. Hit the gardens first, getting there while the morning dew still sits on the plants. You will cross over the Saluda River, the beautiful waterway that runs between the zoo and garden and provides the name *Riverbanks*. The zoo really can be an all-day affair, and the kids (and you) will be exhausted when the park closes at 5 PM. I recommend returning to your hotel—a good affordable one in the city is **The Whitney** (803-252-0845; whitneyhotel.com), 700 Woodrow Street—and freshening up before dinner at **Mr. Friendly's** (803-254-7828, mrfriendlys.com), 2001-A Greene Street, Five Points. This is my absolute favorite restaurant in town. The food is great and won't break you. There are plenty of affordable items for kids and several tasty options for vegetarians.

Five Points is always abuzz with activity after dark, but it's not for kids. If you are traveling without the kids, grab a copy of the *Free Times* or check them out online at free-times.com for a list of performers at the local watering holes. My favorite music venue is actually down on Main Street, **the White Mule** (803-661-8199; thewhitemule.com), 1530 Main Street.

There are two really great ways to spend a hot day in Columbia. First, you can hang out on one of the three rivers (the Saluda and the Broad meet in the city to form the Congaree) that offer great kayaking, canoeing, and fishing opportunities; or you can visit the **South Carolina State Museum/EdVenture** complex (803-898-4921; museum.state.sc.us), 301 Gervais Street, in the Congaree Vista area.

Contact **River Runner Outdoor Center** (803-771-0353; riverrunner .us), 905 Gervais Street, for the best way to get on one of the rivers. This outfitter offers all kinds of tours on the waters in Columbia and can provide everything you need for a safe trip. The Saluda has some potentially dangerous rapids near the zoo, so a guided tour would be best for the novice paddler. Or you could put in later where the water flattens out before heading into **Congaree National Park** (803-776-4396; nps .gov/cong/index.htm), 100 National Park Road, Hopkins. This stretch and the park offer wonderful canoeing.

The State Museum and EdVenture are a great place to take the kids to get out of the heat. The museums offer wonderful touch and interactive exhibits for the youngsters as well as the young at heart. The educational programs that run through the day, such as one on laser technology, are very entertaining and worth the time. You can spend all day at these two locations, with a break between for lunch at **M Vista** (803-255-8878; miyos.com), 701 Lady Street, Suite C, which has the best Asian food in the city. From the museums, you can check out the Three Rivers Greenway, either on the Columbia side of the river at **Riverfront Park & Historic Columbia Canal** (803-545-3100; columbiasc.net), Laurel at Huger Street; or by walking across the Gervais Street Bridge to the **West Columbia Riverwalk**. These parks offer the easiest access to Columbia's rivers and awesome views of the waterway and downtown. The West Columbia park also has an amphitheater where plays and musical events are held throughout the year. If you choose the "West Bank"—as we like to call it West Columbia—check out **116 Espresso and Wine Bar** (803-791-5663; 116state.com), 116 State Street, West Columbia. It's a great place to have some wine and tapas before or after strolling on the Riverwalk.

Upstate 5

SC Department of Parks, Recreation & Tourism, DiscoverSouthCarolina.com

INTRODUCTION

In the past 20 years the South Carolina Upstate has transformed itself from the center of a dying textile industry to a thriving cultural hub for international industries such as BMW and Michelin. The success of these businesses and the variety of people who pass through the area's main city of Greenville give it an upscale, hip flair more at home in a port city like Charleston or a tourist town like Asheville, North Carolina. Still, the influence of fundamentalist Christian Bob Jones University and onetime Baptist-affiliated Furman University make the area the most politically and socially conservative in a very conservative state.

The Greenville metropolitan area, which includes Spartanburg to the east, Anderson to the west, and the college town of Clemson to the north, is where the piedmont meets the mountains. Three main lakes highlight the area: The pristine deep-water Lake Jocassee, created by a dam on the Toxaway River in the 1970s and maintained as a predominantly wilderness area, spills into the more developed Lake Keowee with its many access points. To the west is Lake Hartwell—which is one of many lakes created by dams on the Savannah River, which separates South Carolina from Georgia.

Greenville is just two hours from Charlotte and two and a half hours from Atlanta, making it a wonderful weekend getaway for folks in those cities, particularly during the heat of summer when Greenville typically will be a few degrees cooler. The fall is prime visiting time for the area, as the Cherokee Scenic Highway (SC 11) winds through the hills, past apple orchards and other colorful hardwoods putting on their annual leaf show.

The city mixes natural beauty with some of the best art collections around. The Museum and Gallery at Bob Jones University has a collection of religious-themed art unmatched in the Southeast. The university has a satellite gallery at Heritage Green, a collection of museums just blocks from the city's downtown Falls Park at the Reedy River. Also there is the Greenville Museum of Art with one of the largest Andrew Wyeth collections in the country.

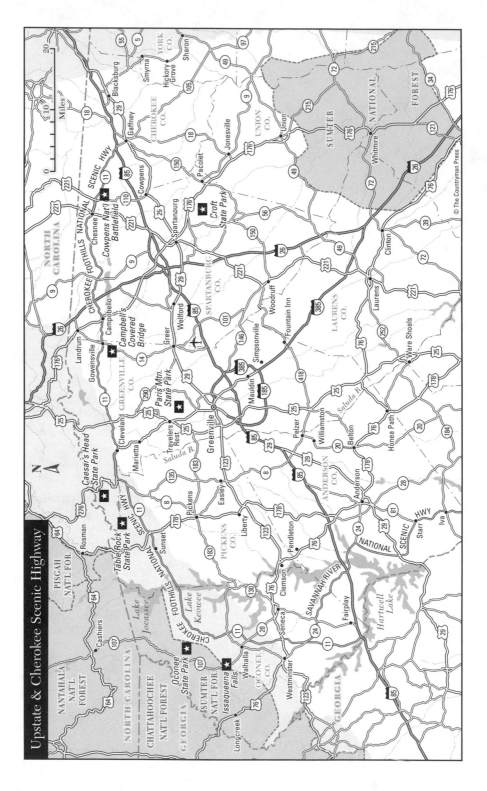

Upstate & Cherokee Scenic Highway

© The Countryman Press

Celebrity chef Tyler Florence was born and raised in Greenville, and the revitalized city center has attracted high-end restaurants, including Soby's, The Lazy Goat, Restaurante Bergamo, Two Chefs, Chophouse '47, and Nantucket Seafood Grill.

But Greenville isn't the only attraction here. The town of Spartanburg is just half an hour away and is home to Cowpens National Battlefield, marking the site where General Daniel Morgan defeated British Colonel Banastre Tarleton near the end of the Revolutionary War. Also a former textile town, Spartanburg's fortune is now aligned with BMW Manufacturing Co. and companies that make products for the automotive industry.

Spartanburg also is home to the Beacon restaurant—a must-see for anyone looking for a big fat slice of South Carolina life. For first-timers, I recommend you split a chili cheeseburger-a-plenty, meaning the ample-sized burger is buried under a mountain of french fries and fried onion rings. If you have kids, this might feed three of them. But be sure to get your own sweet tea. They do it so well here that the stuff has been sold in local grocery stores.

In addition to Furman and Bob Jones in Greenville, Spartanburg has Wofford and Converse Colleges, two private universities that have educated many of the state's leaders, teachers, and musicians over the years. The largest school in the area is Clemson University, whose campus turns into a sea of orange—in the trees and on football fans' backs—in the fall. Clemson is the state's agricultural college, and its dairy operations make some of the finest blue cheese and ice cream you'll ever taste.

THE LAZY GOAT RESTAURANT

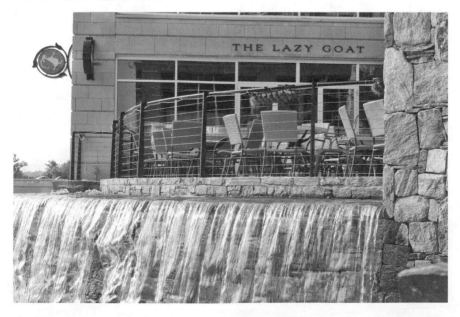

Clemson students cured their first batch of blue cheese in 1941 in Stumphouse Mountain Tunnel, another stop you'll want to make in the Upstate. The tunnel was begun as a way to connect Charleston to the Midwest by rail. Construction was begun in the 1850s but abandoned during the Civil War. The 200-foot Issaqueena Falls is a short walk from Stumphouse Park.

In the lower part of the Upstate are the small towns of Abbeville and Greenwood. Once home to several of the state's textile mills, they have remade themselves as places to go and see a classic Southern downtown with restaurants, shops, and—in Abbeville—a remade opera house.

WHEN TO COME The South Carolina Upstate is a year-round destination, though it's most popular in late summer, when the cooler temperatures provide a refuge from the heat of lower-lying areas, and in the fall, as the hardwood leaves put on a beautiful show. Be warned, though: The Upstate is home to several football-playing colleges, including Clemson, Furman, Wofford, and North Greenville, so some Saturdays in the fall may be very crowded. Late spring also is popular as mountain laurel and other flowers break out in bloom. Summer is the best time for water sports, but hiking and camping may be a little miserable, because South Carolina's summers are hot, humid, and buggy. The winter is generally mild here, as it is across much of the state, though there are occasional snowfalls and severe cold snaps.

GREENVILLE

Greenville has reinvented itself many times over the years. Its rocky foothill terrain was never well suited for farming, but the moving water provided power for industry—especially textiles, which took the cotton from nearby farms and turned it into clothing, bedsheets, and towels. As late as the early 1980s, textiles were the state's number one industry, and Greenville was the center of that. But free trade agreements made it easier to sell goods in the United States that were made outside the country, and those textile jobs began moving first to Latin America, then to Asia—wherever the cheapest labor could be found. It was the same phenomenon that had brought the textile mills to the South in the 1920s and '30s, when plant owners sought to escape higher wages and stricter labor laws in the Northeast.

But Greenville continued to thrive as other, more high-tech industries began making the same move that textiles had made decades earlier. Cheaper land and a relatively inexpensive, but trainable, workforce brought companies such as Michelin and BMW to the area, and Greenville became the hub for a Southern automotive industry. The firms brought with them European executives and engineers, who in turn brought some of their culture to the area.

In 1990 the city's Peace Center for the Performing Arts opened with a 2,100-seat concert hall as well as a 400-seat theater and amphitheater along the river with an open-air pavilion. It was just the beginning of a revitalization of the downtown area that includes Falls Park at the Reedy River, which was dedicated in 2004 with the Liberty Bridge spanning the river to give visitors a bird's-eye view of the park. On one side of the park is the West End, a collection of shops and restaurants; on the other is Main Street, which also has been remade as a dining and shopping district.

Heritage Green brings together several museums and other attractions together in one area. It's now home to the Greenville County Museum of Art, a satellite gallery of Bob Jones University's Museum and Gallery; the

GREENVILLE'S MUSEUM SQUARE AT HERITAGE GREEN

Upcountry History Museum located in the old Coca-Cola bottling building; and the Children's Museum, which opened in summer 2009. Within walking distance are the main branch of the Greenville County Library and the Greenville Little Theater.

GUIDANCE Greater Greenville Chamber-Commerce (864-282-8509; greenvillechamber.org), 24 Cleveland Street. Open 8–5 Monday through Friday.

The Upcountry (864-233-2690; theupcountry.com), The Web-based visitors center offers tourists information about visiting, shopping, and relocating to the Greenville area and offers an electronic newsletter that includes coupons and special deals.

GETTING THERE *By air:* **Greenville-Spartanburg International Airport** (864-877-7426; gspairport.com) offers direct flights to four Florida cities through Allegiant Airlines (702-505-8888; allegiantair.com), and connections to most major airports through carriers American Eagle (800-433-7300; aa.com), Continental Airlines (800-525-0280; continental.com), Delta Air Lines (800-221-1212; delta.com), Northwest Airlines (800-225-2525; nwa.com), United Express (800-241-6522; united.com), US Airways (800-428-4322; usairways.com).

By train: **Amtrak** (800-872-7245; amtrak.com), 1120 West Washington Street. The Crescent runs from New York to New Orleans with stops in Spartanburg, Greenville, and Clemson in the Upstate.

By bus: **Greyhound** (864-235-4741; greyhound.com), 100 West McBee Avenue. Several buses daily arriving and departing.

By car: Greenville is about two hours from Atlanta and two hours from Charlotte, North Carolina, on Interstate 85. Interstate 385 spurs off Interstate 26 south of Greenville for those driving up from Charleston, or from Interstate 95 from the south.

GETTING AROUND The best way to get around Greenville is by car. The city's bus service, **Greenlink** (864-235-4741; ridegreenlink.com), has a dozen routes in and around the city. $1.25 each way, no Sunday service.

✳ To See

MUSEUMS Greenville County Museum of Art (864-271-7570; greenvillemuseum.org), 420 College Street. Open 11–5 Tuesday through Saturday, 1–5 Sunday. Free. This is hands-down one of the best art museums in the state. Its extensive collection of Andrew Wyeth paintings are always being refreshed and repackaged to highlight a certain aspect of his work. Jasper Johns always has a home here as well as artists like Mary Whyte, whose exhibit Working South—looking at the vanishing professions so long associated with Southern workers—will be at the Greenville Museum of Art through the fall of 2011.

Bob Jones University Art Museum and Gallery (864-770-1331; bjumg .org), 1700 Wade Hampton Boulevard. Open 2–5 Tuesday through Saturday. Admission: $5 adults; children younger than 12 are free. This world-famous collection of religious art includes European art from the 14th

MURAL OF THE LAST SUPPER AT BOB JONES UNIVERSITY

through 19th centuries, including works by Rubens, Tintoretto, and van Dyck. The museum also has a collection of antiquities, Russian icons, and seven large canvases from Benjamin West's series *The Progress of Revealed Religion*. The hours at the main museum are limited, so in 2008 the school opened a satellite M&G at 25 Heritage Green Place. Open 10–5 Tuesday through Saturday. Admission: $5 ages 12 to 60; $4 seniors, $3 students, children under 12 free with an adult. This facility features exhibits from the main museum as well as more interactive opportunities for children.

Upcountry History Museum (864-467-3100; upcountryhistory.org), 540 Buncombe Street. Open 10–5 Tuesday through Saturday, 1–5 Sunday. Admission: $5 adults, $4 seniors and college students with valid ID, $3 children ages 4–18; free for children 3 and younger. This museum explores what it means to be part of the geographic region of the state known as the Upcountry in the foothills of the Blue Ridge Mountains and in the northwest corner of the state.

✎ **Children's Museum of the Upstate** (864-233-7755; tcmupstate.org), 300 College Street. Open 9–5 Tuesday through Saturday, 1–5 Sunday. Open Monday in the summer. Admission is $12 for everyone over 2 years old. Opened in 2009, the museum has three floors of exhibits designed mostly for children ages 6–11. Exhibits include Talkin' Trash, which discusses the environment, and a Bi-Lo market to teach kids about nutrition and grocery shopping. There's also a garage band zone, a television studio, and a construction zone. Younger children will enjoy Grandma Betty's Farm and a Toddler Lily Pond. This is a great place to let the kids just touch and learn. The museum also has outdoor garden exhibits. Get here early and plan to spend all day. You and the little ones won't be disappointed.

Museum and Library of Confederate History (864-421-9039; confed eratemuseum.org), 15 Boyce Avenue. Open 10–3 Monday and Wednesday, 1–9 Friday, 10–5 Saturday, and 1–5 Sunday. There is no admission charge, but donations are accepted. This museum is located in the historic Pettigru District near downtown. If you're staying downtown, it's worth a stroll over to this museum to see some of the relics and artifacts from the Civil War including firearms, photographs, clothing, letters, and newspapers. A research library is located here for the more studious visitor.

✎ **Roper Mountain Science Center** (864-355-8900; ropermountain .org), 402 Roper Mountain Road. The observatory is open Friday from 7:30 PM to 10 PM and 9–5 on the second Saturday of the month. The nature trail is open Monday through Friday 8:30–5. Located on 62 acres just off Interstate 385 about 10 minutes from downtown, this wonderful science and nature center includes a planetarium, a science center, an amphitheater, and walking trails. Public programs at the observatory are held on Fridays and the second Saturday of each month. There are two shows each Friday at 7 and 8:45 PM. The "Starry Nights" program is $4 for

ages 6–12 and seniors, and $5 for adults and teens. The second-Saturday programs are at 9 AM and 1 PM and feature a different theme each month. Admission is $5 for ages 6–12 and seniors; $6 for adults and teens. The outdoor areas are open whenever the main gates are open and include an arboretum, butterfly garden, water lily pond, and kitchen and vegetable gardens as well as the walking trails. Admission is $4 for adults and teens; $3 for ages 6–12 and seniors.

PARKS Falls Park at the Reedy River (864-467-4350; fallspark.com), 601 South Main Street. Open 7 AM–9 PM daily. Free. A small river runs through Greenville, and the city built a park around it. The Reedy River has served as a vital lifeline for the city's industries since the first gristmill was opened there in the late 18th century. Unfortunately the same industries—including textile mills—that provided much-needed jobs also contributed to the deterioration over the centuries of the river's water quality. The Carolina Foothills Garden Club bought the land where Falls Park now sits in 1926 and turned it into a 26-acre park. Over the next 60 years, the club and the city, as well as surrounding companies, worked to clean up the park and restore the historic Falls Cottage. In the 1990s the Liberty Bridge was added and the park was fully landscaped and turned into a regional attraction. The garden manager will give a guided tour for $35 per person, by appointment only.

Cleveland Park (864-467-4350; greatergreenville.com), East Washington Street, Greenville. Open daily, sunrise to sunset. This park encompasses 126 acres along the Reedy River and is home to the **Greenville Zoo** (864-467-4300; greenvillezoo.com), as well as the city's Vietnam Veterans

SUSPENSION BRIDGE OVER FALLS PARK AT THE REEDY RIVER

Memorial, the Rock Quarry Garden, and the Fernwood Nature Trail. The park also has tennis and volleyball courts, a playground, a softball field, and ample covered picnic facilities.

OTHER PLACES OF INTEREST Shoeless Joe Jackson Statue, West End, South Main Street. One of the most famous baseball players ever, Joseph Jefferson Jackson (1881–1951)—better known as Shoeless Joe— was a native of Greenville and played for the Greenville Spinners in the Carolina League, where he got his nickname. Seems the new spikes he was wearing for a doubleheader put blisters on his feet, and he decided to take them off. No one noticed until he got a hit and had to run without the shoes. Jackson was at the peak of his game when he was accused along with seven other Chicago White Sox players of conspiring to throw the World Series. All the men were banned from baseball for life even thought they were tried and found innocent. Jackson's play in the series was nearly flawless, with a series-high batting average of .375 and a record 12 hits. He had no errors and hit the series' only home run. He denied the allegations until his dying day in 1951 and remains one of the game's most beloved players.

Charles Townes Statue, Main Street across from the entrance to Falls Park. Though Townes's name is not as immediately recognizable as that of Joe Jackson, almost everyone in the world has benefited from his work: The 1964 Nobel Prize winner developed the laser in 1960. The technology is now used in bar-code scanners at grocery stores, compact disc and DVD players in your home, and laser printers at your office. The invention was born out of a request by the U.S. military to create a radar system with a wavelength that measured in the millimeters. The statue is located near where Townes went to school at Furman University when its campus over- looked the Reedy River downtown. The bench that his likeness is sitting on is from Franklin Square Park in Washington, DC, where Townes had an "Ah-ha!" moment that led to the invention of the laser's predecessor, the maser. Visitors are invited to sit next to the statue in search of their own "Ah-ha!" moment.

✳ To Do

FAMILY-FRIENDLY ACTIVITIES ✐ **Asia Garden at Furman Uni- versity** (864-294-2185; furman.edu), 3300 Poinsett Highway. This garden built around a large pond with waterfall and a stream has Japanese irises, bog plants, bamboo, and several species of Japanese pines, camellias, and cherry trees.

✐ **Greenville Zoo** (864-467-4300; greenvillezoo.com), 150 Cleveland Park Drive. Open daily 10–4:30. Admission: $7.75 for ages 16 and older; $4.50 for children 3–15; free for younger children. A small zoo that includes giraffes, monkeys, and elephants. It's a wonderful way to spend a fall morning.

⚓ **Discovery Island Waterpark** (864-963-4345; greenvillerec.com/parks /discovery-island), 417 Baldwin Road, Simpsonville. Open 10–6 Monday through Saturday and 1–6 Sunday when school is out. Admission is $10 for people 4 feet tall and taller, $8 for shorter guests, and $3 if you don't plan to go in the water. This water park gives you the feel of being in the cool mountain streams that surround Greenville, without the worry about snakes and other critters out in the woods. There's a lazy river, a body slide, a tube slide, and a leisure pool.

GOLF Southern Oaks Golf Course (864-859-6698; southernoaks-golf .com), 105 Southern Oaks Drive, Easley. Open daily year-round. This par-72 course is less than 30 minutes from downtown Greenville. Greens fees: $35 weekdays, $43 weekends; pull cart $3, electric cart $13 per player. Weekday seniors (55 and older) greens and cart $24.

Furman Golf Club (864-294-9090; furman.edu/golf), 3300 Poinsett Highway. This semi-private golf course gives members first crack at tee times, but after that it's anyone's game. The course has recently added a fifth set of tees for senior golfers. This is the home course of the university's men's and women's teams, which have included such greats as Betsy King, Beth Daniel, Dottie Pepper, and Brad Faxon. Par-72, it plays almost 7,000 yards from the back tees. Greens fees range from $15 in the winter to $43 on summer weekends. Cart rental is additional $15.

Verdae Greens Golf Course (864-676-1500; verdaegreens.com), 650 Verdae Boulevard. A relatively new course, Verdae Greens opened in 1991 and plays 6,773 yards from the back tees in a par-72. Greens fees range from $40 to $60 and discounts are given to seniors, active-duty military, and guests at the Embassy Suites Golf Resort.

Saluda Valley Country Club (864-847-7102; saludavalleycc.com), 598 Beaverdam Road, Williamston. This 6,486-yard course is a par-72. Rates $30–35 including cart.

✳ Green Space

PARKS Paris Mountain State Park (864-244-5565; southcarolinaparks .com), 2401 State Park Road. Admission: $2 for adults; $1.25for South Carolina seniors; free for those 15 and younger. Open 8 AM–9 PM during Daylight Saving Time, closes at 6 in the winter. This park was built by the Civil Conservation Corps in the 1930s and offers green space for hiking and biking year-round as well as boating and swimming in the summer. The renovated bathhouse serves as the park's new center, with exhibits on the park's history and a classroom for learning about the local flora and fauna.

✳ Lodging

INNS AND BED & BREAKFASTS

Pettigru Place (864-242-4529; pettigruplace.com), 302 Pettigru Street. For the past six years Lori Donaldson has been the chef and owner of this five-room B&B just blocks from downtown in the Pettigru Historic District. The inn's guests often walk to the restaurants, shops, and other attractions. Rooms rates are $120–200 and include a full breakfast in the morning and complimentary wine and snacks in the evening.

The Garden House Bed & Breakfast (864-963-3379; gardenhousebb.com), 302 South Main Street, Simpsonville. This B&B is just a little south of the main hub of Greenville and offers five guest rooms with a warm breakfast each morning, refreshments in the afternoon, and dessert in the evening.

The home started as a cottage in 1905, but has been renovated and added onto, so it's now about 6,000 square feet. Smoking is allowed on outside porches only and no pets are allowed, but the owners can help you find a place to board your pet if you need.

Ryan Nicholas Inn (864-286-6000; ryannicholasinn.com), 815 Holland Road. This large, newly built mansion is set on 6 acres and specializes in weddings on the weekends. There are four rooms with fireplace and oversized bath, including a whirlpool tub and steam shower; $155 per night Monday through Wednesday.

HOTEL ❦ The Westin Poinsett

(864-421-9700; westinpoinsettgreenville.com), 120 South Main Street. The city's oldest hotel, the Poinsett opened in 1925 but didn't

PETTIGRU PLACE B&B

make money until 1040. The Poinsett was one of the state's most elegant hotels for years, but fell into disrepair; at one point in the 1980s, it was a retirement home. After sitting empty for more than 10 years, it was completely renovated in the late 1990s with more than 200 modern rooms. Rooms start at $140 a night. Pets are allowed for a $50 nonrefundable deposit.

RESORTS Embassy Suites Hotel Greenville Golf Resort and Conference Center (864-676-9090; embassysuites1.hilton.com), 670 Verdae Boulevard. Built on a golf course, this hotel offers all the standard amenities of an Embassy Suites facility. Guests get discounts at the Verdae Greens golf course. Rates around $130 a night for a two-room suite.

CAMPGROUNDS & CABINS Ivy Acres Lodge and RV Park (864-220-9680; ivyacresrvpark.com), 201 Ivy Acres Drive, Piedmont. Set on 75 acres on the Saluda River, this RV park includes a three-bedroom lodge that can sleep up to 10 people. There are no shower facilities for campers. RVs are $30 a night. The lodge is $150 a night Monday through Thursday for up to four people; $200 a night on weekends; $20 a night for each additional person, and $100 cleaning fee. Free WiFi throughout the park.

Solitude Pointe (864-836-4128; solitudepointe.com), 102 Table Rock Road, Cleveland. This RV

park also has six cabins with full kitchen and private bath. Each cabin can sleep four adults and two children. $100–130 a night. The RV park has full hookups as well as bathroom facilities. Pull-through, back-in, and tent sites are available. Rates are $30 a night for two adults and two children. Extra adults are $5 a night; extra children $2.

✳ Where to Eat

DINING OUT Soby's (864-232-7007; sobys.com), 207 South Main Street. Open daily for dinner starting at 5:30. Sunday brunch 10:30–1. Soby's is considered by most to be Greenville's best

THE WESTIN POINSETT HOTEL

restaurant, combining classic Southern cuisine with an international flair. Opened in 1997 in the refurbished cotton exchange building, Soby's is part of the locally owned Court Square Restaurant Group that operates several Greenville restaurants. Entrées range from seasonal local vegetable plate ($15) to New York strip with 5-ounce lobster tail ($40). Reservations recommended.

The Lazy Goat (864-679-5299; thelazygoat.typepad.com), 170 River Place. Open 11:30–2:30 for lunch and at 5 for dinner Monday through Saturday. Sister restaurant to Soby's and overlooking the Reedy River downtown, The Lazy Goat offers Mediterranean-style food and specializes in made-from-scratch cooking down to the zahtar spices on the tables and homemade pasta. Lunch sandwiches and pizzas are $10 or less; dinner entrées range from paella at $18 to roasted grouper with a lobster risotto for $27.

Restaurante Bergamo (864-271-8667; ristorantebergamo.com), 100 North Main Street. Open 5:30–9:30 Tuesday through Saturday. For 22 years, this restaurant has specialized in northern Italian cuisine. The menu includes three veal dishes and plenty of seafood. Bergamo bottles its own limoncello, called Nello Cello for the owner, that sells for $40. There are only 80 seats, so reservations are highly recommended. Entrées range from $18 for pasta dishes to $34 for langostinos.

Chophouse '47 (864-286-8700; centraarchy.com/chophouse47.php) , 36 Beacon Drive. Open at 5 for dinner Monday through Saturday. This is part of a small southeastern restaurant group known as Centra Archy, which was born in Columbia, South Carolina. Chophouse '47 is the only one of its kind in that group and is a classic white-tablecloth steak house. Most entrées are $20–40 and include some seafood, veal, and lamb as well as steaks. All sides are à la carte and average $8.

Nantucket Seafood Grill (864-546-3535; nantucketseafoodgrill .com), 40 West Broad Street. Open daily for dinner at 5, Sunday brunch 11–3. A modern dining room located inside the new Courtyard by Marriott. This locally owned and operated restaurant offers indoor and outdoor dining and puts a dash of Creole or Lowcountry in most dishes. Entrées $20–40.

Pomegranate on Main (864-241-3012; pomegranateonmain .com), 618 South Main Street. Open for lunch and dinner Monday through Saturday starting at 11:30 AM. Owner Ali Saifi knows the restaurant business—he has opened dozens of Subway restaurants in South Carolina. But Pomegranate is more than a business for this native of Iran. "I wanted to serve authentic Persian food without alterations to the menu," he says. "I didn't know whether it was going to go over well with Americans." Saifi needn't

NANTUCKET SEAFOOD GRILL

have worried. His rack of lamb marinated in homemade yogurt is the restaurant's biggest seller. All of his meats are cooked on skewers in an open flame. "We don't even have a fryer in the restaurant," he says. Start with a spread or salad, then go straight for the lamb—rack or kebab. All dishes are served with rice—you can choose from several types—and are gluten-free. Starters are around $6; entrées range $15–25.

EATING OUT Mary Beth's at McBee Station (864-242-2535; marybethsatmcbee.com), 500 E. McBee Avenue, Suite 109. Open daily for breakfast and lunch 7–3; dinner from 5:30 Thursday through Saturday. This great little restaurant is located next to high-end condos and apartments near down-town. The menu is inventive and the food is tasty. It's a wonderful place to take a break from shopping or exploring. Their hibiscus—champagne and cranberry—is a refreshing twist on the morning cocktail. Four types of eggs Benedict for breakfast, quiche every

QUICHE AND SALAD AT MARY BETH'S

day, and the Asian barbecue chicken sandwich with a salad is perfect for lunch at $11. The dinner specialty is a grilled filet with crab, asparagus, and hollandaise for $28.

Henry's Smokehouse (864-232-7774; henryssmokehouse.com), 240 Wade Hampton Boulevard. Fall-off-the-bone ribs, pulled pork barbecue with a variety of sauces. Every plate is served with a thick-cut slice of white bread. Dishes $6–13. Henry's has a small dining room, with plenty of outside seating. Order at the counter and fix your own drinks.

Stax Original (864-232-2133; staxoriginal.com), 1704 Poinsett Highway. Open 7–2 for breakfast and lunch; reopens at 5 for dinner until 8. Take a step back in time at the Original Stax restaurant with low-rise counter seating as it was in the 1950s. Booth and table seating are also available. Most dishes $6–10. There are a couple of other restaurants with the name Stax in the Greenville area that are owned by the same family, but this is the original.

Two Chefs Deli and Market (864-370-9336; twochefsdeli.com), 104 South Main Street, Suite 105. Open 8:30–7:30, Monday through Friday. Two Chefs also has a take-out store at 8590 Pelham Road that also is open on Saturday. Large deli salads with a variety of meat options and classic deli sandwiches as well as wraps and sub-style sandwiches. Everything on the menu is under $10. They also offer six different box lunches that come with a salad or sandwich, side, and cookie, perfect for a picnic in Falls Park.

HENRY'S SMOKEHOUSE

OLD-STYLE BAR SEATING AT STAX ORIGINAL

Cantinflas Restaurant & Bar
(864-250-1300; healthycantinflas
.com), 10 South Main Street.
Open daily 11–10. Cantinflas
offers open-air dining and the
neatest sidewalk café on Main
Street. They serve standard Mexi-
can dishes with a wide selection of
vegetarian options and huge mar-
garitas. Entrées $10–15.

Tommy's Country Ham House
(864-242-6099), 214 Rutherford
Street. Open daily 5 AM–2 PM;
closes at noon on Saturday. Breakfast meats range from bacon and
chicken sausage to mahimahi and
red salmon. Breakfast is served all
day, and all items are less than
$10. For lunch, pick your meat
and as many veggies as you want
at $1.30 each. Meat selections
and specials change daily. A fried
chicken plate with mac and cheese,
pole beans, and collards will run
you about $10 with a glass of tea.

**Addy's Dutch Cafe & Restau-
rant** (864-232-2339), 17 East Coffee Street. Open for dinner
Tuesday through Sunday, starting
at 4:30 PM. Entrées are about

OUTDOOR DINING AT CANTINFLAS
RESTAURANT & BAR

TOMMY'S COUNTRY HAM HOUSE

$10–15 and Wednesday is schnitzel night, but there is some Asian influence here as well. The food is good, but folks seem to love the beer selection. So if Dutch food is not your bag, at least stop by for a beer.

DESSERT Luna Rosa Gelato (864-241-4040; lunarosagelato .com), 9 West Washington Street. Open daily for lunch 11–3, serving gelato until 10 PM. The Luna Rosa serves an interesting array of soups, salads, panini, and pizza all for around $10 per person, but that's not the main reason to come here. Just have the gelato; it's smooth and creamy and comes in a dozen decadent flavors from chocolate velvet to caramel latte crunch. Regular servings about $5.

Brick Street Café (864-421-0111; brickstreetcafe.com), 315 Augusta Street. Open for lunch Monday through Saturday 11–2:30 and for dinner Thursday through Saturday 5:30–9:30. Located in an old belt factory, the Brick Street Café has been around since 1995, though it feels older. The chicken salad is great, as are the Love Muffins for lunch. The café sells sandwiches, soup, and salads for lunch with most meals less than $10. For dinner, there is beef, halibut, shrimp and grits, and vegetarian lasagna—comfort food, with the filet mignon topping the menu at $25. The store has a wooden statue of Abe Lincoln out front.

✳ Entertainment

MUSIC VENUES Peace Center (864-467-3000; peacecenter.org), 300 South Main Street. Located in the heart of the renovated downtown, the Peace Center is one of the city's best attractions. Many visitors build weekend trips around the national shows stopping here. Acts playing here have included Sheryl Crow, a touring company of *Wicked*, Itzhak Perlman, the Doobie Brothers, and Kathy Griffin.

The Handlebar (864-233-6173; handlebar-online.com), 304 East Stone Avenue. Open 11:30 AM– 2 AM Monday through Friday, 5–midnight Saturday. The Handlebar serves food from 11:30–10:30, but is known mostly for its live music, which typically starts around 9 PM. Food is not allowed in the listening room, but there is a bar. Acts are mostly contemporary rock, pop, and blues, but include reggae, bluegrass, and heavy metal. The venue features widely known performers such as David Sanborn and Delbert McClinton and regional acts such as Cravin' Melon and the Blue Dogs (which was formed by high school friends of mine from Florence, by the way). Ticket prices vary depending on the act, but most shows are under $20.

THEATERS Cafe and Then Some (864-232-2287; cafeats .com), 101 College Street. Dinner seatings 6:30 and 7:30; show-only seating 7:45 Wednesday through Saturday. Shows are original comedic creations of the café's staff writer, including a recent hit, *Sanford in Love*, detailing the unhappy events surrounding the former governor's high-profile extramarital affair. Dinner fare ranges from Southern specialties of shrimp and grits and fried

green tomatoes to more unusual dishes like duck burritos. Entrées range from $8 to $25. Show is $15.

Centre Stage (864-233-6733; centrestage.org), 501 River Street. Shows at 8 PM; Thursday through Saturday 3 PM. Sunday shows typically run for three weeks every other month. A professional year-round theater, Centre Stage was founded in 1983 and has 285 seats. The company also performs one show a year by the winner of its annual playwrights' contest. Tickets $25 for nonmuscials; $30 for musicals.

The Warehouse Theatre (864-235-6948; warehousetheatre.com),

LUNA ROSA GELATO

37 Augusta Street. Tickets $15–25 depending on the night and the type of play (musical or not). Located in a converted textile warehouse, the theater puts on at least 15 local productions a year, including the Upstate Shakespeare Festival at Falls Park.

BAND CONCERTS Furman Concert Band Lakeside Concert Series (864-294-3491; furman .edu), 3300 Poinsett Highway. Performances begin at 7:30 PM every summer Thursday by the lake on the Furman University campus. Bring a picnic, a blanket, and some chairs. This is a must-do if you are in the area on a Thursday.

✳ Selective Shopping

ANTIQUES Buncombe Antique Mall (864-268-4498; buncombe antiques.com), 5000 Wade Hampton Boulevard, Taylors. Open 10–5:30 Monday through Saturday. Large antiques mall featuring art, furniture, silver, glass, books, and china. Cash or check only.

Southern Estates Antiques (864-299-8981), 415 Mauldin Road. Open 10–6 Monday through Saturday, 1–5 Sunday. This large antiques mall with more than 100 dealers includes furniture, china, crafts, jewelry, and artwork.

Southern Housepitality (864-299-0045; southernhousepitality .squarespace.com), 110 Mauldin Road. Open 10–6 Monday through Saturday, 1–5 Sunday.

There are bargains to be had at this upscale furniture consignment shop.

Greystone Antiques (864-233-3424; greystoneantiques.net), 1500 Augusta Street, and 101 Piney Mountain Road. Open 10–5 Tuesday through Saturday. An antiques and restoration business with two locations near downtown, Greystone offers a mix of American and European designs.

Galleries of Brian Brigham (864-235-4825; galleriesofbrian brigham.com), 1011 Woods Crossing Road. Open 10–5:30 Monday through Saturday. This business started as an interior design company in 1985; Brian Brigham Lehman has added a retail showroom featuring antiques and new home furnishings.

OTHER SHOPPING Historic Downtown Greenville offers visitors a unique shopping experience with new stores and restaurants mixed in with generations-old retailers. Dozens of these old buildings are attractions in themselves with listings on the National Register of Historic Places and wonderful examples of Victorian architectural styles.

Art Crossing at River Place (864-430-8924; artcrossing.org), 300 River Street. Generally, the studios are open 11–5 Tuesday through Saturday, a little later in summer and until 9 PM on the first Friday of the month. The Art Crossing studios have every style and medium available for purchase. You can talk to the artist directly before deciding on your purchase. If you're not in the buying mood, it's like a free gallery tour.

The Cook's Station (864-250-0091; thecooksstation.com), 659 South Main Street. Open 9–6 Monday through Thursday; until 8 PM Friday through Saturday; noon–5 Sunday. The Cook's Station has every kitchen gadget you think you need and some you didn't know existed. They also sell a selection of wines.

Mast General Store (864-235-1883; mastgeneralstore.com), 111 North Main Street. Open 10–6 Monday through Thursday, 10–9 Friday through Saturday, noon–6 Sunday. As its name implies, this store has a little bit of everything and reminds you of a downtown store from the early 20th century. You'll find outdoor clothing, boots, hiking and camping gear, cast-iron cookware, pottery, soaps, and gourmet food. When you're tired of shopping, pick through their barrels of old-style candies and pull up a rocking chair.

Happy Cow Creamery (864-243-9699; happycowcreamery .com), 332 McKelvey Road, Pelzer. Open 9–7 Monday through Friday; closes at 5 on Saturday. Located a little south of Greenville, the Happy Cow Creamery sells milk bottled at the nearby farm, butter, cheese, sausage, chicken, and organically grown fruits and vegetables.

Greenville State Farmers' Market (864-244-4023; agriculture.sc.gov), 1354 Rutherford Road. Open Monday through Saturday 8–6. The Greenville market offers fresh fruits and vegetables from surrounding counties as well as plants and flowers. You should plan to arrive here early to get the best offerings, especially during the peak summer months. Produce is available inside a 14,400-square-foot building or under a 10,000-square-foot shed. It started off as a tailgate market downtown. As more space was needed, the market moved a little out of town, but still just 10 minutes from Main Street.

✳ Special Events

SPRING *May:* **Artisphere** (864-271-9398; artisphere.us), 16 Augusta Street. This downtown Greenville festival features visual and performing artists from around the world and showcases homegrown artists with a gallery row. Area restaurants sell food at the festival. Free admission. Buy tickets for food and beverages.

✐ **Freedom Weekend Aloft** (864-399-9481; freedomweekend .org), Simpsonville. The event is typically held Friday through Monday and features hot-air balloon competitions as well as kid-friendly entertainment and activities. Admission: $10 per day for adults (13 and older); Monday is free admission. Parking $5 a day.

SUMMER *August/February:* **The Kennel Club Dog Show** (greenvillekc.org) is held twice a year at Carolina First Center, 1 Exposition Drive. More than 3,000 dogs and handlers descend on Greenville for this American Kennel Club–sanctioned event. Free.

SPARTANBURG

Spartanburg lives in the shadow of the larger Greenville, but the city has many of its own charms and prizes. The county is home to BMW Manufacturing Corp., the worldwide headquarters and research center of Milliken & Co., and home base for the largest payday lender in the country, Advance America. It also is the corporate home for restaurant chain Denny's.

Every year, Wofford College hosts training camp for the NFL's Panthers as team owner Jerry Richardson is from Spartanburg and played football for Wofford.

A onetime railroad hub, Spartanburg is often called "Hub City." **The Magnolia Street Train Depot** stands as a testament to that history and serves as the Amtrak station as well as housing the Hub City Railroad Museum and the Hub City Farmers' Market.

GUIDANCE Spartanburg Area Chamber of Commerce (864-594-5000; spartanburgchamber.com), 105 North Pine Street.

The Upcountry (864-233-2690; theupcountry.com). The Web-based visitors center offers tourists information about visiting, shopping, and relocating to the Upstate area and offers an electronic newsletter that includes coupons and special deals.

GETTING THERE *By air:* **Greenville-Spartanburg International Airport** (864-877-7426; gspairport.com) offers direct flights to four Florida cities through Allegiant Airlines (702-505-8888; allegiantair.com), and connections to most major airports through carriers American Eagle (800-433-7300; aa.com), Continental Airlines (800-525-0280; continental.com), Delta Air Lines (800-221-1212; delta.com), Northwest Airlines (800-225-2525; nwa.com), United Express (800-241-6522; united.com), US Airways (800-428-4322; usairways.com).

By train: **Amtrak** (800-872-7245; amtrak.com), 290 Magnolia Street. The Crescent runs from New York to New Orleans with stops in Spartanburg, Greenville, and Clemson in the Upstate.

By bus: **Greyhound** (864-582-5814; greyhound.com), 100 North Liberty Street.

By car: Spartanburg is about three hours from Atlanta and 90 minutes from Charlotte, North Carolina, on Interstate 85. Interstate 26 also passes through the town.

GETTING AROUND The best way to get around Spartanburg is by car.

✳ To See

CHURCHES Nazareth Presbyterian Church (864-576-8034; nazareth presbyterian.org), 680 Nazareth Church Road, Moore. Open Monday through Thursday 9–2; Sunday service at 10:30 AM. This church was established in 1765 and is one of the state's oldest churches and cemeteries not along the coast. Soldiers from the Revolutionary War and every subsequent U.S. war are buried here. Bricks for the current church were handmade near the Middle Tyger River and dried in the sun on a nearby hillside.

HISTORIC SITES Historic Price House (864-576-6546; spartanburg history.org), 1200 Oak View Farms Road, Woodruff. Open Saturday 11–5, April through October; Sunday 2–5, year-round. Admission: $4 adults; $2.50 children 6–17 years; free for children 5 and younger. This building was constructed on a 2,000-acre plantation at the end of the 18th century. There was a general store, a post office, and a tavern and inn that provided a break for stagecoach travelers. Tours of the main house, a slave cabin, and grounds offer a glimpse into the lives of 19th-century business owners.

Seay House (864-596-3501; spartanburghistory.org), 106 Darby Road. Open the third Saturday 11–4 and Sunday 1–4, April through October. No admission is charged, but donations are accepted. This home started as a log cabin built in 1800. Three bedrooms were added during the Victorian period. The story of this house focuses on three unmarried Seay sisters, Ruthy, Patsy, and Sarah, who lived in the home their whole lives. They had a simple life on the farm, and this modest house gives visitors a look how most early-19th-century settlers in the area lived.

Walnut Grove Plantation (864-576-6546; spartanburghistory.org), 1200 Otts Shoals Road, Roebuck. Open Saturday 11–5, Sunday 2–5. Closed for winter. Admission is $6 for adults, $3 for children 6–17, and free for children 5 and younger. This plantation was established on a royal land grant in the 1760s. Charles and Mary Moore raised 10 children in the home, including daughter Kate who was a scout for General Daniel Morgan leading up to the decisive Patriot victory at the Battle of Cowpens. Each October a small skirmish between British soldiers and local militia is reenacted on the plantation's grounds. Tours of the restored buildings let visitors see what life was like for the plantation owners and their enslaved workers in the years leading up to and immediately after the Revolutionary War. In addition to the house, a kitchen, blacksmith's forge, smokehouse, one of the area's first schools, and an early doctor's office also have been preserved. The site also has the original family cemetery and a nature trail.

GARDENS & **Hatcher Garden & Woodland Preserve** (864-574-7724; hatchergarden.org), 820 John B. White Sr. Boulevard. Open daily during daylight hours. No admission is charged, but donations are requested. Located just outside downtown Spartanburg, this 10-acre garden has paved paths that are wheelchair accessible. Walking trails pass a series of ponds and a mix of trees, shrubs, and perennials, with plant identification tags along the way. This is an ideal place for a picnic or peaceful stroll.

MUSEUMS Chapman Cultural Center (864-542-2787; chapman culturalcenter.org), 200 East St. John Street. Open Tuesday through Saturday 10–5. Free. This three-building campus centers on a public plaza and includes a 500-seat theater, art and dance studios, and hands-on science exhibits that the kids will enjoy. The site also includes the **Spartanburg Art Museum** (864-582-7616; spartanburgartmuseum.org). A special art walk is held after hours on the third Thursday of each month. Admission is $4 for adults, $3 for seniors and active military, $2.50 for college students, $2 for students through high school; ages 5 and younger are free. Galleries rotate exhibits every eight weeks. The permanent collection includes 20th-century works by Robert Henri, Elizabeth O'Neill Verner, Hattie Saussy, and August Cook. The site also includes the **Spartanburg County Regional History Museum** (864-596-3501; spartanburghistory .org). Open Tuesday through Saturday10–4:30. The history museum has a $4 admission for adults, $3 for seniors and veterans, and $2 for students; free for children 5 and younger. In addition to traveling exhibits, the museum's permanent collection includes the Pardo Stone (see the sidebar), items from Camp Wadsworth and Camp Croft, textile quilts, and a doll collection.

OTHER PLACES OF INTEREST The Spartanburg Music Trail (spartanburgmusictrail.com). Maps available at **Hub City Books** (864-577-9349; hubcity.org), 186 West Main Street. The trail is made up of decorative signs throughout downtown honoring Spartanburg's music connections—and they are plentiful and varied, from William Walker, who

THE PARDO STONE

The Pardo Stone was found near the small town of Inman in 1935 by a farmer. The face of the stone is a little bigger than a legal-sized notepad, and it's about 4 inches thick. Along with markings that make the stone a historic find are dings from the farmer's harvester that hit the stone. Historian D. D. Wallace wrote in the *Hispanic American Review* in an article published in 1936 that the stone is a relic from the Juan Pardo expedition of 1567.

There are numbers on the stone that can be read as 1567, though the 6 suffered in the meeting with the harvester. There also is an arrow etched into the stone, which looks like granite, but is softer, and a parallelogram below the number. also appear to be radiating lines that could represent a sun.

Wallace describes Pardo's expedition from the Spanish Fort San Felipe on Parris Island near Beaufort to an area about 15 miles southeast of Augusta, Georgia, then due north to the mountains. He then traveled east to the Wateree River in the center of the state and back to Beaufort. Wallace estimates that Pardo followed trails between the settlements of the Cherokee in the foothills and the Catawbas south of Charlotte, North Carolina. The 1567 expedition was to visit Fort San Juan, which Pardo had established a year earlier somewhere in Pickens or Oconee County and about 50 miles west of where the stone was found.

Wallace discredits a theory that the farmer's field workers put the markings on the stone as a joke, saying that would imbue "the farm laborers of South Carolina with a familiarity with Spanish-American history and its critical dates that unhappily they do not possess."

Wallace would no doubt be sad to know that Pardo's expedition is still not taught in South Carolina history classes—at least I don't remember hearing about it until 2011.

first married the words of the poem "Amazing Grace" with the music of "New Britain" to give us the most popular 20th-century version of the hymn, to 1970–'80s country rockers the Marshall Tucker Band. The trail has started with a dozen names and plans to add a dozen more over the next decade. You will be amazed at the number of well-known musicians who have called Sparkle City home.

PARKS Croft State Natural Area (864-585-128; southcarolinaparks
.com), 450 Croft State Park. Open daily 7–6, until 8 on Friday, open
7 AM–9 PM during Daylight Saving Time. Admission: $2 adults; $1.25
South Carolina seniors; ages 15 and younger free. This area is known for
its equestrian facilities including 55 stalls, a show arena, and 20 miles of
horse-friendly trails. Located on an old army training base, the park also
has 12 miles of biking and hiking trails, a playground, and a picnic area, as
well as two lakes for fishing and boating.

✳ Lodging

INN Walnut Lane Inn (864-949-
7230; walnutlaneinn.com), 110
Ridge Road, Lyman. Located
between Greenville and Spartanburg, this six-room inn is an old
cotton plantation and offers visitors a chance to step back to the
turn of the last century. Surrounded by walnut trees, the inn offers a
full breakfast and complimentary
dessert in the evenings. Rooms
start at $130 a night.

✳ Where to Eat

DINING OUT City Range (864-
327-3333; cityrange.com), 774
Spartan Boulevard. Open daily for
lunch and dinner. In addition to
the regular menu of steaks, salads,
and sandwiches, the chef has a
fixed-price menu that changes
every day. The dining areas are
built around a large stone fireplace, and there is a patio for outdoor dining. Dinner entrées range
from $14 to $26.

Four Seasons (864-699-9730; the
fourseasons.biz), 1071 Fernwood-
Glendale Road. Open Monday
through Saturday for lunch and
dinner. This place could be called

the Four Chefs, as a quartet of fel-
las in the kitchen make the menu.
There's Billy from Greece, Italo
from the Dominican Republic,
Tony from Lebanon, and William
from United States. The guys serve
up steaks, seafood, burgers, and
sandwiches. Entrées range from
$15 to $25.

II Samuels Restaurant (864-
596-5080; ribaultcatering.com
/ii-samuels-restaurant), 351 East
Henry Street, Suite A. Open
10:30–3 Monday through Friday
for lunch; Tuesday through Saturday for dinner starting at 5. This is
a local and visitor favorite for its
eclectic mix of gourmet dishes, like
the poached pear salad, with new
spins on Southern favorites, like
fried chicken livers on a yogurt grit
cake. Several dishes come in small
portions for smaller prices, which
top out around $32 for the lamb
chops.

**EATING OUT The Beacon
Drive-In** (864-585-9387; beacon
drivein.com), 255 John B. White
Sr. Boulevard. Open 6:30 AM–
10 PM Monday through Saturday. If

you have high cholesterol or heart problems, don't eat here. For everyone else, dig in. Beacon and founder John B. White Sr. passed away in February 2011, but little has changed at the iconic restaurant where most dishes are served "a-plenty." That is, with a heaping of fries and fried onion rings on top. Study the menu carefully while in line, but know what you want when J. C. greets you with "Talk" and "Walk." He doesn't appreciate a first-timer's questions and may skip over you to the next person in line. He's been doing this for, well, probably since the place opened in 1946. My advice is to split on your first trip. Have one person scope out the tables while the orderer gets in line. Whatever you get—I recommend the chili cheeseburger, but they have everything from a banana sandwich to fried fish—get it "a-plenty." Then order two sweet teas—the house specialty that is so good, they bottle it and sell it at grocery stores. If it's too sweet for you, you can always "cut it" with some unsweet tea at the self-serve refill station. Just start in on the fries and O-rings and don't worry that you can't see your burger. It's under there. Once you uncover it, cut it in half and enjoy. If you are still hungry—and unless you are

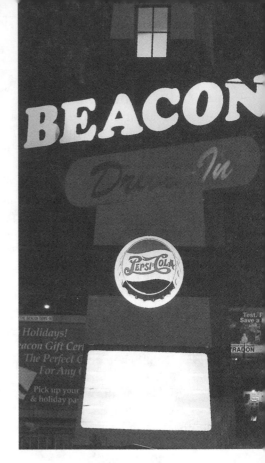

THE BEACON DRIVE-IN SIGN AT NIGHT, SPARTANBURG

an NFL lineman, I doubt you will be—they sell ice cream and milk shakes at the dairy bar. Not recommended for daily eating, but every once in a while won't hurt you. The burger a-plenty is about $8 with an extra $3 for two teas. Just about everything on the menu is less than $10.

CHEROKEE SCENIC
HIGHWAY CORRIDOR

The Cherokee Foothills Scenic Highway follows the southern lip of the Blue Ridge Mountains. The 115-mile SC 11 runs from the Georgia state line at Lake Hartwell up to the North Carolina state line and east to Gaffney. It passes lakes and rivers, apple and peach orchards, and miles of beautiful mountain scenery.

If you were simply to drive it end-to-end, the trip would take about three hours, but you don't want to do that, you will miss so much. Plan to divide and conquer it by making several day trips or a weeklong visit.

GUIDANCE The Upcountry (864-233-2690; theupcountry.com). The Web-based visitors center offers tourists information about visiting, shopping, and relocating to the Greenville area and offers an electronic newsletter that includes coupons and special deals.

GETTING THERE The road is the "there" here. You can get on at either end off Interstate 85 near Gaffney or near the Georgia state line. It crosses several state highways and intersects with U.S. Highways 76, 178, and 276.

GETTING AROUND The only way to get around is in a car.

WHEN TO COME Fall is prime time for this area. It's when the apples are ready, the leaves are turning, and there's just enough nip in the air to make use of the fireplaces in all the B&Bs tucked off the highway.

✳ To See

CHURCHES Old Stone Church (864-654-2061; cityofclemson.org), 101 Stone Circle, Clemson. Grounds open to the public 8–6 daily. This Presbyterian church was built in 1797 by Revolutionary War hero Andrew

Pickens. The sanctuary was damaged by a fire and is no longer used for services, but remains standing over a cemetery that includes some of the Upstate's founding families, including Robert Anderson, who also a Revolutionary War hero.

Symmes Chapel "Pretty Place" (864-836-3291; campgreenville.org /chapel.php), YMCA Camp Road, Marietta. Open daily during daylight hours, but the chapel is typically booked for weddings and worship services on Saturday and Sunday. It is so popular for weddings because of the stunning views of the Carolina mountains from the top of Standing Stone Mountain. The YMCA camp and the chapel sit right along the state line with North Carolina. Anyone can come and enjoy the view, but the chapel is closed to the public during special events, so call ahead to see if it's open. The chapel was built in 1941 and was given to the YMCA Camp Greenville by Fred Symmes. Don't miss this pretty place. But when you go, remember that it is a place of worship and the caretakers appreciate your respect. No alcohol and no smoking are allowed.

GARDENS ✿ **South Carolina Botanical Gardens at Clemson University** (864-656-3311; clemson.edu/public/scbg), 150 Discovery Lane, Clemson. Open daily dawn to dusk. Free admission. The gardens are nearly 300 acres of natural landscape, display plantings, and miles of nature trails and streams. Clemson is an official American Hosta Display Garden and has a 70-acre arboretum as well as nature trails and a wildflower meadow. Yoga classes are offered here three times a week on Tuesday and Thursday evening and Saturday morning. It's only $12 if you just want to drop in for one. The classes focus on breathing. Also, if you're in town on the first Friday of the month between November and March, stop by at 9 AM for a free guided walk through the garden. Participants meet in the Caboose parking lot. There are special programs every month, so check in to see whether there is something to interest you. Clemson is the state's agricultural college, and there is precious little the folks there don't know about gardening. The gardens also have an art gallery and the **Bob Campbell Geology Museum**, open 10–5 Wednesday through Saturday (closed on home football game Saturdays), 1–5 Sunday. This self-guided museum has more than 10,000 rocks, minerals, fossils, and artifacts, including early mining equipment and American Indian tools. A favorite with the kids is Smilodon—Clemson's oldest tiger. The skeletal replica shows the saber-toothed lions that once roamed South Carolina. There also is a fluorescent room with glowing minerals, a light show, and a scavenger hunt for the youngsters. Admission is $3 adults, $2 children; those younger than 2 are admitted free.

MUSEUMS **Fort Hill: Home of John C. Calhoun and Thomas G. Clemson** (864-656-2475; clemson.edu/about/history/properties/fort-hill),

101 Fort Hill Street, Clemson. Open Monday through Saturday 10–noon and 1–4:30; Sunday 2–4:30. Admission is $5 for adults, $4 for seniors, and $2 for ages 6–12. This historic home was built by John C. Calhoun, vice president of the United States under John Quincy Adams and fellow South Carolinian Andrew Jackson (see *Politicians* in "What's Where"). He left his home to his daughter Anna and her husband, Thomas Green Clemson. The Clemsons willed the home and surrounding plantation to the state of South Carolina to create an agricultural college. The home is decorated with period furniture and family mementos.

Antiquers Haven Museum and Shop (864-843-6827), 517 Flat Rock Road, Liberty. Open Wednesday through Saturday 11–5. Opens at 1 PM on Sunday. No admission is charged, but donations are accepted. This quirky little place is a great place to drop in and see a collection of antiques from a variety of eras, from 1690 through the 19th century. From the 19th century, there are newspapers, a barbershop, a tavern, and a pool table, as well as a dentist's office. The museum has 20 automobiles dating from 1904 to 1934 on display.

Anderson County Museum (864-260-4737; andersoncountymuseum .org), 202 East Greenville Street, Anderson. Open Tuesday through Saturday 10–4. Free. This museum tells the story of the people of Anderson County through interactive exhibits and artifacts. There also are county archives for genealogical and local history research. The exhibit Keep the Home Fires Burning focuses on the stories of the local men and women who have fought in various U.S. wars, including the story of **Freddie Stowers**, the only African American awarded the Medal of Honor for bravery during World War I. Corporal Stowers was a 21-year-old squad leader in Company C, 371st Infantry Regiment, 93rd Division. His company was leading an assault on German trenches in the Champagne Marne Sector of France. About half of his company was wounded or injured during the assault and Stowers took charge, "setting such a courageous example of personal bravery and leadership that he inspired his men to follow him in the attack," according to his Medal of Honor citation. Stowers was cited for continuing to lead his men even after being critically wounded. He died of his injuries, but the machine-gun position was destroyed. Stowers was recommended for the Medal of Honor during the war, but the recommendation was not processed until 1990 when it was uncovered during an army review. The award was presented to Stowers's family members in 1991 by President George H. W. Bush. Stowers was born in Sandy Springs, near Anderson.

BMW Zentrum (864-989-5297 or 888-868-7269 for tour information; bmwzentrum.com), 1400 Highway 101, Greer. The museum is free and open Monday through Friday 9:30–5:30. Factory tours are $7 for adults, $3.50 for students, and are arranged by appointment only. The 28,000-

square-foot visitors center is truly impressive and showcases the German automaker's long history of building things that go fast, from motorcycles to cars and aircraft. The museum is located at the company's South Carolina manufacturing plant where several models of BMWs are made. The factory tours are engaging even if you only think about cars when you drive your own.

Anderson Arts Center (864-222-2787; andersonarts.org), 110 Federal Street, Anderson. Open Tuesday through Friday 9:30–5:30. This free art museum is located in a renovated warehouse and has a permanent collection as well as traveling exhibits.

Cherokee County History & Arts Museum (864-489-3988; cherokee countyhistory.org), 301 College Drive, Gaffney. Open Wednesday through Friday 10–4, Saturday 2–5. Admission: $5 for adults ages 13 and older, and $3 for younger kids, seniors, and college students. This museum is located on the site of the historic mustering grounds of the South Carolina Militia and includes exhibits on the area's geology, Indians, and role in the Revolutionary War as well as more modern history that includes textiles, peaches, moonshining, and auto racing. A library and genealogy research room also is available.

Hagood-Mauldin House/Irma Morris Museum of Fine Art (864-898-5963), 104 North Lewis Street, Pickens. Admission $3; students $1. Open the first and third Saturday of the month 11–4 (April through November) and by appointment. Built around 1856 in the original Pickens County seat west of the Keowee River, this classical Greek Revival house was dismantled and moved here when the town was moved in 1868. It houses 17th- and 18th-century furnishings and art collected by the last owner, who left it as a museum.

Lunney Museum (864-882-4811), 211 West South 1st Street, Seneca. Open Thursday through Sunday 1–5. Free. Listed on the National Register of Historic Places, this California-style bungalow was built in 1909 by Dr. and Mrs. W. J. Lunney and occupied continuously by the Lunney family until 1969. Its distinctive Arts & Crafts architecture extends to include a two-story carriage house and a "two-seater" outhouse. This house museum contains a collection of Victorian furniture as well as historic memorabilia from Oconee County.

Oconee Heritage Center (864-638-2224, oconeeheritagecenter.org), 123 Brown Square Drive, Walhalla. Open noon–5 Tuesday, Thursday, and Friday; 10–3 Saturday; and by appointment. This center is located in a 19th-century tobacco factory and features a museum, archives, and classroom. An 18th-century dugout canoe is undergoing preservation. Other exhibits include a Walk-In Stump House Tunnel and a Tenant Farmer's House. All exhibits showcase the history of Oconee County.

Pickens County Museum of Art & History (864-898-5963; co.pickens
.sc.us/culturalcommission), 307 Johnson Street, Pickens. Open Tuesday,
Wednesday, Friday 9–5; Thursday 9–7:30; Saturday 9–4:30. Free. Located
in the old county jail with its turn-of-the-20th-century architecture. A
10,000-square-foot expansion features the story of Pickens County and the
Upstate. Three other galleries hold rotating exhibits featuring regional
artists, themed exhibits, and youth arts programming. A native plant garden is located outside.

HISTORIC SITES Cowpens National Battlefield (864-461-2828;
nps.gov/cowp/index.htm), 4001 Chesnee Highway, Gaffney. Open 9–5
daily. Free admission. This park preserves the scene of a key victory for
the colonists during the Revolutionary War and offers visitors a walking
trail, marked road tour, picnic ground, and visitors center. The 1781 battle
commemorated here lasted less than an hour. General Daniel Morgan
defeated British colonel Banastre Tarleton—known as Bloody Tarleton—
near the end of the Revolutionary War. Most of Tarleton's soldiers were
captured or killed, and the remainder ran away. It was Tarleton's worst
defeat and one of the worst defeats for the British in the South.

Campbell's Covered Bridge, Campbell's Bridge Road, Landrum. Built
in 1909, this is the last covered bridge in South Carolina.

Hagood Mill (864-898-5963; co.pickens.sc.us/culturalcommission), 138
Hagood Mill Road, Pickens. Open Wednesday through Saturday 10–4.
The mill's grounds are available for use as a park during daily hours. The
Historic Site and Folklife Center is home of the historic gristmill that was
built at its current location in 1845. It is one of the oldest operating grist-
mills in the state and has the largest waterwheel (20 feet). The site also
includes a family farm exhibit, a log cabin dating to the 18th century, a
blacksmith shop, and a moonshine still. A large outdoor stage has been
added for musical events held on the third Saturday of each month and
featuring some of the region's best bluegrass, old-time, and blues musicians. It is on the National Register of Historic Places. And, oh yeah, don't
forget to pick up some grits and cornmeal from the mill store.

Issaqueena Falls/Stumphouse Tunnel (864-638-4343; oconeecountry
.com/stumphouse.html), SC 28, 7 miles north of Walhalla. Open 10–5
daily. Free. A county park is located at the abandoned tunnel that was
supposed to provide a railroad connection for Charleston to the Midwest.
Work began in the 1850s and was abandoned when the Civil War began.
An easy walk from the county park will bring you to the 200-foot Issaqueena Falls, where legend says in Indian maiden hid out after warning
a nearby fort of an impending attack.

Ashtabula Historic House (864-646-7249; pendletonhistoricfoundation
.org), 2725 Old Greenville Highway, Pendleton. Open 1–5 Tuesday,

ISSAQUEENA FALLS

Thursday, and Sunday, April through October. Admission: $7 adults, $3 for ages 5–10; free for younger children. This large mansion was originally built in 1825 by Ladson Gibbes and his wife and later owned by their son, naturalist Lewis Reeves Gibbes. On the 10-acre site is a late-18th-century building that was operated as a tavern before the main house was built. The building was later attached to the home by a breezeway and used as a kitchen for the main house. The house has been restored and furnished with 19th-century antiques. Ashtabula is listed on the National Register of Historic Places and is a site on the South Carolina National Heritage Corridor.

Pendleton Village Green (864-646-3782; pendletondistrict.org), 173 East Exchange Street, Pendleton. The visitors center is open Monday through Friday 9–4:30. This district of shops and restaurants is on the National Register of Historic Places and includes Farmer's Hall, which dates to the early 19th century. It was supposed to be a courthouse, but the county seat was changed before the building was finished and it became the Farmer's Society Meeting Hall. Hunter's store, which once was the center of the town's commerce, now houses the Pendleton visitors center at 125 East Queen Street.

Woodburn Historic House (864-646-7249; pendletonhistoricfoundation .org), 130 History Lane, Pendleton. Open Sunday 2–6, April through October. Admission is $6 for adults, $2 for children 5–11, and free for younger children. This plantation was built around 1830 as a summer retreat for wealthy Charlestonians—first by Charles Cotesworth Pinckney, who was a signer of the Constitution of the United States, and later by the Reverend John B. Adger, who added the double piazzas. The 11-acre site includes a carriage house with a period wagon, an 1810 log cabin, and a cookhouse. A reproduction of a slave/tenant cabin has been built, and walking trails lead to ruins of other outbuildings. The tours last about an hour and focus on the life of Jane Edna Hunter, a civil rights activist who was born in the tenant cabin in 1882. Hunter went on to establish a forerunner of the Phyllis Wheatley Society in Cleveland, Ohio. The site is on the National Register of Historic Places and is in the South Carolina National Heritage Corridor.

✷ To Do

Nantahala Outdoor Center (864-647-9014; noc.com), 851A Chattooga Ridge Road, Mountain Rest. Open daily 7–7. Trips start at $90 per person, but there are loads of options depending on what you want to do. This outfitter has been around for almost 40 years and is one of the best for rivers in the mountains of the Carolinas. You can even book your trip online. They can take you on the wildest whitewater in the Southeast on the Chattooga, or you can do a little light kayak paddling on Lake Tugaloo at the end of the rapids.

Wildwater Ltd. (800-451-9972; wildwaterrafting.com), 1251 Academy Road, Long Creek. Wildwater offers a four-hour mini trip along the Chattooga River that runs along the South Carolina–Georgia state line. The Class III mini trip is best for families with small children or older members; $70–80 per person. The full seven-hour trip is $90–110 per person and includes lunch and the Bull Sluice Rapid. Other trips available, including an overnight trip.

Bryson's U-Pick Apple Orchard (864-647-9427; brysonsappleorchard .com), 1011 Chattooga Ridge Road, Mountain Rest. Open 9–6 daily August–November. Come pick your own or let Bryson's pick for you. Fresh apple cider is available as well as jams, jellies, and fresh honey.

Victoria Valley Vineyards (864-878-5307; victoriavalleyvineyards.com), 1360 South Saluda Road, Cleveland. Winery is open 11–5 Monday through Thursday, 11–6 Friday through Saturday, noon–6 Sunday. The vineyards offer wine tastings and tours for $5. Deli-style lunch served daily 11–2. Salads and sandwiches all for under $10.

GOLF Falcon's Lair (864-638-0000), 1308 Falcons Drive, Walhalla. This 6,866-yard course is a par-72 and includes water hazards and ravines. Greens fees $20–32.

Boscobel Country Club (864-646-3991), 6900 US 76, Pendleton. This well-maintained course is a local and visitor favorite at 6,366 yards and a par-71. Rates: $31–39.

Woodhaven Golf Course (864-646-9511), 215 Woodhaven Drive, Pendleton. It's just nine holes, but players say it's a great place to learn at a low price: just $7.50 for nine holes or $12 to play them twice.

The Rock at Jocassee (864-878-2030; golftherock.com), 171 Sliding Rock Road, Pickens. This 6,514-yard, par-72 course has some beautiful scenery, from heavy woods to waterfalls. Rates: $27–36.

The Walker Course (864-656-0236; golfatclemson.com), 110 Madren Drive, Clemson. This 6,911-yard, par-72 course is designed for all skill levels and runs along the shore of Hartwell Lake. If you're not a Gamecock fan, you may enjoy the signature Tiger Paw 17th hole. Rates: $32–50.

Pickens Country Club (864-878-6083), 1018 Country Club Road, Pickens. This par-72, 6,220-yard course is outlined by dense hardwoods and evergreens. Rates: $30–37.

PARKS Oconee State Park (864-638-5353; southcarolinaparks.com), 624 State Park Road, Mountain Rest. Open daily 7–6, extended to 9 PM during Daylight Saving Time. Admission $2 adults, $1.25 South Carolina seniors; free for ages 15 and younger. This park has two small lakes for boating and fishing and eight trails for walking or hiking.

Table Rock State Park (864-878-9813; southcarolinaparks.com), 158 East Ellison Lane, Pickens. Open daily 7–6, extended to 9 PM during Daylight Saving Time. Admission $2 adults, $1.25 South Carolina seniors; free for ages 15 and younger. Named for the towering Table Rock Mountain, this 3,083-acre state park has challenging hiking trails and two lakes as well as a campground and rustic mountain cabins.

Calhoun Falls State Recreation Area (864-447-8267; southcarolina parks.com), 46 Maintenance Shop Road, Calhoun Falls. Hours: 6–6, extended to 8 during Daylight Saving Time. Admission: $2 adults ages 16 and older; $1.25 South Carolina seniors; ages 15 and younger free. This park on Lake Russell offers camping, picnicking, tennis, playground, hiking trails, swimming, and fishing.

Oconee Station State Historic Site (864-638-0079; southcarolinaparks .com), 11500 Oconee Station Road, Walhalla. Open 9–6 daily from April through November; Friday through Sunday only, December through March. Historic structures open 1–5 Saturday through Sunday only, with guided tours available. Free admission. Buildings date back to the late 18th century when this site was a military outpost for fighting Cherokee Indians. A trading post was later added. The site also has a fishing pond

OCONEE STATION STATE HISTORIC SITE

SC Department of Parks, Recreation & Tourism, DiscoverSouthCarolina.com

SC Department of Parks, Recreation & Tourism, DiscoverSouthCarolina.com

TABLE ROCK STATE PARK

and 1.5-mile nature trail that leads into Sumter National Forest and the Station Cove Falls, a lovely 60-foot waterfall. This park is best in spring when the wildflowers bloom, or fall when the leaves are turning.

Pleasant Ridge County Park (864-288-6470; greenvillerec.com), 4232 SC 11, Marietta. This park was originally established by the state in the 1940s for black visitors during the days of segregation in South Carolina. When the parks were integrated, this park was donated to Greenville County. Although it is a favorite getaway for local residents, it is a great way to get that wilderness experience within a short 40-minute drive of downtown Greenville. The park has a wonderful fishing lake, a hiking trail, some small waterfalls, and the remains of a gristmill. A large cabin with kitchen and fireplace that sleeps six rents for $275 per weekend or $500 for Monday through Friday. Pets are not allowed in the cabin. This park also has campsites with water and electricity and a bathhouse for about $20 a night.

Lake Hartwell Recreation Area (864-972-3352; southcarolinaparks .com), 19138-A SC 11 South, Fair Play. Lake Hartwell is a 56,000-acre reservoir with almost 1,000 miles of shoreline that sits on the Georgia–South Carolina state line and was built by the U.S. Army Corps of Engineers between 1955 and 1963. There are 80 boat access points for water-skiing, fishing, canoeing, kayaking, or just spending a day on the water. The lake also has several designated swim and picnic areas. Hartwell gets very crowded on summer weekends, so if you prefer more quiet, come during the week or in the off-season. Fall is especially lovely as the leaves on the hardwoods surrounded the lake turn vibrant colors.

Chattooga National Wild and Scenic River (864-638-9568; fs.fed.us /r8/fms or chattooga-river.net), 112 Andrew Pickens Road, Mountain Rest. The address is for the Andrew Pickens Ranger Station in the Sumter National Forest, which surrounds the Chattooga—designated a National Wild and Scenic River more than 30 years ago. This river provides the best whitewater rafting in the state as well as wonderful waterfalls and hiking opportunities. The best way to see the start of the river is at **Ellicott Rock Wilderness Area**—the point at which both Carolinas and Georgia meet. The area is maintained by the USDA Forest Service. It was established in 1875 and covers more than 9,000 acres. The terrain is very steep and the area gets a lot of rain, so if you want to hike or camp here, be prepared for wet ground conditions and possible showers. It's also a good bit cooler up here than in nearby towns, which can be a joy in the summer, but in the cooler months, again, be prepared. There is no boating allowed north of the SC 28 bridge, but this is where the hiking is good and a dozen waterfalls are located. The easiest to reach—and therefore the most popular—is **Spoonauger Falls**. This 50-foot waterfall is particularly beautiful in the summer with all the greenery. It's just a 20-minute hike from the Chattooga Trail parking area on Burrells Ford Road in Oconee County. Just follow the signs from the parking lot. South of SC 28 is the start of the rapids that increase in difficulty to navigate until you get dumped into Lake Tugaloo. The first 8 miles south of the SC 28 bridge are very calm; you can take a boat or even an inner tube. There are a couple of take-outs along the way, but if you pass Long Bottom Ford, you must continue on to Earl's Ford. There is a Class II rapid known as Big Shoals on the way, but you can walk around it. After that, the Chattooga is not for novices unless you take a guided raft tour—and even then, the extreme hydraulics can be dangerous with names like Screaming Left Hand Turn, Corkscrew, Sock-em Dog, and Dead Man's Pool just below the Five Falls area. Obstacles include large boulders such as Deliverance Rock. That last name comes from the movie *Deliverance*, which was filmed on the river and made it infamous. The movie starred Burt Reynolds and was written by the late James Dickey, once the state's poet laureate and a very popular professor at the University of South Carolina. The movie tells a brutal story about a group of friends making a trip down the river. Not everyone survives and no one gets out undamaged. If you do make the run through the most dangerous rapids, you will find yourself in Lake Tugaloo. If you've been wise and hired a guide, you will get a quick tow to shore. Otherwise, it is an almost 3-mile paddle to the take-out.

Walhalla State Fish Hatchery (864-638-2866; dnr.sc.gov), 198 Fish Hatchery Road, Mountain Rest. Open daily 8–4. This facility was built in the 1930s by the Civilian Conservation Corps and is the only trout hatchery in South Carolina, raising more than 150,000 pounds of rainbow, brown, and brook trout each year to stock the state's rivers and lakes. If you are going to be in the Chattooga River area, it's worth the extra short drive up here to see this amazing "farm."

✳ Lodging

INNS Laurel Mountain Inn (864-878-8500; laurelmountaininn .com), 129 Hiawatha Trail, Pickens. Each room offers a king-sized or two full beds and all the modern amenities, including microwave and wireless Internet access. Rates: $85–105 a night.

The Inn at Table Rock Bed & Breakfast (864-878-0078; theinn attablerock.com), 117 Hiawatha Trail, Pickens. Rates $100–180 a night. The inn sits on 4 wooded acres in the foothills with wonderful views, especially of Table Rock. There's a wraparound porch with a swing and rocking chairs.

Candleberry Inn B&B/Day Spa (864-201-1411; candleberryinn.us), 105 Marshland Lane, Greer. Guests can choose from a variety of spa options, including mani/pedi ($90) or full-body massage $100. Breakfast is separate unless you've booked a package. Rooms are from $110 to $160.

James F. Martin Inn (888-654-9020; clemson.edu/centers-intitutes /madren/inn), 230 Madren Center Drive, Clemson. This is Clemson University's hotel, so don't plan on finding a room during fall weekends when the Tigers are in town. Located on the Walker Golf Course, the inn has 89 rooms, including 27

suites, overlooking Hartwell Lake. There is an outdoor swimming pool, tennis courts, restaurant and lounge, and free continental breakfast. A bridal suite offers living space, separate sleeping room, and dressing parlor, as well as a whirlpool tub.

BED & BREAKFASTS Fieldstone Farm Inn Bed and Breakfast (864-882-5651; fieldstonefarm inn.com), 640 Fieldstone Farm Road, Westminster. Located on 23 acres less than 10 miles from Clemson University, this B&B provides a full breakfast buffet with your stay and complimentary evening beverages. Horses are available for trail riding on the property at $25 an hour, or you can book an all-day ride in the Sumter National Forest with lunch and drinks for $150 a horse. Four rooms, starting at $80 a night Sunday through Thursday and ranging up to $115 on weekends. Two cottages and one log cabin are available at $135 a night.

Walhalla Liberty Lodge Bed and Breakfast and Restaurant (864-638-8239; walhallaliberty lodge.com), 105 Liberty Lane, Walhalla. This Victorian-era home was a wedding gift from Judge John J. Norton to his daughter in

1884. The lodge is run by sisters Betty Dowell and Patsy Dowell Sims. Five rooms are available, but only three have private bath; about $100 a night on weekends includes full breakfast. During the week, rooms are $10 cheaper but come with coffee only. The lodge has an outdoor pool, and the restaurant is open 5–8 PM Thursday through Saturday, and 11–2 for Sunday buffet.

Magnolia Manor Bed & Breakfast (864-647-8559; magnolia manorbb.com), 207 Westminster Highway, Westminster. This Greek Revival–style mansion has four second-floor rooms and a third-floor suite. Rates start at $90 during the week and continue up to $125 on the weekends. The Magnolia Manor specializes in wedding packages, including ceremony space, a reception area, catering, and even the DJ and a photographer.

The Amethyst Inn (864-878-6771; theamethystinn.com), 4870 SC 11, Pickens. Open year-round. October has a two-night minimum stay. With Table Rock State Park as this inn's backyard, it is easy to see what draws visitors. The entire property is nonsmoking, and the inn cannot accommodate children, pets, or people who cannot comfortably climb stairs. Two rooms with shared bath at $85 a night; two rooms with private bath $110–150. Rooms come with a full breakfast.

Oconee Belle Bed and Breakfast (864-638-2238; oconeebelle inn.com), 302 South College Street, Walhalla. This small B&B has just three rooms from $85 to $105 a night. Full breakfast in the morning and wine in the evening are included in the room price.

CAMPGROUNDS/CABINS
Lake Hartwell Camping and Cabins (864-287-3223; camplake hartwell.com), 400 Ponderosa Point, Townville. This facility has 120 camping sites, 80 pull-through sites with full hookup; the rest are for tents and pop-ups. All campsites have fire rings. Rates starting at $32 for electric hookups up to $90 for large motor homes. There also are seven equipped cabins and one rustic cabin. Cabin rates: $55–120 a night. Pontoon boat rentals also available for $115 for a half day including gas and taxes; canoes rent for $50 for a full day.

Lake Hartwell Recreation Area (864-972-3352; southcarolina parks.com), 19138-A SC 11 South, Fair Play. This recreation area has 115 paved RV and camping sites for about $20 a night. The park also has two rustic cabins that have electricity but no running water. Bathroom facilities that are available for campers are also available for those in the cabins, which rent for less than $40 a night.

Fall Creek Cottage (864-647-2336; fallcreekcottage.com), 250 Fall Creek Road, Mountain Rest. Open year-round. This three-bedroom, two-bath cottage in the Sumter National Forest is a wonderful jumping-off spot for a large family to explore the outdoors. It's near the Chattooga River for rafting, and bring your own bike to explore the mountain forest complete with nearby waterfalls. Rents for $690 a week and sleeps up to nine people.

✳ Where to Eat

DINING OUT Pixie & Bill's (864-654.1210; tigergourmet .com/pixie_home.htm), US 123, Clemson. Open for lunch Monday through Friday 11:30–1:30; dinner Monday through Saturday 5:30–9:30. Pixie & Bill's has been open for more than 40 years and is probably Clemson's oldest fine-dining restaurant. If you can't find something on the menu here, you're not trying. Appetizers include a tuna spring roll, Fontina cheese baked in a puff pastry, and spanakopita, a Greek spinach pie. The main entrée is prime rib, but there are a variety of other dishes, including steaks, seafood, veggie pizza, and pasta. The restaurant sits on Lake Hartwell and can be accessed by land or water. The restaurant has a unique house-blend coffee that is roasted at Electric City Coffee Roasters in nearby Anderson. Dinner entrées range $18–30.

Pumpkintown Mountain (864-836-8141; pumpkintownmountain .com), 3414 SC 11, Pickens. Open 11–5 Wednesday through Sunday for lunch and early dinner. Saturday at 7 PM they have dinner and a show. Shows range from dancing

and comedy to a murder mystery. Dinner includes salad, entrée, beverage, and dessert for $25.

Seasons by the Lake (864-656-7444; clemson.edu), Madren Center, Clemson University. Open for lunch and dinner 11:30–2 and 5–9 Monday through Thursday, 11:30–2 and 5–10 Friday through Saturday; 11:15–2 for Sunday brunch. Renovated in early 2011, Seasons by the Lake specializes in seafood, poultry, and beef, using local ingredients such as Clemson Blue Cheese. Seasons overlooks Lake Hartwell and the 18th green of the Walker Golf Course.

1826 On the Green (864-646-5500; 1826onthegreen.com), 105 Exchange Street, Pendleton. Open Thursday through Saturday 11:30–2 for lunch, and for dinner starting at 5. Situated on this small town's village green, 1826 On the Green is a wonderful place for a lunch break from antiquing. In nice weather their patio seating is just perfect. Owner-chef Lorett offers classic dishes for lunch and dinner, including her famed Rusty's chicken salad. Dishes include smoked Gouda macaroni, seafood, and pasta in a cream sauce. Dinner entrées range from $10 to $23. This elegant setting is not really for kids.

EATING OUT Aunt Sue's Country Corner (864-878-4366; aunt sues.com), 107 Country Creek Drive, Pickens. Open 11–7 Tuesday through Thursday, 11–9 Friday through Sunday. Aunt Sue's offers weekend breakfast buffets and Sunday lunch buffets. Dinner is a Southern delight of a meat and your choice of sides—or you could go sides-only. They use locally produced meats and vegetables when available. Everything on the dinner menu is under $10. The Sunday lunch buffet is $11. Save room for dessert, as Aunt Sue specializes in ice cream creations from a scoop of vanilla to banana splits.

The Hot Dog House (864-878-4366; auntsues.com), 107 Country Creek Drive, Pickens. Open 11–7 Tuesday through Sunday. Located at Aunt Sue's Country Corner, the Hot Dog House sells an interesting selection of hot dog creations, such as the Ruben Dog with sauerkraut, Thousand Island dressing, and Swiss cheese, all for less than $2. They also have snow cones.

Mac's Drive In (864-654-2845), 404 Pendleton Road, Clemson. Open Monday through Saturday 10:30 AM–11 PM. This place is an institution among Clemson University students, ballplayers, and even famed national-championship-winning football coach Danny Ford. Burgers, fries, and beer-battered onion rings are the highlights of the menu. All items less than $10.

✳ Selective Shopping

'55 Exchange (864-656-2155; clemson.edu/icecream), Hendrix Student Center—East End at Cherry and McMillan Roads,

Clemson. Open 11:30–6 Monday through Friday, 1–6 Saturday through Sunday. This is the best ice cream you will ever eat. The exchange was established in 2005 by Clemson University's class of 1955 (hence the name). The shop is staffed by students and the ice cream comes from the college's dairy program. This is also where you will find **Clemson Blue Cheese** (864-656-3242; clemson bluecheese.com), 118 Newman Hall, Clemson. Open Monday through Friday 8–2. This is some of the most flavorful blue cheese you will ever have. It's not cheap, but it's well worth the price. The cheese can also be ordered online or by phone, but try it locally first to make sure you like the bite. Clemson Blue Cheese was first cured in 1940 in the damp air of the nearby Stumphouse Tunnel near Walhalla by a Clemson dairy professor. The tunnel was deemed unsafe at the time. It now is open for tourists, and the cheese-curing operations moved in 1958 to Newman Hall on campus. Air-conditioned rooms re-create the temperature and humidity of the tunnel. In 2009 it was among the best blue cheeses in the nation, according to ratings from the U.S. Championship Cheese Contest in Green Bay, Wisconsin.

Split Creek Farm (864-287-3921; splitcreek.com), 3806 Centerville Road, Anderson. Open Monday through Saturday 9–6 and Sunday 2–5. Split Creek Farm is a goat dairy and offers artisan cheeses, fudge, and soaps. The farm has a herd of 350 goats and is open to the public daily. In addition to its goat's-milk products, the farm shops also sell folk art and antiques. Farm tours are available by appointment only at $5 per person.

The Stores at Aunt Sue's Country Corner (864-878-4366; aunt sues.com), 107A Country Creek Drive, Pickens. Open 11–7 Tuesday through Thursday, 11–9 Friday through Sunday These stores and the restaurant offer the "critical mass" needed to make them worth a stop as you are touring the area. **Wood/Animal House** (864-878-5604) has gifts from handcarved wood bowls to wooden toys and wind chimes. **Candle House** (864-878-9888) sells all things scented from essential oils, Yankee Candle to reed diffusers. **Glass House** (864-878-2850) offers a collection of lamps, sun catchers, and jewelry. **Wild Bird House** (864-878-3212) is just what is says with locally made birdhouses and feeders. **Rock House** (864-878-5570) has minerals, fossils, and semiprecious gemstones.

Prime Outlets-Gaffney (864-902-9900; primeoutlets.com /gaffney), 1 Factory Shops Boulevard, Gaffney. Open Monday through Saturday 10–9, Sunday 1:30–7. This is a typical outlet shopping location with dozens of brand-name stores, including Ralph Lauren, Coach, Pottery Barn, Nike, J. Crew, and Ann Taylor. They have a children's playground area to keep the little ones busy, and the food court is indoors.

Suber's Corn Mill (864-877-5616), 2002 Suber Mill Road, Greer. Open Monday through Friday 8–5, Saturday 8–noon. You can watch an old-time gristmill at work and buy the finished grits or cornmeal at the end. The mill has been owned and operated by the same family since 1908, and the process for turning shelled corn into grits hasn't changed much. It's like stepping back in time and worth the stop.

✳ Special Events

April: **Pendleton Spring Jubilee** (864-646-3782; pendletondistrict .org), 125 East Queen Street, Pendleton. This juried arts and crafts festival started in 1978 to bring visitors to Anderson, Oconee, and Pickens Counties. Now more than 300 artists apply for the 90 spaces available and thousands of visitors come each year. Artworks include paintings, stained glass, pottery, and wood sculptures. Live entertainment plays throughout the festival, and plenty of food vendors are around to keep you happy. This one is definitely worth planning a trip around.

JOCASSEE GORGES

This is one of the jewels of South Carolina and it is largely "undiscovered," meaning that even in the heat of summer, when most of the state's lakes are filled to capacity with boaters, anglers, and swimmers, Lake Jocassee feels like it belongs only to you.

Created in the 1970s by a dam on the Toxaway River, Lake Jocassee is a deep-water lake (up to 400 feet at its deepest point). North Carolina–based Duke Energy Co. owns the lake and manages it for hydroelectric generation. Much of the land surrounding the lake is managed by the state as a wilderness area.

There are a few private homes on the lake, and the state Parks, Recreation and Tourism Department operates lake access, cabins, and villas here as well as primitive campsites. When the lake's parking lots fill up on busy weekends, access is closed, so there are never too many people on the water.

If you don't have your own boat, don't worry. The Jocassee Outdoor Center on the way to the lake can rent you kayaks, canoes, and pontoons. If you are unfamiliar with the lake, I recommend you start your vacation with a guide-led tour on your first day—about $300 for four hours—and then you can decide how you want to enjoy the lake for the rest of the trip.

GUIDANCE Jocassee Gorges Visitors Center (864-868-2605; state parks.com), 108 Residence Drive, Sunset. Open daily 11–noon, 4–5 PM. Located in the Keowee-Toxaway State Natural Area. This facility has limited hours and is located in a former Baptist church. The center offers information about the gorges and how to enjoy it.

GETTING THERE The only way to get here is by private car, and the only public access to Jocassee Lake is through Devil's Fork State Park, which is located near SC 130 at the Cherokee Foothills Scenic Highway (SC 11).

Christy Watts Gentry

ONE OF SEVERAL WATERFALLS AT LAKE JOCASSEE

GETTING AROUND The only way to get around is by car or by boat. Although some industrious folks hike here via the Palmetto Trail, they still need a boat ride to get to the park.

✳ To See

Yellow Branch Falls and Trail. From Walhalla, drive west on SC 28 for 6.8 miles, then turn left into Yellow Branch Picnic Ground. Open daily 6 AM–10 PM. This moderately difficult trail circuit takes you to the base of a 50-foot waterfall. During wet conditions, the hiking can be difficult along the edges of deep ravines. During dry spells, however, the falls may look more like a leaking faucet.

Lower Whitewater Falls, SC 130, Salem. Open daily, dawn to dusk. This 200-foot waterfall is part of the Whitewater Falls chain along the state line between North and South Carolina. There are signs directing you to the parking at the Duke Power Bad Creek Project about 10 miles north of SC 11. From the parking area, it is a 2-mile hike to the falls over-look with some beautiful stopping points along the way and a bridge over the river. It is up- and downhill a fair bit, with the last half mile a pretty significant climb. During hunting season (October to December), much of the trail is open to vehicles, reducing the hike. Also, if you can't make the climb, the Bad Creek project has an overlook that may do you. There are portable potties at the trailhead, but there is no potable water, so bring your own.

✳ To Do

Jocassee Outdoor Center (864-944-9016; jocasseeoutdoorcenter.com), 526 Jocassee Lake Road, Salem. Open 6–6 daily. This store is your last stop before Devil's Fork State Park and Lake Jocassee, and it rents of all kinds of watercraft from pontoon boats and Jet Skis to canoes and kayaks. A guided tour of Jocassee's waterfalls will cost about the same as a daylong pontoon rental ($300 for up to 10 people). Ray Hawkins and his crew also will shuttle hikers to three water-access-only trailheads on the Foothills Trail and will come pick up tired kayakers. There is a sandwich shop on site and plenty of snacks available. Boats with motors start at $200 for a half day; fees go up to $400 for a whole day on a ski boat. People-powered boats rent for a whole day and are $45 for a single kayak up to $75 for a canoe. Skis, wakeboards, kneeboards, and tubes also are for rent at $30 a day. Motorboat prices do not include gas.

The Scuba Shop (864-585-5694; scubashopsc.com), 333 Whitney Road, Spartanburg. Open 10–6 Monday through Friday, 10–2 Saturday, from May through September. Lake Jocassee's depths make it a perfect place for learning and practicing scuba diving. The Scuba Shop and Jocassee

JOCASSEE OUTDOOR CENTER

Outdoor Center team up for these chartered dive trips. Call either for reservations.

FISHING Jocassee's deep waters offer visitors a variety of fishing opportunities. Anglers can catch anything from rainbow trout to smallmouth bass. Several trout streams surround the lake, including the Eastatoe, Thompson, and Whitewater Rivers and Laurel Fork, Corbin, and Howard Creeks. A valid South Carolina fishing license is required.

Devils Fork State Park (864-944-2639; southcarolinaparks.com), 161 Holcombe Circle, Salem. Opens daily at 7 AM year-round; closing times vary by season and day of the week. Admission: $2 adults; $1.25 South Carolina seniors; ages 15 and younger are admitted free. This is the only public access to Lake Jocassee.

Lake Jocassee Charters (864-280-9056; jocasseecharters.com). Fishing excursions can be tailored to your abilities and needs. Jocassee Charters specializes in deep-water trolling for big brown and rainbow trout. Rates include all tackle and bait. Guests will need to provide food, drinks, and their own fishing license. Fishing rates: $275 for four hours, up to four people. Lake tours are available for $200 for three hours, up to eight people.

HUNTING Jocassee Gorges is one of very few areas in South Carolina where hunters can shoot bear. The area also has plenty of deer, wild turkeys, raccoons, and feral hogs that are popular among hunters. Almost all of the properties are inside the state **Natural Resources Department's Wildlife Management Area** (dnr.sc.gov/wma/index.html) and available for public hunting. You have to have a WMA permit and should consult the state agency's rules and regulations for when and how you can hunt. Generally speaking, bear season is two weeks in October; dogs can be used only one of those weeks. Most of the other large game is in-season from October through the end of the year, with turkey season in April.

FAMILY-FRIENDLY ACTIVITIES ✔ **The Happy Berry Inc.** (864-868-2946; thehappyberry.com), 510 Gap Hill Road, Six Mile. Located on the eastern shore of Lake Keowee in Pickens County, the Happy Berry Inc. is a pick-your-own small fruit farm with blackberries, blueberries, elderberries, grapes, and figs. They also will pick for you, but what's the fun in that. The season is typically June 1 to early September.

TENNIS Belton Tennis Center (864-338-1374; beltontennis.com), 104 Brown Avenue, Belton. Open 8 AM–10 PM Monday through Saturday, noon–10 Sunday. The center is home to several statewide tennis tournaments throughout the year and offers five lighted courts and a clubhouse in downtown Belton. It also is the home court for the **South Carolina Tennis Hall of Fame** (864-338-7400; beltontennis.com), 50 North Main Street, Belton. Open Wednesday through Saturday 10–4. This free museum is located in the Belton Depot and features tennis artifacts from throughout the state as well as honoring outstanding players, coaches, officials, and volunteers. The inductees' gallery includes a portrait of each inductee and a memento from their tennis career.

HIKING The Foothills Trail (864-467-9537; foothillstrail.org) is an 80-mile footpath extending from Table Rock State Park in the east to Oconee State Park in the west. Its route takes the hiker through the heart of the Jocassee Gorges with scenic mountain views and shady spots with some very interesting plant life. The trail crosses or follows several major streams and rivers including Laurel Fork Creek, Toxaway River, Horsepasture River, Thompson River, Whitewater River, East Fork Creek, and the Chattooga River.

Devils Fork State Park Trails (864-944-2639; southcarolinaparks.com), 161 Holcombe Circle, Salem. The park has two main trails: The Bear Cove Trail, 2 miles, loops through hardwood forests and begins and ends in the picnic area. The Oconee Bell Nature Trail is an easy 1-mile loop named for the wildflowers that marks the path.

UPSTATE

✳ Green Space

PARKS Devils Fork State Park (864-944-2639; southcarolinaparks
.com), 161 Holcombe Circle, Salem. Located along the southwestern
shore of Lake Jocassee, this park is the premiere lake access point. Visitors
also can camp along the lakefront or access the Foothills Trail; some areas
are accessible only by boat. The park has 20 villas for rent ranging from
$100 to $170 a night. No pets in the villas area. You'll also find public restrooms, snack bar, and changing areas. Signs at the park try to dissuade
swimming because there are no lifeguards and bottom footing can be pre-
carious. But swimming is not prohibited.

Keowee-Toxaway State Natural Area (864-868-2605; southcarolina
parks.com), 108 Residence Drive, Sunset. This 1,000-acre park sits on
the banks of Lake Keowee and features stunning views of the Blue Ridge
Mountains. One three-bedroom cabin with a floating dock on Lake Keowee
is available at $90–160 a night depending on day of the week and season.
There also are paved and primitive campsites and trails.

Caesars Head State Park (864-836-6115; southcarolinaparks.com), 8155
Geer Highway, Cleveland. Open daily 7–6, extended to 9 PM during Day-

DEVILS FORK STATE PARK

SC Department of Parks, Recreation & Tourism, DiscoverSouthCarolina.com

CAESARS HEAD STATE PARK

light Saving Time. Admission: $2 adults; $1.25 South Carolina seniors; free for ages 15 and younger. Some of the best mountain views in South Carolina can be had from here. This is a must-see if you're in the area in the fall, when the park hosts a hawk-watch program from a perch 3,200 feet high. Raven Cliffs Falls can be accessed from one of Caesars Head's trails leading to a suspension bridge over the falls.

Jones Gap State Park (864-836-3647; southcarolinaparks.com), 303 Jones Gap Road, Marietta. Open daily 7–6, extended to 9 PM during Daylight Saving Time. Admission: $2 adults; $1.25 South Carolina seniors; free for ages 15 and younger. Jones Gap and Caesars Head form the Mountain Bridge Wilderness area. Jones Gap focuses on the Middle Saluda River, which was the first in South Carolina to be designated a scenic river. The park offers trout fishing and camping, and is an access point for the Foothills Trail.

Sadlers Creek State Recreation Area (864-226-8950; southcarolina parks.com), 940 Sadlers Creek Road, Anderson. Admission: $2 adults; $1.25 South Carolina seniors; free for ages 15 and younger. Open 7–6 daily; two hours later on Friday. This park sits on a peninsula in Lake Hartwell and offers boat access and lakeside camping.

JONES GAP STATE PARK

✳ Lodging

BED & BREAKFASTS Three Pines View (864-280-0482; three pinesview.com), 151 Shack Hollow Road, Salem. If you're not paying attention, you might miss the turnoff for this B&B on your way to Lake Jocassee. The Three Pines is a new build with five rooms. Stay comes with breakfast, and you also can have lunch and dinner (with 24-hour notice to your hosts Diane and Steve Hayes). Boats are available for rent on site. Rates are $190–250 a night.

🐾 **Sunrise Farm B&B** (864-944-0121; bbonline.com/sc/sunrise farm), 325 Sunrise Drive, Salem. Guests can rent a farmhouse room or one of two cottages. Cottages allow some pets for additional $20 fee. Cottages are breakfast-optional.

Breakfast is included in all farmhouse room rates, which start at $110.

CAMPGROUNDS/CABINS Devils Fork State Park (864-944-2639; southcarolinaparks .com), 161 Holcombe Circle, Salem. Twenty villas for rent ranging from $100 to $170 a night. No pets in the villas area. The main lakeside camping area has 59 paved sites with water and electrical hookups. Some sites can accommodate RVs up to 36 feet. Rates about $20 a night.

Keowee-Toxaway State Natural Area (864-868-2605; southcarolina parks.com), 108 Residence Drive, Sunset. One three-bedroom cabin with a floating dock on Lake

Keowee is available at $90–160 a night, depending on day of the week and season. Camping is available at paved sites with electricity and water at $15 a night, tent pads with water only $10 a night; trailside camping is allowed on the Raven Rock Hiking Trail for $7–9 a night per person. Registration is required.

The Mountain Bridge Wilderness Area (864-836-364; south carolinaparks.com), 303 Jones Gap Road, Marietta. Trailside backcountry camping is available at 24 primitive sites for $8–20 a night. Fires are allowed only in provided fire pits.

Sadlers Creek State Recreation Area (864-226-8950; southcaro linaparks.com), 940 Sadlers Creek Road, Anderson. Lakeside camping is available. $15–20 a night for sites with electricity and water. Tent sites rent for $11–13 a night.

CONDOS/VILLAS Keowee Key Rentals (800-537-5253; keowee keyrentals.com), 1209 C Stamp Creek Road, Salem. Two-bedroom, two-bath condos and villas are available for two-night minimum stays at $350 up to $1,800 for the month. The rentals offer lakefront or wooded locations.

✳ Where to Eat

EATING OUT Grits and Groceries (864-296-3316; gritsand groceries.com), 2440 Due West Highway, Belton. Open 7 AM–2 PM Tuesday through Friday, and 6 AM–2 PM for Saturday brunch. Carolinas natives Joe and Heidi Trull returned to their roots after a decade in New Orleans, working with Emeril Lagasse and Heidi running her own place, Elizabeth's. Everything on the menu is less than $10 and includes locally grown produce and homemade ice cream.

THREE PINES VIEW B&B

The Spot on the Alley Sports Bar & Restaurant (864-985-0102; thespot.us), 122 Ram Cat Alley, Seneca. Bar food, plus a gluten-free menu, beer, and pool tables in the historic shopping district of Seneca. Open 11:30 AM Monday through Saturday; closing at 1 AM Monday through Thursday, 2 AM Friday, and midnight Saturday. Most items less than $10.

Hoyetts Café (864-944-9016; jocasseeoutdoorcenter.com), 526 Jocassee Lake Road, Salem. Located in the Jocassee Outdoor Center, this little café serves up "Hoyt" dogs, sandwiches, and ice cream.

GREENWOOD/ABBEVILLE

These two small cities were built around the textile industry in the early 20th century. By the end of that century they'd begun to turn to tourism to help replace the jobs and money lost when those mills moved overseas.

In Greenwood the bulk of the mills were owned by the Self family, which has remained in the town and started new enterprises, made philanthropic donations, and built the area's hospital. Some mills do still operate, but by and large the industry is dying in South Carolina as it has across the country.

In Abbeville the town has created a tourism industry based on its Opera House, which hosts local and touring shows in a turn-of-the-20th-century facility.

Either makes a great weekend getaway built around a show at the Opera House or the South Carolina Flower Festival. The two towns are only 20 miles apart, so you could do both in one long weekend.

I recommend Greenwood in the spring and early summer to see the gardens at the Park Seed Co. in full bloom. Lake Greenwood has plenty of water sports opportunities for the heat of summer. Abbeville is better in spring and fall.

GUIDANCE Greenwood Area Chamber of Commerce (864-223-8431; greenwoodscchamber.org), 110 Phoenix Street, Greenwood.

Greater Abbeville Chamber of Commerce (864-366-4600; visitabbe villesc.com), 107 Court Square, Abbeville. Open 10–4 Monday through Friday and 10–3 Saturday.

Old 96 District Tourism Commission (864-984-2233; sctravelold96 .com), 204 East Public Square, Laurens. Open 8:30–4:30 Monday through Friday.

GETTING THERE Greenwood and Abbeville are two of the most difficult places to reach in South Carolina. There are no major airports, train stations, or bus stops within an hour's drive. Even the nearest interstate access is 45 minutes away. A car is your best bet for getting here and getting around. The nearest airport is **Greenville-Spartanburg International Airport**. The nearest train is in Clemson and the nearest bus stop is in Greenville. All are about 60 miles away.

By car: U.S. Highways 25, 178, and 221 run through Greenwood. Abbeville is reachable only by state highway, and the best one is SC 72 from Greenwood.

✳ To See

Greenwood Museum (864-229-7093; greenwoodmuseum.org), 106 Main Street, Greenwood. Open 10–5 Wednesday through Saturday. Adults $5, children $2. Three floors of exhibits including a look at the history of the area from the days of the Indians through industrialization.

Greenwood Arts Center (864-388-7800; greenwoodmuseum.org), 120 Main Street, Greenwood. Open 8:30–5 Monday through Friday, 9:30–1:30 Saturday. Free. Artists' studios are located in the basement of the renovated federal building that is home to this neat little arts center with high ceilings, large windows, and great lighting.

Burt-Stark Mansion (864-366-0166; burt-stark.com), 400 North Main Street, Abbeville. Open 1–5 Friday through Saturday or by appointment.

ARTISTS' STUDIOS IN THE BASEMENT OF THE GREENWOOD ARTS CENTER

Tours take about an hour and cost $10. This home is the site of the last meeting of Jefferson Davis's war council at the end of the Civil War when the president of the Confederacy realized that "All is indeed lost."

Benjamin Mays Historic Site (864-223-8434; mayshousemuseum.org), 237 North Hospital Street, Greenwood. Open 9–2 Monday, Tuesday, and Thursday or by appointment. The son of former slaves, Benjamin Mays grew up in rural South Carolina and went to a one-room schoolhouse for black children in the early 20th century. He went on to become the president of Morehouse College in Atlanta and mentor to civil rights leader the Reverend Martin Luther King Jr. His books, including *Seeking to Be a Christian in Race Relations*, published in 1957, focused on religion in the African American culture. His civil rights influence focused on the dignity of all human beings.

✴ To Do

Abbeville Opera House (864-366-2157; theabbevilleoperahouse.com), 100 Court Square, Abbeville. Box office opens 10–2 Monday through Friday. Shows at 8 Friday and Saturday nights, with a 3 PM Saturday matinee. Tickets are $17 with a $1 discount for seniors and group tickets. More than 100 years old, the Opera House began as a touring stop for plays, musicals, and vaudeville productions. It turned into a movie house with the advent of moving, then talking pictures. Abandoned in the 1950s, the Opera House was restored in the late 1960s as the home of the Abbeville Community Theater. Michael Genevie's traveling theater company took up residence here in 1979, and he remains as executive director. The Opera House has a community theater winter season and a repertory company. It still hosts the occasional traveling shows as it did when it opened in 1908. There are about 40 live shows a year.

Greenwood Community Theater (864-299-5704; greenwoodmuseum .org), 110 Main Street, Greenwood. This theater has five performances during their winter and spring season. Tickets are $8–18. The theater is centrally located in Greenwood's cultural district.

STATE PARKS Baker Creek State Park (864-443-2457; southcarolina parks.com), 863 Baker Creek Road, McCormick. Open 9–9, seven days a week; the park is open mid-March through November. $2 adults; $1.25 South Carolina seniors; free for children 15 and younger. This 1,300-acre park sits on Strom Thurmond Lake, which is known as Clarks Hill Lake on its Georgia shores. There are two 50-site campgrounds, one with water and electricity, one with water only. Baker Creek State Park offers access to fishing and boating on the lake as well as hiking and biking trails. The park is surrounded by the Sumter National Forest.

GREENWOOD COMMUNITY THEATER

☸ **Hickory Knob State Resort Park** (864-391-2450; southcarolinaparks .com), 1591 Resort Drive, McCormick. Open 24 hours a day; office open 7 AM–11 PM. Free admission. This 1,000-acre park is South Carolina's only full-service resort state park. Hickory Knob offers 18 one-bedroom cabins, more than 70 lodge rooms, and 44 campsites. There is a full-service restaurant and a golf course. Located on Strom Thurmond Lake, the park also has a boat ramp, campgrounds, and mountain biking trails. Pets are not allowed in lodge rooms or cabin areas but are allowed in most other outdoor areas on a leash.

Lake Greenwood State Recreation Area (864-543-3535; southcarolina parks.com), 302 State Park Road, Ninety Six. $2 adults ages 15 and older; $1.25 South Carolina seniors. Open daily 6–6, extended to 10 PM during Daylight Saving Time. The park sits on the shores of Lake Greenwood with ample, boating, fishing, and hiking opportunities.

GOLF Hickory Knob State Resort Park (864) 391-2450; southcarolina parks.com), 1591 Resort Drive, McCormick. This Tom Jackson–designed course sits along Lake Thurmond. Weekdays $15, weekends $20; cart fee $13 per person.

✳ Lodging

INNS Bernibrooks Inn (864-366-8310; bernibrooksinn.com), 200 West Pinckney Street, Abbeville. This four-room inn takes its name from the family that runs it now, Don and Karen Berni, and the woman who owned it back when, Maggie W. Brooks, and it's listed under her name on the National Register of Historic Places. Miss Maggie ran a boardinghouse in the home following the Civil War. Room rates range $65–115 a night and include breakfast in the morning and an evening glass of wine, dessert, and coffee.

BED & BREAKFASTS Hearthside Manor Bed & Breakfast (864-366-6555; hearthsidemanor .com), 1304 North Main Street, Abbeville. This home was built in the late 1860s and offers guests five rooms ranging from $75 a night for a room with twin beds to $130 for a king room with a private porch entry. The wraparound porch has rockers and a swing. Complimentary drinks and snacks for guests throughout their stay in addition to a hot breakfast each morning. Historic downtown Abbeville is an easy walk of less than a mile away. Bikes are available. Packages include tickets to the Abbeville Opera House and a voucher for dinner on the town.

Veranda On Main (864-366-9540; verandaonmain.com), 802 North Main Street, Abbeville. This place's name says it all: Large porches on the first and second floors make this place a rocker's dream. Room rates $90–130 includes breakfast.

COTTAGES ⚓ Smith's Vacation Cottages (864-333-5198; modoc retreat.com), 119 McCarty Drive,

HICKORY KNOB STATE RESORT PARK

SC Department of Parks, Recreation & Tourism, DiscoverSouthCarolina.com

A TRIP TO GILLEBEAU HOUSE AT HICKORY KNOB

We stayed at the Gillebeau House in the woods of Hickory Knob State Park and I have to say "Wow!" The park itself is far beyond anything I have ever seen in South Carolina. The golf course, the lake, the lodge with restaurant—it's what you want a state park to be. The Gillebeau House is an 18th-century cabin that was home to French Huguenots. The house was owned by the same family for generations before being donated to the state and moved to its current location in the park in the 1980s.

It rents for less than $150 a night in season, but a weeklong stay is required during summer months. However, if you are traveling on short notice, it's worth a call to the park to see whether it's available for a long weekend. The online reservation system won't let you book for less than a week, but the fine folks at the park would rather have you in it for a few days than let it sit empty all week. Also, if you do stay here, be prepared for some curiosity-seekers. The Gillebeau House is open for visitors if no one is renting it. We had to turn away one family who wanted a tour while we were still in our pajamas.

The Gillebeau House is one of those places that's really hard to describe. On the one hand, it's ancient. It's like staying in a historic house. On the other hand, it has been fixed up rather nicely with some 20th- and 21st-century amenities, including WiFi. We drove up and there sat our little cabin in the woods, so quiet, so simple. The back door was covered in spiderwebs and bugs—a bad sign to start—but when we got in, it was very clean and mostly bug-free. (You can never be truly bug-free in the South Carolina woods no matter what time of year.)

The kitchen/dining room area was added on after the original cabin was moved. It has wonderful antiques, including an icebox—which is purely for decoration, because the kitchen has all the modern conveniences including refrigerator, microwave, coffeepot, and an electric stove that looks like a wood-burner from days gone by. The vaulted ceiling makes the room feel larger and offers a wonderful display for hundreds of kitchen gadgets from the past 200 years. The dining table seats four comfortably.

A door that looks like it might lead to a pantry actually leads up some rather irregular stairs to the loft. There you'll find a full bath, sitting area, and twin beds under a very low ceiling. This area would really be comfortable only for children or people less than 5 feet tall.

Back downstairs in the original portion of the cabin is the den. There is a couch, recliner, large fireplace with gas logs, rocking chair, and television set with cable channels. The master bedroom has a bath, double bed, and dresser. It's a bit of a tight fit for full-sized people, but you won't be spending much time in here anyway.

The front porch is glorious with a picnic table, swing, and rockers. There also is plenty of room to park your bikes out of the weather.

The house has many windows making it fairly well lit during the day, but at night its minimal lighting, coupled with the compact fluorescent bulbs, leave it a little dark.

The cabin sits on one of the park's three nature trails. Less than half a mile away is one of two boat ramps where you can rent kayaks and canoes. The golf course is visible (and audible) from the cabin's yard and is a beautiful, hilly, well-maintained course.

The park sits on a peninsula in Lake Thurmond with the park office, lodge, restaurant, and cabins at the very tip. Some of the cabins overlook the lake, while the lodge rooms overlook the pool.

We came to the park with a very active agenda: hiking, biking, and boating. We arrived on a Friday afternoon and settled in before biking around the lodge area and strolling to the nearest boat ramp where we sipped adult beverages, dangled our feet in the water, and watched the sun slip behind the woods. The next morning we were up early, had breakfast in the lodge (a buffet for two, less than $15 with tax and tip), and were ready to tackle the 7-mile Lakeview Trail, marked for bikers and hikers. We packed lots of water, some snacks, bug spray, and fortitude. After four hours in the woods, we emerged exhausted, but proud of ourselves for hiking the whole trail. Novice hikers can handle it with some water, good shoes, and a snack; some parts seemed a little tough for novice bikers. Beaver Run Trail is a little better for biking, though we had to stop on occasion to walk our bikes on the uphill parts. (Note: The Beaver Run Trail is listed at 2.5 miles, but it's not a loop, so if you walk it end-to-end it's a 5-mile round trip—or maybe a little less if you take the road.)

After working up such an appetite, we decided to grill steaks out on Saturday night. We bought charcoal and some other essentials at a grocery store in nearby Lincolnton, Georgia, but we had brought our own steaks with us. The grill at the Gillebeau House is very simple, but easy to work and roomy. We took our own cooking grate so we wouldn't have to worry about cleaning off the park's grill, but we were able to cook two steaks, two ears of corn, broccoli, and a Vidalia onion all at the same time. Cooking everything outside kept the house cool and allowed us some more outdoor time to watch the sun set through the trees. We even heard a wild turkey. We didn't see him, mind you, but we did hear him.

We had planned to rent a canoe or a couple of kayaks on Sunday (less than $15 for a full-day rental), but we were a little weary after Saturday's hike, so we rode our bikes on the Beaver Run Trail, then took a dip in the pool to cool off. Checkout was Monday morning, and we had breakfast in the cabin before heading out. It was so peaceful and relaxing. I think the Gillebeau cabin is best for couples, although families with children old enough to walk the trails on their own might enjoy it as well. Just keep in mind that once the kids are old enough to venture out on their own, they might be too tall for the loft.

Modoc. These two-bedroom, two-bath lakeside cottages with full kitchen are ideal for hunters and anglers, but also great for families. There is a boat ramp nearby and plenty of room for parking boats and other water toys. Cottages rent for $500 for a week, $100 a night Friday and Saturday, and $85 a night during the week. A two-night minimum stay is required, and rates are higher during the week of the Master's golf tournament in nearby Augusta, Georgia.

CABINS/CAMPGROUNDS
Hickory Knob State Resort

Park (864-391-2450; southcarolina parks.com), 1591 Resort Drive, McCormick. This state park with an 18-hole golf course has 70 lodge rooms ranging from $50 a night during the week to $140 on weekends. The park has one- and two-bedroom cabins at $70–105 a night. There are campsites with water and electric for $20 a night.

Lake Greenwood State Recreation Area (864-543-3535; southcarolinaparks.com), 302 State Park Road, Greenwood. The park has 125 campsites with electric and water for $20–25 a night.

✳ Where to Eat

DINING OUT Windows on Main (864-366-3505), 101 South Main Street, Abbeville. Open for lunch 11:30–2:30 Monday through Saturday, dinner 5–9 Tuesday through Saturday. Windows on Main provides an excellent people-watching opportunity along with quality food at a small-town price. Crab-stuffed mushrooms and steaks are favorites. Entrées $15–25.

EATING OUT Yoder's Dutch Kitchen (864-366-5556), 809 East Greenwood Street, Abbeville. Timing is everything when you come to Yoder's. If you wait too late, you'll be standing in line. Southern comfort foods—fried chicken and fish, greens, macaroni and cheese—on an all-you-can eat buffet, with plenty of sweet tea to wash it down. Save room for dessert.

✳ Selected Shopping

The Park Seed Co. (800-213-0076; parkseedco.com), 1 Parkton Avenue, Greenwood. The Park Seed Co. has been in Greenwood since 1924, and its annual seed catalog has been the harbinger of spring since George Park began selling seeds as a teenager from his parents' home in Pennsylvania in the late 1800s. The company was sold in 2010 to a firm that guaranteed it would continue operating in Greenwood for at least three years. The company's trial gardens with more than 1,000 varieties of annuals, perennials, and vegetables are on display during the South Carolina Festival of Flowers held every June in Greenwood.

✳ Special Events

June: **South Carolina Festival of Flowers** (864-223-8411; scfestival offlowers.org), Greenwood. Ticket prices vary by event and typically go on sale May 1 at the chamber of commerce. Events include musical performances, dances, a beauty pageant, wine tasting, and, of course, a tour of Park Seed Co.'s famed trial gardens.

SUGGESTED ITINERARIES

The South Carolina Upstate is a wonderful place for outdoor activities, especially in warmer months when the region tends to feel a little cooler than the rest of the state.

Let's start in Greenville with its myriad art galleries, museums, and wonderful **Falls Park at the Reedy River** (864-467-4350; fallspark .com); 601 South Main Street. This is a great place to take an early-morning walk. For places to stay, I recommend **The Westin Poinsett** (864-421-9700; westinpoinsettgreenville.com), 120 South Main Street, or **Pettigru Place** (864-242-4529; pettigruplace.com), 302 Pettigru Street. Although the Westin is a chain, its location is unique and provides a great location from which to explore the city. Pettigru Place isn't too far off the main drag and feels like you are staying at a friend's house. If you need breakfast away from where you're staying, check out **Mary Beth's at McBee Station** (864-242-2535; marybethsatmcbee.com), 500 East McBee Avenue, Suite 109. The quiche is great. Try a hibiscus—champagne and cranberry juice—to get your day started. From there, walk around Falls Park before heading to the **Greenville County Museum of Art** (864-271-7570; greenvillemuseum.org), 420 College Street, which I think is the state's best art museum—and it's free. If you're traveling with the kids, try the **Children's Museum of the Upstate** (864-233-7755; tcmupstate.org), 300 College Street, and the **Upcountry History Museum** (864-467-3100; upcountryhistory.org), 540 Buncombe Street, all in the Heritage Green area. **Bob Jones University Art Museum and Gallery** (864-770-1331; bjumg.org), 1700 Wade Hampton Boulevard or 25 Heritage Green Place, has a world-famous collection of religious art. The on-campus location has limited hours, so you may want to try the satellite location at Heritage Green. When you are ready for lunch, I like **Brick Street Café** (864-421-0111; brickstreetcafe.com), 315 Augusta Street. The chicken salad is fantastic here in a rehabbed old belt factory with high ceilings and wonderful ambience. There is some good shopping downtown as well as great restaurants. I love the **Mast General Store**

(864-235-1883; mastgeneralstore.com), 111 North Main Street. It's like taking a step back in time, and I never leave without buying something. For dinner, I have to recommend **The Lazy Goat** (864-679-5299; the lazygoat.typepad.com), 170 River Place. It's right on the water, has wonderful patio dining, and you've just got to try the paella.

The Cherokee Foothills National Scenic Highway—SC 11—is simply a fantastic drive. Start your day at **BMW Zentrum** (864-989-5297 or 888-868-7269 for tour information; bmwzentrum.com), 1400 SC 101, Greer. Call ahead to make sure they are offering tours. This is a very interesting look at the history of one of the world's foremost automakers. For lunch, you must try the **Beacon Drive-In** (864-585-9387; beacondrivein.com), 255 John B. White Sr. Boulevard. Order one chili cheeseburger-a-plenty for every two people and enjoy. While that's digesting, drive over to Gaffney (less than an hour). There's the Peachoid—you'll know it when you see it—**Cowpens National Battlefield** (864-461-2828; nps.gov /cowp/index.htm), 4001 Chesnee Highway—site of a key colonial victory during the Revolutionary War—and for shopping, **Prime Outlets— Gaffney** (864-902-9900; primeoutlets.com/gaffney), 1 Factory Shops Boulevard, Gaffney. From here, turn west onto SC 11 and head to **Campbell's Covered Bridge**, Campbell's Bridge Road, Landrum—the only covered bridge in South Carolina. From here, you will head toward the North Carolina state line and **Symmes Chapel "Pretty Place"** (864-836-3291; campgreenville.org/chapel.php), YMCA Camp Road, Marietta. This is a great place to visit when the sun is setting, but be sure to check in to make sure there are no weddings planned for when you want to visit. You will probably be exhausted by now, so I recommend staying at **Three Pines View** (864-280-0482; threepinesview.com), 151 Shack Hollow Road, Salem. You'll be perfectly located to spend Day 2 of your trip at Lake Jocassee, paddling, boating, swimming, or hiking around the lake. Three Pines View can provide you with paddle-power boats, or you can try **Jocassee Outdoor Center** (864-944-9016; jocasseeoutdoorcenter.com), 526 Jocassee Lake Road, Salem. The JOC has everything you could need—including a guide to take you out on the water if you don't want to drive the boat yourself. Call in advance for reservations. You can pack a lunch from the inn or from the JOC and have a picnic on the water. Dinner is at the inn.

For Day 3, head over to **Issaqueena Falls/Stumphouse Tunnel** (864-638-4343; oconeecountry.com/stumphouse.html), SC 28, to see where Clemson Blue Cheese was first made and view an early transportation project that never got finished. You can stop at **The Happy Berry Inc.** (864-868-2946; thehappyberry.com), 510 Gap Hill Road, Six Mile, or **Bryson's U-Pick Apple Orchard** (864-647-9427; brysonsappleorchard .com), 1011 Chattooga Ridge Road, Mountain Rest, for fresh fruit. If it's spring or early summer, stop in at the Happy Berry. The Apple Orchard is better in the fall. A great stop for lunch is **1826 On the Green** (864-646-5500; 1826onthegreen.com), 105 Exchange Street, Pendleton, which is a lovely town for antiquing. There also is the small town of Clemson, home of Clemson University. Highlights here include the lovely campus (maybe check it out in summer when there are fewer students), the South Carolina Botanical Garden, and the Bob Campbell Geology Museum. For history buffs, there is **Fort Hill: Home of John C. Calhoun and Thomas G. Clemson** (864-656-2475; clemson.edu /about/history/properties/fort-hill), 101 Fort Hill Street. Don't forget to stop at **'55 Exchange** (864-656-2155; clemson.edu/icecream), Hendrix Student Center—East End at Cherry and McMillan Roads, for ice cream and Clemson Blue Cheese. For dinner, try **Pixie & Bill's** (864-654-1210; tigergourmet.com/pixie_home.htm), US 123.

For your final day in the South Carolina Upstate, I highly recommend a whitewater rafting trip. It's just the thing to get your heart pumping. The **Nantahala Outdoor Center** (864-647-9014; noc.com), 851A Chattooga Ridge Road, Mountain Rest, is the best place to stop for guided tours of the river.

INDEX